Frederick H. A. Scrivener

The Authorized Edition of the English Bible

Its Subsequent Reprints and modern representatives

Frederick H. A. Scrivener

The Authorized Edition of the English Bible
Its Subsequent Reprints and modern representatives

ISBN/EAN: 9783337170004

Printed in Europe, USA, Canada, Australia, Japan

Cover: Foto ©Lupo / pixelio.de

More available books at **www.hansebooks.com**

THE AUTHORIZED EDITION

OF THE

ENGLISH BIBLE (1611).

London: C. J. CLAY, AND SON,
CAMBRIDGE UNIVERSITY PRESS WAREHOUSE,
AVE MARIA LANE.

Cambridge: DEIGHTON, BELL, AND CO.
Leipzig: F. A. BROCKHAUS.

THE
AUTHORIZED EDITION

OF THE

ENGLISH BIBLE (1611),

ITS SUBSEQUENT REPRINTS
AND MODERN REPRESENTATIVES.

BY

F. H. A. SCRIVENER, M.A., D.C.L., LL.D.

PREBENDARY OF EXETER AND VICAR OF HENDON.

EDITED FOR THE SYNDICS OF THE UNIVERSITY PRESS.

CAMBRIDGE:
AT THE UNIVERSITY PRESS.
1884

PREFACE.

THE following pages comprise in substance a reprint of the author's Introduction to the Cambridge Paragraph Bible of 1873, with such additions and corrections as more recent studies have enabled him to make. The original work was the result of seven years' continuous labour, and has been generally recognized as the only attempt hitherto made to construct a critical edition of the Authorized Bible of 1611.

One interesting portion of his previous work, the discussion of the Greek text underlying the Authorized Bible and embodied in Appendix E, has been virtually re-written, in the hope of attaining a higher degree of accuracy than he or others have reached aforetime. The author has been blamed for stating that Beza, late in life, and through mere forgetfulness, asserted a claim to the revision of the Greek text which appeared in parallel columns with his Latin Version of 1556. Yet it is hard to put any other construction on the language of his Preface to his own latest edition, dated *Calendis Augusti* 1598 :

> Annus agitur quadragesimus secundus, Christiane lector, ex quo Novi Testamenti Latinam interpretationem emendare sum aggressus, Græco contextu, non modò cum novemdecim vetustissimis quàm plurimis manuscriptis et multis passim impressis codicibus, sed etiam cum Syra interpretatione collato, et quàm optima potui fide ac diligentia, partim cum veterum Græcorum ac Latinorum patrum scriptis, partim cum recentioribus, tum pietate, tum eruditione præstantissimorum Theologorum versionibus, et variis enarrationibus comparato.

HENDON, *February*, 1884.

TABLE OF CONTENTS.

	PAGE
Preliminary explanation	1
Section I. History of editions of the Authorized Bible, 1611–1863	3
Section II. Its marginal notes and original texts	40
Section III. Its use of Italic type	61
Section IV. Its punctuation	81
Section V. Its orthography and grammar	93
Section VI. Parallel references in the margin	116
Section VII. Miscellaneous observations	127
Appendix A. List of wrong readings of the Bible of 1611 amended in later editions	147
Appendix B. Variation between the two issues, both bearing the date of 1611	203
Appendix C. List of original readings of the Bible of 1611 restored, later alterations being withdrawn	215
Appendix D. Dr Blayney's Report to the Delegates of the Clarendon Press	238
Appendix E. The Greek text adopted in the Bible of 1611 examined and arranged	243
Note on the Synod of Dort	264
Original Epistle of the Translators to the Reader, with notes	265
Index of Persons and Subjects	305

CORRIGENDA.

THE AUTHORIZED EDITION OF THE ENGLISH BIBLE (1611),
ITS SUBSEQUENT REPRINTS AND MODERN REPRESENTATIVES.

A CRITICAL edition of the Authorized Version of the English Bible, having reference to its internal character rather than to its external history, and indicating the changes for good or ill introduced into the original text of 1611 by subsequent reprints, would have been executed long ago, had this Version been nothing more than the greatest and best known of English Classics. And such a design has been rendered all the more necessary by the fact that a formal revision of the Translation itself is now in progress, having been undertaken about fourteen years ago under the auspices of the Convocation of the Province of Canterbury. If a judgment may be formed from previous experience in like cases, the revised and unrevised Versions, when the former shall be at length completed, are destined to run together a race of generous and friendly rivalry for the space of at least one generation, before the elder of the two shall be superseded in the affections of not a few devout persons, who, in so grave a matter as the daily use of Holy Scripture, shall prove slow to adopt changes which yet they will not doubt to be made, on the whole, for the better. With so sharp a struggle before it, it is only right that the Authorized or King James's Bible should be represented, as far as may be, in the precise shape that it would have assumed, if its venerable Translators had shewn themselves more exempt than they were from the failings incident to human infirmity; or if the same severe accuracy, which is now demanded in carrying so important a volume through the press, had been deemed requisite or was at all usual in their age. The purpose of the present work is to discuss, within as moderate a compass as the subject will permit, the principles which have been adopted in editing the following pages, the reasons whereon they are grounded, and the difficulties which have been encountered in the prosecution of an arduous but by no means a wearisome task. For the reader's convenience it will be divided into seven Sections, the chief contents of which are here subjoined.

Section I. On the history of the text of the Authorized Version, from A.D. 1611 down to the present time.

Section II. On its marginal notes; and on the original texts, both Greek and Hebrew, employed by the Translators.

Section III. On the use of the Italic type by the Translators, and on the extension of their principles by subsequent editors.

Section IV. On the system of punctuation adopted in 1611, and modified in more recent Bibles.

Section V. On the orthography, grammatical peculiarities, and capital letters of the original, as compared with modern editions.

Section VI. On the references to parallel texts of Scripture which are set in the margin.

Section VII. Miscellaneous observations relating to the present edition, and general Conclusion.

To this short treatise is annexed, besides several other

Appendices, a full Catalogue of the places in which the text of modern Bibles differs from that of the standard of 1611, with the dates at which the variations were severally adopted, so far as by diligent care they have been ascertained.

The Translators' address to the Reader, prefixed to the edition of 1611, is reprinted at the end of this volume.

SECTION I.

On the history of the text of the Authorized Version of the English Bible, from A.D. 1611 *down to the present time.*

MOST readers will be aware that numberless and not inconsiderable departures from the original or standard edition of the Authorized Translation as published in 1611, are to be found in the modern Bibles which issue from the press by thousands every year. Some of these differences must be imputed to oversight and negligence, from which no work of man can be entirely free; but much the greater part of them are deliberate changes, introduced silently and without authority by men whose very names are often unknown. Now, if such alterations had been made invariably for the worse, it would have been easy in future editions to recall the primitive readings, and utterly to reject the later corruptions. This, however, is far from being the case. Not a few of these variations, especially those first met with in Cambridge folio Bibles dated 1629 and 1638, which must have been superintended with much critical care, amend manifest faults of the original Translators or editors, so that it would be most injudicious to remove them from the place they have deservedly held in all our copies for the last 250 years[1]. A full and, it may be hoped, a fairly

[1] On a question of so great importance as that of retaining changes for the better already made by previous editors of the Authorized Version, it is safe to be fortified by the judgment of so

complete list of these changes is given in Appendix A at the end of this volume, to which the student is referred once for all: the attempt therein made to assign the period at which they were severally admitted into the text, although great pains have been bestowed upon the investigation, must be regarded as sometimes only approximately successful. Other copies, of an earlier date than that cited, may occasionally have anticipated it in making the given correction; but these inaccuracies will hardly affect the general results, or impair the conclusions to which they lead. One class of variations has been advisedly excluded from the Catalogue, as seeming rather curious than instructive or important; namely, that arising from errors which, having crept into editions later than that of 1611, after holding a place in a few or in many subsequent issues, have long since disappeared from the Bibles now in use. Of this kind is that notorious misprint in the Cambridge folio of 1638, once falsely imputed to ecclesiastical bias, "whom ye may appoint over this business" ("ye" for "we".) Acts vi. 3; a blemish which obstinately maintained its ground in some copies, at least as late as 1682[1]. The several editions of

cautious and well-informed a writer as Dr Cardwell: "There is only one case, perhaps, in which it would become the duty of the privileged editor to enter into questions of criticism, without some express authority to support him. If a given mistake of the Translators had already been corrected before his time, if the public opinion had concurred, either avowedly or tacitly, in the change, he might reasonably hope that the general acknowledgment of the truth would relieve him from the obligation of returning into error. I say nothing of the boldness which first made the alteration; I only commend the sound judgment which, after it was generally adopted, did not hesitate to retain it" (*Oxford Bibles*, 1833, p. 2, by Edward Cardwell, D.D., Principal of S. Alban's Hall, Oxford).

[1] Hartwell Horne, to whose *Introduction* all English students of the Bible owe more than they can ever duly acknowledge, adds another instance of less importance (though he does not quite know its true history), which shall serve as a sufficient specimen of the whole class. In 1 Tim. iv. 16 for "the doctrine" of the books from 1611 to 1630, we read "thy doctrine" in 1629 (Camb.) down to

the Authorized Version which have been used in the formation of our Catalogues and in our suggested revision of the text are chiefly, though not exclusively, the following.

(1) The standard or primary one published in 1611, "Imprinted at London by *Robert Barker*, Printer to the Kings most Excellent Majestie." Here, however, we are met on the threshold of our researches by the perplexing fact that at least two separate issues bear the date of that year, yet differ from each other in so many minute particulars, that we cannot help raising the question which is the earlier or more authoritative, and consequently the more suitable to be taken as the model to which subsequent reprints ought to be accommodated. On this subject, so interesting to students of the English Bible, much information has been imparted by Mr Fry of Bristol, whose materials will be thankfully used by many that feel unable to adopt his conclusions, and might desire a little more scholarlike precision in the method of his investigations[1]. The two chief issues of 1611 may be respectively represented by a folio now in the British Museum (3050. g. 2), and another in the same Library (3050. g. 1) of which Mr Fry says in a manuscript note that "it is every leaf correct, and may be taken as a standard copy of this issue." There is yet a third class of books, bearing date the same year, containing (some more, some less) sheets of six leaves or twelve pages each, or occasionally only two or four leaves of a sheet, which appear to be reprints of portions of one or the other of the aforenamed issues, the preliminary matter being made up from the folio of 1617 or elsewhere, a circumstance which compli-

---

1762. Blayney (1769) restored "the," but Horne has seen "thy" in Bibles of the commencement of the present century. *Introduction*, Vol. II. Pt. II. p. 79 note (1834).

[1] *A Description of the Great Bible*, 1539,......*also of the editions, in large folio, of the Authorized Version of the Holy Scriptures, Printed in the years* 1611, 1613, 1617, 1634, 1640. By Francis Fry, F.S.A., folio, London, 1865.

cates the question not a little, so that in what we have to say it will be advisable to exclude all considerations respecting these reprinted portions[1]. This may be done the better, inasmuch as Mr Fry's researches have discovered only six such leaves in the Pentateuch, five in the Apocrypha, none in the New Testament. These reprints are bound up with and form a complete book with portions of each issue in two other Bibles in the Museum (1276. l. 4 and 3050. g. 3) respectively. The textual differences between the two original issues have been diligently collected below in Appendix B, from which only very manifest misprints of both books have been excluded: by a careful examination of our collation, in those portions where there are no known reprints, the student can form an independent judgment respecting the internal character of each of them. In preparing the present volume, a Bible belonging to the Syndics of the Cambridge University Press (A. 3. 14, wanting sheet A containing the Title-page, Dedication, and part of the Translators' Preface) has been substituted for the Museum book 3050. g. 2, and for 3050. g. 1 the Oxford reprint of 1833, as being a well-known publication which exactly resembles it in all places consulted, and was itself taken verbatim, with unusual care for insuring accuracy, from a Bible in the Library of the Delegates of the Oxford Uni-

---

[1] Gen. xlvi. 12—xlix. 27; Num. xxi. 2—xxvi. 65; Josh. x. 9—xi. 11; xv. 13—xvii. 8; Judg. xiv. 18—xx. 44; Ruth i. 9—2 Sam. ix. 13; xi. 26—xiv. 19; xv. 31—xvii. 14; xix. 39—xxii. 49; 1 Kin. i. 17—xvi. 3; xvii. 20—xxii. 34; 2 Kin. i. 15—2 Chr. xxix. 31; Ezra ii. 55—Job xxii. 3; xxv. 4—xxxi. 28; xxxiv. 5—xli. 31; Ps. vi. 3—Prov. vi. 35; ix. 14—xiv. 28; xvii. 3—Eccles. ii. 26; vi. 1—Cant. vii. 1; Isai. i. 1—xxxii. 13; xli. 13—lxiii. 1; Jer. i. 7—vii. 26; xi. 12—xv. 10; xxvi. 18—Ezek. xiv. 22; xvii. 22—xx. 44; Zech. xiv. 9—Mal. ii. 13; 1 Esdr. iv. 37—v. 26; Ecclus. xvi. 7—xx. 17; Baruch iii. 1—iv. 28; Song, ver. 20—Hist. Susanna, ver. 15 : in all 244 leaves (but not so many in any one copy), distinguished by the comparison of B. M. 3050. g. 2 with 44 other copies, in respect to initial letters and minute typographical variations (*Fry*, Table 2).

versity Press at that time in actual use. Copies of both issues or recensions of 1611 survive in great numbers in private as well as in public hands, since, when the Translation was completed, every Church had to be furnished with at least one without delay. Fifteen copies of that which it followed, twelve of the other, are enumerated in the Advertisement which preceded the publication of the Oxford reprint (dated Jan. 14, 1834), and Mr Fry has seen at least seventy, although he seldom gives us information as to where they are severally located[1].

The question which of the two recensions is the earlier must be decided partly by external, partly by internal considerations. The latter will speak for themselves, and it may be taken for granted that no one will doubt the great superiority on the whole of the text of the Oxford reprint to the other, or hesitate to mark in it many designed improvements and corrections which betray a later hand (Appendix B § II.), while the instances in which the Syndics' book is superior or not inferior to the other (App. B § I.) are scanty, slight, and incapable of suggesting the converse inference[2].

[1] Besides those named above the author has examined (not to mention some in private hands) resembling Camb. Synd. A. 3. 14, S. John's Coll. Cambridge (T. 2. 24); King's College (53); Jesus Coll. Cambridge (A. 7. 7 with the *false* date of 1613 on the title-page of the O. T.); Lambeth Muniment Room: resembling the Oxford reprint, Brit. Mus. (466. i. 6); Sion College Arch. x. 3; Cambridge University Library (I. 15, 16); Emmanuel College (B. I. 23), and the very fine copy in the Bodleian.

[2] A few instances are as good as a thousand, if only they be unequivocal. We would press Ezek. xliv. 29, where what we call the first issue treats the final *mem* as if it were double; Amos vi. 7, where the second issue corrects the wrong number of the first; but 1 Macc. x. 47 seems conclusive, where *our* second issue, deeming "true peace" too strong a rendering of λόγων εἰρηνικῶν, banished "‖True" into the margin. There are no reprints in these leaves. It is fair to add two instances in App. B which we have found tending to an opposite conclusion, in the false arrangement of the margins of Wisd. iii. 14; Mark vii. 4, in the Oxford reprint. But the general drift of the internal evidence sets strongly the other way.

Both contain innumerable errors of the press, some peculiar to a single issue[1], not a few (including nearly all the false textual references in the margin, see below Sect. vi.) common to both. It is useful to remember one characteristic *erratum* of each, which will enable us to determine at a glance to which recension a particular volume in our hands belongs. The Syndics' copy and its fellows have "Judas" instead of "Jesus" in Matt. xxvi. 36; the Oxford reprint and its associates read twice over the following words (forming three complete lines) in Ex. xiv. 10 "the children of Israel lift up their eyes, and behold, the Egyptians marched after them, and they were sore afraid: and" the printer's eye wandering back from the second "the children of Israel" in the verse, to the first[2]. Yet in spite of this portentous blunder, the recension which contains it is decidedly the more correct of the two, and irresistibly forces on the mind of any one that has minutely studied both, that whether we regard emendations of the sense or comparative exemption from typographical oversights, it had undergone revision, fitful and superficial perhaps, but not the less real on that account. Hence it seems not quite reasonable, in answer to the enquiry "Which of the two issues was first printed?" to say with Mr Fry, "I do not think that any evidence on this point can be adduced, from the existence of an error in one, and the absence of it in another copy" (*A Description*, &c. p. 23). Not certainly from noting a single error or from noting twenty, for such an argument is cumulative in its weight, and can only be appreciated by patient enquirers:

---

[1] In compiling a list of errata in the Syndics' copy (A. 3. 14) much aid was given by the corrections made in that book by Gilbert Buchanan, LL.D., of Woodmansterne, Surrey, in the winter of 1813—4, when engaged in revising for the King's Printer his quarto edition of 1806.

[2] It deserves notice that this could easily be done if the type were set up from the Syndics' copy, where "the children of Israel" begins a line in both parts of the verse.

but if, out of two books substantially the same, one shall prove on examination more free than the other from mechanical imperfections and printers' *errata*, and at the same time full of small yet unequivocal corrections whether of the style or the matter of the performance, we cannot doubt that, in the absence of any considerable proof to the contrary, the common consent of mankind would pronounce that the better executed volume must needs be the later of the two.

And what considerable proof to the contrary has Mr Fry been able to allege? Direct evidence on the subject there is none, for never was a great enterprise like the production of our Authorized Version carried out with less knowledge handed down to posterity of the labourers, their method and order of working. There still remains the bibliographical branch of this investigation, and it will demand some attention. The first point we take up makes little in favour of Mr Fry's view of the priority of that issue which the Oxford reprint follows with such faithful exactness. All copies of the other issue, if they have a title-page at all, exhibit a respectable and elaborate woodcut (repeated before the New Testament with the necessary change in the printed words) that had often done duty before, notably in the Bishops' Bible of 1602. It represents the four Evangelists with their proper emblems at the top and bottom of the cut, the tents and armorial bearings of the twelve tribes on the left of the letter-press, the twelve Apostles on the right of it, the Paschal Lamb slain on the altar beneath it, the Lamb Triumphant under the Incommunicable Name surmounting all. But in many copies of the recension to which the Oxford reprint belongs the title-page is of a totally different character. It is a very elegant copper-plate engraving, of whose refined beauty Mr Fry's reproduction on stone (Plate 34) gives but a poor idea. Here Moses stands *cornutus* on the left of the letter-press title, Aaron on the right, the Apostles and Evangelists above and below in attitude and form quite different from the conventional manner of artists; above, the Incommunicable Name, the Dove, the Lamb Triumphant; below, the Pelican and her young; at the foot of this masterpiece the subscription *C. Boel fecit in Richmont,* Cornelius Boel of Antwerp then working at Richmond in Surrey. Now the point to be noted is this. It is admitted by Mr Fry and by every one else that in no copy of what he calls the second issue is there an engraved title, whereas some copies of *his* first issue have the engraved plate, others the woodcut, a few possibly, though not certainly, both, prefixed to the Old Testament. The inference seems a natural one that Boel's plate not being ready when the earliest copies of our Authorized Version were published, the old woodcut was made to serve in its place for a while, and that those copies of Mr Fry's first and our second issue which contain Boel's copper-plate, are in all probability the latest of any. If there be any more simple solution of the matter, it would be well to state it.

But that which is most dwelt upon by such as would invert what internal evidence points out as the true order of the two issues rests on facts relating to the reprinted leaves which Mr Fry has demonstrated with great pains and ingenuity. Out of 25 copies of *his* first issue which he examined, 23 were leaf for leaf alike, agreeing entirely with each other: in one copy two leaves, in another six, were of the rival issue. Forty-five copies of this latter issue were then collated, of which the large number of 41 were found to vary from each other in some of the reprinted leaves supplied (see p. 6 note), and only two pairs were entirely identical. "I have now shewn" he proceeds to sum up "from the actual comparison of a very large number of the

Bibles of 1611, as many as seventy, that one issue is unmixed (with the exception of eight leaves in two copies out of 25 examined), and that the other issue is made up in a very remarkable manner, not only with reprints, but that it is often mixed with the other issue, with the preliminary leaves of 1613, 1617, and 1634. Is not this conclusive evidence that the Bibles No. 1 and No. 2 before alluded to[1] are respectively of the 1st issue and of the 2nd issue[2]?" (*Description*, &c. p. 25.) Certainly not, if we understand what is meant by *conclusive evidence*. The facts established by Mr Fry (and we can confirm many of them from our own experience) are sufficient to raise a strong presumption that not very many copies of the earliest printed issue were bound up at once and sent out to Parish Churches, for which reservation their shameful inaccuracy will abundantly account. After the great and immediate demand was satisfied by that better edition which the Oxford reprint exhibits, and after the Translators were dispersed and had ceased to

---

[1] As usual, Mr Fry does not indicate what and where are the copies he used. He only says just before, "I placed my two best copies side by side, the one with the error of three lines in Ex. xiv. 10, the No. 1 copy..., and the other with the verse correctly printed, No. 2 copy... (p. 22)," which is vague enough. He tries also to make something of "the obvious difference in the condition of the rules with which the black lines [inclosing the letter-press] are printed. In No. 1 they are straight and generally true at the corners; in the 2nd Issue they are not so true, and are more open, shewing the effect of use" (p. 25). The difference will not appear so conspicuous to every one who inspects these early Bibles; from the original leaves supplied at the end of the Syndics' copy of his own book, and from comparing various parts of Brit. Mus. 3050. g. 1 and g. 2, quite an opposite conclusion might be drawn: but if the difference were ever so great, it would only prove that the lines were repaired for a new issue. It is even doubtful, on close inspection, whether the same lines were used for both.

[2] "Because those Bibles which were printed and bound up before the 2nd Issue was printed (and no doubt there were such) could have leaves of no other Issue or edition inserted" (p. 22). This consideration he calls "almost absolute proof" of his opinion. It shews, of course, that his theory is self-consistent, but nothing more.

have any control over their work, the printer seems to have gradually put forth the unused sheets that had been first struck off and deliberately laid aside, supplemented by reprinted leaves and other portions of later books.

"Why these 244 leaves were required to be printed a second time we can only conjecture" (*ibid.* p. 24). In truth the difficulty presses equally upon every possible hypothesis that can be maintained. Almost the only real information available which bears even remotely on the matter is Dr Anthony Walker's Life of John Bois[1] [1560—1643], who was a member first of the fourth, afterwards of the second Company. Of him we are told

" Four years he spent in this service[2], at the end thereof (the whole work being finished, and three copies of the whole Bible being sent to London, one from Cambridge, a second from Oxford, and a third from Westminster), a new choice was to be made of six in all, two out of each company, to review the whole work, and extract one out of all the three, to be committed to the press. For the despatch of this business Mr Downes[3] and he, out of the Cambridge company[4], were

[1] Harleian MS. 7053, printed also in Peck's *Desiderata Curiosa*, Vol. II. Book VIII. 1732. The Harleian manuscript is written by the hand which records a list of Degrees conferred by George II. at Cambridge, April 25, 1728: Peck derived his materials from one of the Baker papers, which John Lewis also cited in 1739. The two manuscript authorities are independent, each preserving passages not found in the other. Both contain incidental statements, hitherto unnoticed, which might lead to the supposition that the different Translators took to themselves separate books (Harl. pp. 104, 105), as was really the case with the Bishops' Bible.

[2] So that we need not take literally the "twice seven times seventy-two days and more," about two years and nine months, as Canon Westcott notes (*General View of History of English Bible*, p. 154), which *The Translator to the Reader* speaks of. Elsewhere Anthony Walker says of Bois's labours, "Five years were spent in the Translation, which makes no noise, because it carries no name" (Peck, *ubi supra*, p. 53).

[3] " Though Mr Downes would not go, till he was either fetcht or threatened with a Pursuivant." Walker in *Peck*. The Harleian copy does not mention this story, so characteristic of the times.

[4] So that " two out of each company," mentioned just before, must mean two out of each *place ;* and the final Committee consisted of six persons, not of twelve, as was

History of the Text. 13

sent for up to London, where meeting their four fellow-labourers, they went daily to Stationers' Hall, and in three quarters of a year fulfilled their task. Whilst they were employed in this last business, he, and he only, took notes of their proceedings, which he diligently kept to his dying day."

Could these notes be recovered[1], they would solve, not only the problem discussed by Mr Fry, but many other questions of great interest. If Dr Walker can be trusted, it would seem that every part of each Company's task had in some fashion been revised by each of the rest, a statement which neither the time employed, nor the results obtained, render very likely (see Sect. VII.). At all events it is clear, unless we reject his evidence altogether, that the printing, so far as the Translators superintended it at all, must have been begun and ended within the short period of nine months, which seems wholly inadequate for the accomplishing of all they had in hand[2].

---

stated at the Synod of Dort (1618). Compare, however, Anderson, *Annals of the English Bible* (1845), Vol. II. pp. 381—2, and my friend Dr John Eadie's noble and almost posthumous *English Bible*, Vol. II. p. 201. Bp Miles Smith, the author of the Preface, and Bp Bilson of Winchester, "whose name does not appear among the revisers, superintended the work at press." See below p. 264.

[1] Harl. 7053 contains John Bois's will dated the year he died (1643), wherein he bequeaths his books and papers, on which he set great store, to his daughter, Anne Bois, "to her best use and commodity," and requests his curate, John Killingworth, to be "aiding and helpful in the disposing" of the same. They were no doubt sold, and may yet be found in some private collection.

[2] A ray of fresh light has been thrown upon the history of the version by a letter referred to, so far as we know, for the first time by Mr J. H. Blunt, *Annotated Bible*, Introduction, p. xliv. note 1 (1878). The volume which contains it, the gift to the Bodleian (Rawlinson, C. 849) of Archbishop Ussher's grandson, James Tyrrell, consists of large abstracts of learned books in the Primate's cramped handwriting, one sheet being written, after the poet Pope's fashion, on the back of the letter in question, which has thus been preserved for our use. The writer, William Eyre, Eyers, or Ayers (the name being spelt each way), as the courtesy of Dr Luard, the University Registrary, enables me to know, was Fellow of Emmanuel College, Cambridge, B.A. 1595—6, M.A. 1599, B.D. 1606, and afterwards Prebendary of Ely. Its chief purpose is civilly to decline a proposal made to him by Ussher, then Chancellor of S. Patrick's Cathedral, to accept

Although we have not been able to resist the pressure of the internal evidence which assures us that the issue represented by Synd. A. 3. 14 is the earlier of the two, yet the influence of our error (if any shall still judge it to be an error) upon the text of the present volume, as given in our Appendices A—C, is infinitesimally small. It is strictly confined within the limits indicated in Appendix B, § 1, the great majority of which variations are either purely indifferent, or would have been received on their own merits, without reference to the prior claims of the copy that contains them.

Respecting Appendix C, wherein are registered the joint readings of the two issues of 1611 which in later times have been displaced but ought now to be restored, not a few of them are quite insignificant in themselves, but are re-established as a matter of right, and as a kind of protest against

a Fellowship at the infant College in Dublin. Dating from Emmanuel College Dec. 5, 1608 "W. Eyre" writes as follows: "Sr It pleased God to bring us in safety to Cambridge before the last day of November...In my absence there was an order taken from the King's Majestie by the Arch B of Cantuar that the translation of the Bible shall be finished and printed as soon as may be, but two of the entire company are chosen to revise and conform (*sic*) the whole at London. Hereupon I am earnestly requested to get again that copy of our part which I lent you for D[?] Daniel his use, for albeit there be two fair written copies out of it: yet there will be use of it because I noted in the margent by *rashe tevoth* (ר״ת) of the places which were doubted of. And this צריק עיון [i.e. it wants consideration. Cf. Zanolini, *Lex. Chald.-Rabbin.* Patavii, 1747. *Rashe tevoth* seems to mean *head marks*] is not in the others. Wherefore I am to request you so soon as you can after my letters come to your hands to send that copy forthwith by some that may either deliver it to myself, or send me word where I may gain it." The D [or G?] Daniel to whose judgment the revision had been submitted must have been William Daniel, Fellow of Trinity College, Dublin, 1593, translator into Irish of the N.T. (1602), and of the book of Common Prayer (1608), Archbishop of Tuam 1609—28. The name of Eyre is not in the list of translators, yet we see that the work of the Cambridge Company was subjected to his criticism, and by him imparted to others. The "two of the entire company" who were to finish the work in London, leaves that point just as ambiguous as ever. See above, p. 12 note 4.

the unnecessary, the almost wanton changes, in which certain editors of the Bible have been pleased to indulge. Examples of this kind will be seen in Judg. xix. 29; 1 Sam. xx. 5; 2 Sam. vii. 7 *marg.*; 1 Kin. xv. 27; xvi. 19; 2 Kin. viii. 19; Isai. vi. 8; Hos. xiii. 3; 1 Esdr. viii. 75; 2 Esdr. xv. 22; 2 Macc. viii. 33; Luke xix. 13 *marg.*[1]

We now proceed to describe the principal editions of the Authorized Bible which have appeared since 1611, especially those which seem to have been prepared with some degree of care, or have largely influenced the text of succeeding impressions.

(2) The Holy Bible of 1612, copies of which are in the British Museum (1276. b. 6) and at Trinity College, Cambridge (A. 8. 51), is beautifully printed in a small clear Roman type in octavo, the woodcut of the first issue of 1611 (above, p. 9) being reproduced in a reduced size. On examining the collation we have made of this the earliest reprint of the Authorized Version (Appendices A, B, C below), it may be considered to depart but seldom from the issue represented by the Oxford reprint, except to correct some grave mistake (e.g. Mark vii. 4 *marg.*). In such a case it is usually followed by the edition of 1616, also printed in Roman type, but rarely influences the black-letter Bibles of 1613 or 1617. In 1 Kin. iii. 4; 1 Esdr. viii. 39; Rev. xx. 13 *marg.* this edition stands alone. The

---

[1] Students should be aware that the representation given of the New Testament of 1611 in Bagster's *Hexapla*, 1841 cannot be implicitly relied upon. There are two issues of that book, with two several Introductions, and the stereotyped plates bear marks of alterations in what seems the later (Matt. xiii. 45). Thus, for example, in John viii. 4 "said" suits neither form of the Bible of 1611: sometimes the text follows our first issue, as in Matt. xiii. 4, 31, 45; xviii. 30; xxii. 24; Mark xv. 46; Acts iv. 27; xvi. 7, 19; xxi. 2; xxv. 1; Rom. vi. 21; x. 21; xi. 22; Eph. vi. 21; 1 Thess. i. 9; James v. 4; 2 Pet. ii. 6: sometimes that which Mr Fry counts the earliest, as in Luke ii. 24; x. 36; John xiv. 23; Acts vi. 12; xv. 11; 1 Pet. i. 22. In Rom. x. 19 "will I anger" Bagster seems to stand alone.

following are examples of improvements brought into it, which immediate successors have overlooked: Ps. xcix. 2; 2 Esdr. ii. 7 *marg.*; Judith xvi. 24; 1 Macc. v. 9; Matt. v. 22; Acts xiii. 19; 1 Cor. vii. 32; 2 Cor. v. 20. We reject the grammatical corrections in Dan. v. 31; John xi. 18 *marg.*

(3) The Holy Bible of 1613 is the more generally known from a collation of the smaller black-letter folio copy of it at the University Press at Oxford with the Oxford reprint of the book of 1611, annexed to that very useful publication[1]. This book is readily distinguished from both issues of 1611, inasmuch as it contains 72 lines of smaller type in a column, to their 59[2]. It is plain that no formal revision of the text, italics, or margin, was attempted thus early. Out of the 412 variations which the Oxford collation records, just 70 arise from the following of the Syndics' copy (A. 3. 14) in preference to the other issue, but this includes corrections of some 20 evident misprints of the Oxford reprint issue. In about four places (Ezra iii. 5; Ezek. xxiv. 7; 1 Macc. iv. 29; 2 Thess. ii. 15) we find manifest improvements on the standard editions: in Dan. ix. 12 the reading of the Hebrew margin or *keri* is adopted ("word") against the other books:

---

[1] We have used for our own purpose a copy in the Syndics' Library, Cambridge (A. 3. 13). To the variations recorded in the Oxford reprint we have been able to add in passing Ruth iii. 15 "she went" Synd. (A. 3. 14), 1613, but "he went" Oxon.; Ps. lxxviii. 60 *marg.* "1 Sam." Synd. (a reprint), 1613, "1 King." Oxon.; Jer. xl. 1 "||chains" 1613, "||captaine" Oxon.; Ezek. xvi. 16 "Of thy garments" 1613, "And of thy garments" Oxon.; Wisd. ix. 15 "earthly" 1613, "earthy" Oxon.; 2 Cor. iii. 3 "fleshly" 1613,

"fleshy" Oxon. In Josh. xii. 11; 2 Sam. xvii. 25; Neh. xi. 14 *marg.*; 1 Esdr. v. 20 *marg.*; Judith iii. 5 —vii. 16 (Olofernes), Proper names are differently spelt, but the Oxford collation does not profess to include these.

[2] A few copies of what we regard as the first issue of 1611 are said to bear on the Old Testament title-page, but not on the New, a genuine date of 1613: that being no doubt the year they were bound up. There was at that time no inducement to antedate falsely, but rather the contrary.

nearly all the other variations arise from the glaring misprints of this handsome but inaccurate volume. Such are the omissions of clauses by reason of their having the same beginning or ending as those immediately preceding (1 Kin. iii. 15; Matt. xiii. 8; xvi. 11; John xx. 25), and of two whole verses, Ecclus. xvi. 13, 14, as also the putting "delighted" for "defiled" Ezek. xxiii. 7, the omission of "thou" in Mark ix. 24, the leaving out of "not" in 2 Tim. iv. 16, and other errors almost as gross. That this book was set up from *our* first issue appears likely, as well from many other resemblances to be seen in Appendix B, as from the printer's mistaking "y^t" in that book for "the" in Acts xxi. 38. The other issue has "that Egyptian" in full[1].

The next two books were used at Tregothnan (R. 4 and R. 7), by the kind permission of their owner, Viscount Falmouth.

(4) The Holy Bible in small folio Roman type 1616, with the Prayer Book and Genealogies, Map, &c. prefixed, the metrical Psalms with musical notes (dated 1612) and Private Prayers at the end, with their first leaf lost. This seems a somewhat rare book, not particularly intended for Church reading, is beautifully printed, and in a very perfect state. It appears to be the first edition of the Authorized Version which was submitted to any considerable revision. Its value will be seen from the study of Appendices A and B, and it should be remarked all along, that improvements brought in from time to time in Bibles of the Roman type seem to have had very slight influence with the printers of the black-letter books of 1617, 1634, 1640, who continued to set the press from one or the other of the issues of 1611, almost regardless of subsequent changes for the better.

[1] Other copies, by no means rare, are from S. Luke's Chapel, in the Precinct, Norwich (bought 1618), now in the Chapter Library there, and Brit. Mus. 469. g. 10, with Boel's frontispiece, and an inserted title page of 1611.

Some of the corrections of 1616 were received into the great folio of 1617, but the following, among others, were overlooked: Gen. xxii. 7; 2 Sam. xxiii. 20; 1 Kin. xx. 3; 1 Chr. i. 5, 47; vii. 13; xxvi. 5; xxvii. 33; 2 Chr. xi. 20; xxx. 6; xxxii. 20; Neh. viii. 10; Eccles. vii. 26; Cant. v. 12; Jer. xxxv. 13; Tobit iv. 12; Ecclus. li. 12; 1 Macc. viii. 8; ix. 35; xi. 34, 56; xv. 23; Matt. xvi. 19; Mark xiv. 32; Luke xxiii. 19; Acts iv. 17; xxvii. 18; Rom. vi. 12; vii. 13; xvi. 10. Dr Corrie, Master of Jesus College, Cambridge, has a rare 8vo. in Roman type, dated 1619.

(5) The Holy Bible, large folio, black letter, 1617, a much more pretentious but less valuable edition[1]. As its leaves have got much mixed with those of the other folios, especially of our first issue of 1611, it is proper to apply Mr Fry's tests before using any copy (*A Description*, &c. plates 46, 47), so far as for critical purposes it is worth using at all. The large paper copies may be expected to be pure for obvious reasons. The Tregothnan book does not answer Fry's tests in three leaves up to Ps. xxii[2]. Among its few original corrections are Mal. iv. 2; 2 Tim. ii. 19. The Bible of 1617, like that of 1612, usually abides by the issue of 1611 represented by our Synd. A. 3. 14, while that of 1616 follows the Oxford reprint standard, even in such obvious errors as Hos. vi. 5.

The public demand must have been satisfied with these several editions, especially of the large size, which were published so near each other. Some years elapsed before the appearance of other chief Bibles, whereof three several pairs can most conveniently be discussed according to their

---

[1] Other copies are numerous: e.g. Brit. Mus. (1272 h. 4) and (3052. b.); a copy given by "Thomas Hobson, Carrier of Cambridge, to Benet Parish," Trin. Coll. Cambridge (A. 12. 34), large paper, very fine; S. John's Coll. Camb. (T. 6, 26); Caius Coll. (H. o. 26).

[2] They are Xx 3 (Neh. vii. 11—viii. 9), which is taken from our first issue; Zz (Job i. 17—iv. 16), and Ccc 2 (Ps. xix. 2—xxii. 31), whence derived Mr Fry's list fails to shew.

relation to each other, rather than in the chronological order,—the two of 1629, those of 1630, 1634, 1638, 1640.

(6) The Holy Bible, small quarto, 1629 "Imprinted at London by *Bonham Norton* and *John Bill* Printers to the King's most excellent Majestie." Also in folio with the same readings and the same setting up. Dr Newth tells me of one copy at New College, Hampstead; another is possessed by the Rev. W. L. Manley, Vicar of Treleigh, Redruth.

(7) The Holy Bible, also small quarto, 1630 "Imprinted at London by *Robert Barker*, Printer to the King's most Excellent Majestie: and by the Assignes of *John Bill*."

These two books are of the same size, have the same title-page, though different tail-pieces at the end of the Prophets, correspond with each other page for page, line for line, with the closest exactness, even to the peculiar shape of the letters used in the same places (compare, however, Num. xxii. 31; Ezek. xx. 37 *marg.*; Dan. viii. 18 *marg.*), so that the type from which the two were printed off was, at least in my opinion, set up but once. The volume of 1629, however, is printed on much worse paper, and does not contain the Apocrypha[1], although APO- still remains, as in its fellow, below the tail-piece at the end of Malachi. At the end are the metrical Psalms with musical notes, and the date of 1630. It would never be suspected, prior to actual trial, that the text in these two books is not absolutely identical. Yet an inspection of Appendices A, B, C will shew that this is not the case: e.g. Gen. xlvi. 12; xlvii. 18; Lev. xviii. 30; xxv. 5 *marg.*; Num. v. 20; 1 Kin. xviii. 28;

---

[1] Thus early began the practice of leaving out the Apocrypha, although it had been forbidden by Archbishop Abbot in 1615 on pain of a year's imprisonment (C. R. Rivington, *Records of Stationers' Company*, p. 21). It was hardening into fixed habit when Selden said, "The Apocrypha is bound with the Bibles of all churches that have been hitherto. Why should we leave it out?" (*Table Talk*, p. 10). The copies used by me are also in the Syndics' Library, A. 5. 22 and 25.

xx. 3; 1 Chr. i. 38; vii. 27; xxiv. 11; 2 Chr. xxvi. 18; Esther viii. 5 *marg.* (*devised* 1630, for *the device*); Ps. xxiv. 10; Jer. xl. 1; Ezek. i. 2; xvi. 59; xxxvi. 2; Dan. v. 4 (dranke 1629, drunke 1630 after 1611); Rom. x. 21; xvi. 10; 2 Cor. vii. 3 (yee are 1629, you are 1630 after 1611); ix. 4 (haply 1629, happily 1630 after 1611); Gal. i. 6 (removen 1629); Eph. vi. 21, 24; 1 Thess. i. 9; 1 Pet. v. 12. Instances such as these help to justify Mr Fry's assertion, which to an inexperienced reader might appear somewhat unlikely, "The absence of a particular error in one copy, is no proof that it is of a different edition from the one with the error; for I have observed many errors in one copy corrected in another of the same edition, in other Bibles than those here described" (*A Description,* &c. p. 23), meaning those of 1611 and their near contemporaries. The Bible of 1630 has some readings that seem peculiar to itself, e.g. 1 Macc. x. 20 "require of thee"; xii. 53 *fin.* "them" for "men."

Thus far the reprinting of the Authorized Version had been entirely in the hands of the King's Printers. They had made changes in the text, slight indeed and far from numerous, yet enough to shew that they doubted not their competency to make more if they had taken the trouble. The italic type and textual references in the margin they left untouched, with all the obvious faults of both uncorrected, only that occasionally a false quotation was set right. The next stage in the history of our Translation is more interesting, and the Cambridge University printers, Thomas and John Buck in 1629, Thomas Buck and Roger Daniel in 1638, published two important folios which have largely (and on the whole beneficially) influenced our Bibles to this day.

(8) and (9)[1]. The first Cambridge editions of the Holy

---

[1] These editions are not at all rare. We have used for the one of 1629, Camb. University Library, I. 14. 12; for that of 1638,

History of the Text.

Bible shall be considered together, inasmuch as that of 1629, which is the smaller of the two, and has the Prayer Book prefixed to it, and the metrical Psalms with musical notes bound up at the end, inaugurated that course of systematic revision of the text, of the italics, and of the margin, which nine years afterwards was more fully and consistently carried out. It is not a little remarkable, that the subject of the internal character of our English Bible, as distinct from its external history, had excited so little attention for the space of two centuries, that the high merit of these books has been understood only within the last forty years. "For this beautiful edition," Lea Wilson writes most truly of the elder of the two, "the text appears to have undergone a complete revision, although I can find no record of such having been done by authority" (*List of Bibles*, &c. 4to. 1845). "So far as I can judge" says Bp. Turton of its compeer of 1638 "the edition was carefully superintended" (*Text of the English Bible considered*, 2nd edition, 1833, p. 35). As he becomes better acquainted with it, his language grows more decided, as well it might: "A revision of the text of 1611... it is now certain, was carried into effect, from the beginning of the Volume to the end, at Cambridge, in 1638" (p. 126). "The revision indeed was a work of great labour" (p. 91), but he always speaks of it as commenced and carried out in the same volume. What Turton did not know, but only regarded as possible, that it might "hereafter appear that an earlier revision had taken place" (*ibid.*), is a fact that no one will doubt as regards the text who shall examine the contents of our subjoined Appendices. The task seems to have been executed between the two sets of editors in no unequal shares. What the one party left undone, by reason of haste or human oversight, the others in a good measure

Syndics' Library, A. 3. 8. The page of the New Testament.
date of the latter is on the title

supplied, by inserting words or clauses, especially in the Old Testament, overlooked by the editors of 1611; by amending manifest errors; by rendering the italic notation at once more self-consistent, and more agreeable to the design of the original Translators (see below, Sect. III.). What persons were concerned in the edition of 1629, as Lea Wilson notices, we are wholly ignorant, but if similarity of plan and spirit afford us any ground for conjecture, one at least of them must have had a share with others in preparing the subsequent book of 1638, and these latter, as we learn from a manuscript note in the Jesus College copy, in the handwriting of Richard Sterne, Master of the College, and Vice-Chancellor that selfsame year, were Dr Goad of Hadley, Dr Ward (see below, p. 264), Mr Boyse[1], and Mr Mead[1]: men whose obscure diligence in a grave and delicate work was doubtless rewarded with honour more excellent than fame can give or take away[2].

With this pair of editions began the habit of adding to the parallel textual references in the margin: the Bible of 1638 admits also one or two fresh marginal notes (1 Macc. iv. 15; ix. 36). We have seldom to hesitate about the propriety of receiving their emendations of the text (see Appendix C, 2 Sam. xvi. 8; Ps. cxix. 42 *marg.*), as in the case

---

[1] Doubtless meaning John Bois or Boys, spoken of above (p. 12, &c.), and the illustrious Joseph Mede (d. 1638) from whose *Works* (p. 767) Dean Burgon supplies the following curious extract: "Compare Acts ix. 7 (where it is said, *They heard Paul's voice,*) with Acts xxii. 9 (where it is said, *They heard not the voice of him that spake unto him*) and take heed here of some of our English Bibles, which have put in a [*not*] where it should not be, as they have done the like in other places. Fie upon such careless printers."

[2] Kilburne calls the book of 1638 "the Authentic corrected Cambridge Bible, revised *Mandato Regio,*" whatever that may mean (*Dangerous Errors in several late Printed Bibles to the great scandal and corruption of sound and true religion. Discovered by Wm. Kilburne, Gent.*, 8vo., Finsbury, 1659, p. 6). His little pamphlet of 15 pages produced a great effect, and is full of weighty matter. A copy is in the British Museum (1214 a. 9).

of some of their successors: their corrections command our assent by their simple truth. One of the changes introduced in 1638 it would have been better to have finally adopted, "and the truth" with the Greek in John xiv. 6. The "and" held its place beyond Blayney's revision of 1769, but has disappeared in Bibles from D'Oyly and Mant (1817) downwards. The following *errata* have been noticed in these two admirable books, most of which blemishes have been perpetuated to modern times.

1629. 2 Chr. ix. 11 *marg.*; Jer. xxxiv. 16; Ezek. xxxi. 14; Ecclus. xvii. 24; 2 Macc. ix. 18 (see Appendix C for all these); Judith i. 6 ("Hydaspe:" so also 1638 [not 1744], 1762, 1769, all moderns down to our model [below, p. 38], which restores "Hydaspes" of 1611); Baruch vi. 8 ("gold," all the editions just named, with 1744 added: here again our model restores "silver" of 1611); 2 Cor. viii. 7 ("in utterance," repeated in 1638, 1699, "*in* utterance" 1762: but 1743, 1769 and the moderns restored "and utterance" of 1611); 1 Tim. iv. 16 (see p. 4, note). Notice also that this edition has misled every subsequent one by placing the reference to Ps. xxii. 6 in Job xxv. 6 over against the first "worm" instead of the second.

1638. Neh. xii. 3 *marg.* (see Appendix A); Ezek. xviii. 1; Hos. xiii. 3 (see for these Appendix C); Acts vi. 3 (see p. 4); Rev. ii. 20 ("Jezabel," the Greek form, followed by 1699, 1743: but "Jezebel" was restored in 1762).

In the matter of the italic type, to which much attention is paid in these two Bibles, one or other of them has led later copies wrong in the following places:

2 Sam. xxiv. 12 *do it* (1629), corrected in the American (1867) only; Isai. v. 9 *marg.* This is (1638); 25 *were* torn (1638); xxxviii. 12 *from the* thrumme (1638); Jer. xxv. 18 and the princes (1638); Ezek. xl. 4 *art* thou brought (1629); Zech. vi. 3 and bay (1638); 1 Esdr. viii. 58 is a vow (1629); Matt. xv. 9 *for doctrines* 1638, *for* doctrines 1762, &c.; Eph. v. 26 cleanse it (1629). All these are merely uncorrected *errata*[1].

---

[1] Professor Grote (*MS.* p. 36) speaks of a small 4to., Cambridge, 1637, in Trinity College Library, "which has none of the additions

The next pair comprises the black letter folios of the King's Printer, dated (10) 1634 [B. M. 1276 l. 5. 1—2] and (11) 1640 [B. M. 1276 l. 7]. The former is much mixed with later issues of the books of 1611 and 1617, and may be discriminated by the use of Mr Fry's elaborate tests (*A Description*, &c. Plates 46, 47). The latter is at once detected by its use of Roman letters instead of italics in the marginal notes, nor does the type run quite line for line with the earlier folios. Speaking generally, these books contain none of the improvements found in the two Cambridge editions, although a few changes for the better may be met with here and there. Thus the edition of 1634 anticipates the emendations of 1638 in 1 Chr. i. 20; John vii. 16 (see Appendix A): in Hagg. i. 12 it reads "Joshuah," in Rev. xxi. 20 "sardonyx." In Ecclus. xxxv. 18; xlix. 4; Acts iv. 17; vii. 10 (see Appendix A) that of 1640, but not the other, adopts the readings of 1629. A fuller examination would no doubt make known a few more instances, equally insignificant.

The volume of 1640 proved to be the last of the Bibles of its class; the Great Rebellion leaving men neither inclination nor means for costly undertakings of this nature. "You may well remember," writes William Kilburne (see above, p. 22, note 2) in 1659, to the honourable and elect Christians whom he addresses, "the zeal and care of the late Bishops (especially of reverend and learned Doctor Usher) was such, that for the omission in one impression of the

of Buck, 1638." From the specimen Bp. Lightfoot gives of its reading in 1 Cor. xii. 28 (*On a Fresh Revision*, &c. p. 129, note), it does appear to contain the changes or improvements of Cambridge, 1629. Such is the case also in Gen. xxxix. 1; Deut. xxvi. 1; Job iv. 6. The valuable manuscript notes of Professor Grote, from which we shall hereafter make several extracts, though scarcely in a state suitable for publication in full, were obligingly placed at my disposal by his representatives, and throw much light on the internal history of the printing of the Authorized Bible.

History of the Text. 25

Negative word [not] in the seventh Commandment, the Printer was fined £2000 or £3000 in the late King's time, as I have heard[1], which happened long before the late wars began: in which time, through the absence of the King's Printers, and cessation of Bible-printing at London, many erroneous English Bibles were printed in and imported from Holland[2]; which being diligently compared by the late Assembly of Divines were reported to the Parliament in 1643 to be corrupt and dangerous to Religion" (*Dangerous Errors*, &c. p. 5[3]). This importation indeed was expressly prohibited by statute, without much good effect; "Moreover, during the time of the late Parliament great numbers of Bibles in a large 12" volume were imported from Holland in 1656 with this false title (*Imprinted at London by Robert Barker, Anno* 1638)...being contrary to the several Acts of Parliament of 20° Sept. 1649 and 7 Janu. 1652 for regulating of Printing" (*ibid*. p. 12). Kilburne furnishes a really painful

---

[1] This notorious book, referred to by Addison (*Spectator*, No. 579), was published by the King's Printers, Robert Barker and Martin Lucas, in 1632: the real fine was £300, to be expended on a fount of fair Greek type. It was inflicted by Archbishop Laud (whom even on the eve of the Restoration Kilburne does not care to name) in the High Commission Court. The impression was of course called in, but a single copy is said to survive in the Library at Wolfenbuttel. Mr J. H. Blunt (*Annotated Bible*, Introduction, p. lvii., note) finds the same error in a German Bible of about 1731. Mr Stevens (*Athenæum*, June 20, 1874) speaks of similar copies dated 1632, possessed by Mr Lenox of New York and by the British Museum. I do not find this error in B. M. 1276 k.

5, folio, or 3052 b. 22, 8°.
[2] While on the table before them was lying unopened a Bible Ponderous, bound in leather, brass-studded, printed in Holland.
Longfellow, *Miles Standish*, IV. But the Dutch counterfeit of Field's edition, 24°, 1658 (B. M. 3051 a. 7) is clearer and (I think) more correct than Field's own (B. M. 1159 b. 12).
[3] This statement is confirmed by Whitelocke (*Memorials*, p. 89, 1732): "1644, By advice of the Assembly of Divines, an erroneous print of the English Bible at Amsterdam sent over hither, was suppressed by order of Parliament." So again (p. 167) "Aug. 19, 1645. Ordered that no foreign impressions of English Bibles be vended here, without perusal of the Assembly."

list of the inaccuracies of these foreign Bibles ("thirty grand faults in part of Genesis, a hundred in Isai. i—xxvii."), but shews plainly that the privileged printers, Henry Hills and John Field, were scarcely a whit more careful. They had, in truth, to pay for their privilege a bribe of £500 per annum to certain men in power, "whose names, out of respect to them, I forbear to mention" (*ibid.* p. 14), and reimbursed themselves for that shameful outlay by taking no measures for the due correction of the press. In their Bibles of 1653, 1655 (two editions), 1656 (two editions), and 1657 (reputed to be the worst of all), Kilburne computes that he discovered twenty thousand faults, some (which he particularises) being intolerably gross. On the other hand, he praises several editions in 8vo. and 12mo. issued "by Authority of Parliament" in 1646, 1648, 1651, &c., by Wm. Bentley of Finsbury, based upon the Cambridge folio of 1638.

Of the Bibles published during the latter part of the seventeenth century, that of Hills and Field, small 8vo. London, 1660, is remarkable for certain additions to the original marginal notes of 1611, subsequently improved upon in a Cambridge quarto of 1682—3 (see Sect. II.) bearing the name of John Hayes, the University Printer, who had previously put forth a well-known edition in 1677. The later of Hayes's two contains a great number of fresh textual references, the reputed work of Dr Anthony Scattergood, and mostly taken from his Bible, also published at Cambridge in 1678. But the most celebrated edition of the period was that undertaken on the motion of Archbishop Tenison, and at the alleged request of Convocation in 1699, by the eminently learned William Lloyd [1627—1717], successively Bishop of S. Asaph and of Worcester, under whose superintendence appeared

(12) The Holy Bible, large folio, 3 vol. "London, Printed by *Charles Bill* and the Executrix of *Thomas*

Newcomb deceased, Printers to the King's most excellent Majesty, 1701."

This splendid but somewhat cumbersome book is the first that contains the marginal dates (see Sect. VII.), and sundry marginal annotations, of doubtful merit, discussing chronological difficulties and imparting other information (Sect. II.). Annexed are Bp. Cumberland's Tables of Scripture measures, weights, and coins (first published in 1685), Tables of Kindred, Time, and Offices and Conditions of men. The textual references also are increased, but not very materially, and in respect to punctuation many parentheses were restored, which had been gradually removed from the text (see Sect. IV.). On the whole, this hasty labour added little to the fame of the veteran Lloyd, and in 1703 the Lower House of Convocation made a formal *Representation* to the Upper respecting the many errors it contains[1]. Except in regard to the dates, no principal edition so little influenced succeeding Bibles as this, notwithstanding the high auspices under which it came forth.

It was doubtless through the care of Archbishop Wake (who, though himself not a very powerful writer, had the spirit of a true scholar) that persons from whom so little could be expected as George I. and his great minister, were induced to issue four salutary Rules, dated April 24, 1724, to the King's Printers[2], with a view to the more

---

[1] Our authority for this statement must be Lewis (*Complete History of Translations of the Bible*, 2nd ed. 1739, p. 350), inasmuch as on searching the Records of the Proceedings of both Houses of Convocation, now deposited in the Archiepiscopal Library at Lambeth, I can find no trace of synodical action about a new edition of the Bible either in the Registers or in the Schedules for 1699, which, however, for that year are incomplete. Those for 1703 (the year then ending on March 24) are all preserved, and in a long list of *Gravamina*, brought to the Upper House on Feb. 11, one article declares "That in some late editions of the Holy Bible, and of the Liturgy of the Church of England, several gross errors have been committed." If this be all, Lewis seems to have made too much of what actually occurred.

[2] Lewis (*ubi supra*, p. 351).

effectual removal of misprints from their copies of the Authorized Version. One of these rules strikes at what was beyond question the root of the mischief in the evil days of Hills and Field, and prescribes that those employed on so grave a work should receive competent salaries for their pains and skill. In the middle of the eighteenth century the Bibles of the Basketts, at once the King's and Oxford University Printers, earned a fair name both for the beauty of their typography and their comparative freedom from misprints. Their quarto of 1756 is particularly commended, and will supply the student with a knowledge of the exact state of our Bibles just before the commencement of the kindred labours of Paris and Blayney, which yet remain to be described. In preparing the present work we have used another of their editions, in substance almost identical with that of 1756.

(13 a.) The Holy Bible, quarto, with "above two hundred historys curiously engraved by J. Cole from designs of the best masters," "Oxford, Printed by *Thomas Baskett* and *Robert Baskett* Printers to the University 1744" (Old Testament). For the New Testament: "London, Printed by *Thomas Baskett* and *Robert Baskett*, Printers to the King's most excellent Majesty 1743."

(13 b.) The Holy Bible, quarto, London, "Printed by Thomas Baskett, Printer to the King's more excellent Majesty, and by the Assigns of Robert Baskett," 1756 (B. M. 464 b. 3).

We now come to the last two considerable efforts to improve and correct our ordinary editions of Holy Scripture, made in 1762 by Dr Paris, Fellow of Trinity College, Cambridge, and still commemorated in the list of the Benefactors of the College, and by Dr Blayney, whose labours were published in 1769, both anonymously. The latter, however, has left a very interesting account of his work and the principles upon which it was executed in a brief *Report* to the Vice-Chancellor and Delegates of the Clarendon Press, reprinted below (p. 238) as Appendix D, and well deserving of attentive perusal. Dr Paris's name is not mentioned therein in such terms as might have been expected from the liberal use made of his materials by his successor: in fact his book is almost unknown even to Biblical students, although it has contributed more than that which appeared but seven years later towards bringing the text, the marginal annotations, the italics, and the textual references of modern Bibles into their actual condition. The truth is that Paris's edition had no real circulation, partly because it was so soon superseded by Blayney's, chiefly by reason of a large portion of the impression having been destroyed by fire in Dod's the publisher's warehouse[1].

(14) The Holy Bible, folio and quarto, 2 vol. Cambridge, "Printed by Joseph Bentham, Printer to the University. Sold by Benjamin Dod, Bookseller...London, 1762."

(15) The Holy Bible, quarto and folio[2], 2 vol. Oxford, "Printed by *T. Wright* and *W. Gill*, Printers to the University: 1769." With Prayer Book prefixed.

It will be seen when we come to discuss the italic type (Sect. III.) that the use of it was considerably extended in these two Bibles, notably in the later one, by a more full carrying out of the system of the Translators than they

---

[1] "Only six copies were preserved from a fire at the printers," MS. note in the British Museum folio copy. But more than six in quarto undoubtedly survive, as may appear from the Catalogues of various booksellers. The statement may be true of the large paper or folio issue. We have used Camb. Synd. A. 4. 3^b, 3^c for 1762; A. 4. 16 for 1769.

[2] In the folio copy in the Bodleian, but not in that in the British Museum (1276 l. 9), the Apocrypha is bound up so as to follow, not precede, the New Testament, and the signatures to the sheets suggest this unusual arrangement. Those in the Old Testament end with 7 T, those in the New Testament begin on the fifth page with 7 X, whereas the signatures in the Apocrypha extend afresh from A to O.

would probably have sanctioned themselves. The marginal annotations also, which had been growing in some Bibles since 1660 but were excluded from others (see Sect. II.), were finally received into the place they have occupied ever since, sundry new ones being added, the great majority in 1762. Bp. Lloyd's dates and chronological notes were also received and added to at the same time, and the two editions contributed largely, in about equal proportions, to swell the catalogue of textual references to parallel passages of Scripture. An inspection of our Appendices A and C will shew how far each of them helped to amend or corrupt the Translators' text, and it cannot be doubted that these two editors are the great modernizers of the diction of the version, from what it was left in the seventeenth century, to the state wherein it appears in modern Bibles. Much of the labour described in Sect. v. has been rendered necessary for the undoing of their tasteless and inconsistent meddling with archaic words and grammatical forms. On the whole, Dr Paris, who has been kept so utterly out of sight, performed his task with more diligence, exactness, and moderation than his Oxford successor. Yet, much as they left undone or did amiss, their editions of the Bible are monuments of genuine industry and pious zeal, all the more conspicuous in an age when shallow superciliousness was too often made a substitute for generous criticism and scholarlike precision: they might either of them have cheered the heart of worthy Archbishop Secker, on whose suggestion Blayney's labours are believed to have been undertaken. In point of typographical correctness, as is already well known, the quarto (and to a slightly less extent the scarce folio[1]) of 1769 are conspicuously deficient: on one page of the Apocrypha there are no less than three typographical errors

---

[1] Here again, as in the case of the folio edition of Dr Paris, a fire at the printers or publishers destroyed most of the copies.

(Esth. xi. 2 "Nison;" 8 "upon earth," "the" being omitted; xii. 6 "the eunuchs," "two" being omitted), so that the commonly estimated number of 116 such *errata* would seem below the truth. In Rev. xviii. 22 occurs an omission of a whole clause, for the same cause as was spoken of in regard to the Bible of 1613 (above, p. 17): "And no craftsman, of whatsoever craft *he be*, shall be found any more in thee¹." Some of Blayney's needless changes are in Ps. cxv. 3; cxli. 9; 2 Pet. i. 9 (see Appendix C): certain of a better character occur in Prov. vi. 19 (see App. A); Ecclus. xxix. 17 "[in danger]" for "in [danger]" of 1611, &c.; 2 Cor. iii. 3 "fleshy" of 1611 restored, for "fleshly," which had held its ground since 1613. On the other hand, in Ezek. xxiii. 4 (his own margin) *His tent* should have been *Her tent*. In regard to italics, whereof at times he is somewhat lavish, he rightly prints in Ps. xiii. 3 "the *sleep of* death," instead of "*the sleep* of death," as from 1611 downwards; in 1 John iii. 16 "*of God*" is italicised for the first time: his oversights in this matter will be noticed hereafter (p. 34). In the Bible of 1762 also the following errors should be noted: 2 Kin. x. 31 "for" instead of "*for*" of 1611—1744; xxv. 4 "of war fled" for "of war *fled*" of 1611—1744; Ps. lxix. 12 "I *was*" for "*I was*" 1611—1744. The second and grossest is amended in the American Bible 1867, otherwise they remain untouched to this day.

The following list of errors which we have incidentally detected in Dr Paris's edition of 1762 deserves the more notice, because they are nearly all repeated by Blayney, as we have indicated by adding the date 1769 within marks of parenthesis. They occur oftenest in the marginal annotations added in this pair of Bibles, and can be best accounted

---

¹ Three complete lines, as above p. 8. The omission occurs both in the folio and in the quarto, not (as has been stated) in the latter only.

for by supposing that Blayney's sheets were set up by Paris's, used as copy.

Ex. xxvi. 24 *marg.* and xxxvi. 29 *marg. twined.* See Appendix B (1769); Num. xxvi. 13 (marg. of 1762) *Zohar* (1769); Deut. x. 2 brakedst (1769); Josh. xvii. 2 (marg. of 1762) *Jezer* (1769); Judg. iii. 15 *marg. Gemini* (1769); xviii. 7 (marg. of 1762) *Leshen* (*Leshem* 1769); 1 Sam. xvi. 6 (marg. of 1762) 13, called *Elihu*. (13. Called *Elihu*, 1769); 2 Sam. vi. 2 (marg. of 1762) *Baalab* (1769); 2 Kin. xvi. 7 (marg. of 1762) *Tilgath-pileser* (1769); 1 Chr. i. 51 (marg. of 1762) *Avah* (*Alvah* 1769); iii. 8 *marg. Beeliada* (*Beeliada* 1769); Ps. cxxxv. 5 "our LORD" of 1611—1630 restored instead "our Lord" of 1629 Camb., 1638, 1744 (1769, but moderns from Oxf. 1835 have "our Lord"); Prov. xxxi. 14 merchant (merchants 1769: see Appendix A); Jer. xl. 1 the word that (1769); xliv. 28 *marg.*; *or them* (1769); Ezek. xiii. 9 *marg. council* (1769); Dan. ix. 24 (marg. of 1762) Axtaxerxes (not 1769); 27 *marg.* See Appendix A; Nahum iii. 16 fleeth (1769); Hab. iii. 19, see Appendix A (1769); 1 Esdr. ix. 22 *marg. Josabad* (1769); Baruch i. 1 Checias (1769, D'Oyly and Mant 1817, Oxf. 1835); ii. 16 thine holy (1769, &c.); 2 Macc. iv. 41 next in hand (1769, &c.); Acts vii. 28 "killedst" for "diddest," a designed but needless correction, rejected by 1769, &c., as also is "*things* strangled," Acts xxi. 25, a correction of the same class. Blayney also refuses Paris's "be *ye* warned and be *ye* filled," James ii. 16 ("be you warned and filled", 1611—1743), though he wrongly italicises the first "ye," which he retains. In Gal. ii. 6 1762 recalls from the Bible of 1683 the reading "those who," which had been afterwards neglected for the inferior reading of 1611, "these who" (*Grote MS.* p. 133). Paris was followed by Blayney and others up to a very recent period (Bagster 1846, American 1867). Our model (Camb. 1858) falls back upon "these who," which we would not disturb.

Some other emendations of Dr Paris are a little too bold (e.g. Ps. cvii. 19, see App. C below, p. 223), and one at least of his marginal notes is very questionable (Acts vii. 45). His punctuation is often good: he was the first to substitute a full stop and a moderate space for the colon of 1611, &c., at the great break in Zech. xi. 7 "And I took unto me two staves." For a specimen of his successor's merits in this respect see Sect. IV. (2 Cor. v. 2).

It is now necessary to subjoin an incomplete, yet overlong list of the errors other than bare misprints which have met us in habitually consulting Blayney's quarto of 1769. We must not suppress the notice of faults, some of which have led his successors grievously wrong, through the vain fear of detracting from the honour of a learned and diligent student of Holy Writ. All accuracy is only comparative, as every true scholar knows well; and if we be at a loss to account for the unusual number of his oversights, we may fairly impute much to the comparatively short time—between three and four years—spent by him in accomplishing, or at least in attempting, the burdensome task which his *Report* describes (Appendix D, below p. 238). The reader will refer to our Appendices A and C for further details.

Ex. vi. 21; Josh. xix. 2, 19; 2 Sam. xxiii. 37; 1 Kin. xv. 2 (marg. of 1769) *Michaia;* 1 Chr. ii. 47; vii. 1 (an error revived); 2 Chr. iv. 12 (the second "the top of" omitted[1]): Job xli. 6 (see Appendix C): Ps. xviii. 47 "unto" for "under[2];" xxiv. 3; lx. 4 "feared" for "fear[2];" lxxviii. 66 "part" for "parts[2]:" so a Scotch edition (Coldstream) as late as 1845; cxlviii. 8; Prov. xxv. 24; Ezek. v. 6, the comma placed before "and my statutes" in 1629 is removed, for want of looking at the Hebrew; Hab. iii. 13 (an error revived) "†by discovering" for "by †discovering;" 1 Esdr. iv. 29; v. 13 *marg.*; 20 "Ammidoi" for "Ammidioi[3];" vii. 9 "service" for "services[3];" viii. 56 "sixty" for "fifty[3];" 2 Esdr. i. 15 "to you" for "for you[3];" 38 "come" for "cometh[3];" iv. 21 "upon the heavens" for "above the heavens[3];" v. 15 "upon" for "up upon[3];" 27 "of people" for "of peoples[3];" Judith ii. 20; Esther xiv. 14 "help" for "helper[3];" Wisd. vii. 25 *marg.*; Ecclus. xvii. 5 comma removed after "seventh[3];" xxvii.

---

[1] *Report from the Select Committee of the House of Commons on the Queen's Printers' Patent*, 1859, Mr Child's Evidence, 1859, p. 28; a blue-book full of most interesting information on the whole subject of modern Bibles.

[2] These *errata* held their ground until they were corrected before 1845 under the direction of Bp. Turton. See below, p. 36.

[3] These *errata*, after holding their place in the text of D'Oyly and Mant (1817), Oxford 1835, and other Bibles, are amended in our model for the Apocrypha, Camb. 4to. 1863. See below, p. 38.

13 "in" omitted before "the wantonness[1];" xlv. 8 *marg.*; Hist. of Susanna, ver. 37 "was there" for "there was[1];" Bel and Dragon, ver. 3 "was spent" for "were spent[1];" ver. 6 "a living God" for "a living god" (1611—1762), as all in ver. 24 after 1744; 1 Macc. ix. 68; x. 30 "of Jerusalem" for "at Jerusalem[1];" John xi. 34; Rom. vii. 20 "Now if do;" xi. 23 om. "still" (thus many later Bibles, but not our model, Camb. 1858: see below, p. 38); 1 Cor. iv. 13 "the earth" for "the world;" 2 Cor. vii. 16 "con-|dence" for "confidence;" xii. 2 "about" for "above," repeated in later Bibles up to Bagster, 1846: but the American and our model restore "above;" this change seems intentional. 1 Tim. iv. 10 "the saviour;" Rev. vii. 6, see Appendix A; Rev. xviii. 22 (see p. 31).

In regard to the use of italic type Blayney's edition is very careless, although he had evidently taken some pains about the subject. Some of his errors are:

Deut. viii. 17 "*mine* hand;" xv. 20 "eat *it;*" I Kin. xvii. 24 "*and* that" for "and *that;*" 1 Chr. xviii. 16 "*was*" 1611—1762, but "was" 1769; 2 Chr. xx. 34 "*is* mentioned;" xxiv. 26 "these are they" for "these *are* they" (1762); Ps. viii. 4 "What is man" for "What *is* man" of 1611—1762; xvii. 6 "*hear* my speech;" xlix. 7 "his brother" for "*his* brother" of 1611—1762; lxxv. 1 "is near" for "*is* near" of 1611—1762; ver. 5 "*with* a stiff neck;" Prov. ix. 8 "wise man" and Isai. xxix. 8 "thirsty man," against his own practice, although 1638—1762 italicise "*man;*" Eccles. viii. 11 "sentence against," but "sentence *against*" 1611—1762; Isai. xxxvi. 3 "which was" for "which *was*" 1611—1762, as even 1769 in ver. 22; Jer. xxxiii. 12 "which is desolate" (after Camb. 1629), "which *is* desolate" 1611—1630, "*which is* desolate" 1638—1762; xxxvi. 19 "ye be" for "ye *be*" 1611—1762; Ezek. x. 1 "that was above" for "that *was* above" 1611—1762; Dan. viii. 3 (*bis*), 6, 20 "*two* horns," though the noun is dual; Hab. i. 10 "shall be a scorn" for "*shall be* a scorn" 1611—1762; Hagg. ii. 19 "Is the seed" for "*Is* the seed" 1611—1762; Judith xiii. 14 "(I say)" 1611—1762, which is the method employed in the Apocrypha for indicating what is omitted in the Greek, he regards as parenthetical, and accordingly the marks ( ) are removed in 1769; Matt. xxii. 10 "highways" for "*high*ways" (ὁδοὺς) of 1638—1762; Luke xiv. 4 "let him go" for "let *him* go" of 1638—1762; Rom. iii. 14 "*is* full" (γέμει); 1 Cor. iii. 23 "ye are Christ's" for "ye *are* Christ's" of 1638—1762; Gal. v. 10 "his judgment" for "*his* judgment" of 1611—1762.

[1] Refer back to p. 33, note 3.

Out of this whole list of blunders in regard to the italic type, some of them being very palpable, the American Bible of 1867 corrects those in Ps. xvii. 6; lxxv. 5, Professor Scholefield (whose care on this point will be noticed again, Sect. III., p. 79, note 1) the last two. Blayney is followed in the rest by the whole flock of moderns, without inquiry and without suspicion.

For many years which followed the publication of the edition of 1769, even after its glaring imperfections had become in some measure known, the King's Printer and the two English Universities continued to reproduce what was in substance Dr Blayney's work, when the public attention was claimed in 1831 by Mr Curtis of Islington, who complained that all modern reprints of Holy Scripture departed widely from the original edition of 1611, to the great deterioration of our Vernacular Translation[1]. It is needless to revive the controversy that ensued, in which the case of the privileged presses was successfully maintained by Dr Cardwell in behalf of Oxford, by Dr Turton for Cambridge, in the pamphlets which have been already cited in this Section. The consequent publication of the standard text in the Oxford reprint of 1833, which we have found so useful, virtually settled the whole debate, by shewing to the general reader the obvious impossibility of returning to the Bible of 1611, with all the defects which those who superintended the press had been engaged, for more than two centuries, in reducing to a more consistent and presentable shape. One result of the communication at that time entered upon between the Delegates of the Oxford and the Syndics of the Cambridge Presses was a letter written by Dr Cardwell to Dr Turton in 1839 respecting a more exact accordance

---

[1] *The Existing Monopoly an inadequate protection of the Authorized Version of the Scripture*, &c., &c. By Thomas Curtis, London, 1833, 8vo.

between editions of the Authorized Version as published by the two Universities. These learned men were instructed to confer together on the subject, although it is not easy to point out any actual result of their consultation. The only papers at Cambridge at all bearing on the subject have been placed at my disposal, but they amount to very little, though it is to them that I am indebted, when in the Appendices or elsewhere I speak of an alteration as having been made by the direction of Bp. Turton[1].

The revision of the Canonical Scriptures projected (1847—1851) by the American Bible Society was a more ambitious enterprise, which until lately has hardly been heard of in England[2]. A Committee of seven, on which we recognize the honoured name of Edward Robinson, engaging as their collator James W. McLane, a Presbyterian minister in the state of New York, superintended his comparison of a standard American Bible with recent copies published in London, Oxford, Cambridge, and Edinburgh, as also with the book of 1611. Where the four modern British volumes proved uniform, the new revision was conformed to them, or, in matters of punctuation, to any three united. Other rules drawn up for McLane's guidance shew laudable care on the part of the Committee, who felt and confessed that some restraint (even though a light one) was peculiarly

---

[1] It would be ungrateful not to notice the minute and unpretending diligence of those who prepared Bagster's editions of the Holy Bible. We have consulted the miniature quarto of 1846, wherein we found anticipated many a small discovery we had supposed to be original. The instances cited in Appendix A will explain what we mean. The revision seems due in the main to Wm. Greenfield, F.A.S., of the British and Foreign Bible Society, although he died as far back as 1831.

[2] The only detailed account which has reached England is given in a scarce Tract in the Library of the British and Foreign Bible Society (U. 4. 23): *Report on the History and Recent Collation of the English Version of the Bible: presented by the Committee of Versions to the Board of Managers of the American Bible Society, and adopted, May* 1, 1851, pp. 32, [New York] 1851.

needed by their citizens, since "the exposure to variations is naturally greater, wherever the printing of the Bible is at the option of every one who chooses to undertake it, without restriction and without supervision; as in this country since the Revolution" (*Report*, p. 8). To this task the good men devoted themselves for three years and a half, and finally presented their Report and revision to the Board of Managers which had appointed them. *Ibi omnis effusus labor:* adopted at first, the work was rejected the very next year (1852) by a majority of the same body, "on the ground of alleged want of constitutional authority, and popular dissatisfaction with a number of the changes made[1]." Some small fruits, however, of their faithful toil remain in the editions of the Bible published by the American Bible Society since 1860, to which reference is frequently made in the course of the present treatise and its Appendices[2]. It is not easy to persuade ourselves that very much has been lost by the failure of the praiseworthy effort just described. The plan of operation was not sufficiently thorough to produce any considerable results. Between the five recent Bibles that were collated the differences would be slight and superficial, but when the standard of 1611 came to be taken into account, it is very credible that the recorded variations, solely in the text and punctuation, amounted to 24,000 (*Report*, p. 31). No attempt seems to have been made to bridge over the wide gulf between the first issues of the Authorized version and those of modern times by the use of such intermediate editions as have been examined in the present Section; nor does the general tone of their *Report* encourage the belief that the previous studies of the revisers had lain in that direction. Hence followed of necessity, or

---

[1] Philip Schaff, D.D. *Revision of the English Version*, &c. New York, 1873, p. xxxi. note.

[2] The edition we have used is the beautiful Diamond Ref. 24mo. of 1867.

at any rate in practice, so complete a postponement of Bibles of the seventeenth century to those of the nineteenth, that wheresoever the latter agreed together, their very worst faults, whether relating to the text or to the italic type (and more especially to the italics), were almost sure to escape detection, and never did come to the knowledge of the Committee, save by some happy accident.

It remains to state that the model or standard copy adopted for the purposes of the present work is the Cambridge 8vo edition, small pica (with marginal references) 1858. This standard may be pronounced to be accurately printed, inasmuch as close and repeated examination has enabled us to note only the following *errata* in the text or margin.

1 Chr. iv. 24 (margin of 1762) *Zoar* for *Zohar;* 2 Chr. i. 4 Kiriath; Ezra i. 7 his god (presumably by accident, yet it looks true: compare in Hebrew 2 Kin. xix. 37; Dan. i. 2); Esther i. 7 gave them; Job xv. 35 mischiof; xxi. 26 worm; Ps. xxxi. 7 adversity; xlv. 11 thy lord; Hos. ii. 1 Ru-hamah; Jonah i. 4 was †like (see Appendix C); Luke iv. 7 *marg. fall* down (so Camb. nonpareil, 1857).

Since this Bible of 1858 does not contain the Apocrypha, a Cambridge 4to. 1863 has been adopted for the model of that portion of our work. Besides correcting the mistakes of Blayney and his successors in the passages indicated in pp. 33, 34 and notes, this book alone (so far as we know) has the following changes for the better:

1 Esdr. v. 5 *marg.* "Or," set before "*Joacim;*" 2 Esdr. vi. 49 *marg.* "Or," set before "Behemoth;" Ecclus. iv. 16 "generations" for "generation" of 1611, &c. For Tobit iv. 10; Judith i. 6; 2 Macc. ix. 18, see Appendix C.

This book contains also the following errata:

1 Esdr. v. 72 and Judith iv. 7 "straight" for "strait;" 1 Esdr. vi. 22 "our Lord" for "our lord;" viii. 32 *marg.* "*Shechanaiah*" for "*Shechaniah;*" ix. 4 "bear" for "bare;" 26 *marg. Porosh* for *Parosh;* 2 Esdr. vii. 17 "shall" for "should;" Judith x. 8 and xiii. 5; Ecclus.

xxxvii. 16; 2 Macc. xiv. 5 "enterprizes:" but "enterprises" in 1 Macc. ix. 55; Judith xvi. 11 ‖with "these," instead of with the first "they;" Wisd. i. 6 "a witness" for "witness;" v. 23 "dealings" for "dealing;" vi. 11 "affections" for "affection;" xiii. 11 "‖a carpenter" for "a ‖carpenter;" Ecclus. iii. 27 "sorrow" for "sorrows;" xlvi. 7 "murmurings" for "murmuring;" Song, ver. 5 "upon us" (second); 1 Macc. iv. 20 "hosts" for "host;" 34 "above" for "about;" vii. 45 "‖Then they" for "Then they;" x. 54 "son-in-law" for "son in law:" Comp. Tobit x. 12 and ch. xi. 2; xiv. 27 "hight priest;" ver. 32 "the ‖valiant" for "‖the valiant;" 2 Macc. i. 23 "priest" for the second "priests;" xiii. 23 *marg.* "‖Or, *rebelled*" over against ver. 24; *ibid.* "entreated" for "intreated" (as six times before); xiv. 25 "‖and" for "and‖."

The Epistle of "The Translators to the Reader[1]," which follows the Dedication in all principal editions of the Authorized Version, has been illustrated in this volume by such notes as seemed necessary. The reputed author of this noble Preface (for, in spite of the quaintness of its style and the old fashion of its learning, it deserves no meaner epithet) is Dr Miles Smith of the first Oxford Company, who would naturally be one of the six final revisers (p. 12 note 4), and became Bishop of Gloucester in 1612. The Calendar and Tables of Lessons usually annexed to this Preface are no more a part of the Version than the Book of Common Prayer and the metrical Psalms which are sometimes placed at the beginning and end of the Bible. The Genealogical charts, accompanied with a Map of Canaan and its Index, the work of John Speed, were issued separately in various sizes, that they might be bound up with the Bibles, without any option of the purchaser. Mr Fry prints (*A Description*, &c. p. 40) a patent granting to him this privilege dated in the eighth year of James I., to hold good "only during the term of ten years next ensuing," at an additional charge of not more than two shillings for the large folio size.

[1] See p. 265.

SECTION II.

On the marginal notes and the original texts of the Authorized Version of the English Bible.

BESIDES those references to parallel texts of Scripture which will be spoken of elsewhere (Section VI.), the margin of most of our English Bibles, including the Authorized Version, contains certain brief annotations, the extent and character of which will now be described. The practice was begun by Tyndale, in whose earliest New Testament of 1525, the poor fragments of whose single known copy enrich the Grenville Library in the British Museum, notes rather expository than relating to interpretation are extant in the margin. In some places, and yet more in his version of the Pentateuch (1530 and subsequent years), these notes become strongly polemical, and breathe a spirit which the warmest admirers of their author find it easier to excuse than to commend. In Coverdale's Bible (1535), which was put forth in hot haste to seize a fleeting opportunity, only five out of the eighteen notes found in the New Testament are explanatory, the rest having reference to the proper rendering: in the earlier pages of his Bible they occur much more frequently. Annotations of this kind are quite a distinctive feature as well of the Geneva New Testament of 1557, as of the Geneva Bible of 1560; and, mingled with others which are purely interpretative, are strewn somewhat unequally over the pages of the Bishops' Bible (1568, 1572). One of the most judicious of the Instructions to the Translators laid down for their guidance by King James I., and acted upon by them with strict fidelity, prescribed that "No marginal notes at all be affixed, but only for the explanation of the Hebrew or Greek words, which cannot, without some circumlocution, so briefly and fitly be expressed in the text." It had by that time grown intolerable, that on the self-same page with the text of Holy Scripture, should stand some bitter pithy comment, conceived in a temper the very reverse of that which befits men who profess to love God in Christ.

In the Old Testament the marginal notes in our standard Bibles of 1611 amount to 6637, whereof 4111 express the more literal meaning of the original Hebrew or Chaldee (there are 77 referring to the latter language): 2156 give alternative renderings (indicated by the word "||Or" prefixed to them) which in the opinion of the Translators are not very less probable than those in the text: in 63 the meaning of Proper Names is stated for the benefit of the unlearned (e.g. Gen. xi. 9; xvi. 11): in 240 (whereof 108 occur in the first Book of Chronicles) necessary information is given by way of harmonizing the text with other passages of Scripture, especially in regard to the orthography of Hebrew names (e.g. Gen. xi. 16, 20, 24): while the remaining 67 refer to various readings of the original, in 31 of which the marginal variation (technically called *Keri*) of the Masoretic revisers of the Hebrew is set in competition with the reading in the text (*Chetiv*). Of this last kind of marginal notes a list is subjoined, as many of them are not readily distinguishable from the alternative renderings, being mostly, like them, preceded by "||Or". They are

Deut. xxviii. 22. Josh. viii. 12 (*Keri* in marg.); xv. 53 (*Keri* in marg.). 1 Sam. vi. 18 (אֶבֶן for אָבֵל, with the Targum and Septuagint); xxvii. 8 (*Keri* in text). 2 Sam. xiii. 37 (*Keri* in text); xiv. 22 (*Keri* in marg.). 1 Kin. xxii. 48 (*Keri* in text). 2 Kin. v. 12 (*Keri* in marg.); xx. 4 (*Keri* in text); xxiii. 33 (*Keri* in text). 1 Chr. 1. 6; 7. 2 Chr. 1. 5. Ezra ii. 33; 46 (*Keri* in text); viii. 14 (*Keri* in marg.); x. 40 [1].

---

[1] Strangely enough, this is the earliest marginal note relating to various readings, noticed by Bp. Turton in his *Text of the English*

Neh. iii. 20 (*Keri* in marg.). Job vi. 21 (*Keri* in text); xxxiii. 28 (twice as *Keri* in text). Ps. ix. 12 (*Keri* in text); x. 12 (*Keri* in text); xxiv. 6 (marg. with the Septuagint, Syriac, and Latin Vulgate); lxiv. 6; lxviii. 30; c. 3 (*Keri* in marg.); cii. 3; cxlvii. 19 (*Keri* in marg.). Prov. xvii. 27 (*Keri* in text); xx. 30 (*Keri* in marg.); xxi. 29 (*Keri* in marg.); xxiv. 19; xxvi. 17. Cant. v. 4. Isai. x. 13 (*Keri* in marg.?); xiii. 22; xviii. 2; xxx. 32 (*Keri* in marg.); xli. 24; xlix. 5 (*Keri* in marg.); lxiii. 11 (marg. with Aquila and the Vulgate); lxv. 4 (*Keri* in text). Jer. ii. 20 (*Keri* in text); iii. 9 (text with the Septuagint); vii. 18 and xliv. 17 (לִמְלֶכֶת for לִמְלֶאכֶת, apparently from conjecture); xvi. 7; xviii. 4; xxiii. 31 (probably a conjectural reading, חלק for לקח); xxxiii. 3; xlix. 1 and 3 (marg. with the Septuagint); l. 9 (שׁ text, שׂ marg.); 26 (לֹ text, לֹ marg.); li. 59 (marg. מְנֻחָת? παρὰ Σεδεκίου, Septuagint). Ezek. vii. 11; xxiii. 42 (*Keri* in marg.); xxv. 7 (*Keri* in text); xxx. 18 (שׁ text, שׂ marg.); xxxvi. 14 (כשל *Chetiv* in marg., שׁכל in text, but *Keri* is quite different, viz. שׁלך); ver. 23 (marg. with the Masora, Septuagint, and some Hebrew manuscripts, against the commonly printed text); xl. 40; xlii. 9 (*Keri* in marg. "he that brought"). Dan. ix. 24 (*Keri* in text, "to make an end"). Amos iii. 12 (Hebrew manuscripts varying between דַּמֶּשֶׂק of the printed text, which is represented by marg., and the name of the city דַּמֶּשֶׂק). Zech. xi. 2 (*Keri* in text). Mal. ii. 15 (marg. שְׁאֵת "excellency," being the rendering of Coverdale, "an excellent spirit").

Where the variation in the reading was brought prominently into view by the Masoretic notes, it was only natural that the Translators should refer to it in their margin. Respecting the Hebrew text which they followed, it would be hard to identify any particular edition, inasmuch as the differences between early printed Bibles are but few. The

Bible Considered. He gives Ezra x. 40. Ps. cii. 3. Cant. v. 4 for the Old Testament, and eight references to the New, adding, "I will not positively affirm that no other Various Readings than the following are to be found in the Margin, but the impression of my mind is that no others do exist there" (p. 128, second edition). But, in truth, his whole treatise is a notable example of what wary tact and dialectic skill may accomplish, when wielded by one who does not know too much about the matter at issue, and is fortunate enough to encounter opponents who know considerably less.

Complutensian Polyglott, however, which afforded them such important help in the Apocrypha, was of course at hand, and we seem to trace its influence in some places, e.g. in 2 Chr. i. 5, שָׁם "there" of the Complutensian text the Septuagint and Vulgate, being accorded a place in the margin; as also in Job xxii. 6 אָחִיךְ "thy brother," where later editors give the plural, as do the Targum, Syriac, Septuagint, and Vulgate. Yet the Complutensian throws no light on the reading in many other passages, where some other text must have been before the Translators: e.g. 1 Chr. vi. 57 ("of Judah" added); Ps. lxiv. 6, where the marginal rendering ought to be taken in preference. In Job xxx. 11, 22 the Authorized prefers *Keri* to *Chetiv*.

It has been sometimes alleged that the alternative renderings (introduced by "||Or") which are set in the margin of the Authorized English Version, are superior, on the whole, to those in the text[1]. It would be indeed a conspicuous instance of bad judgment on the part of the Translators, if it could be justly alleged that where two or more senses of a passage were brought fairly before them, they mostly, or even frequently, put the worst into the body of their work. But no competent scholar who has carefully examined the matter will think that they have gone so far wrong. On the other hand, he will perhaps feel disposed to complain that so many of these marginal notes assign a sense to the sacred record which cannot possibly be accepted as true. Some of these, no doubt, are taken either from the text or margin of the Bishops' Bible, which had been read in Churches for about forty years when the Authorized Version was made, and which King James had

---

[1] "The Translators...have placed some different significations in the *Margent*; but those most-what the *better;* because when *truth* is tryed by *most voyces*, it is commonly out-voted." Dr R. Gell's *Essay toward the amendment of the last English Translation of the Bible*, 1659 (Preface, p. 24).

expressly directed "to be followed, and as little altered, as the truth of the original will permit." But far the greater part must be traced to another source, to which adequate attention has not hitherto been directed. Of the several Latin translations of the Old Testament which were executed in the sixteenth century, that which was the joint work of Immanuel Tremellius [1510—80], a converted Jew (the proselyte first of Cardinal Pole, then of Peter Martyr), who became Professor of Divinity at Heidelberg, and of his son in law Francis Junius [1545—1602], was at once the latest and the most excellent. Originally published in 1575—9. and after the death of Tremellius revised in 1590 by Junius. who added a version of the Apocrypha of which he was the sole author, a large edition printed in London in 1593 soon caused it to become very highly esteemed in this country for its perspicuity and general faithfulness. One great fault it has, a marked tendency, in passages either obscure in themselves, or suggesting some degree of difficulty, to wander into new paths of interpretation, wherein it ought to have found few to follow or commend it. This version must have lain open before the Translators throughout the whole course of their labours: it has led them into some of the most conspicuous errors that occur in their text (2 Chr. xx. 1; Job xxxiv. 33), while as regards the margin, whensoever a rendering is met with violently harsh, inverted, or otherwise unlikely, its origin may be sought, almost with a moral certainty of finding it, in the pages of Tremellius and Junius. These statements are made with reference to every part of the Old Testament (e.g. Gen. xl. 13, 16, 19, 20. Ex. xvii. 16; xxix. 43. Judg. ix. 31. 2 Sam. i. 9, 18; xxi. 8. Lam. iii. 35; iv. 14; 22¹), but, for the sake of brevity,

---

¹ Dr Ginsburg (*An Old Testament Commentary for English Readers*, 1882) would adopt their margin in Lev. xviii. 18. but one would doubt whether they were the first to propose it. The very

the proof of them shall be drawn from one distinct portion, the books of the Minor Prophets. To these authorities solely, so far as the writer has observed, are due the supplying of *"for nought"* in Mal. i. 10, and the textual rendering of Mal. ii. 16: as are also the following marginal notes, scattered among others of a widely different type: Hos. i. 6; 10 (*"instead of that"*); vi. 4 (*"kindness"*); x. 10; xii. 8 (*"all my labours,"* &c.); xiv. 2. Joel iii. 21. Amos iv. 3; v. 22; vii. 2; Obad. 7 (*"of it"*). Mic. vii. 13. Nah. i. 12; iii. 19. Hab. i. 7; ii. 11 (second). Zeph. iii. 1. Zech. v. 3; ix. 15 (twice); 17 (*"speak"*); x. 2; xi. 16 (second); xii. 5; xiv. 5; 14 (first). Mal. i. 13; ii. 9 (but ἐδυσωπεῖσθε πρόσωπα Symmachus); 11.

Thus far no marginal notes have been taken into consideration except those given in the primary issues of 1611; but 368 others have been subsequently inserted by various hands, which ought to be distinguished in our Bibles from those of earlier date by being printed within brackets. Of these the Cambridge folio of 1629 contributes that on Jer. iii. 19; the folio of 1638 that on Ezek. xlviii. 1: thirty-one others were inserted in the course of the century that followed, viz. 1 Kin. xxii. 41, 51. 2 Kin. i. 17; viii. 16; ix. 29; xiii. 9, 10; xiv. 23, 29; xv. 1, 8, 10, 30 (*bis*), 37; xvii. 1; xxiii. 23. 2 Chr. xx. 36; xxi. 1, 3, 5, 12, 18. Job i. 1. Ps. xi. 6. Dan. i. 21; xi. 7, 10, 25. Hos. vii. 7; xiii. 16. As many as 269 are due to Dr Paris (1762), and 66 to Dr Blayney (1769), who is usually credited with them all. Many of them are not destitute of a certain value (especially in such explanations relating to Proper Names as occur in Gen. ii. 23)[1], although a persistent resolution to set right the regnal years of the

---

improbable margin in Lev. xxvii. 12, also derived from Tremellius and Junius, is certainly countenanced by 2 Kin. ix. 5.

[1] The first of these later marginal notes that occurs in the Authorized Bible (Gen. i. 20, †Heb. *let fowl fly*) is taken from the Geneva Bible (1560), and seems as good as most of its date—1762.

Jewish kings, commenced in 1701, and fully carried out in 1762, leads on their authors to expedients which are at times rather daring than satisfactory: e.g. 2 Kin. xv. 1, 30. The American revisers of 1851 (see p. 36) not unreasonably condemned notes like these and those on Judg. iii. 31; xi. 29; xii. 8, 11, 13; xiii. 1; xv. 20 (all from the Bible of 1762), as "containing merely conjectural and unwarranted commentary," and expunged them accordingly from the margin of their book; but they all came back again with the other restorations which public opinion forced upon the New York Bible Society. In one instance (Dan. ix. 27) Dr Paris has ventured to substitute a marginal rendering of his own in the place of that of 1611 ("Or, *with the abominable armies*"), and has been followed by all modern Bibles.

The marginal notes appended to the Apocrypha, which have next to be examined, differ not inconsiderably in tone and character from those annexed to the text of the Canonical Scriptures. They are much more concerned with various readings, as was indeed inevitable by reason of the corrupt state of the Greek text of these books, which still await and sadly need a thorough critical revision, chiefly by the aid of materials that have recently come to light. Authorities also are sometimes cited by name in the margin, a practice not adopted in the Old Testament[1]. Such are Athanasius, 1 Esdr. iv. 36: Herodotus, Judith ii. 7: Pliny's History, Benedicite or the Song, ver. 23: Josephus, 1 Esdr. iv. 29. Esther xiii. 1; xvi. 1. 1 Macc. v. 54; vi. 49; vii. 1; ix. 4, 35, 49, 50; x. 1, 81; xi. 34; xii. 7, 8, 19, 28, 31. 2 Macc. vi. 2: in the Maccabees after the example of Coverdale. Even Junius, the Latin translator (above, p. 44),

---

[1] The apparent exceptions of Josephus, quoted Gen. xxii. 1; 2 Kin. xiv. 8, are respectively due to the editors of 1701 and 1762. The reference to "Usher" in 2 Kin. xv. 30 forms part of a note added in 1701.

is appealed to eight times by name: 2 Esdr. xiii. 2, 13. Tobit vii. 8; ix. 6; xi. 18; xiv. 10. Judith iii. 9; vii. 3.

The texts from which the Apocryphal books were translated can be determined with more precision than in the case of the Old Testament, and were not the same for them all. The second book of Esdras, though the style is redolent of a Hebrew or Aramaic origin, exists only in the common Latin version and in Junius' paraphrase, which is cited for the reading in ch. xiii. 2, 13. In this book some excellent Latin manuscripts to which they had access (ch. iv. 51 marg.), as also the Bishops' Bible, must have had great weight with its revisers. The Prayer of Manasses had to be drawn from the same source, for the Greek was first published in Walton's Polyglott (1657) as it appears in the Codex Alexandrinus, the earliest that contains it, which did not reach England before 1628. The first book of Esdras ('Ο ἱερεύς as the Greeks call it), is not in the Complutensian Polyglott (1517), so that Aldus's Greek Bible (1518) was primarily resorted to, as is evident from the margin of ch. ii. 12, the typographical error there described being that of Aldus (παρεδόθησαν ἀβασσάρῳ for παρεδόθη Σαναβασσάρῳ), which had misled the Bishops' Bible. Besides this edition, our Translators had before them the Roman Septuagint of 1586[1], to which they refer, without as yet naming it, in ch. v. 25; viii. 2. For the remainder of the Apocrypha they had access also to the Complutensian, which in the books of Tobit, Judith, Wisdom and

---

[1] An excellent account of this edition is contained in the *Prolegomena* to Tischendorf's *Septuagint*, pp. xix.—xxviii. (1869). Although the work itself is not quite what it professes to be, "exemplar ipsum" (the great Codex Vaticanus) "de verbo ad verbum representatum:" yet both the Epistle of Cardinal Carafa, who superintended it, and the Preface of his assistant, Peter Morinus, display an insight into the true principles of textual criticism, quite beyond their age.

Ecclesiasticus seems almost a copy of Cod. Vatican. 346 (Cod. 248 of Parsons)[1], but they used with it the Aldine and Roman editions[2]: the latter "copy" they cite by name Tobit xiv. 5, 10; 1 Macc. ix. 9; xii. 37, as they also do "the Latin interpreters" in 2 Macc. vi. 1. By means of these Greek authorities they were enabled to clear the text of Tobit of the accretions brought into the Old Latin version, which had been over-hastily revised by Jerome. As a small instalment of what remains to be done for the criticism of that noble work, two passages in Ecclesiasticus (i. 7; xvii. 5) are inclosed within brackets in the books of 1611. The former is found in no Greek text our Translators knew of, but only in the Latin and Bishops' Bible: the latter occurs complete only in some late manuscripts, though the Complutensian and Cod. 248 have the last two lines of the triplet. These preliminary statements will enable the reader to understand the marginal notes in the Apocrypha which treat of various readings. They are no less than 156 in number, besides 13 of latter date.

1 ESDRAS i. 11 (τὸ πρωϊνόν Greek, בֹּקֶר for בָּקָר); 12 (*cum benevolentiâ* Vulg., i.e. μετ' εὐνοίας); 24 (ἐν αἰσθήσει: om. Roman); ii. 12 (above, p. 47); v. 25 (217 as Roman edition: Vulg. has 227); v. 46; see below, p. 198 note 1; vi. 1 *fin.* (if this be intended for a various

---

[1] This manuscript contained also 1 Esdras, if it be the same as that for which Cardinal Ximenes gave a bond in 1513 to the Librarian of the Vatican (Vercellone, *Præf. to Mai's Cod. Vat.* Vol. I.). So that he must have designedly kept back a book which the Council of Trent afterwards refused to declare Canonical.

[2] Our Translation often adopts the Aldine text in preference to those of the Complutensian and Roman editions jointly: e.g. Judith iii. 9; viii. 1. Ecclus. xvii. 31; xxxi. 2; xxxvi. 15; xxxix. 17; xlii.

13; xliii. 26; xlvii. 1. Bel and Dragon, ver. 38. 2 Macc. i. 31; viii. 23; xii. 36; xiv. 36. On the other hand the Roman is followed rather than the Complutensian and Aldine text united in 1 Macc. iii. 14, 15, 18, 28; iv. 24; v. 23, 48; vi. 24, 43, 57; vii. 31, 37, 41 (*bis*), 45; viii. 10; ix. 9 (avowedly); x. 41, 42, 78; xi. 3, 15, 22, 34, 35, &c.; xii. 43; xiii. 22, 25; xiv. 4, 16, 23, 46; xv. 30; xvi. 8. 2 Macc. viii. 30; xv. 22. Aldus is followed in preference to the Bishops' Bible in 1 Esdr. v. 14: cf. 1 Esdr. viii. 39.

reading, no trace of it remains); 23 (τόμος Ald., τόπος Rom. Vulg. Bishops'); vii. 8 (φυλαρχῶν Ald. Rom., φυλῶν Old Latin, Vulg. Bishops'); 10 (margin as Cod. 248, Vulg. Bishops'); viii. 1 ('Αξαρίου Vulg. Coverdale only); 2 ('Οξίου Rom., 'Εξίου Ald. Bishops'); *ibid.* (three names omitted in Rom. Vulg. Coverdale, not in Ald. Bishops'); 20 (ἄλλα Ald. Vulg. Coverdale, Bishops': but Old Latin, Junius ἄλα, as Ezra vii. 22 [non habet Cod. Vaticanus]); 29 (Αττούς Ald., Άττούς Rom., *Acchus* Vulg. Coverdale, *Hattus* Bishops', *Chartusch* Junius, טבחים Ezra viii. 2); 34 (80 Vulg. Junius, Coverdale with Ezra viii. 8, against Ald. Rom. Bishops'); 35 (212 Ald. Rom. Vulg. Coverdale, Bishops': 218 Junius, Ezra viii. 9); 38 ('Ακατάν Ald. Rom. Bishops', *Ecetan* Vulg., *Ezechan* Coverdale, *Katan* Junius: cf. Ezra viii. 12); 39 (60 Junius, Ezra viii. 13 only); 88 (margin requires μὴ ὀργισθῇς, for which there is no known authority); 96. See Appendix C; ix. 20 (ἀγροίας Rom. Vulg. Coverdale, *reatu* Junius, ἀγρείας Ald. Bishops').

2 ESDRAS i. 22 (margin from the Bishops' margin: so Junius, in the form of a conjecture); ii. 15 (*columba* Vulg. Junius, *columna* Coverdale, Bishops'); 16 (text as Vulg. Coverdale, Bishops', though Fritzsche's three Latin MSS. STD[1] read *in illis*, the margin is from Junius); 32 (text as Clementine Vulg. Junius, Coverdale, Bishops': but margin with Fritzsche's STD); 38 (*in convivio* Vulg. Coverdale, Bishops' text: *ad convivium* Junius; "||Or, *for*" Bishops' marg.); iii. 19 (text Vulg. Coverdale, Bishops': margin is fashioned from Junius and Bishops' margin); 31 (*memini* Vulg., Fritzsche's STD: *percive* Coverdale, Bishops': *venit in mentem* Junius, *conceive* margin); iv. 11 (*corruptionem* Vulg. Junius, Coverdale, Bishops': *incorruptionem* Fritzsche's SD, but the whole passage is in confusion); 36 (*Huriel* Fritzsche's T only: all the rest *Jeremiel*); 51 (*quid erit* Vulg. Junius, Coverdale, Bishops': but *quis erit* Fritzsche's STD, so that our Translators might well appeal to a "Manuscript" here); vi. 49 (*Enoch* Vulg. Coverdale, Bishops': *Be-*

---

[1] S is Codex Sangermanensis at Paris of the ninth century, T at Turin is of the thirteenth, D at Dresden of the fifteenth, all collated afresh for or by Fritzsche (*Libri Apocryphi V. T.* 1871, pp. xxvii. xxviii.). Mr R. L. Bensly also collated S for his *Missing Fragment of the fourth book of Esdras* (1875). This *Missing Frag-ment* (ch. vii. 36—105) was obtained from the *Bibliothèque Communale* at Amiens (10), and a transcript of the same passage was made from a manuscript in Spain by J. Palmer, Professor of Arabic at Cambridge (1804—19), and discovered in 1877 among his papers at S. John's College.

hemoth Junius, Bishops' margin, Syriac and Æthiopic in Fritzsche); vii. 30 (*judiciis* Vulg. Junius, Coverdale, Bishops': *iniciis* Fritzsche's STD); 37 (*Achaz* Vulg., *Achas* TD, Coverdale, Bishops': *Hacan* Junius, עָכָן Josh. vii. 1, &c.; עָכוֹר Josh. vii. 26); 52 (*tardè* Vulg., *considerate* Junius, *patient* Coverdale, Bishops': but *castè* SD); 53 (*securitas* Vulg. Junius: *freedom* Coverdale, Bishops' ["Or, *safety*" Bishops' margin]: *saturitas* Fritzsche's SD); 69 (*curati...contentionum* Vulg. Junius, Coverdale, Bishops': *creati...contemptionum* Fritzsche's STD); viii. 8 (*quomodo* Vulg., *like as* Coverdale: but *quando* Junius, *quoniam* Fritzsche's STD, *when* Bishops'); ix. 9 (*miserebuntur* Vulg. Junius, Bishops'; *be in carefulness* Coverdale: *mirabuntur* Fritzsche's STD); 17—19 (*quoniam tempus erat...mores corum*. The whole passage is hopelessly corrupt, and no English version affords even a tolerable sense. In ver. 19 Coverdale reads *creator* with Vulg., *mense* with Fritzsche's TD: *creatorum* (κτισθέντων) seems a conjecture, adopted by the Bishops' version and our own: our margin reads *messe*, and so probably the text and Bishops' *seed:* the Syriac must have read *mensâ*); xii. 42 (*populis* Vulg. Junius, Coverdale, Bishops': *prophetis* Fritzsche's SD); xiii. 2, 13 (Junius stands alone: see above, p. 44); 3 (*millibus* Vulg. Junius, Bishops': *nubibus* Fritzsche's SD, Coverdale); 20 (*in hunc* Vulg., *in hunc diem* Junius: but *in hæc* Fritzsche's D, the Syriac and Æthiopic, *in hac* ST, *in these* Coverdale, *into these* Bishops', set in their substitute for italic type); 45 (the margin is only a bold guess of Junius[1]); xiv. 44 (904 Fritzsche's STD: he himself reads 94 from the versions); 47 (*flumen* all authorities. Perhaps *lumen* is conjectural); xv. 36 (text as *suffraginem* S, *suffragmen* D, *fragmen* T: *avertam* Junius: but *substramen* Vulg., *litter* Coverdale, Bishops'); 43 (text *exterrent* Coverdale, Bishops': but margin *exterent* Vulg. Junius); 46 (*concors in spem* Vulg. Junius [Coverdale, Bishops']: *consors specie* or *in specie* Fritzsche's SD); xvi. 68 (very perplexing: *fede the ydle with Idols* Coverdale: *cibabunt idolis occisos* Vulg., *shall slay you for meat to the idols* Bishops'. Fritzsche notes no variation of his manuscripts). Three like marginal notes (the first two of importance), due to the Bible of 1762, may be conveniently added in this place. 2 Esdr. xii. 32 (*ventus* Vulg. Coverdale, Bishops'; *Spiritus* Junius: *Unctus* Fritzsche's STD); xiv. 9 (*consilio* Vulg. Junius, Coverdale, Bishops': *filio* Fritzsche's STD); xvi. 46 (*in captivitatem* Junius, but the margin hardly rests on his sole authority).

---

[1] "Etsi quid si corruptè est Eretz Ararat, id est, regio Armeniæ. Docti viderint." Junius *in loco*.

Marginal notes and original texts. 51

Tobit i. 2 (κυρίως Cod. 248. Compl.: Κυδίως Ald. Rom.); 5 (δυνάμει 248. Compl.: δαμάλει Ald. Rom., but *Bahali deo* Junius); 7 ('Ααρών Compl. Ald.: Λευὶ Rom.); 14 (ἐν ἀγροῖς τῆς Μηδείας Ald., ἐν 'Ραγοῖς τῆς Μηδ. Rom., *in Rages civitatem Medorum* Vulg. See Appendix A); 17 (ἐπὶ τοῦ τείχους Compl. Ald.: ὀπίσω τοῦ τ. Rom.); ii. 10 (στρουθία LXX., *hirundines* Vulg., whom Coverdale and the Bishops' follow closely throughout Tobit); vii. 17 (ἀπεδέξατο LXX.: ἀπεμόρξατο two Old Latin manuscripts in Parsons); ix. 6 (Vulg. rather favours the daring conjecture of Junius); xi. 18 (the margin is only another guess of Junius[1]); xiii. 10 (εὐφράνη Compl. Ald., εὐφρᾶναι Rom.); xiv. 5 (εἰς πάσας τὰς γενεὰς τοῦ αἰῶνος Compl. Ald. Junius: omitted by Rom. Vulg.); 10 (ἔπηξαν Comp. Ald. Junius; ἔπηξεν Rom.)[1]; 11 (ἔθαψεν Compl. Junius: ἔθαψαν Ald. Rom.). The book of 1762 adds, ch. i. 2, *Shalmaneser*, from the Old Latin, Vulg. Syriac.

Judith iii. 9 and iv. 6 (*Esdrelom* refers to ch. i. 8, where only LXX. has that form); iii. 9 (Δωταίας LXX. Junius, *Dothan* Syr.: but Ἰουδαίας Ald.); iv. 3 (ἐκ τῆς ἰουδαίας 248. Compl. Ald., but Rom. omits ἐκ); v. 14 (ὄρος 248. Compl. Ald. Junius, ὁδὸν Rom., *deserta Sina montis* Vulg.); vii. 3 (ἐπὶ LXX. Vulg.: Junius alone has *a*); viii. 1 (Σαμαηλ Ald., Σαμαλιηλ 248. Compl., Σαλαμιηλ Rom., *Salathiel* Vulg., *Sammiel* Junius); 22 (φόνον Rom., φόβον 248. Compl. Ald.); xvi. 1 (καινὸν Vulg., Roman edition, against Cod. Vaticanus: καὶ αἶνον 248. Compl. Ald.); 13 (καινὸν Rom. with Cod. Vaticanus, Vulg. Junius: καὶ αἶνον Ald.).

Esther xiv. 12 (θεῶν Ald. Rom. Vulg.: ἐθνῶν Compl. Junius); xv. 7 (προπορευομένης Rom. Compl. Junius: πορευομένης Ald.: *went with her* Coverdale, Bishops').

Wisd. iii. 14 (ναῷ all authorities: cf. Isai. lvi. 5. Whence came λαῷ of margin?); v. 11 (διαπτάντος Compl. Ald., but διιπτάντος Rom. Vulg. Junius); 14 (χοῦς Rom. Coverdale's and Bishops' margins: χνοῦς Compl. Ald. Vulg. Junius, Coverdale, Bishops'); vii. 9 (τίμιον 248. Compl. Vulg. Junius: ἀτίμητον of margin, Ald. Rom.); 15 (δέδωκεν Compl. Ald. Old Latin, Vulg. Junius: δῴη Rom.); *ibid.* (δεδομένων Rom. Junius, διδομένων Compl. Vulg., εὐδομένων Ald., λεγομένων Fritzsche, after the Syriac and other versions, Codd. Sinaiticus and Alexandrinus); ix. 11 (δυνάμει Vulg. Coverdale, Bishops' only, for δόξῃ); xv. 5 (ὄρεξιν Comp. Vulg. Junius: ὄνειδος Ald. Rom.). The text of

---

[1] "Hunc locum sic legendum suspicor, **Ἀχίχαρος ὁ καὶ Νισβᾶς.**" Junius *in loco*. The change made by Junius in ch. xiv. 10, with a reference to this place (*Nitzba* for *Manasses*), is quite gratuitous.

4—2

this book is far purer than that of Ecclesiasticus, which is largely interpolated through the influence of the Complutensian Polyglott and its prototype, Cod. 248.

ECCLUS. Prolog. II. l. 36 (ἐφόδιον Grabe, *viaticum* Junius, whence the margin: ἀφόμοιον LXX.); ch. i. 13 (εὑρήσει χάριν Ald. Rom.: εὐλογηθήσεται Compl. Vulg. Junius, Coverdale, Bishops'); vii. 26 (μισουμένῃ Compl. [Ald. Rom. have not the line] Vulg. &c. No trace of "light," except it be a euphemistic paraphrase); xiii. 8 (εὐφροσύνῃ LXX. Junius: ἀφροσύνῃ Vulg. Coverdale [*simpleness*], Bishops'); 11 (ἔπεχε LXX., *des operam* Junius: ἄπεχε *retineas* Vulg., *withdraw* Coverdale, Bishops'); xiv. 1 (πλήθει 248. Compl. Junius: λύπῃ Ald. Rom. Vulg., *conscience* Coverdale, Bishops'); xix. 12 (κοιλίᾳ LXX. Junius: καρδίᾳ Vulg. Coverdale, Bishops'); xx. 19 (ἄνθρωπος ἄχαρις, μῦθος ἄκαιρος· both clauses are in LXX. &c.); xxii. 9 (τροφήν 248. Compl., τέχνην manuscripts named by Arnald in his elaborate *Critical Commentary* on the Apocrypha, the only considerable one in English. In Ald. Rom. Vulg. &c. ver. 9, 10 are wanting); 17 (τοίχου ξυστοῦ Ald. Rom. with the margin: 248. Compl. prefix ἐπὶ, Vulg. *in*. The rendering of ξυστὸν as a noun is from *winter house* Coverdale, Bishops', *xysti* Junius); xxiii. 22, 23 (ἄλλου Compl. Junius: ἀλλοτρίου Ald. Rom. Vulg., but Coverdale and the Bishops' vary in the two verses); xxiv. 11 (ἠγαπημένη Ald. Rom.: ἠγιασμένῃ 248. Compl. Vulg. Junius, Coverdale, Bishops'); 14 (ἐν αἰγιαλοῖς Ald. Rom.: ἐν Γαδδὶ 248. Compl. [Syr. Junius]: *Cades* Vulg. Coverdale, Bishops'); xxv. 9 (*amicum verum* Vulg. Coverdale, Bishops': φρόνησιν LXX. Junius, Bishops' margin); 17 (σάκκον Ald. Rom. Bishops': ἄρκος 248. Compl. Vulg. Junius, Coverdale); xxx. 2 (εὐφρανθήσεται 248. Compl. Junius, Coverdale, Bishops': ὀνήσεται Ald. Rom.); xxxiv. 18 (δωρήματα 248. Compl. Junius, μωμήματα Ald., μωκήματα Rom. Vulg. Coverdale, Bishops'); xxxvi. 14 (ἆραι τὰ λόγιά σου Compl. Ald. Junius, ἀρεταλογίας σου Codd. Sinaiticus, Alexandrinus, Vaticanus [cf. Field, LXX. *Collatio*, p. 204], *inerrabilibus verbis tuis* Vulg., *thine unspeakable virtues* Coverdale, Bishops'); 15 (προφήτας 248. Compl. Vulg. Junius: προφητείας Ald. Rom. Coverdale, Bishops'); 17 (οἰκετῶν Compl. Vulg. Syriac, Junius, Coverdale, Bishops': ἱκετῶν Ald. Rom.); xxxvii. 20 (τροφῆς Ald. Rom., *re* Vulg. Coverdale, Bishops': σοφίας 248. Compl. Junius); 26 (δόξαν 248. Compl. Vulg. Junius: πίστιν Ald. Rom. Coverdale[1], Bishops'); xxxviii. 2

---

[1] It is worthy of notice how Coverdale (1535), whose version of the Apocrypha was the first printed in English, though leaning much on the Latin Vulgate, follows Aldus in preference in these readings.

(τιμὴν 248. Compl. Junius: δόμα Ald. Rom. Vulg. Coverdale, Bishops'); 22 (μου 248. Compl. Vulg., *tui* Junius: αὐτοῦ Ald. Rom. Coverdale, Bishops'); xxxix. 13 (ἀγροῦ Ald. Rom. Coverdale, Bishops': ὑγροῦ 248. Compl. [Vulg.] Junius); xlii. 8 (περὶ πορνείας of the margin is found in no edition or version, and in only three unimportant manuscripts); 18 (κύριος Ald. Rom. Vulg. Coverdale, Bishops': ὕψιστος 248. Compl. Junius); xliii. 5 (κατέπαυσε 248. Compl. only, for κατέσπευσε); xliv. 12 (δι' αὐτοὺς Rom. and all others, except μετ' αὐτοὺς Compl. Ald. Junius); xlvii. 3 (ἔπαιζεν Ald., *lusit* Vulg. Coverdale, Bishops': ἐπεξένωσεν 248. Compl., whence *peregrinus conversatus est* Junius: ἔπαισεν Rom.); 11 (βασιλέων Ald. Rom.: βασιλείας 248. Compl. Vulg. Junius, Coverdale, Bishops'); xlviii. 11 (κεκοιμημένοι 248. Compl. Junius: κεκοσμημένοι Ald. Rom. Vulg. Coverdale, Bishops'); xlix. 9 (κατώ‚θωσε 248. Compl., *correxit* Junius: ἀγαθῶσαι Ald. Rom. Coverdale, Bishops').

Add a various reading of 1762; ch. xlviii. 8 (*thee* Vulg. Junius, Bishops': αὐτὸν LXX. Coverdale). In ch. li. 11 καὶ of the Greek is rendered by Junius *quòd;* hence *because* 1762 marg.

BARUCH i. 5 (ηὔχοντο Rom. Vulg. Coverdale, Bishops': but Compl. Ald. Junius add εὐχὰς); vi. 61 (καὶ πνεῦμα of text Ald. Rom. Vulg., but Compl. with margin omits καὶ).

BEL AND DRAGON, ver. 27 (ἴδε Compl. Ald. Vulg. Junius, Coverdale, Bishops': ἴδετε Rom. with margin).

PRAYER OF MANASSES, line 38 (ἄνεσις Cod. Alexandr., but the Latin version [which is not Jerome's] and Bishops' Bible read *respiratio*, i. q. ἀνάπνευσις).

1 MACC. i. 1 (χεττιείμ or -ειείμ LXX., *Chethim* Vulg., *Cethim* Coverdale, Bishops', *Chettim* Bishops' marg.); 4 (τυράννων Rom. Vulg. Coverdale, Bishops': τυραννιῶν Compl. Junius, τυραννικῶν Ald.); ii. 2 (Καδδίς Rom. Junius, 'Ιαδδίς Compl., Γαδδίς Ald. Old Latin, Vulg. Coverdale, Bishops'); 5 (Αὐαρὰν Compl. Rom., 'Αναράν Ald., *Habaran* Junius, *Abaron* Vulg. Coverdale, Bishops'); 66 (πολεμήσει Rom. Vulg. Coverdale, Bishops': πολεμήσετε Compl. Ald. Junius); iii. 29 (φόροι Codd. Sinaiticus and Alexandrinus, Old Latin, Vulg. Coverdale, Bishops': φορολόγοι Compl. Ald. Rom. Junius); 41 (παῖδας LXX.: πέδας Josephus, *Ant*. XII. 7, 3 and Syriac); v. 3 ('Ακραβαττίνην Compl. Ald. Rom. Junius, *Arabathane* Vulg. Coverdale, Bishops'); 26 (Βόσσορα Ald., Codd. Alexandrinus and Vaticanus: Βόσορα Cod. Sinaiticus with 1611: Βόσοππα Compl., *Abosor* Vulg., *Barasa* Coverdale, Bishops'); *ibid.* (Χασφὼρ Rom. Vulg. Coverdale: Χασκὼρ Compl. Ald., *Casbon* Bishops'. In ver. 36, as the margin of 1762 notes, Χασφὼν is read by Compl. Ald. Rom., but

Chasbon by Vulg., *Casbon* by Coverdale, Bishops'); 28 (Βόσοππα Compl. Ald., Βοσὸρ Rom. Vulg. Coverdale, Bishops'); vi. 38 (φάλαγξιν Old Latin, Vulg. Syriac, Junius, Coverdale, Bishops': φόραγξιν Compl. Ald. Rom.); vii. 31 (Χαφαρσάλαμα Rom. Vulg. Coverdale, Bishops': Καφαρσάραμα Compl. Ald., *Capharsama* Old Latin, *Carphasalama* Bishops' margin); ix. 2 (*Galilea* is a mere guess of Drusius, according to Cotton); 9 (much confusion exists in Compl. Ald. which read ἀλλ' ἢ σώζωμεν τὰς ἑαυτῶν ψυχάς. τὸ νῦν ἐπίστρεψον. καὶ οἱ ἀδελφοὶ ἡμῶν ἀπερρύησαν, καὶ πολεμήσομεν... which Junius follows: this virtually agrees with Vulg. Coverdale, Bishops'. Our version justly professes to follow Rom. ἀλλ' ἢ σώζωμεν τὰς ἑαυτῶν ψυχὰς τὸ νῦν, καὶ ἐπιστρέψωμεν μετὰ [*ad* Vulg. &c.] τῶν ἀδελφῶν ἡμῶν καὶ πολεμήσωμεν...); 37 (Ναδαβὰθ Ald. Rom., Ναβαδὰθ Compl., *Madaba* Vulg. Coverdale, Bishops', *Medeba* Junius); 66 ('Οδομηρὰ Compl. Ald., 'Οδοααρρὴν Rom., *Odaren* Vulg. Coverdale, *Odomeras* Bishops' text, *Odareb* margin. *Odonarkes* has absolutely no authority, as Canon Westcott notices); xi. 63 (χώρας Compl. Ald. Bishops': χρείας Rom. Old Latin, Vulg.: *from meddling in the realm* Coverdale); xii. 37 (ἔπεσε Ald. Old Latin, Vulg. Coverdale, Bishops': ἤγγισε Compl. Rom. Junius): xiv. 9 (*de bonis terræ* Vulg. Coverdale, Bishops' only: περὶ ἀγαθῶν LXX.); 34 (*Gaza* Coverdale, Bishops' only: *Gazaris* Bishops' margin); xv. 22 ('Αριαράθη Rom. Junius, 'Αράθη Compl. Ald., *Arabe* Vulg., *Araba* Coverdale, Bishops'); 23 (Σαμψάμῃ Compl. Rom. Vulg., *Samsanes* Coverdale, *Samsames* Bishops', σαμψάκῃ Ald. See ten lines below, 1762); *ibid.* (τὴν Βασιλείδαν Cod. Alexandrinus only).

The Cambridge Bible of 1638, which very seldom adds to the marginal notes, in this book cites ch. iv. 15 'Ασσαρημώθ, the reading of Compl. Ald., and ch. ix. 36 'Αμβρὶ of Compl. The Bible of 1762 adds (besides two rectifications of dates) ch. iv. 24 (*bonus* Vulg. Junius, Coverdale, Bishops'); v. 13 (Τωβίου Rom., τοῦ βίου Compl. Ald., *Tubin* Vulg. Coverdale, Bishops'); xiv. 22 (ταῖς βουλαῖς LXX. Vulg. Coverdale, τοῖς βιβλίοις one unimportant Greek manuscript, *libris* Junius, *public records* Bishops'); xv. 23 (*Lampsacus* Junius, adding "sic placuit legere ex conjecturâ."); 39 (*Gedor*, a like conjecture of Junius, approved by Grotius and Dr Paris).

2 MACC. iii. 24 (πνῶν [i.q. πνευμάτων] omitting κύριος, Compl. Syr. Junius: *Spiritus omnipotentis Dei* Vulg. Coverdale, Bishops': πρων [i. q. πατέρων] Ald. Rom.); iv. 40 (Αὐράνου Cod. Alexandrinus, Compl. Junius: Τυράννου Ald. Rom. Vulg., "tyrant" Coverdale, Bishops'); vi. 1 ('Αθηναῖον LXX. Bishops' margin: *Antiochenum* Old Latin, Vulg.

Junius, Coverdale, Bishops'); ix. 15 (Junius stands alone here in rendering *Antiochenis*); xi. 21 (Διοσκορινθίου LXX. Junius, Coverdale, Bishops': *Dioscori* Old Latin, Vulg. Syriac); 34 (ἀνθύπατοι, if that word be meant in the margin, has no authority: these men were not consuls at all, but *legati* to overlook affairs in Syria); xii. 12 (if the margin represents a various reading, no trace of it remains); 39 (τρόπον [Ald.] Rom.: χρόνον Cod. Alexandrinus, Compl. Junius: but Vulg. Coverdale, Bishops' omit both words); xiii. 14 (Κτίστῃ Compl. Rom. Vulg.: Κυρίῳ Ald. with three manuscripts only).

The Bible of 1762 notes one various reading: ch. xii. 36 (Γοργίαν Ald., five manuscripts, Coverdale, Bishops' text: Ἐσδριν all other Greek, Vulg. Syriac, Junius, Bishops' margin).

To these 156 various readings indicated by the Translators of 1611 in the Apocrypha we must add 138 marginal notes, which express the exact meaning of the Greek, and three of the Latin of 2 Esdras. In 505 places varied renderings are alleged (the word "‖Or" being prefixed to them), many taken from Junius (besides those where he is expressly named, p. 46), from the Bishops' Bible and other Old English versions. In 174 places (167 of them in 1 Esdras) alternative forms of Proper Names are given for the reader's guidance, to which must be added 42 notes containing more or less useful information. Hence the sum total of the notes due to the original Translators in the Apocrypha appears to be 1018. Besides these, two were annexed in the Cambridge Bible of 1638 (see above, p. 54), 18 in that of 1762, one (Tobit iv. 20) in 1769, in all 21. To these might very well be added, set within brackets, at Ecclus. xviii. 30; xx. 27; xxiii. 7, summaries of contents, extracted from the best Manuscripts, resting on authority quite as good and nearly identical with any in favour of those inserted by the Authorized version in Ecclus. xxiv. 1; xxx. 1, 14; xxxiii. 24; xxxiv. 1; xliv. 1; li. 1.

We come at length to the New Testament, the marginal

annotations on which in the first edition amount to 767, so that together with the 6637 in the Old Testament, and the 1018 in the Apocrypha, the number in the whole Bible is no less than 8422. Of the 767 in the New Testament 37 relate to various readings, and will be detailed presently (p. 58); 112 supply us with a more literal rendering of the Greek than was judged suitable for the text; no less than 582 are alternative translations, 35 are explanatory notes or brief expositions. Of later notes, the Bible of 1762 added 96, that of 1769 no more than nine. Taking in therefore the 368 noted in the Old Testament (p. 45), and the 21 in the Apocrypha, these additional marginal annotations amount in all to 494, few of them of any great value, some even marvellously trifling, but all of them ought in editions of the Bible to be readily distinguished from the work of the original Translators by being placed within brackets. Those who shall look almost at random into the multitude of Bibles published between 1638 and 1762 (a branch of enquiry which our plan does not lead to the necessity of examining very minutely), will probably find the germ of some of these later notes in Bibles of that period, put forth as it were tentatively, and withdrawn in later copies. Thus the later margins of Matt. xxviii. 19 (slightly altered in 1683, 1701) and of Acts xiv. 21, first appeared in Field's Bible of 1660, then in the Cambridge edition of 1683. To the same Bibles may be traced the notes on Matt. x. 25; xiv. 6; xxi. 19; xxii. 26. Mark xi. 17. Luke xxii. 42. Acts vii. 44; viii. 13. 1 Cor. vii. 32. 2 Cor. viii. 2; x. 10. James iii. 6. 2 John 3. The Cambridge Bible of 1683 first gave those on Matt. i. 20. Mark iii. 3; vii. 22. Luke vii. 8; xi. 36; xviii. 2; xxi. 8. Acts ix. 2; xv. 5; xvii. 3; xviii. 5. 1 Cor. vii. 16. Eph. ii. 5; vi. 12. 1 Tim. iii. 16. 2 Tim. *postscript.* Heb. x. 34; xii. 10. James iv. 2. 2 Peter i. 1, 8: many of which were obviously the work of the same mind. Two more appear in Lloyd's Bible of 1701, 1 Cor. xii. 5. Heb. i. 6[1]. These 38 notes at least must accordingly be deducted from the 96 imputed to Dr Paris, and they are among the best of this class. After having been swept away from the ordinary Bibles whereof ours of 1743—4 is a type, he brought them back again into their former places.

As Tremellius had special influence with the revisers of the Old Testament, and Junius with those of the Apocrypha, so Beza had considerable weight with those of the New Testament. Some of their worst marginal renderings come from his Latin version, such as Mark i. 34. Luke iv. 41. Acts i. 8. Rom. xi. 17. 1 Cor. iv. 9, though this last belongs to 1762. The earlier versions also often gave rise to the margin. Thus 2 Cor. v. 17 is alleged to this effect by Bp. Turton[2], where the Genevan Bible of 1560 led the Translators to insert a note in opposition to their own judgment, fortified as it was by Beza, and all the English translations save that one. Particular attention was naturally paid to the Bishops' Bible, which was the basis of the Authorized. Sometimes its renderings both in text and margin are retained unchanged, e.g. 2 Cor. viii. 22: or the margin alone is kept, after the text is changed, e.g. Heb. xii. 2: or the Bishops' rendering, although removed from the text where it once stood, is retained for a margin, e.g. Gal. iii. 4. Eph. iv. 1. 2 Thess. iii. 14. 2 Tim. iv. 5, 15. In that primary passage Heb. ii. 16 the text and margin are both virtually the Bishops', with their places reversed. It is

---

[1] All these particulars (a little revised) are derived from p. 10 of Professor Grote's valuable Manuscript, for which see above, p. 23, note. He includes in his list Acts xvii. 19, but this is as old as 1611. The note on Eph. ii. 5 "*by* whose *grace*", taken from a various reading of certain manuscripts of the Vulgate *cujus gratiâ*, seems due to Scattergood (see p. 26), and is suggested in that portion of *Poli Synopsis* of which he is the reputed author (Grote *MS.* p. 41).

[2] *Text of English Bible*, p. 71 note.

58 Sect. II.] *Authorized Version of the Bible* (1611).

needless to pursue this subject further, however curious the questions it suggests, since, after all, every rendering must be judged upon its own merits, independently of the source from which it was drawn.

The following marginal notes relating to various readings occur in the New Testament in the two issues of 1611. They are nearly all derived from Beza's text or notes.

S. MATT. i. 11; vii. 14; ix. 26 (perhaps αὐτοῦ of Codex Bezæ [D] is represented in the text: "the fame of this" Bishops'); xxiv. 31; xxvi. 26. S. MARK ix. 16 (αὐτούς Beza 1565, afterwards changed by him to αὐτοῖς). S. LUKE ii. 38; x. 22 (the words in the margin are from the Complutensian edition and Stephen's of 1550); xvii. 36. S. JOHN xviii. 13 (the words of this margin, except the reference to ver. 24, are copied from the text of the Bishops' Bible, where they are printed in the old substitute for italic type).[1] ACTS xiii. 18; xxv. 6. ROM. v. 17; vii. 6; viii. 11. 1 COR. xv. 31[2]. 2 COR. xiii. 4[3]. Gal. iv. 15 (*ubi* Vulg. text., τίς marg. with Greek). *ibid.* 17 (ὑμᾶς Compl. Erasm. Steph. Beza 1565, ἡμᾶς Beza 1589, 1598). EPH. vi. 9 (ὑμῶν καὶ αὐτῶν Compl.). 1 TIM. iv. 15 (om. ἐν text, with Vulg.). HEB. iv. 2 (συγκεκραμένους margin, with Compl. Vulg.); ix. 2 (ἄγια text, with Compl. Erasm. Beza: ἁγία marg. with Steph.): see below, p. 253; xi. 4 (λαλεῖ text, with Erasm. Aldus, Vulg. English versions: λαλεῖται margin, Compl., Stephen, Beza[4]). JAMES ii. 18 (χωρὶς text, Colinæus 1534, Beza's last three editions, Syr. Vulg.: ἐκ margin, Compl. Erasm. Stephen, Beza 1565, all previous English versions). 1 PET. i. 4 (ἡμᾶς Steph.); ii. 21 (ὑμῶν Beza 1565, not in his later editions: this marginal

---

[1] It is doubtful whether even in the Bishops' Bible the words are designed to indicate a various reading, or are a simple comment on the passage, compared with ver. 24. There is Syriac and some other though very slender authority for inserting them, but that of Cyril alone would be known to our Translators, who doubtless took them from Beza's Latin version (1556).

[2] For the last three passages see Appendix E.

[3] But as no early edition reads σύν, the margin may only suggest a different rendering for ἐν. Beza says "Sed ἐν pro σύν positum esse vel illud declarat, quod in proximo membro scriptum est σὺν αὐτῷ," and so he translates *cum 'eo*, ἐν αὐτῷ.

[4] Beza's Latin is like the Vulgate "loquitur:" perhaps λαλεῖται was not regarded by him as passive.

note is also in the Bishops' Bible). 2 PET. ii. 2 (ἀσελγείαις marg. Compl.); 11 (marg. as Vulg. Great Bible); 18 (ὀλίγον Compl. Vulg.). 2 JOHN 8 (εἰργάσασθε...ἀπολάβητε marg. Vulg.). REV. iii. 14 (margin as Compl., all previous English versions); vi. 8 (αὐτῷ margin, with Compl. Vulg. Bishops' Bible); xiii. 1 (ὀνόματα margin, with Compl. Vulg. Coverdale); 5 (margin adds or prefixes πόλεμον to ποιῆσαι of the text, with Compl. Colinæus 1534, but not Erasm., Beza, Vulg. or English Versions); xiv. 13 (marg. ἀπάρτι λέγει ναί τὸ Πνεῦμα with Compl. Colinæus); xvii. 5 (marg. is from Vulg. and all previous English versions).

To these 37 textual notes of 1611, the edition of 1762 added fifteen, that of 1769 one.

1762. S. MATT. vi. 1; x. 10; 25; xii. 27 († "Gr. *Beelzebul,*" and so ver. 24") now dropped. S. LUKE xxii. 42 (incidentally excluding παρένεγκε). ACTS viii. 13. 2 COR. x. 10. HEB. x. 2 (see Appendix E); 17 (probably from the Philoxenian Syriac version, then just becoming known). JAMES iv. 2, revived from the Bible of 1683 (φθονεῖτε Erasm. 1519, Luther, Tyndale, Coverdale, Great Bible, Geneva 1557, Bishops', but perhaps no manuscript). 2 PET. i. 1 (see Appendix E). 2 JOHN 12 (ὑμῶν Vulg.). REV. xv. 3 (ἁγίων text, after Erasm., English versions: the alternative readings in the margin being ἐθνῶν of Compl., which is much the best supported, and αἰώνων of the Clementine Vulgate, of some Vulgate manuscripts, and the later Syriac); xxi. 7 (margin ταῦτα Compl. Vulg. rightly); xxii. 19 (marg. ξύλον for second βιβλίου Compl. Vulg. rightly).

1769. S. MATT. xii. 24 taken *mutatis mutandis* from the marginal note of 1762 on ver. 27.

In Appendix E has been brought together all that can throw light on the critical resources at the command of our Translators in the prosecution of their version of the New Testament. That these were very scanty is sufficiently well known, and, if for this cause only, a formal revision of their work has become a matter of necessity, after the lapse of so long a period. None of the most ancient Greek manuscripts had then been collated, and though Codex Beza (D) had been for many years deposited in England, little use had been made of it, and that single document, from its very peculiar character, would have been more likely to mislead than to instruct in inexperienced hands. It would be unjust to allege that the Translators failed to take advantage of the materials which were readily accessible, nor did they lack care or discernment in the application of them. Doubtless they rested mainly on the later editions of Beza's Greek Testament, whereof his fourth (1589) was somewhat more highly esteemed than his fifth (1598), the production of his extreme old age. But besides these, the Complutensian Polyglott, together with the several editions of Erasmus, and Stephen's of 1550, were constantly resorted to. Out of the 252 passages examined in Appendix E, wherein the differences between the texts of these books is sufficient to affect, however slightly, the language of the version, our Translators abide with Beza against Stephen in 113 places, with Stephen against Beza in 59, with the Complutensian, Erasmus, or the Vulgate against both Stephen and Beza in 80. The influence of Beza is just as perceptible in the cases of their choice between the various readings which have been collected above (p. 58): the form approved by him is set in the text, the alternative is mostly banished to the margin. On certain occasions, it may be, the Translators yielded too much to Beza's somewhat arbitrary decisions; but they lived at a time when his name was the very highest among Reformed theologians, when means for arriving at an independent judgment were few and scattered, and when the first principles of textual criticism had yet to be gathered from a long process of painful induction. His most obvious and glaring errors their good sense easily enabled them to avoid (cf. Matt. i. 23; John. xviii. 20).

SECTION III.

On the use of the Italic type by the Translators, and on the extension of their principles by subsequent editors.

THE practice of indicating by a variation of type such words in a translation of the Bible as have no exact representatives in the original is believed to have been first employed by Sebastian Munster in his Latin version of the Old Testament published in 1534[1]. Five years later this diversity of character ("a small letter in the text" as the editors describe it) was resorted to in the Great Bible, in order to direct attention to clauses rendered from the Latin Vulgate which are not extant in the Hebrew or Greek originals. A good example of its use occurs in Matt. xxv. 1 where "*(and the bride)*" is added to the end of the verse from the Old Latin, not from any Greek copy known in that age. As the readings of the Vulgate came to be less regarded or less familiar in England, subsequent translators applied the smaller type to the purpose for which Munster had first designed it, the rather as Theodore Beza had so used it in his Latin New Testament of 1556. Thus the English New Testament published at Geneva in 1557, and the Genevan Bible of 1560, "put to that word, which lacking made the sentence obscure, but set it in such letters, as may easily be discerned from the common text[2]." The same expedient was adopted by the translators of the Bishops' Bible (1568, 1572), somewhat too freely indeed in parts.

---

[1] Bp. Turton's *Text of the English Bible Considered* (p. 111, second edition). In this branch of the subject the Bishop was quite at home, and has given a view of the italics which is only not complete.

[2] *To the Reader*, p. 2, N.T. 1557.

It is one of the most considerable faults of this not very successful version, that its authors assumed a liberty of running into paraphrase, the ill effects of which this very difference in the type tended to conceal from themselves. From these two preceding versions, then held in the best repute, the Geneva and the Bishops' Bibles, the small Roman as distinguished from the black letter (now and as early as the Bible of 1612 respectively represented by the Italic and Roman type) was brought naturally enough into the Bible of 1611, and forms a prominent feature of it, whether for good or ill.

On this last point, namely, the wisdom or convenience of printing different words in the same verse or line in different kinds of type, with a view to the purpose explained above, it is not necessary for an editor of the Authorized Bible to express, or even to hold, an opinion. Italics, or whatever corresponds with them, may possibly be dispensed with altogether (though in practice this abstinence will be found hard to maintain); or they may be reserved for certain extreme cases, where marked difference in idiom between the two languages, or else some obscurity or corruption of the original text, seems to forbid a strict and literal translation. It is enough for the present purpose to say that our existing version was plainly constructed on another principle. Those who made it saw no objection to the free use of a typographical device which custom had sanctioned, and would have doubtless given a different turn to many a sentence had they been debarred from indicating to the unlearned what they had felt obliged to add of their own to the actual words of the original; the addition being always either involved and implied in the Hebrew or Greek, or at any rate being so necessary to the sense that the English reader would be perplexed or go wrong without it. Taking for granted, therefore, the right of the Translators

The Italic type. 63

thus to resort to the italic type, and the general propriety of their mode of exercising it, the only enquiry now open to us is whether they were uniform, or reasonably consistent, in their use of it.

And in the face of patent and well ascertained facts it is impossible to answer such a question in the affirmative. Undue haste and scarcely venial carelessness on the part of the persons engaged in carrying through the press the issues of 1611, which are only too visible in other matters (see above, p. 8), are nowhere more conspicuous than with regard to this difference in the type. If it be once conceded that the Translators must have intended to use or refrain from using italics in the selfsame manner in all cases that are absolutely identical (and the contrary supposition would be strange and unreasonable indeed), their whole case in this matter must be given up as indefensible. There is really no serious attempt to avoid palpable inconsistencies on the same page, in the same verse : and those who have gone over this branch of their work will be aware that even comparative uniformity can be secured only in one way, by the repeated comparison of the version with the sacred originals, by unflagging attention so that nothing however minute may pass unexamined. This close and critical examination was evidently entered upon, with more or less good results, by those who prepared the Cambridge Bibles of 1629 and more especially of 1638 (for before these appeared the italics of 1611, with all their glaring faults, were reprinted without change[1]), and in the next century by Dr Paris in 1762, by Dr Blayney and his friends in 1769 (see Appendix D). The rules to be observed in such researches, and the principles on which they are grounded, must be gathered

---

[1] There may be more alterations, but we can name only Gal. i. 3, "*be*" italicised in 1613, but not in later Bibles before 1629 (Cambridge).

from the study of the standard of 1611, exclusively of subsequent changes, regard being paid to what its authors intended, rather than to their actual practice.

The cases in which the italic character has been employed by the Translators of our Authorized Bible may probably be brought under the following heads:—

(1) When words quite or nearly necessary to complete the sense of the sacred writers have been introduced into the text from parallel places of Scripture. Six such instances occur in the second book of Samuel:

ch. v. 8. "And David said on that day, Whosoever getteth up to the gutter, and smiteth the Jebusites, and the lame and the blind, *that are* hated of David's soul, *he shall be chief and captain.*" The last clause is supplied from 1 Chr. xi. 6.

ch. vi. 6. "And when they came to Nachon's threshing-floor, Uzzah put forth his *hand* to the ark of God." Rather "*his hand*" (as in 1638) from 1 Chr. xiii. 9.

ch. viii. 4. "And David took from him a thousand *chariots*, and seven hundred horsemen, and twenty thousand footmen." We derive "*chariots*" from 1 Chr. xviii. 4.

ibid. 18. "And Benaiah the son of Jehoiada was *over* both the Cherethites and the Pelethites" (*was over* 1629). In 1 Chr. xviii. 17 "*was* over" (1611).

ch. xxi. 19. "...slew *the brother of* Goliath the Gittite." In 1 Chr. xx. 5 we read "slew Lahmi the brother of Goliath the Gittite."

ch. xxiii. 8. "the same *was* Adino the Eznite: *he lift up his spear* against eight hundred, whom he slew at one time." 1 Chr. xi. 11 supplies "he lift up, &c."

Thus Num. xx. 26 is filled up from ver. 24; Judg. ii. 3 from Num. xxxiii. 55 or Josh. xxiii. 13; 1 Kin. ix. 8 from 2 Chr. vii. 21; 2 Kin. xxv. 3 from Jer. xxxix. 2 and lii. 6; 1 Chr. ix. 41 from ch. viii. 35; 1 Chr. xvii. 25 from 2 Sam. vii. 27; 1 Chr. xviii. 6 from 2 Sam. viii. 6; 2 Chr. xxv. 24 from 2 Kin. xiv. 14; Ezra ii. 6, 59 from Neh. vii. 11, 61. In the Bible of 1638 Jer. vi. 14 "*of the daughter*" is italicised, as taken into the text from ch. viii. 11. This is the simplest case, for the words supplied in italics are doubtless lost in the one ancient text, while they are preserved in the other.

(2) When the extreme compactness of the Hebrew language produces a form of expression intelligible enough to those who are well versed in it, yet hardly capable of being transformed into a modern tongue. One or two of Bp. Turton's (*Text*, &c. pp. 50, 51) examples will illustrate our meaning:

Gen. xiii. 9. " Separate thyself, I pray thee, from me: if the left hand, then I will go to the right; or if the right hand, then I will go to the left."

Ex. xiv. 20. "And it was a cloud and darkness, but it gave light by night."

Every one must feel that something is wanting to render these verses perspicuous ; the latter indeed we should hardly understand, without looking closely to the context. It seems quite right, therefore, that supplementary words should be inserted in such places, and equally fit that they should be indicated by some contrivance which may shew that they form no part of the Hebrew original. In our version accordingly the verses stand as follows, except that, in the former, "thou" (twice over) was not in italics before 1629; italicise also the second "to":

"If *thou wilt take* the left hand, then I will go to the right; or if *thou depart* to the right hand, then I will go to the left."

"It was a cloud and darkness *to them*, but it gave light by night *to these*."

To this class we may most conveniently refer the numerous cases wherein what grammarians call the *apodosis* (that is, the consequence resulting from a supposed act or condition) is implied rather than stated, yet in English requires something to be expressed more or less fully: such are the following texts:

Gen. xxx. 27. "If I have found favour in thine eyes, *tarry*."

2 Chr. ii. 3. "As thou didst deal with David my father, and didst send him cedars...*even so deal with me.*"

Dan. iii. 15. "If ye be ready that at what time ye hear the sound of the cornet,...ye fall down and worship the image which I have made, *well.*"

Luke xiii. 9. "And if it bear fruit, *well.*"

Occasionally our Translators, with happy boldness, have suppressed the *apodosis* entirely, as in the original (Ex. xxxii. 32; Luke xix. 42). In some few passages the seeming necessity for such insertion arises from a misunderstanding either of the sense or the construction: such is probably the case in Neh. iv. 12, and unquestionably so in Matt. xv. 6; Mark vii. 11.

(3) Just as little objection will probably be urged against the custom of our Translators in italicising words supplied to clear up the use of the grammatical figure known as the *zeugma*, whereby, in the Hebrew no less than in the Greek and Latin languages, an expression which strictly belongs to but one member of a sentence, with some violation of strict propriety, is made to do duty in another.

Gen. iv. 20. "And Adah bare Jabal: he was the father of such as dwell in tents, and cattle." Supply, "*of such as have* cattle."

Ex. iii. 16. "I have surely visited you, and that which is done to you in Egypt." Our version here, with less necessity, inserts "*seen*" after "and."

Ex. xx. 18. "And all the people saw the thunderings, and the lightnings, and the noise of the trumpet, and the mountain smoking." Here the order of the clauses renders it impossible to supply any single word which would not increase the awkwardness of the sentence: the passage is accordingly left as it stands in the original. Not so the sharper language of the parallel place:

Deut. iv. 12. "Ye heard the voice of the words, but saw no similitude, only a voice." After "only" insert with 1611 "*ye heard.*"

2 Kin. xi. 12 (so 2 Chr. xxiii. 11). "And he brought forth the king's son, and put the crown upon him, and the Testimony." Insert "*gave him*" before "the Testimony."

Luke i. 64. "And his mouth was opened immediately, and his tongue," add "*loosed.*"

1 Cor. xiv. 34. "It is not permitted unto them to speak, but to be under obedience." After "but" insert "*they are commanded.*" So "*and commanding*" before "to abstain" in the exactly parallel passage, 1 Tim. iv. 3.

The following examples, taken from the Apocrypha, have been neglected by all editors up to the present date:

2 Esdr. ix. 24. "Taste no flesh, drink no wine, but *eat* flowers only."

xii. 17. "As for the voice which thou heardest speak, *and that thou sawest* not to go out from the heads." This rendering, taken from the Coverdale and Bishops' Bible, is possibly incorrect.

Ecclus. li. 3. "According to the multitude of *thy* mercies and *greatness* of thy name."

(4) Akin to the preceding is the practice of inserting in the Authorized Version a word or two, in order to indicate that abrupt transition from the *oblique* to the *direct* form of speech, which is so familiar to most ancient languages, but so foreign to our own:

Gen. iv. 25. "And she bare a son, and called his name Seth: for God, *said she,* hath appointed me another seed instead of Abel."

Ex. xviii. 4. "And the name of the other *was* Eliezer; for the God of my Father, *said he, was* mine help."

2 Sam. ix. 11. "As for Mephibosheth, *said the king,* he shall eat at my table."

Jer. xxi. 11. "And touching the house of the king of Judah, *say,* Hear ye the word of the Lord."

Judith v. 23. "For, *say they,* we will not be afraid of the face of the children of Israel."

Acts i. 4. "Which, *saith he,* ye have heard of me."

The inconvenience of a sudden change of person, unbroken by any such words supplied, may appear from Gen. xxxii. 30, "And Jacob called the name of the place Peniel: for I have seen God face to face, and my life is preserved." Just as abrupt is the construction in Gen. xli. 52 (compare ver. 51); Tobit viii. 21. In 2 Macc. vi. 24 "said he" continued in Roman type till 1638.

(5) Another use of italics is to indicate that a word or clause is of doubtful authority as a matter of textual criticism. Of this in the Authorized Version we can produce only one unequivocal instance in the Canonical books, 1 John ii. 23 (see Appendix E, p. 254); for it is not quite certain that the change of type in Judg. xvi. 2; xx. 9, employed to point out words borrowed from the Septuagint, intimates any suspicion of a *lacuna* in the text. Some doubt also hangs over 1 Cor. xiv. 10 "none *of them*" (see Appendix E, pp. 245, 251, where the italics were removed in 1638). In subsequent editions occur the following instances, most of them being due to the Cambridge edition of 1638, those that are not so having another date affixed to them:

Deut. xxvii. 26 ("*all*"). Josh. xxii. 34 ("*Ed*"). 1 Sam. ii. 16 ("*Nay*" 1629 Camb.)[1]. 2 Kin. xix. 31 ("*of hosts*")[2]; xx. 13 (the second "*all*" appears in most Hebrew Bibles, and we should restore the Roman character). 2 Chr. v. 1 ("*all*"); xvii. 4 ("*LORD*"). Job x. 20 ("cease then, *and*," 1611 inconsistently: we should read with 1638, "cease *then, and*," or leave all in Roman as 1629 Camb., since both particles are found in *Keri*). Ps. xli. 2 ("*And* he shall be," *Chetiv*, not *Keri*); lxix. 32 ("*and* be glad"). Prov. xx. 4 (*therefore:* but ו of *Keri* is in Symmachus and the Vulgate, so that we should restore the type of 1611). Jer. xiii. 16 ("*and* make," yet ו of *Keri* is in the Septuagint and Vulgate). Lam. v. 7 ("*and are* not;" "*And* have." These two conjunctions are both wanting in *Chetiv*, but present in *Keri*, yet 1769 italicises the first, not the second). Mark viii. 14 ("*the disciples*,"

---

[1] This is inevitable, as the reading is either לֹו "to him" (*Chetiv*), or לֹא "Nay" (*Keri*), not both. The two words are confused in 18 other places, of which Delitzsch points out 17.

[2] The addition in this passage and others is from the Hebrew *Keri* or margin; but *Keri* is received without italics where we should not wish to insert them now: e.g. Judg. xx. 13 "the children;" Ruth iii. 5, 17 "to me." In ver. 37 of this chapter (2 Kin. xix.) we should italicise Keri "*his sons*" for the sake of consistency. In the parallel place Isai. xxxvii. 38 "his sons" stands in *Chetiv*, or the text.

first italicised in 1638). Mark ix. 42 (see Appendix E). John viii. 6 (1769: see Appendix E). In Acts xxvi. 3 "*because I know*," and the first "*and*" in ver. 18, the italics are due to 1769. 1 John iii. 16 (see Appendix E, p. 255).

Thus in the Apocrypha 1629 italicises *on me* in Tobit xi. 15, με being wanting in the Complutensian, but we had better return to the Roman type. For similar cases examine Ecclus. iii. 22 (1629 and 1769); 1 Macc. iii. 18 (1638); x. 78 (1638); xi. 15 (1638, *partim recte*); xiv. 4 (1638).

To these passages we may add 2 Chr. xv. 8 "*of* Oded[1]," to point out the doubt hanging over the reading or construction in that place. Also in Ecclus. i. 7; xvii. 5, italics have been substituted, as was stated above (p. 48), in the room of brackets, as a mark of probable spuriousness in the lines so printed. The portion of 1 John v. 7, 8 which is now for the first time set in italics in the Cambridge Paragraph Bible, is probably no longer regarded as genuine by any one who is capable of forming an independent judgment on the state of the evidence.

(6) The last class to which we may refer the italicised words in our version, is that wherein the words supplied are essential to the English sense, although they may very well be dispensed with in the Hebrew or Greek; nay more, although very often they could not be received into the original without burdening the sentence, or marring all propriety of style. This last head comprises a far greater number of cases than all the rest put together, and it may reasonably be doubted whether much advantage accrues from a change of type where the sense is not affected to an appreciable extent. Whether we say "the folk that are with me" (Gen.

---

[1] וְהַנְּבוּאָה עֹדֵד הַנָּבִיא (contrast ch. ix. 29 וְעַל־נְבוּאַת אֲחִיָּה). The absolute state of הַנְּבוּאָה seems connected with a break in the sense, such as occurs in ver. 11;

ch. xvi. 9. The Vulgate has here *Azariæ filii Oded*, as all in ver. 1. Thus again in Prov. xv. 22, by italicising "they," one may intimate that "thoughts" is probably not the real nominative to תָּקֵם.

xxxiii. 15) with the Bible of 1611, or "the folk that *are* with me" with the Cambridge edition of 1629, could make no difference whatever, except to one who was comparing English with Hebrew idioms, and such a person would hardly need to carry on his studies in this fashion. One thing, however, is quite clear, that if it be well thus to mark the idiomatic or grammatical divergences between languages, all possible care should be devoted to secure UNIFORMITY of practice; cases precisely similar should be treated in a similar manner. Now this is just the point at which our Authorized Version utterly fails us; we can never be sure of its consistency for two verses together. To take one or two instances out of a thousand: why do we find "*it be hid*" in Levit. v. 3, 4, and "it be hidden" in ver. 2, the Hebrew being the same in all? Or why should the same Hebrew be represented by "upon all four" in Levit. xi. 20, but by "upon (or "on") *all* four" in ver. 21, 27, 42? Even in graver matters there is little attempt at uniformity. Thus οὗτος Heb. iii. 3 is "this *man*" in 1611, but "this man" in Heb. viii. 3, a variation retained to this day; in 1 Pet. iv. 11 "*let him speak*" is italicised in 1611, but the clause immediately following "*let him do it*" not before 1629. The foregoing gross oversights, with countless others, are set right by the revisers of 1629 and 1638, yet these later editors have been found liable to introduce into the printed text nearly as many inconsistencies as they removed. Thus, for example, whereas "which were left" Lev. x. 16 adequately renders the Hebrew article with the participle of the Niphal conjugation, and so in 1611 was printed in ordinary characters, the edition of 1638 wrongly italicises "*which were*" here, but leaves untouched "that were left" in ver. 12, a discrepancy which still cleaves to our modern Bibles. The same must be said of "ye *are* to pass" ("*are*" first italicised in 1629) Deut. ii. 4 compared with "thou art to pass" ver. 18: "*even* unto Azzah" ver. 23 ("*even*" correctly italicised in 1638, indeed the word is expressed in ver. 36), but "even unto this day" left untouched in ver. 22: "the slain *man*" ("*man*" first in 1629) Deut. xxi. 6, but "the slain man" ver. 3: "*their* backs" ("*their*" first in 1629) Josh. vii. 12, but "their backs" ver. 8[1]. The reader will find as many instances of this nature as he cares to search for in any portion of our modern Bibles he may please to examine, and from the whole matter it is impossible to draw in the main any other conclusion than this:— that the changes introduced from time to time have been too unsystematic, too much the work of the moment, executed by too many hands, and on too unsettled principles, to hold out against hostile, or even against friendly criticism.

Dr Blayney in his Report to the Oxford Delegates (Appendix D) appeals to the edition of Dr Paris (1762) as having "made large corrections in this particular," adding that "there still remained many necessary alterations, which escaped the Doctor's notice" and had to be set right by himself and his friends. And it cannot be doubted that the two Bibles of 1762 and 1769 between them largely increased the number of the words printed in italics, although the effect was rather to add to than to diminish the manifest inconsistencies of earlier books. Thus Blayney (and after him the moderns) in Luke xvii. 29 (ἅπαντας) italicises "*them*"

---

[1] In the Bible of 1638, with all its merits, we occasionally notice a strange want of critical skill. In Prov. iii. 18 our version happily changes "he" of the Bishops' version into "every one," to express the plural participle, to which the feminine pronoun is affixed; yet this book, followed by all the rest, actually sets "*every one*" in italics. In Cant. iv. 2 "even shorn" is designed to translate הַקְּצוּבוֹת (ὁλοκλήρων, Symmachus: *of the same bigness*, Bishops'), yet "*even*" is set in italics, as if it were a conjunction. In Heb. xi. 36 we may retain, yet not without hesitation, the italics first used for the word *cruel* in 1638, since all the earlier English versions were satisfied with "mockings:" *ludibria*, Vulg.

before "all," yet leaves untouched "them all" ver. 27: in Luke xix. 22 he reads "*thou* wicked servant," retaining "thou good servant" in ver. 17. Nor can the correctness of Dr Paris be praised overmuch. In putting into Roman type the "*good*" of 1611, Eccles. vii. 1, he has been blindly followed by the rest, though a glance at the Hebrew would have set them right: yet some of his errors in italics were removed in 1769, e.g. "way-*side*" Matt. xiii. 4; Mark x. 46; Luke viii. 5. Hence it becomes manifest that, in preparing a critical edition of our vernacular Translation, which shall aim at meeting the wants and satisfying the scholarship of the present age, nothing less than a close and repeated comparison of the sacred originals, line by line, with the English Bible, will enable us to amend the mistakes which lack of time and consideration has led certain of the most eminent of preceding editors to pass by unnoticed, or even to exaggerate while attempting to remedy them.

In the Apocrypha indeed the work would have to be done almost afresh, inasmuch as the Company of Translators to whom these books were assigned took no sort of pains to assimilate their portion of the work to that executed by the others. They introduce this difference of type only 54 times in the whole Apocrypha, in fact only three instances occur at all later than Ecclus. xlv. 4, after which brackets [ ], or sometimes ( ) are substituted in their room. No improvement worth mention seems to have been attempted before 1638, when 96 fresh instances of italics were added (e.g. Judith xiv. 18, but Tobit iv. 13 in 1629), and most of the brackets were displaced for italics, though a few yet survive in modern Bibles (2 Esdr. iii. 22. Wisd. xii. 27; xvii. 2, 3, 4. Ecclus. vi. 1, 2; viii. 11; xi. 30; xii. 5; xiv. 10[1]). About ten places more were subsequently italicised

---

[1] In Ecclus. xliv. 22 the brackets [ ] can only be intended for marks of parenthesis ( ), since no copy omits the enclosed words.

(e.g. Wisd. v. 17; viii. 2. Baruch iii. 33. 2 Macc. xi. 33 "*and*," all in 1769), so that the italics of modern Bibles are but 273 in all. Those that are employed are of much the same character as in the Canonical Scriptures; some for pointing out the *zeugma* (above p. 66), as 1 Macc. vii. 19[1]; x. 20, 24; 2 Macc. xi. 14: or for indicating a transition in the form of speech (Judith v. 23. Ecclus. ii. 18. 1 Macc. i. 50; xvi. 21; so 1 Esdr. i. 4 in 1629, and 2 Macc. vi. 24 in 1638): some for supplying a real or seeming grammatical defect (1 Esdr. iv. 11. Tobit viii. 10. Ecclus. xii. 5): one for calling attention to uncertainty in the reading (Tobit x. 5[2]; see above, p. 68): a few for no reason that is apparent (Wisd. vi. 9 *O kings*. Ecclus. xl. 4; xlv. 4[3]), it would seem in mere error. Since our version of the Apocrypha is so imperfectly revised as to resemble the Bishops' version in other respects more closely than we find in the inspired books, so does it in this over-free use of italic type by way of commentary. The interpolations in Wisd. ii. 1; xvi. 10; 1 Macc. vii. 32 are derived from this source; that in Ecclus. vi. 2 from the note of Junius (*ferociens incerto et vago impetu*): and too many others are conceived in the same spirit, e.g. Wisd. x. 10; xiv. 12; xix. 14. Ecclus. viii. 11; xi. 30; xlvi. 6. 1 Macc. viii. 18. In 1 Macc. ix. 35, after Coverdale and the Bishops' Bible, our Translation actually brings a Proper Name into the text "[John]," avowedly on the

---

[1] But we should set in ordinary character "[have they cast out]" of 1611 in ver. 17, inasmuch as the ellipsis is only accidental, arising from the order of the words cited from Ps. lxxix. 2, 3 in the Septuagint, and indeed in the Hebrew.

[2] In 1611 we read "*Now I care for nothing*, my son, *since I have let thee go*," οὐ μέλει μοι, τέκνον, ὅτι ἀφῆκά σε, but Junius would have us read οἶ for οὐ (Drusius persuades even Fritzsche to adopt σὺ μέλει), from the Vulgate *heu heu me, fili mi, ut quid te misimus*. The italic type should be changed into Roman, since the passage may very well stand unaltered.

[3] In the original edition the first four words of Ecclus. viii. 8 are italicised by a like oversight. They were set in Roman type in 1629.

authority of Josephus, for the slight evidence now alleged in its favour (the Syriac and three recent Greek copies) was unknown to them.

After this general survey of the whole subject, it is proper to state certain rules, applicable to particular cases, which a careful study of the Bible of 1611 will shew that our Translators laid down for themselves, but which haste or inadvertence has caused them to carry out very imperfectly in practice. It will be seen that many of their omissions were supplied in one or other of those later editions which display care in the matter, while almost as many have remained to be set right by their successors. "Whether the Translators, if they had foreseen and fully considered how far the system of italics which they adopted, when carried out, would lead, would have adopted it,...may be a question. And whether the abundance of the italics...does not in a measure defeat its own purpose by withdrawing attention from them, is perhaps a question also. But as it was, the course adopted by the editors of 1611 having been to mark by italics not important insertions only, but to aim at marking in this manner everything, even trifling pronouns and auxiliary verbs, not in the originals, carrying out however their intention very imperfectly: the choice for after editors lies between adopting a different system, and carrying out theirs to the full[1]." Between these alternatives few perhaps will censure those who have chosen the latter without much hesitation.

The following observations, therefore, grounded on the practice of our Translators, will guide us in a vast number of doubtful cases.

(1) The English possessive pronoun, when it renders the Hebrew or Greek article, should be set in italics. Compare in 1611 Judg. iii. 20. 2 Sam. vi. 7; xvii. 23. 2 Kin.

[1] Grote MS. p. 24. See above, p. 23, note.

ix. 35; xiii. 3. 2 Chr. xiii. 10. Job i. 5; ii. 13. 1 Cor. i. 1.
2 Cor. i. 1. Gal. v. 10. Eph. iv. 28. Phil. ii. 13. So in
1629, Gen. xxvi. 11. Neh. xii. 42: in 1638, Matt. viii. 3;
x. 24; xii. 10, 33; xiii. 15 (*ter*); xiv. 19, 31; xv. 5, &c. *passim:*
in 1762, Matt. xii. 46; xxi. 31; xxvi. 23, 51; xxvii. 24: in
1769, Matt. xv. 8; xxv. 32. Mark v. 29; x. 16, &c.

(2) Since the definite article is only the unemphatic form of the demonstrative 'that,' and has itself a demonstrative force[1], it might not appear necessary to set "that" in italics when it represents the Greek or Hebrew article. In 1611, however, it is thus printed so often as to prove that our Translators designed to do so always with "this" and "that." For their practice compare Gen. xviii. 32. Ex. ix. 27; xxxiv. 1. Num. xi. 32. Josh. iii. 4. 1 Sam. xiv. 8; xxv. 24. 1 Chr. xviii. 11; xxi. 22. 2 Chr. xx. 29; xxxvi. 18. Ezra ix. 2; x. 9. Eccles. vi. 12. Luke viii. 14. 2 Tim. ii. 4. In 1629 many more were added, e.g. Gen. xxxi. 43 (*"these"* ter); xliii. 16 (*bis*): in 1638, 1 Chr. vi. 64; vii. 21. 2 Chr. xxviii. 22. Ezra x. 4. Neh. viii. 10. Job xxxii. 5. Ps. li. 4. Eccles. viii. 8; ix. 9. Isai. xxxvii. 30 (yet not 2 Kin. xix. 29). Jer. ix. 26; xxxviii. 12. Ezek. xliv. 3; xlvi. 2, 8. Hab. i. 6. Mark iv. 11; ix. 42. John v. 13. Acts xxiv. 22. Rom. xvi. 22. 1 Cor. ix. 12; xi. 27. 2 Cor. v. 1, 4. 2 Thess. i. 11. 1 Tim. vi. 7, 14. 2 Pet. i. 14: a few in 1769, 2 Sam. xvi. 11; xviii. 32. Hos. ix. 10. Yet in the New Testament this rule is even now greatly neglected.

(3) The idioms of the English and the Hebrew differ so widely that no attempt has been made, in the great majority of cases, to print the English definite article in italics when the Hebrew one is wanting. The only apparent instance of such distinction being kept up by our Translators occurs in 1 Sam. xxvi. 8, and is a mere error, the Hebrew article being present: hence "the" is put into Roman type

[1] Bain, *English Grammar*, p. 34.

in 1638[1]. Occasionally, however, the sense is so much affected, perhaps for the worse, by the presence of the English article, that we should be careful to note its absence in the Hebrew: e.g. Ps. xlv. 1. Ezek. iv. 1; x. 20; xxiii. 45. Hos. ii. 4; viii. 7; x. 10; xii. 4. Joel ii. 6. Amos vii. 10. Jonah iv. 10 *marg.* Mic. v. 5. In thus dealing with the Greek article rather more freedom may be assumed, regard being always had to the anarthrous style of certain of the sacred writers, and to the licence which permits the omission of the article in certain constructions. Compare Ecclus. xliv. 18. Rom. i. 6; ii. 14. 1 Cor. ix. 20. Gal. iv. 31. 1 Thess. ii. 6. 1 Tim. ii. 5. Heb. ii. 5. 1 Pet. i. 12; iv. 10. 1 John ii. 1. 3 John 3. Rev. xiv. 9; xv. 2; xxi. 17. The English indefinite article[2], or none at all, would better suit most of these places.

(4) Annexed to proper and common appellations of places the Hebrew ה, the old accusative termination, is regarded as denoting *motion to*, and its absence, or that of a corresponding preposition, is indicated by italics: e.g. Job xxx. 23; Ps. v. 7 in 1611. But ה prefixed, which may be the article, and sometimes accompanies ה annexed (compare 2 Sam. xiii. 10), is not so regarded. Prepositions of motion in English, which have no Hebrew equivalent, should be systematically set in italics, the rather since it is not always certain that the right one is employed, e.g. 1 Sam. xxiii. 25. 2 Kin. xvi. 8.

(5) When an article is prefixed to a participle, but not otherwise, and it is rendered by "which are," "that is" &c. ("such as were" Eccles. iv. 1), these words are best printed

---

[1] In Job xi. 16 also Synd. A. 3. 14, B. M. 1276. l. 4 and 3050. g. 3 read "*the* misery," but this is probably a misprint for "*thy* misery" of the other issue.

[2] It is, of course, quite unmeaning to italicise our indefinite article, as 1611 seems never to have done, but only 1638 in Acts x. 2, and 1762 in Acts xxiv. 5.

without italics, as in 1611 they are pretty uniformly, e.g. Lev. x. 16. Deut. xx. 11; xxv. 6, 18; xxix. 29[1]. In 1638 italics came to be employed in some cases of this kind, e.g. "*that was* built" Judg. vi. 28; "*which is* shed" Ps. lxxix. 10; "she *that* looketh" Cant. vi. 10; "*one* that accuseth" John v. 45. In Judg. xi. 30 *marg.* "*that* which *cometh forth*" of 1611 is properly changed in 1629 into "*that which cometh forth.*"

(6) But even if the article be prefixed to an adjective, the correct practice is to italicise the words supplied. Thus in 1611 "*that are* wise," "*that are* mighty" Isai. v. 21, 22; "*who is* holy" Heb. vii. 26, in which passages there is no article. In Judg. viii. 15, where the article is found, we have "that *are* weary" in 1611, "that are weary" 1629, "*that are weary*" 1638 correctly. This last edition is very careful on the point, having rightly put into italics what had previously been Roman in 1 Sam. xv. 9. Neh. iv. 14. Ps. lxxxv. 12. Ezek. xxii. 5. Yet in Judg. xvii. 6; xxi. 25 and such like passages some adopt (not very consistently) "*that* which *was* right," to intimate the presence of the article, as 1 Sam. ix. 24 in 1638.

(7) In such phrases as "and it came to pass...that," if the Hebrew copulative ו be not expressed at the beginning of the second clause, its absence is denoted by italicising "that," which otherwise would stand in Roman type. This nice distinction is observed by our Translators with as much consistency as they display in greater matters. Thus 1611 in Gen. iv. 14. Ex. xxxiii. 8. Num. xvi. 7. 2 Kin. xviii. 1. 1 Chr. xiv. 15. Esther v. 2. Isai. x. 12, 20, 27; xxiv. 18. So in 1629, Ex. xxxiii. 7. Lev. ix. 1. Num. xvii. 5: in 1638, Neh. iv. 16: in 1762, Matt. xiii. 53; xix. 1. Luke xx. 1. Compare Luke v. 1, 17; vii. 12; viii. 1, &c.

---

[1] In the concise style of poetry we may often willingly overlook the absence of the article before the present participle.

(8) The personal pronoun, when omitted with the Hebrew infinitive (occasionally with some risk of ambiguity in the sense) should always, when supplied in the version, be printed in italics. This comprehensive rule is abided by in 1611 at Gen. vi. 19, 20 "to keep *them* alive;" Ex. xxx. 12 (second case, but overlooked in the first), 15; xxxi. 13. Deut. xxvi. 18. 1 Kin. xii. 6 ("*I*" overlooked by 1629 and later Bibles). 1 Chr. xxviii. 4. 2 Chr. xxxv. 6. Isai. l. 4 ("*I*" again overlooked in 1629 and its successors). Thus also in 1629, Ex. xxviii. 28. Esther iv. 11: in 1638, Gen. iii. 6. Acts xii. 19. Rom. xiii. 5: in 1769, Ex. xxxv. 1. Deut. xxix. 29. Heb. xii. 10.

(9) Where in Hebrew the first of two nouns is in the state of construction, the word "of" between them is not italicised in English: but if the preceding noun be susceptible of a change by reason of the state of construction, and yet be not so changed, "of" or its equivalent is italicised. Compare, for example, Ex. xxxvii. 24 with Ex. xxv. 39. The Masoretic points are necessarily taken for true under this head.

(10) It would seem natural to italicise "own" in the expression "your own," "his own," &c. where the original has but the simple possessive pronoun. Yet in 1611 we find it so printed only in 2 Sam. xviii. 13. Job v. 13; ix. 20. Prov. i. 18 (*bis*). Blayney has "his *own*" in Gen. i. 27, and in no other place, as if he shrank from making about 200 changes in respect to one word. We should italicise "own" only in Job xix. 17, where its presence excludes one very possible sense, and in Acts xxi. 11, where it is important to mark that ἑαυτοῦ is not in the text.

(11) The Hebrew preposition ל "to," with or without the verb "to be," is considered as equivalent, idiom for idiom, with the English verb "to have." It is so treated in the book of 1611 usually (e.g. Gen. xii. 20; xvi. 1), but

not always (e.g. Gen. xi. 6 "they *have*," ver. 30 "she *had*"). But "pertained" in such phrases is always italicised, as Judg. vi. 11 in 1611. Hence we would not follow Scholefield[1], who reads "what *have* I" 1 Cor. v. 12.

(12) We have adopted, with some hesitation, Mr Gorle's[2] refined distinction, confirmed by 1611 in Jer. xli. 16, between אַחַר "after *that*" and אַחֲרֵי־כֵן "after that;" not however with infinitives, as 2 Chr. xxvi. 2. Jer. xxxvi. 27; xl. 1.

(13) When in different parts of Scripture a phrase or expression is given with more or less fulness, it is right to distinguish the shorter form, by setting the missing part of it in italics. Examples are in 1611 "dead *men*" Ex. xii. 33; "*mighty* man" Ps. cxx. 4 *marg.* (compare Ruth ii. 1. 1 Sam. xiv. 52. Jer. xli. 16, where "man" is expressed): in 1638, Job xvii. 8, 10. Isai. xxix. 8; xliv. 25: in 1769, Isai. xli. 2. Again in 1611, "fill *with*" Gen. xliv. 1. Ps. lxxi. 8 (*bis*); lxxii. 19, a preposition being supplied after the verb (מָלֵא) in Ex. xvi. 32. 2 Kin. ix. 24. Ezra ix. 11. Job xli. 7. Ezek. xxxii. 6. Care, however, should be taken to put in italics no more than is really wanting: thus in Matt. viii. 25 προσελθόντες ought to be "came to *him;*" Matt. x. 1 προσκαλεσάμενος "called unto *him,*" as it is given in 1762, not as the same word is represented by 1769 in Matt. xv. 32 "called *unto him.*" This rule extends very widely, and is difficult to be observed with perfect consistency.

---

[1] In the Greek and English New Testament, published at Cambridge by Professor Scholefield (new edition, 1836), many words were printed in italics for the first time, chiefly such as bear on our first rule, that regarding pronouns. The changes he introduced evidence great care, but seem not to have influenced other editions of the Bible published since his time.

[2] The Rev. J. Gorle, Rector of Whatcote, submitted to the Syndics of the University Press, in or about 1864, very valuable and elaborate notes on the use of italics in our Bibles, which proved of great service in the preparation of the Cambridge Paragraph Bible.

(14) The verb substantive is italicised before the participle passive (*Paül*), to distinguish it from the Niphal conjugation of the verb (e. g. Gen. xxix. 31, 33 "*was* hated" in 1629 Camb.); but more licence has been granted to the auxiliaries that render the active participle (*Poel*). In Num. x. 29 we prefer "we *are* journeying," though in other places the present "is", "are", &c. is in Roman type, but not "*was*" or "*were*."

Such are the principal rules which the Translators of the Authorized Version designed to follow in the arrangement of italics for the standard Bible of 1611. How little what they printed was systematically reviewed and corrected in the preparation of later editions is evident from the numerous glaring errors, committed by them, which have remained undetected down to this day. The reader will perceive what is meant by comparing the original Hebrew or Greek with any modern Bible in 1 Chr. vii. 6. 2 Chr. x. 16. Neh. v. 19. Job i. 5; xxii. 24; xxx. 5; xxxiv. 14; xli. 20. Ps. lv. 21. Prov. xv. 26. Cant. v. 12. Isai. xxii. 18 ("*like*" a little doubtful); Jer. xi. 4, 7; xxxvi. 22; xlvi. 13. Ezek. iv. 4, 9; xiii. 18; xxii. 20 *marg.*; xxxix. 11; xliii. 3 *marg.* Dan. i. 7; viii. 26; ix. 23 *marg.* Obad. 6. Hab. iii. 9. 1 Esdr. viii. 63. Tobit. iii. 3. Wisd. ii. 1; xix. 14. 1 Macc. viii. 18; x. 24; xii. 37. Tit. ii. 3. 3 John 12. Indeed some more recent corrections are positively false, e.g. 2 Chr. iii. 11 "one wing *of the one*" (1638): Luke x. 30 "*man*" (1762).

What Blayney intended to do and seems to have lacked time for (Appendix D), has been regarded as a matter of imperative duty by the compiler of the present work. He has made out a full list of all the changes with respect to italics, in which the Cambridge Paragraph Bible as edited by him differs from his standard, the Cambridge small pica octavo of 1858 (see above, p. 38), together with such

The Punctuation.

reasons for them as each case might require; and has deposited the list for future reference in the Library of the Syndics of the University Press.

SECTION IV.
On the system of punctuation adopted in 1611, and modified in more recent Bibles.

"THE question of punctuation," to employ the language of Professor Grote[1], "has two parts: one, respecting the general carrying it out for purposes of rhythm and distinction of sentences, independent of any question as to the meaning of the words; the other respecting the particular cases where different punctuation involves difference of meaning." In regard to the first of these parts, much variety of practice will always exist, according to the age in which a writer lives, or the fashion which he has adopted for himself. Thus the edition of 1611 abounds with parentheses[2] which are largely discarded in modern Bibles, wherein commas supply their place, unless indeed they are left unrepresented altogether. The note of admiration, which is seldom met with in the old black-letter copies (wherein the note of interrogation usually stands in its room: e.g. Prov. xix. 7) is scattered more thickly over Blayney's pages than the taste of the present times would approve. Upon the whole, while the system of recent punctuation is heavier and more elaborate than necessity requires, and might be lightened to advantage[3], that of the standard of 1611 is too scanty to afford the guidance needed by the

---

[1] Grote MS. p. 25. See above, p. 23, note.
[2] In Synd. A. 3. 14, these marks of parenthesis often seem to have been inserted with a pen, in places where the Oxford reprint has them; thus supplying another minute argument for the priority of the Syndic's copy (see above, pp. 8, 9).
[3] For instance, in such expressions as "and behold," "and lo," "for lo;" we should omit the comma set by Blayney, &c. between the two words.

voice and eye in the act of public reading. "It is a torture to read aloud from, as those who have had to do it know[1]." Grote contrasts it in this particular with a Cambridge edition of 1683, into which more changes in the stops were admitted than later books cared to follow, and whose punctuation differs in fact but little from that in vogue in recent times.

The case in which difference of punctuation involves difference of meaning cannot be thus summarily dismissed. Since interpretation is now concerned, rather than arbitrary liking or convenience, the principles laid down in the First Section are strictly applicable here (pp. 3, 14). The stops found in the original ought not to be altered unless the sense they assign be not merely doubtful, but manifestly wrong[2]. Modern changes, if still abided by, should be scrupulously recorded, and their retention can be justified only by the consideration that it is at once pedantic and improper to restore errors of the standard Bible which have once been banished out of sight. The following list will be found to contain all divergencies of punctuation from that prevailing in recent editions, not being too insignificant to deserve special notice, which can be supposed to influence the sense. They naturally divide themselves into two classes, those which are, and those which are not, countenanced by the two issues of 1611.

I. The stops of 1611 are retained in preference to those of later Bibles, there being no strong reason to the contrary, in

Gen. xxxi. 40. "*Thus* I was in the day, the drought consumed me," 1611, after Masoretic stops, LXX., Vulg., against the Bishops', 1638—1769, moderns, who have "*Thus* I was; (, 1638—1762) in the

---

[1] Grote MS., *ubi supra*.
[2] Thus no stronger stop than a colon (as in 1611) is proposed after Jesaiah, 1 Chr. iii. 21, though Dr Pusey's view seems very maintainable (*Book of Daniel*, p. 300), that quite another line than Zerubbabel's now follows.

day the drought consumed me." | Lev. iv. 2, "*(concerning things* which ought not to be done)." Here 1769 and the moderns reject the parenthesis of the earlier books, which, though not found in vv. 13, 22, 27, tends to relieve a hard construction. Joshua iii. 16, "very far, from the city Adam," 1611—1630. In 1629 Camb. and subsequent editions the comma after "far" is removed, but the other distribution is not less probable. 1 Kin. xii. 32, "and he ‖ offered upon the altar (so did he in Bethel,) ‖ sacrificing." The moderns, after 1769, punctuate "and he ‖ offered upon the altar. So did he in Bethel, ‖ sacrificing:" against the Hebrew stops, *Zakeph-katon* standing over both "altar" and "Bethel;" and rendering the margin (which provides for וַיַּעַל being the Kal rather than the Hiphil conjugation) quite unintelligible. xix. 5, "behold then, an angel" (וְהִנֵּה־זֶה) : "behold, then an angel," 1769, moderns. Neh. ix. 4, "upon the stairs of the Levites," (עַל־מַעֲלֵה הַלְוִיִּם) : "upon the stairs, of the Levites," 1769, moderns. ver. 5, "Jeshua and Kadmiel," (cf. Ezra ii. 40): "Jeshua, and Kadmiel," 1769, moderns. Job xix. 28, "persecute we him?...found in me." 1611—1617. But 1629 Lond., 1630 place the interrogative also after "me:" 1629 Camb., 1638, moderns, transfer the second clause into the *oratio obliqua* "persecute we him,...found in me?" xxxi. 30. This verse is rightly set in a parenthesis in 1611—1744, which 1762 and the moderns remove. xxxiii. 5, "If thou canst, answer me," as in ver. 32. The first comma is removed in 1629 Camb. (not 1629 Lond., 1630) and all modern books. xl. 24 *marg.*, "*or bore*," 1611: "or *bore*," 1629, 1638, Bagster 1846. But 1744, 1762, moderns, " or, *bore*," quite absurdly. Psalm ii. 12, "but a little: Blessed," 1611—1744, "but a little. Blessed," 1762 mod ;[1]. lxxix. 5, "wilt thou be angry, for ever?" Cf. Ps. xiii. 1; lxxxix. 46. The comma is removed by 1616 (not 1617, 1630), 1629 Camb., &c. ver. 11, "come before thee, According to the greatness of thy power: Preserve thou." Thus 1611—1744, following the Hebrew punctuation: "come before thee; According to the greatness of thy power (, 1762 only) Preserve thou" 1769, moderns, very boldly, though approved by Dean Perowne. lxxxix. 46, "How long, LORD[2], wilt thou hide thyself,

---

[1] The two lines of the couplet are closely connected, as the parallelism shews. Here, and in some other places (notably in Ps. iii. 5; lxiv. 7), the Masoretic punctuation is at variance with the poetical structure. So in Ps. xl. 12, *Rebiah* has tempted 1762 to change the comma after "head" into a semicolon, 1769 moderns into a colon, where we prefer the comma of 1611—1744.

[2] So read instead of "LORD?" of 1769 mod.

for ever?" The third comma is removed in 1629 London and Camb. (not 1630), 1638, 1744, 1769 mod. In 1762 this comma is strengthened into a semicolon. Prov. i. 27. The final colon of 1611—1630 is clearly preferable to the full stop of 1629 Camb., moderns. xix. 2. Restore the comma before "sinneth", discarded in 1762: also in xxi. 28, that before "speaketh," removed in 1769: both these for the sake of perspicuity. xxx. 1 *fin*. The full stop is changed into a comma by 1769 mod. Eccles. ii. 3, "(yet acquainting mine heart with wisdom)." In 1769 mod. the marks of parenthesis are rejected and a semicolon placed after "wisdom." Cant. vii. 9, ", For my beloved, that" 1611, &c. (", For my beloved that," 1629 Lond., 1630: almost preferable; cf. Heb.): "For my beloved, that" 1769, moderns. viii. 2, ", of the juice" 1611—1630: "of the juice" 1629 Camb., 1638, &c. Isai. xxiv. 14, "they shall sing",. The comma is found only in 1611 (Oxford reprint, not Synd. A. 3. 14), and acknowledged by Vulg. and Field ("*jubilabunt;*") as representing the Hebrew *Athnakh*. xlviii. 12, ", O Jacob, and Israel my called;" 1611—1630. But 1629 Camb., 1638, place commas after "Israel," 1769 and the moderns join "Jacob and Israel," against the Hebrew stops. Lam. ii. 4, "pleasant to the eye," (cf. Heb. stop): 1769 mod. remove the comma. iv. 15, ", when they fled away and wandered:" (, for: in 1769 mod.). Hosea vii. 11, "a silly dove, without heart." In 1629 Camb. and the moderns, the comma (which represents the Hebrew accent) is removed, as if "without heart" referred exclusively to the dove. Hagg. i. 1, 12, 14; ii. 2, remove the comma of 1769 mod. after "Josedech." Cf. Zech. i. 1.

2 Esdr. viii. 39, "and the reward that they shall have." (*et salvationis et mercedis receptionis*, Vulg., but *et salutis, et recipiendæ mercedis* Junius): but 1762 mod. place a comma after "reward," as if *receptionis* of Vulg. belonged also to *salvationis*. xii. 2, "and behold, the head that remained, and the four wings appeared no more." In 1762 a comma is inserted after "wings:" in 1769 mod. both commas are removed. There is a pause in the sense after "remained," such as a semicolon would perhaps better represent, before the vision in ch. xi. 18, &c., is repeated. Judith iv. 6, "toward the open country near to Dothaim (κατὰ πρόσωπον τοῦ πεδίου τοῦ πλησίον Δωθαΐμ, LXX.). Here 1629 Camb., 1630, &c., insert a comma before "near." viii. 9, 10. In 1769 mod. the marks of parenthesis are withdrawn, to the detriment of perspicuity. xiv. 17, "After, he went" (καὶ εἰσῆλθεν, LXX.): 1629 Camb. (not 1630), 1638 mod. remove the necessary comma. Ecclus. xxxvii. 8, "(For he will counsel for himself):" .1769 mod. reject the

marks of parenthesis, setting a semicolon after "himself". ver. 11, ", of finishing" (περὶ συντελείας, LXX.): 1769 mod. obscure the sense by rejecting the comma. Baruch vi. 40, "that they are gods?" In 1629, &c., "gods," the interrogation being thrown upon the end of the verse. But compare the refrains ver. 44, 52, 56, 65, to justify our arrangement of the paragraph. 1 Macc. vi. 51, "to cast darts, and slings." The comma is removed in 1638 mod.

S. Matt. ix. 20—22, are inclosed in a parenthesis by 1611—1762, which 1769 rejects[1]. S. Mark iii. 17, and v. 41. The marks of parenthesis (of which 1769 mod. make too clean a riddance) are to be restored from 1611—1762. S. John ii. 15, "and the sheep and the oxen," thus keeping the animals distinct from πάντας ("them all...with the sheep and oxen," Bishops'). In 1630 (not 1638, 1743), 1762 mod., a comma intrudes after "sheep." xviii. 3, "a band *of men*, and officers," 1611—1762, thus distinguishing the Roman cohort from the Jewish ὑπηρέται (*Archb. Trench*). In 1769 mod. the comma is lost. Acts xi. 26, "taught much people, and the disciples were called," 1611—1630: both verbs depending on ἐγένετο. Yet 1638—1743 substitute a semicolon for the comma, while 1762 mod. begin a new sentence after "people," as if the editors had never glanced at the Greek. xviii. 18, "and Aquila: having shorn *his* head"; Paul being the person referred to in κειράμενος. By changing the colon into a semicolon, 1762 mod. render this more doubtful. Rom. i. 9, ", always in my prayers," 1611, 1612, 1613. The first comma is removed in 1629 Camb. and London, 1630, &c.: the second changed into a semicolon by 1769 mod. Cf. 1 Thess. i. 2; Philem. 4. iv. 1, "Abraham our father, as pertaining to the flesh," 1611—1762. In 1769 mod. the comma is transferred from after "father" to before "our." v. 13—17 were first inclosed in a parenthesis by 1769, which is followed by all moderns, even by the American Bible of 1867, though the American revisers of 1851 (see p. 36) had removed it. It is worse than useless, inasmuch as it interrupts the course of the argument. viii. 33 *fin*. The colon of 1611—1762 is almost too great a break, yet 1769 mod. substitute a full stop. The semicolon of *The Five Clergymen* is quite sufficient. xv. 7, "received us," 1611—1743. The comma is removed in 1762 mod. 1 Cor. vii. 5, "prayer," 1611—1630. But 1638 mod. substitute a semicolon for the comma, as if to drive us to take the various reading συνέρχησθε of Beza

---

[1] The parenthesis is absent from the parallel passage of S. Mark. It is not so much wanted in Luke viii. 42—48, but we may retain it from 1611—1743, though 1762 mod. reject it.

86 Sect. IV.]   Authorized Version of the Bible (1611).

1598 (note, not text), and the Elzevirs. viii. 7, "with conscience of the idol unto this hour," 1611—1762, as if the reading ἕως ἄρτι τοῦ εἰδώλου were accepted ("with the yet abiding consciousness of the idol,"), or cf. Phil. i. 26, and Dr Moulton's *Winer*, p. 584. In 1769 mod. the comma is deleted. 2 Cor. xiii. 2, "as if I were present the second time," 1611—1762. In 1769 mod. a comma is put in after "present," through an obvious misconception. Eph. iii. 2—iv. 1, "of the Lord," is wrongly set in a parenthesis by 1769 mod. (not American, 1867). Rather connect ch. iii. 1 with ver. 14. Phil. i. 11, "by Jesus Christ unto the glory..." In 1762 mod. a comma is inserted before "unto." Col. ii. 11, "of the flesh," the two clauses beginning with ἐν τῇ being parallel (cf. *var. lect.*), so that 1762 mod. wrongly remove the comma after "flesh." 1 Thess. iii. 7, ", by your faith " 1611—1630, but 1629 London and Camb. and all after them wrongly omit the comma. 2 Thess. i. 8, "in flaming fire," 1611—1762, connecting the words with ἐν τῇ ἀποκαλύψει, ver. 7. In 1769 mod. the comma is absent. Titus ii. 8, "sound speech that cannot..." The comma after "speech" in 1769 mod. obscures, rather than helps, the English. ver. 12, "teaching us that denying ungodliness and worldly lusts we should live..." Thus the sentence runs in the Oxford reprint of 1611 and in 1612, and this is the safest plan in such a construction, but Synd. A. 3. 14 places a comma after "lusts," and is followed by 1613 and the rest. In 1629 Camb., &c. another comma is set after "us," which 1769 mod. do not improve upon by transposing it to after "that." Heb. ii. 9, "lower than the angels,". In 1769 mod. this comma is removed, so as to *compel* us to take διὰ τὸ πάθημα τοῦ θανάτου with the preceding clause, to which it hardly seems to belong. iii. 7—11. Reject the marks of parenthesis introduced into modern Bibles in 1769. The American Bible of 1867 has them not. x. 12, "for ever, sat down." So 1611—1630, plainly rejecting "is set down for ever" of Bishops' Bible. This arrangement is supported by our standard Cambridge edition of 1858, and the American (1867), by Bp. Christ. Wordsworth, &c., and is surely safer than "for ever sat down" of 1638—1769 and most moderns. xii. 23. Restore the comma of 1611—30 after "assembly": see below, p. 253. xiii. 7. Restore the full stop of 1611 at the end of this verse, which 1762 mod. change to a colon. 2 Pet. ii. 14. The Greek compels us to reject the comma after "adultery" of 1743 and mod. Jude 7, "the cities about them, in like manner..." The comma after "them" is injudiciously removed by 1638, 1699 (not 1743), while 1762 mod. increase the error by placing it after "in like manner."

It would be endless, and would answer no good purpose, to enumerate all the cases wherein minute but real improvements in the punctuation, introduced into editions subsequent to 1611, have been universally acquiesced in (e.g. Jer. xvii. 3; Dan. xi. 18; Bel & Drag. ver. 10; Matt. xix. 4; Rom. ii. 13—15; 1 Pet. v. 13). Some very strange oversights of the standard Bible, in this as in other particulars (see pp. 3, 4), were permitted to hold their place quite late. Thus in John xii. 20 "And there were certain Greeks among them, that came up to worship at the feast:" the intrusive comma lingered till 1769. The comma, which originally stood after "about midnight," Acts xxvii. 27, was removed and set after "Adria" later than 1638. In regard to weightier matters, the comma put by 1611 after "God" in Titus ii. 13 is fitly removed by 1769 mod., that "the great God and our Saviour" may be seen to be joint predicates of the same Divine Person. Luke xxiii. 32 affords us a rare instance of an important change in the stops subsequent to 1769 (we have not been able to trace it up earlier than D'Oyly and Mant's Bible of 1817) "And there were also two other malefactors," where recent editors insert a comma before "malefactors," in order to obviate the possibility of mistake in the meaning of a phrase which is rather Greek than English. They were rightly unwilling to adopt the alternative of changing the plural "other" into "others," as the American Bible (1867) has unfortunately done[1]. The following chief additional changes in punctuation recommended by us, like those affecting the text itself (for

---

[1] Luke x. 1, is exactly parallel in this use of *other*, but that antiquated plural is very common in our version: Josh. viii. 22; xii. 19; 2 Sam. ii. 13; 1 Esdr. vii. 6; 2 Esdr. x. 6, 57; xi. 18; xvi. 22; Tobit vi. 14; Wisd. xi. 10, 13; 2 Macc. vii. 34; xi. 7, 11, 20; Matt. xxiii. 23; Luke xi. 16, 42; xviii. 9; John xix. 18; Acts xvii. 9 (but *others* ver. 34); 1 Cor. xiv. 29; 2 Cor. xiii. 2; Phil. i. 17; ii. 3; iv. 3, most of which remain unchanged in modern Bibles.

which see Appendix A), though usually sanctioned by respectable authority, occasionally by some recent Bibles, must ultimately depend on their own merits for justification.

II. Passages in which the stops, as well of 1611 as of most later Bibles, have been altered in the Cambridge Paragraph Bible.

Ex. xi. 1—3 is placed within a parenthesis, thus referring ver. 4 to ch. x. 29. Josh. vi. 1 might well be treated in the same manner. Josh. xv. 1, "*even* to the border of Edom" is better followed by a comma, as in 1762, than by the semicolon of 1611—1744: both stops are removed in 1769. 1 Kin. vii. 19, and xxi. 25, 26, should be set in parentheses, so as to connect closely the preceding and following verses in either case. xxi. 20. With 1617 (only) place a comma at the end of this verse, the *protasis* beginning with יַ֫עַן, ver. 20, the *apodosis* with וְהָיָ֫ה, ver. 21, just as in ch. xx. 36. Cf. also ch. xx. 42; xxi. 29. 2 Kin. xv. 25. Set a semicolon after "Arieh," in place of the comma of 1611, &c. The "him" following refers to "Pekah," not to "Arieh." So Tremellius after Heb.[1] Job iv. 6. See Appendix A. vi. 10, "Yea, I would harden myself in sorrow; let him not spare:" forms one line in the stichometry (*Delitzsch*). This does not appear in 1611—1744, which set a comma after "spare," or in 1762 mod., which punctuate " : let him not spare." xxviii. 3. Lighten the colon of 1611, &c., after "perfection" into a comma. "The stones" is governed by "searcheth out," whether we consider לְכָל־תַּכְלִית to be used adverbially, or no. Ps. cv. 6. "Ye children of Jacob, his chosen." Unless the comma be inserted, "his chosen" would not be understood as plural. In 1 Chr. xvi. 13, a comma is inserted by 1769 mod. without much need. Ps. cvii. 35. End in a semicolon: yet all our Bibles have a full stop. Ps. cviii. 5, 6. All our Bibles except that of the Tract Society (1861) join these two verses, which seems an impossible arrangement (*Perowne*). Substitute a full stop for the colon of 1611 (which is

---

[1] In Neh. xii. 24, we would substitute a semicolon instead of a full stop at the end of the verse, and perhaps ought to change the comma after Obadiah, ver. 25, into a colon. It would seem from 1 Chr. ix. 15—17; ch. xi. 17—19, that the list of the singers ends with Obadiah, that of the porters begins with Meshullam.

made a semicolon by 1629 Camb. and the moderns) at the end of ver. 5, and a semicolon for the colon after "delivered," as 1611 has in Ps. lx. 5. Prov. vi. 2. Since this verse, as well as ver. 1, is plainly hypothetical (*Bp. Christ. Wordsworth*), in spite of LXX., Vulg., and Tremellius, a comma must take the place of the full stop of 1611, &c. after "mouth." viii. 2, "high places by the way." Transfer the comma of 1611 from after "place" to after "way." Eccles. iv. 1, "and behold," 1629 Camb.—1762. In 1769 mod. the comma is removed though it is really wanted. Even the Hebrew has a distinctive mark (¹) here. Cant. iii. 2, "in the streets and in the broad ways,". So LXX., the Hebrew punctuation and parallelism. In 1611, &c., the comma is transferred to a place after "streets," thus joining the second clause with what follows. Isai. xi. 11, "his people, which shall be left from Assyria,". So the Hebrew stops, the analogy of ver. 16 (recognized by 1611—1762, not by 1769 mod.), LXX., Vulg., Lowth, Field: "his people that shall be left, from Assyria" 1611—1762: in 1769 mod. another comma follows "people." xxxii. 9. This verse is a distich, the true division of which after "voice" is plainer in Hebrew than in English. It is variously punctuated in our Bibles, but all agree in suggesting a false division into three lines, ending respectively at "ease," "daughters," "speech." xxxviii. 10, "I said,". All insert the comma in ver. 11. Jer. xlviii. 29. Instead of the parenthesis which encloses "*he is exceeding proud*" in all our Bibles, substitute a semicolon before, a colon after the words, as in Isai. xvi. 6 in 1762 mod. Ezek. v. 6, "my judgments, and my statutes." The comma, imperatively required by the Hebrew, was inserted from 1629 (both editions) to 1762, discarded in 1769 mod. xxi. 29, "that are slain of the wicked." The comma after "slain", apparently employed by 1611, &c. to aid the voice, fails to represent the *status constructus* of the Hebrew. xlvi. 18, "by oppression to thrust them out" renders a single Hebrew word (*oppressione deturbando eos*, Trem.). Yet 1611—1630 separate the English by placing a comma after "oppression," which 1762 mod. restore after it had been rejected by 1629 Camb., 1744. xlviii. 30, "of the city:" so the Hebrew stops. The Bishops' Bible and 1611—1630 have a comma after "city," which 1629 Camb. and the moderns omit altogether (cf. *Wordsworth*). Hosea ix. 15, "in Gilgal:" the colon of 1611 and the rest is too strong for the sense and the Hebrew accent. xii. 10. Remove the comma of 1611 &c. after "similitudes." Cf. Heb. Micah vi. 5, "; from Shittim" the inserted semicolon representing the Hebrew *Athnakh* (cf. *Wordsworth*). The Bishops' Bible separates these words from the preceding, though only by a comma[1].

2 Esdr. ii. 15 *marg.* " , *as a dove*," with 1629—1744. In 1611 we have "*as a dove:*" in 1630 " , *as a dove:*" against the Latin. In 1762 mod. " , *as a dove*" but our way seems safer. vii. 42, "is not the end, where..." Without the inserted comma, our version is hardly intelligible; *in co* sc. *sæculo*, not *fine.* Judith viii. 21, "if we be taken, so all..." Junius and 1611, &c. join οὕτως closely to the preceding words. (Cf. Moulton's *Winer*, p. 678). Wisd. xiii. 13, "the *very* refuse among those, which served to no use," (τὸ δὲ ἐξ αὐτῶν ἀπόβλημα εἰς οὐδὲν εὔχρηστον). If, with 1611, &c., we omit the comma, "those" will inevitably be taken as the antecedent to "which." xvii. 11—13. Place these verses within a parenthesis. Prayer of Manasses, ll. 17, 18, " : Thou, O Lord,..." The very long English sentence is so constructed (differently from the Greek, this Prayer having been rendered from the Old Latin, see p. 47), that the *apodosis* does not begin before this point; yet 1611 and all its successors put a full stop before "Thou." We adopt a colon from the Bishops' Bible. 1 Macc. vi. 36, "every occasion, wheresoever the beast was:" far preferable to "every occasion: wheresoever the beast was," of 1611, &c. ix. 34 *marg.* " *understood on the sabbath day*," 1629—1744. In 1762 mod. the false punctuation of 1611—1630 is revived ("*understood, on the sabbath day*"), against the Greek, which is not in the same order as in ver. 43. We set ver. 35— 42 in a parenthesis. x. 1, "Antiochus, *surnamed* Epiphanes" ὁ ἐπιφανής, the comma after "Antiochus" distinguishing the text from that of Josephus, namely τοῦ ἐπιφανοῦς, as mentioned in the margin. 2 Macc. x. 29, "men upon horses with bridles of gold" (ἐφ' ἵππων χρυσοχαλίνων ἄνδρες). In 1611, &c., a comma, worse than idle, is set after "horses." xiii. 2, "a Grecian power, of footmen, &c." In 1611, &c. we have "a Grecian power of footmen[2]."

S. Matt. xix. 28, "which have followed me, in the regeneration, when &c." So 1630 alone of our old Bibles, with Nourse (*Paragraph Bible*, Boston, 1836), Bagster, 1846, Scholefield (English), Lachmann, Tischendorf, Tregelles. This is at any rate the safest course. The second comma is wanting in 1611, 1612, 1613, 1616, 1617, 1629

---

[1] Tremellius seems anxious that no mistake should be made as to his judgment, rendering thus: "et quid responderit ei Bilham filius Behoris; ut agnoscens justè facta Jehovæ a Schittimis Gilgalem usque, dicas..."

[2] Yet it must be confessed that the Roman edition reads ἱππεῖς immediately afterwards, while our punctuation represents ἱππέων of Codex Alexandrinus.

(London), most modern Bibles, D'Oyly and Mant (1817), Tract Society's (1861), Blackadder (1864), American (1867), Newberry (1870), and Alford. The first comma is absent in the Bishops' Bible, the books from 1629 (Camb.) to 1769, and Scholefield's Greek text. S. Luke i. 55, "(as he spake to our fathers)". Thus with Nourse, the Tract Society, and Blackadder (*see last note*), indicate by a parenthesis the change of construction. Ver. 70 is also parenthetic[1]. Acts xxiii. 8, "neither angel nor spirit:". Even though the true reading be μήτε...μήτε instead of μηδέ...μήτε, angel and spirit comprehend together one class, resurrection the other, the two classes together comprising ἀμφότερα. The comma after "angel" in 1611—1630, abolished from 1629 (both editions) to 1743, is restored in 1762 mod. xxvii. 18. See below, p. 190. Rom. viii. 20, ", in hope." We can hardly do more in this doubtful passage, than relax the connection of ἐπ' ἐλπίδι with what precedes, by inserting the comma before it, and lightening the stop after it from a colon to a comma, as in 1769 mod., thus with Mr Moule (*Romans* in loco) regarding "in hope" as forming a brief clause by itself. xi. 8, from "according" to "hear" is rightly set in a parenthesis in 1769, as approved by the *Five Clergymen*. 1 Cor. xvi. 22. See below, p. 191, Appendix A. 2 Cor. i. 14, ", in the day" 1611. But later Bibles rightly omit the comma, since the clause that follows it relates only to what goes immediately before. v. 2, "we groan, earnestly desiring..." The adverb is doubtless intended to represent the intensive force of the preposition in ἐπιποθοῦντες (rendered *coveting* by Wicklif, but simply *desiring* by the later versions), so that this punctuation, first found by Prof. Grote in Field's Bible of 1660, but afterwards lost sight of, is that to be received, although through mere oversight, rather than with a view to render *ingemiscimus* of the Vulgate, the comma is placed after, not before, "earnestly" in 1611—1762, the final correction being due to 1769, from which the moderns adopt it. See p. 191, note 2. ver. 19, "God was in Christ reconciling..." All the Bibles from 1611 downwards, except that of 1743, insert a comma after "Christ." Eph. iv. 12, "for the perfecting of the saints for the work of the ministry, for..." (πρὸς...εἰς... εἰς). The comma of 1611, &c. after "saints" would be tolerable if the three prepositions were truly parallel. Phil. ii. 15, "the sons of God without rebuke," The comma set after "God" in 1611, &c. would inevitably suggest a different gender for ἀμώμητα or ἄμωμα. Col. ii. 2, "of God and of the Father and of Christ." The Received text can

---

[1] It would be well also to place Acts i. 18, 19 within a parenthesis, even though the words be still regarded as S. Peter's. It is quite possible that the citation in ver. 20 is appealed to in ver. 16.

hardly stand here, but the translation (taken *verbatim* from the Bishops' Bible) is unquestionably very inferior to that of Tyndale, Coverdale, the Great Bible, and Geneva (1557), "of God the Father, and of Christ." The Bishops' and our own Bibles from 1611 downwards, make bad worse by adding a comma after "God." Titus ii. 13, omit the comma after "God" with some moderns. Heb. iv. 6, 7, "unbelief, again..." The *apodosis* begins with πάλιν. This is not so apparent if with 1611, &c. we set a colon after "unbelief." vii. 5, "they that are of the sons of Levi who receive the office of the priesthood..." The comma set after "Levi" by 1611, &c. might easily suggest the inference that all Levites were priests. 2 Pet. i. 1—5. All our Bibles, following 1611, in their arrangement, place a comma at the end of ver. 2, a full stop at the end of ver. 4. Yet it seems evident that vv. 1, 2 form a separate paragraph, as Nourse, the Tract Society, Blackadder, Wordsworth, and Tischendorf represent them; and if ver. 3 must be connected with ver. 5 (Moulton's *Winer*, p. 771), a colon suffices at the end of ver. 4. ii. 22, "and, The sow" a new proverb beginning. Thus 1638—1762, American 1867: but 1769 mod. return to "and the sow" of 1611—1630. Rev. viii. 12. Remove the stop, whether colon (1611—1630) or comma (1638 mod.), after "darkened," since the following verb also is governed by ἵνα.

As the result of his investigations on this subject Prof. Grote infers that "With respect to the punctuation in general, independently of its affecting the meaning of particular passages, it is, in the editions before 1638, comparatively little *graduated*, colons and semicolons being much fewer in number than commas and full stops......That edition made the punctuation much more graduated, and introduced one practice not common in the earlier ones, that of a full stop in the middle of a verse." "The *graduation* of the punctuation; i.e. the placing of colons and semicolons, is not materially different in Blayney's edition (1769) from what it was in that of 1683 (see above, p. 82). This latter (which is pointed, as printers say, very *low*) improved greatly in this respect upon 1638, as 1638 had improved upon the earlier ones[1]."

---

[1] Grote MS. pp. 83—85, where will also be found some interesting matter, rather foreign to our immediate purpose, on the gradual disuse in our Bibles of what the writer calls "the *cæsural* comma,

Section V.

On the orthography, grammatical peculiarities, and capital letters of the original, as compared with modern editions.

ONE of the salient points which distinguish the early editions of our Bibles from those of modern date, is their wide divergency of practice in regard to modes of spelling. It would be nothing remarkable, but rather analogous to what we observe in the case of all modern and probably of some ancient languages, that the customary orthography, even of very familiar words, should vary considerably at different periods of their literary history. But this is not the phenomenon we have mainly to account for in regard to English books printed in the sixteenth and seventeenth centuries. Judged by them, it would hardly be extravagant to assert that our ancestors had no uniform system of orthography whatsoever, since there are comparatively few words, except a few particles of perpetual occurrence, that are not spelt in several fashions in the same book, on the same page, sometimes even in the same line[1]. The licence extended,

a comma dividing any longish proposition into two balancing parts, and distinguishing the main members of it from each other, as the voice very frequently does, so that the comma marks a real vocal pause." Just as, for instance, there is a comma in John v. 23 after the second "Son" in 1611—1743, which 1762 and the moderns discard. Nor ought I to quit the subject of the present Section without acknowledging my obligations to the late Rev. G. C. Waller, M.A., and R.N., for the use of some acute and weighty notes on the punctuation of the Epistles, in the course of which that earnest student is frequently found to advocate a return to the practice of 1611, *without being aware of the fact.*

[1] The American G. P. Marsh (*Lectures on the English Language,* Lect. xx. p. 313), ascribes the variation of spelling in the same line to the mere convenience of the printer. Cardwell (*Oxford Bibles*, p. 4), had taken the same view before him. To Marsh's example, they shall lie down together, they shal, Isai. xlii. 17,

as is well known, even to Proper Names : men of the highest culture (Shakespeare for a conspicuous example, if we give credit to certain of his biographers,) varying the orthography of their own signatures in three or four several ways. This circumstance affords a conclusive answer to the demand that has sometimes been urged by ill-informed persons, that our modern Bibles should be exact reprints of the standard of 1611; and it was partly to silence such a demand that the Oxford reprint of 1833 was undertaken (see above, p. 35). A glance at that volume must have convinced any reasonable person that more recent editors were right in the main in gradually clearing the sacred page of uncouth, obsolete, and variable forms, which could answer no purpose save to perplex the ignorant, and to offend the educated taste. Whether the judgment of those who are responsible for the Bibles of 1762 and 1769 (for these were the great and most thorough modernizers) was always as true as might be wished for, we shall have to consider in the sequel.

The general rule laid down in the preparation of the Cambridge Paragraph Bible is a very simple one :—whensoever an English word is spelt in the two issues of 1611 in two or more different ways, to adopt in all places that method which may best agree with present usage, even though it is not so found in the majority of instances in the older books. Thus, though *charet* is the form employed in

many might be added, e.g. thereof, the locks therof, and the barres, Neh. iii. 3: tread with shouting, their showting shall, Jer. xlviii. 33: staned from dew, and the earth is staied, Hagg. i. 10, without coming nearer to a solution of the problem. A word is often differently spelt in the text and margin, as in Gen. iii. 16, where Coverdale has "huszbande" in the body of his version, "husbande" in the foot-

note: Gifford in his *Memoirs of Ben Jonson* complains of the same negligence in that scholarly author. Nor is the date of a writer any safe criterion. The best manuscripts of Chaucer, and especially of Gower, as also the Paston letters, written about 1470, approach nearer our present standard of spelling than the Bible of 1611 (Marsh, p. 312).

the vast majority of instances, that Bible has uniformly taken *chariot* as in Ecclus. xlix. 8; 1 Macc. i. 17; viii. 6. *Kinred* is probably the correct mode of spelling, and is by far the most frequent in the standard Bible, yet it is best to abide by *kindred*, as it is found in Ecclus. xiv. 4; 2 Macc. v. 9; 1 Tim. v. 8 *marg.* We would take *caterpillar* from Joel i. 4; elsewhere in 1611 it is *caterpiller*. *Cieled* and *Cieling* are due to the Cambridge Bible of 1629, *sieled* and *sieling* being the form of 1611 in all the eight places where they occur: possibly the American *ceiled* and *ceiling* would be better, as the root seems to be *cælo*, not *ciel*. Again, *forrest* occurs everywhere else, but *forest* Isai. xxi. 13. For *fain*, the ordinary form, we see *feign* in Neh. vi. 8 only. *Ghest* occurs mostly, as in Matt. xxii. 10, but *guests* in ver. 11. *Iron* appears in Ecclus. xxxviii. 28, instead of *yron*, the common form in 1611. *Linen* is found in 1 Kin. x. 28; 1 Esdr. iii. 6, but *linnen* elsewhere. *Miter* is almost constant in 1611, yet we may adopt *mitre* from Ex. xxxix. 31; Zech. iii. 5. We find *oake* Josh. xxiv. 26, elsewhere *oke*. Between *burden*, *murder*, *household*, and *burthen*, *murther*, *houshold*, the usage is more divided: we prefer the former. *Pedegree* occurs thrice, but *pedigree* in Heb. vii. 3 *marg.*, 6 *marg.* *Pelican* appears in Ps. cii. 6, elsewhere *pellicane* or *pellican*. After 1611, in Ecclus. xxxviii. 25 we should give *plough* for the noun, but *plow* for the verb and its compounds in the 26 places where it occurs: the American (1867) has *plough* always. *Pray* (præda) is almost always used, but *prey* Job ix. 26. Again, *surfeited*, the modern form, occurs only Wisd. v. 7 *marg.*, *surfetting*, &c. elsewhere. We find *profane* in Ezek. xxiii. 38, 39; 1 Macc. iii. 51; 2 Macc. vi. 5; Acts xxiv. 6: elsewhere the incorrect *prophane*. Instead of *renowned* (Num. i. 16; Ezek. xxvi. 17; 1 Macc. iii. 9; v. 63; vi. 1) we oftener meet with *renowmed* (Ecclus. xliv. 3, &c.). Such examples might be multiplied indefinitely. On the other hand, for the modern *scent*, we would boldly print *sent*, following the ordinary, if not the universal practice of the seventeenth century, inasmuch as *sent* is true to the etymology, and is invariably used in all the five places where the word occurs, Job xiv. 9; Isai. xi. 3 *marg.*; Jer. xlviii. 11; Hos. xiv. 7; Wisd. xi. 18. For omitting the *c* in *scythe* we have good authority, as well as the practice of our Translation in the margins of Isai. ii. 4; Jer. l. 16; Joel iii. 19; Mic. iv. 3. We must return to *rye* of 1611, which occurs but twice (Ex. ix. 32; Isai. xxviii. 25), though *rie* is in both Bibles of 1629. Probably, too, *lancers* should be restored in 1 Kin. xviii. 28: it came from the Bishops' Bible (*launsers*), but occurs nowhere else, and was not altered into *lancets* before 1762. For *andirons* Ezek. xl. 43 *marg.*, which is etymologically true, 1638, 1769 and the moderns have *endirons; end irons* of 1744, 1762 is a bad guess. The Bishops' margin has *trevets*. Another word, used but once, is *ebeny*, Ezek. xxvii. 15, which is so spelt both in Hebrew and Greek: *ebony* of the moderns is more recent than 1638. Thus too, *turbant*, Dan. iii. 21 *marg.* only, the form adopted by Milton and Dryden, was not changed into *turbans* before 1762. So *imbers*, Tobit vi. 16 *marg.* Since *sailer*, Rev. xviii. 17, is pronounced by Johnson to be more analogical than *sailor*, and held the ground till after 1638, we may take courage to revive it. In Nahum ii. 4 also *justle* of 1611 may be restored, instead of *jostle* of some moderns. Of words met with but twice, neither *alleaging* (Wisd. xviii. 22) nor *alleadging* (Acts xvii. 3) can stand; *ambassage* Luke xiv. 32 should be adopted rather than *embassage* 1 Macc. xiv. 23; *scrole*, Isai. xxxiv. 4, is to be preferred to *scrowle*, Rev. vi. 14; but it is not possible to take either *champion*, Deut. xi. 30, or *champian*, Ezek. xxxvii. 2 *marg.*; either *musitian*, Ecclus. xxxii. 4, or *musition*, Rev. xviii. 22; or *scholler*, 1 Chr. xxv. 8; Mal. ii. 12. Nor would *anker, bal-*

The Orthography. 97

lance, *threed*, suit the modern eye, although they are never met with in what to us appears the only correct form.

The same liberty must be taken in regard to *soldier* and *vinegar*, which the standard Bibles, contrary to their derivation, invariably spell *souldier* and *vineger*. What is spelt *haply* in five other places, in 1611 was *happily* 2 Cor. ix. 4 (πως): though changed in both books of 1629, *happily* was brought back in 1630, but can hardly hold its ground. The particle of comparison *than* is uniformly *then* in the Bible of 1611, as in many books far into the seventeenth century: this fashion, of course, could not be imitated now. Although *saphir* or *saphire* does not vary in the same Bibles, the original will not dispense with *pph*. Nor can we retain *cabbins*, used but once, Jer. xxxvii. 16: though we might venture upon *fauchin* of 1611, Judith xiii. 6; xvi. 9. The strange form *chawes* for *jaws* Ezek. xxix. 4, suggests a questionable etymology. *Traffique* (the verb used once, the noun four times) and *traffiquers* Isai. xxiii. 8 must also be refused[1].

Those English words which, whether from custom or difference of origin, vary in their signification according to the modes in which they are severally spelt, are invariably confused in the standard Bible of 1611. *Travel* and *travail* afford a familiar example of the fact, inasmuch as the fault has not yet been completely removed from modern editions, e.g. Num. xx. 14, where *travel* of 1629 (Camb.) and recent Bibles, though the Hebrew is הַתְּלָאָה, would just make sense, and has been substituted for *travail* of 1611. In Wisd. x. 10 also the latest Bibles, after that of 1629, erroneously render μόχθοις by *travels*, in the room of *travails* of 1611.

---

[1] In regard to the spelling of Proper Names, absolute uniformity need not be aimed at, but the Hebrew should be followed in each case as it arises. The result of this would be to keep up apparent inconsistency in some places: e.g. Josh. xiii. 27, compared with ch. xix. 35.

In Lam. iii. 5 *travel* is given for תְּלָאָה, as in Num. xx. 14, in all the books from 1611 to the American (1867), which has *travail*: although many like errors of the original edition have been corrected by its successors. The case between *twined* and *twinned* is stated below (Appendix B, p. 207 and note 3). The distinction between *morter* (Gen. xi. 3) and *mortar* Num. xi. 8; Prov. xxvii. 22, was first taken in 1638: by spelling both *morter*, the Bible of 1611 confounds words which have only an accidental resemblance. We should also discriminate carefully between *naught* (בְּלִיַּעַל) 2 Kin. ii. 19; Prov. xx. 14, and *nought* (i.e. nothing) Gen. xxix. 15, &c.: they were both spelt *nought* previously to 1638[1]. In spite of the analogy of *nought*, it is probably right to spell *aught* in such places as Gen. xxxix. 6, as the American revisers have done. Nor should we venture on the fine distinction between *veil*, an article of dress, and the *Vail* of the Sanctuary, but retain in all cases (even in Wisd. xvii. 3; Ecclus. l. 5 *marg.*) *vail* of 1611 in preference to *veil* of later editions. In Job xiv. 17 the great oversight of 1611 *sowest* for *sewest* was left in our Bibles till 1762. The similar error *sow* for *sew* in Eccles. iii. 7; Mark ii. 21, remained till 1629; in Ezek. xiii. 18 it survived beyond 1638. Between *intreat* (to pray) and *entreat* (i.e. to treat) there is a broad difference of sense, properly recognized in 1762: yet in 1611 the former is spelt *intreated* Job xix. 16, but *entreated* in the next verse; while in Job xxiv. 21 the second is *intreateth*. In Jer. xv. 11 text and margin, *intreat* and *entreat* actually change places in 1611, and are not put right until 1638. Between *enquire* and *inquire*, on the contrary, the choice is purely indifferent; the former is chiefly adopted in 1611 (but *inquired* Deut. xvii. 4 Oxford reprint; Ps. lxxviii. 34; Ezekiel xx. 31 *bis*;

---

[1] The spelling of 1611, &c. up to 1638 "at naught," Luke xxiii. 11, is a mere error. It occurs also

[2] Esdr. ii. 33 in Synd. A. 3. 14 and 1613, not in Oxford 1611.

John iv. 52, &c.: *inquiry* Prov. xx. 25), the latter is derived from our model (1858: see above, p. 38) and the recent Cambridge Bibles. Thus also we will take *informed* with 1611 in Acts xxv. 2, rather than *enformed* as in 2 Macc. xiv. 1; Acts xxiv. 1; xxv. 15: but *enrolled* of 1611 in 1 Macc. x. 36 in preference to *inrolled* of the margins of Luke ii. 1; Heb. xii. 23. In Isai. v. 11 *enflame* is in 1611, but *inflaming* in Isai. lvii. 5; modern Bibles reverse this, yet all keep *inflamed* of 1611 in Hist. of Susanna ver. 8. Many words, the exact orthography of which is quite indifferent, should be carefully reduced to a uniform method. Thus *ankles*, the usual modern practice, which may be taken in all five places, is found in 1611 only in Ps. xviii. 36 *marg.*, but *ancles* in 2 Sam. xxii. 37 *marg.*; Ezek. xlvii. 3 *text and marg.*; Acts iii. 7: in 1629 *ancles* is set in the first place, *ankles* in the third and fourth, later Bibles recalling this last correction, but bringing *ankles* into 2 Sam. xxii. 37 *marg.* Sometimes the later Bibles issuing from different presses exhibit their characteristic varieties of spelling. Instead of *inquire*, noticed above as a peculiarity of the Cambridge books, those of Oxford (1857) and London or the Queen's Printer (1859) read *enquire:* for *axe* (which word is thus spelt ten times in 1611) these last, after the example of their predecessors from 1629 (Camb.) downwards, wrongly print *ax*, against the modern Cambridge editions. In 1 Kin. v. 9; 2 Chr. ii. 16; 1 Esdr. v. 55 we find *flotes* in 1611, but recent Cambridge Bibles have needlessly changed it into *floats*. These last are again wrong in *soap*, which, after 1611, the Oxford and London Bibles spell *sope* in both places (Jer. ii. 22; Mal. iii. 2). The truer form *rasor* occurs seven times in 1611 and the Cambridge text, while those of Oxford and London have *razor*. In Judg. ix. 53 the Oxford editions, with 1611, adopt *scull*, but the Cambridge, and indeed 1611 in all other places, prefer *skull*. The Cambridge books, after 1611, have *gray* (*greyhound* Prov. xxx. 31, rightly so spelt in 1629 Camb. and 1630, has no connection with it), the Oxford and London *grey*. With the Cambridge Bible we may also spell *counseller* (not *counsellor* with those of Oxford and London), as does also that of 1611 except in three places, where it has *counsellours* (Ezra viii. 25; Prov. xii. 20; xv. 22). *Council* (variously spelt *councill*, *councel*, *councell* in 1611) is ordinarily distinguished from *counsel* or *counsell*, but the latter is put for the former in 1 Esdr. iii. 15 *marg.* (χρηματιστηρίῳ); Matt. v. 22; Mark xiv. 55, all subsequently set right. Since *ours, yours, theirs* are possessive cases plural of the personal pronouns, the apostrophe set before *s* in the editions of 1762 and 1769, as also in the London and Oxford Bibles to this day, is positively incorrect: hence the Cambridge practice, which never admitted the apostrophe, should be followed in this respect.

Again, there are forms not wholly banished from our modern books, though their number is diminished in later times, whose presence tends to lend richness and variety to the style. Such is *marish* Ezek. xlvii. 11; 1 Macc. ix. 42, 45, for the more familiar *marsh:* the pathetic *astonied*, still standing for the more common-place *astonished* in Ezra ix. 3, 4; Job xvii. 8; xviii. 20; Jer. xiv. 9; Ezek. iv. 17; Dan. iii. 24; iv. 19; v. 9, is restored to its rightful place in the great passage Isai. lii. 14, whence a false taste has removed it subsequently to 1638. *Stablish* also might be brought again into twelve places (e.g. Lev. xxv. 30; Deut. xix. 15) instead of *establish* of later books: *grin* or *grinne* (Job xviii. 9; Ps. cxl. 5; cxli. 9) may be treated as a legitimate modification of *gin* or *ginne* (Job xl. 24 *marg.*; Isai. viii. 14; Amos iii. 5), though cast out in 1762. Once only, it would appear, a superficial difficulty is attempted to be concealed by a slight change in the spelling. In Gen. l. 23 *marg. borne*, which in 1611 was equivalent to *born*[1], was sufficiently correct to convey no wrong impression. To ensure clearness the final *e* was dropped in 1629 (Camb.), but restored again in 1762, by which time it would be sure to suggest a false meaning.

Enough has been said of those changes in orthography which are due to accident or the caprice of fashion. Other variations, more interesting, spring from grammatical inflections common in the older stages of our language, which have been gradually withdrawn from later Bibles, wholly or in part, chiefly by those painful modernizers, Dr Paris (1762) and Dr Blayney (1769). Yet it is not always easy to distinguish these from forms involving a mere change in spelling, and different persons will judge differently about them at times. Thus we cannot well retain *growen* 1 Kin. xii. 8, 10, while we alter *knowen* 1 Kin. xiv. 2, &c. To reject, however, such words as *fet* by substituting the modern *fetched*, is a liberty far beyond what an editor of our version ought ever to have assumed: hence restore *fet* in 2 Sam. ix. 5; xi. 27; 1 Kin. vii. 13; ix. 28; 2 Kin. xi. 4; 2 Chr. xii. 11; Jer. xxvi. 23; xxxvi. 21; Acts xxviii. 13: it is full as legitimate as *fetcht* of 2 Sam. xiv. 2; 2 Kin. iii. 9; 2 Chr. i. 17, and even of our latest Bibles in Gen. xviii. 7. The editors of 1762 and 1769 bestowed much evil diligence in clearing our English Translation of this participle in -*t*, Blayney following in the steps of Paris and supplying many of his deficiencies, yet, with characteristic negligence, leaving not a few untouched. Thus *burned* is substituted by them for *burnt* in some 93 places (*burnt* being left untouched in 2 Kin. xvi. 4; xvii. 11, &c). For *lift* they put *lifted* 95 times, once (Dan. iv. 34, where *lift* is past tense indicative) with some show of reason; sometimes (e.g. Zech. i. 21, where *lift up* is the present), to

---

[1] So in 1 Sam. ii. 5 we read in 1611 "the barren hath borne seven," but "born" in modern Bibles.

the detriment of the sense. Similar cases are *built* Neh. iii.
1 (*builded* ver. 2, 1611): *clapt* 2 Kin. xi. 12: *clipt* Jer. xlviii.
37: *cropt* Ezek. xvii. 4: *crusht* Num. xxii. 25: *deckt* Prov.
vii. 16; 2 Esdr. xv. 47; 1 Macc. iv. 57: *dipt* Lev. ix. 9;
1 Sam. xiv. 27; 2 Kin. viii. 15; Rev. xix. 13 (*dipped* also in
1611 Gen. xxxvii. 31): *girt* 1 Sam. ii. 4 (*girded* ver. 18 in
1611): *leapt* 1 Kin. xviii. 26 (text, *leaped* marg.); Wisd. xviii.
15 (*leaped* 1611 in ch. xix. 9); 1 Macc. xiii. 44; Acts xix.
16: *mixt* Prov. xxiii. 30; Isai. i. 22; Dan. ii. 41 (*sic* 1611,
not ver. 43, the second time); 2 Esdr. xiii. 11: *past* 2 Cor.
v. 27 (so even moderns in 1 Pet. iv. 3; in Eph. ii. 11 we
have *passed* in 1611, *past* 1769): *pluckt* 1 Chr. xi. 23; Ezra
ix. 3; Neh. xiii. 25; Job xxix. 17; Prov. ii. 22 *marg.*; Dan.
vii. 4, 8; xi. 4; Amos iv. 11; Zech. iii. 2; 2 Macc. xiv. 46
(*plucked* 1611 in Gal. iv. 15): *puft* Col. ii. 18: *pusht* Ezek.
xxxiv. 21: *ravisht* Prov. v. 19, 20 (*ravished* 1611 in Zech.
xiv. 2): *ript* 2 Kin. xv. 16; Hos. xiii. 16; Amos i. 13: *slipt* 1
Sam. xix. 10; Ps. lxxiii. 2; Ecclus. xiii. 22; xiv. 1: *stampt* 2
Kin. xxiii. 6, 15: *start* Tobit ii. 4 (*started* 1762, but it might
be present, ἀναπηδήσας ἀνειλόμην): *stopt* 2 Chr. xxxii. 4
(*stopped* ver. 30; Zech. vii. 11 in 1611): *stript* Ex. xxxiii. 6;
1 Sam. xviii. 4; xix. 24; 2 Chr. xx. 25; Job xix. 9; Mic. i. 8:
watcht Ps. lix. title: *wrapt* 1 Sam. xxi. 9; 2 Kin. ii. 8; Job
xl. 17; Ezek. xxi. 15; Jonah ii. 5. These archaic preterites
contribute to produce a pleasing variety in the style of a version, and are grammatically just as accurate as the modern
forms; which, however, is hardly the case with *rent* when it
is used not as a preterite only, but as a present, as in Lev.
xxi. 10 (*sic* 1611); 2 Sam. iii. 31; 1 Kin. xi. 31; Eccles. iii.
7; Isai. lxiv. 1 (*sic* 1611); Ezek. xiii. 11, 13; xxix. 7; Hos.
xiii. 8; Joel ii. 13; Matt. vii. 6; John xix. 24. Other antiquated preterites are *begun* Num. xxv. 1 (*began* 1611 in Gen.
iv. 26): *drunk* Gen. xliii. 34 (text not margin); Dan. v. 4:
shaked Ecclus. xxix. 18: *sprang* Gen. xli. 6 (*sprung* ver. 23):

stale Gen. xxxi. 20; 2 Kin. xi. 2 (*stole* 2 Sam. xv. 6; 2 Chr. xxii. 11 in 1611): *strooke* 1 Sam. ii. 14; 2 Chr. xiii. 20 (*sic* 1611); 1 Esdr. iv. 30 (but *stroke* 2 Macc. i. 16; Matt. xxvi. 51; Luke xxii. 64; John xviii. 22, also *strake* 2 Sam. xii. 15; xx. 10, never *struck*): *stunk* Ex. vii. 21 (*stank* ch. viii. 14 in 1611): *sung* Ezra iii. 11: *sunk* Num. xi. 2 *marg.* and seven other places (*sank* Ex. xv. 5, 10): *swore* 1 Macc. vii. 35: *wan* 1 Macc. i. 2; xii. 33 (*sic* 1611); 2 Macc. x. 17; xii. 28 (*won* 2 Macc. xv. 9 in 1611). Among past participles may be noted (*wast*) *begot* Ecclus. vii. 28: (*his*) *hid* (*things*) Obad. 6: (*have*) *sit* Ecclus. xi. 5. It would be well to retain *lien* (which even modern Bibles keep in Ps. lxviii. 13) for *lain* in Num. v. 19, 20, as also in the three places, Judg. xxi. 11; Job iii. 13; John xi. 17. Other verbal forms deserving notice are *oweth* Lev. xiv. 35; Acts xxi. 11, and *ought* Matt. xviii. 24, 28; Luke vii. 41, which were not changed into *owneth* and *owed* respectively till after 1638: *leese* (*lose* 1762) 1 Kin. xviii. 5. The noun *flixe* (*flix* 1629) was corrupted into *flux* in Acts xxviii. 8 as early as 1699. In Ex. xxxv. 19 modern Bibles, after Blayney, have *cloths of service*, but *cloathes* of 1611 was rightly changed into *clothes* as early as 1629 Camb. and retained up to 1762 inclusive. There is a real distinction, as Dr Field notices, between *cloths* and *clothes*.

It is hard to discover any intelligible principle which guided the editors of 1762 and 1769 in their vexatious changes of several particles into their cognate forms. Thus for *amongst* they print *among* 81 times, for *towards* they print *toward* 121 times, for *besides* they give *beside* 44 times[1], yet keep so often the forms they reject elsewhere that it is plain

[1] In Josh. xxii. 29 the change of *besides* of 1611 to *beside* by 1629 (Lond.), 1630, 1769, moderns (but not by 1629 Camb., 1638, 1744, 1762) will not affect the sense, as may be seen from ver. 19, where the Hebrew is virtually the same. Both forms of the English word then meant "except," which is the signification here.

they have no design to disuse them altogether. Such wanton, or perhaps merely careless, variations should be cancelled without mercy. Nor can there be any good ground for turning *sith* into *since* as does Dr Paris in Jer. xv. 7; Zech. iv. 10 *marg.*; 2 Esdr. vii. 53, and Blayney in Jer. xxiii. 38, the rather as *sith* is in our modern Bibles (Ezek. xxxv. 6): *sithence* in 2 Esdr. x. 14 was modernized into *since* as early as 1616, so that it must have been going out of use even then. All our Bibles preserve *whiles* in 2 Macc. ix. 9; x. 36, yet in Ps. xlix. 18 *while* is printed in 1762; in Isai. lxv. 24 *whiles* in 1769 becomes *while;* *whilst* becomes *while* in Heb. iii. 15; ix. 17 in the books of 1629; in 2 Macc. vii. 24 *whilst* is substituted for *whiles* in 1629. The interchanges between *to* and *unto* in Gen. xxv. 33 (1629 Lond.); 1 Kin. xxii. 53 (1616); 1 Macc. vii. 20 (1629 Camb.); Luke xx. 42 (1616); 2 Cor. ix. 9 (1629 Camb.), are not very intelligible. Amidst all this unmeaning tampering with the text, the several editors, especially those of 1762 and 1769, carried out to the full at least two things on which they had set their minds: they got rid of the quaint old *moe* for *more* (spelt *mo* in the Bible of 1638) from the 35 places in which it occurs in the standard copies, and in 364 places (e.g. 1 Cor. xiv. 18) they have altered the nominative plural *you* into *ye*, besides that Blayney makes the opposite change in *Build you* Num. xxxii. 24; *Wash you* Isai. i. 16; *Get you* Zech. vi. 7; *Turn you* Zech. ix. 12. In one particular the orthography of modern Bibles may well be acquiesced in. The word *midst* is often spelt in the Authorized Bibles as *middest;* about Ezekiel and some of the later Prophets almost constantly for a time. This form, however strange to our eyes, would have the advantage of suggesting the true character of the word as a superlative adjective; but the spelling varies so much between *midst, middest, midest* (Judith vi. 11), *middes* (Ps. cxvi. 19; Acts xxvii. 21; Phil. ii. 15), and *mids* (Jer. xxxvii.

12; Hist. of Susanna ver. 34, 48, &c.), that it seems safer to fall back on our general rule of adopting that one out of several forms which best suits the modern usage.

The practice of the Authorized Version with respect to placing the indefinite article *a* or *an* before a word beginning with *h* calls for some consideration, the rather as modern Bibles, with the exception of the American (see above, p. 37) which conforms to present usage, have made no systematic or important changes regarding it. It would seem indeed as if *a* were but an abridged form of *an*, the *n* being dropped before an initial consonant proper, and only subsequently, under certain limitations, before *h* aspirated. Thus Chaucer's use of *an halle, an hare, an herth*, is uniform, and the fashion maintained its ground far into the sixteenth century. In the earliest draft of our English Litany, contained in the King's Primer of 1545, we read, "*an heart to love and dread thee,*" as it still remains in the Book of Common Prayer; and such cases as *a harpe* 1 Sam. x. 5; *a hert* Ecclus. xvii. 6 in Coverdale's Bible of 1535 are quite rare, though no doubt the custom of dropping the *n* had already begun. In the Authorized Version of 1611 we mark a further step in the same direction. As a general rule *an* is there retained before the sounded *h*, though the exceptions are more numerous than some have supposed, and suggest to a modern editor the propriety of conforming the Bible to the now universal habit of the best English writers. The following list will shew how the matter stands in the original books:

An habergeon Ex. xxviii. 32; xxxix. 23[1]: *an habit* Heb. v. 14 marg.: *a habitation* Jer. xxxiii. 12 up to 1629 Camb., 1630, but *an* in 8

---

[1] This is apparently correct, if Dean Alford's rule be true: "When the accent is on the second, or any following syllable of the word, we may use *an*, because the first syllable, by losing its accent, also loses some portion of the strength of its aspiration" (*The Queen's English*, p. 43).

places : *an Hachmonite* 1 Chr. xi. 11 : *a hair* 1 Kin. i. 52¹; Luke xxi. 18 up to 1629 Camb. and Lond., 1630, *an* in 3 places : *a hairy* Gen. xxvii. 11, *an* twice : *a half* Ex. xxv. 10 (1st and 3rd, *an* in 2nd until 1629), 17, 23; xxxvi. 21; xxxvii. 1 (*ter*), 10; Ezek. xl. 42 (2nd); 2 Esdr. xiii. 45, but *an* in 16 places : *a hammer* Jer. xxiii. 29, *an hammer* Judg. iv. 21 : *a hand* Ex. xix. 13 up to 1638, but *an* 5 times : *an handbreadth* 7 times : *an handful* 5 times : *a handmaid* Gen xxix. 24 up to the two editions of 1629, but *an* twice : *an hanging* thrice : *a happy* 2 Macc. vii. 24 : *a hard* 2 Kin. ii. 10; Ps. xxxi. 18 *marg.*; Ecclus. xl. 15, but *an* 4 times : *a harlot* Joel iii. 3 up to 1769, but *an* in 21 places : *an harmless* Wisd. xviii. 3 : *a harp* 1 Sam. x. 5; 1 Chr. xxv. 3, but *an* 4 times : *an hart* Isai. xxxv. 6 : *an harvest* Hos. vi. 11 : *an hasty* Ecclus. xxviii. 11 (*bis*) : *a hat* 2 Macc. iv. 12 : *a haven* 2 Esdr. xii. 42, but *an* thrice : *a haughty* Ecclus. xxiii. 4, but *an* Prov. xvi. 18.

An he (*lamb* or *goat*) thrice : *a head* Judith xiv. 18, *an* Josh. xxii. 14 : *an head-tyre* 1 Esdr. iii. 6 : *an healer* Isai. iii. 7 : *an healing* Dan. iv. 27 *marg.* : *a heap* Isai. xvii. 11; Ecclus. xi. 32, but *an* in 15 places : *a hearer* Wisd. i. 6; James i. 23 : *a heart* 1 Chr. xii. 33 *marg.* (*bis*); Ecclus. xiii. 26; xvii. 6; xxii. 17, but *an* 15 times : *a hearth* Zech. xii. 6 up to 1762, *an hearth* Ps. cii. 3 : *an heathen* Matt. xviii. 17 : *an heave* (*offering*) 11 times : *an heavenly* Heb. xi. 16 : *a heavy* Ecclus. xxv. 23 up to 1629, but *an* 5 times : *an Hebrew* 10 times : *an Hebrewess* Jer. xxxiv. 9 : *an hedge* 4 times : *an heifer* 9 times : *an heinous* Job xxxi. 11 : *an heir* 3 times, correctly by modern usage : *an helmet* 5 times : *a help* Ps. xliv. 26 *marg.*; Ecclus. xxxiv. 16 until 1762; xxxvi. 24, but *an* 5 times : *a helper* Ps. xxii. 11 *marg.*, but *an* thrice : *a hen* Matt. xxiii. 57; Luke xiii. 34 : *an herald* Dan. iii. 4 : *an herb* Isai. lxvi. 14 is probably right : *an herd* twice : *an herdman* Amos vii. 14 : *an heretick* Tit. iii. 10 : *an heritage* occurs 14 times, and we should retain *an*, regarding the *h* as mute; compare *heir, herb, honest, honour, honourable, hour, humble*².

An hidden Job iii. 16 : *a hiding* Isai. liii. 3 *marg.* up to 1762, but *an* Deut. xxxii. 38 *marg.*; Isai. xxxii. 2 : *a high* 1 Sam. xxii. 6 *marg.*; Isai. xxx. 13; 2 Esdr. ii. 43, but *an* 32 times : *a highway* Isai. xix. 23; xl. 3, but *an* Isai. xi. 16; xxxv. 8 : *a hill* Josh. xxiv. 33; Isai. xxx. 17 up to both Bibles of 1629, but *an* 5 times : *an hin* always (21 times):

¹ Synd. A. 3. 14, not Oxford reprint.
² Of these words whose initial *h* is unaspirated, *humble* and perhaps *herb* are a little doubtful; but they have all one property in common, in that they are Latin words coming to us through the French.

The Indefinite Article. 107

an hire Gen. xxx. 18 *marg.*: *an hired* 7 times: *an hireling* 9 times: *an hissing* 6 times: *an Hittite* Ezek. xvi. 3, 45.

An hold Judg. ix. 46; 2 Sam. xxiii. 14: *a hole* Ex. xxxix. 23 up to 1769; 2 Kin. xii. 9; Jer. xiii. 4; Ezek. viii. 7, but *an hole* Ex. xxviii. 32; 2 Macc. iv. 14 *marg.*: *a hollow* 2 Macc. i. 19 up to 1762, *an hollow* Judg. xv. 19; 2 Macc. ii. 5 : *a holm tree* Hist. of Susanna ver. 58, up to 1762 : *a holy* Lev. xxvii. 23; Isai. xxx. 29; Wisd. xviii. 9, but *an holy* no less than 45 times: *a home-born* Jer. ii. 14: *an homer* always (10 times): *an honest* 5 times, *an honour* thrice, *an honourable* 4 times, and rightly (see *heritage* above) : *an honeycomb* 5 times: *an hoof* Ex. x. 26: *an hook* 4 times : *a horn* Dan. viii. 5 *marg.*, but *an horn* 1 Kin. i. 39; Luke i. 69: *an horrible* always (6 times): *an horror* Gen. xv. 12 : *a horse* 2 Macc. iii. 25 up to 1629, but *an* 7 times: *a horseman* 2 Macc. xii. 35, but *an* 2 Kin. ix. 17 : *an host* 15 times : *an hostage* 1 Macc. i. 10 : *an hostile* Acts xii. 20 *marg.*: *a hot* Lev. xiii. 24; Ecclus. xxiii. 16; 1 Tim. iv. 2, but *an hot* 2 Esdr. iv. 48 : *an hour* 6 times, and rightly : *a house* Ex. xii. 30; Lev. xiv. 34 (not ver. 55 before 1769); 2 Sam. xx. 3 *marg.* (*an* 1762); 1 Chr. xvii. 5 (*an* both Bibles of 1629) ; Ps. lxviii. 6 *marg.*; Ecclus. xxi. 18; 1 Macc. vii. 37 ; Mark iii. 25 ; Luke xi. 17 (*bis*), but *an house* 84 times : *an householder* Matt. xiii. 52 ; xx. 1 : *an howling* Jer. xxv. 36; Zeph. i. 10.

An huckster Ecclus. xxvi. 29 : *an humble* Prov. xvi. 19 ; Song ver. 16, is probably true, and is so represented in the American Bible: *a hungry* Isai. xxix. 8 up to 1762, 2 Esdr. xvi. 6 up to 1629, but *an* Ecclus. iv. 2 : *a husband* Ruth i. 12 (once out of 3 times, but *an* thrice in 1762); Jer. xxxi. 32 *marg.* (not text) up to 1629 Camb.; Ecclus. iv. 10, but *an* 15 times: *an husbandman* Gen. ix. 20; Zech. xiii. 5.

An hymn Matt. xxvi. 30; Mark xiv. 26 : *an hypocrite* Job xiii. 16; Prov. xi. 9; Isai. ix. 17; Ecclus. i. 29; xxxiii. 2: *an hypocritical* Isai. x. 6.

This variable and inconsistent practice of the Authorized Bible, rather concealed than remedied in later editions, will probably be allowed to justify the rejection of *n* of the indefinite article, whensoever modern usage shall demand it. In the case of the word *hundred* alone this can hardly be done, as well because that out of the 150 places or more, wherein *hundred* occurs, *a* is found before it only in six (Ex. xxxviii. 9; Judg. xx. 10 *once;* 1 Kin. vii. 2; Isai. xxxvii. 36; Ecclus. xli. 4; 1 Macc. vii. 41), whereof all but Isai. xxxvii. 36 are corrected in subsequent copies, as especially because *an hundred* is still found in some recent writers conspicuous for purity of style. The choice between *an hungred* (Matt. iv. 2; xii. 1, 3; xxv. 35, 37, 42, 44; Mark ii. 25; Luke vi. 3) and *a hungred*, which latter does not occur in 1611, is more precarious, inasmuch as here *an* or *a* is probably not the article at all, but a prefix expressive of a continued state, as "a building" 2 Chr. xvi. 6, 1 Esdr. vi. 20; "a coming" Luke ix. 42; "a dying" Luke viii. 42, Heb. xi. 21; "a fishing" John xxi. 3; "a preparing" 1 Pet. iii. 20 (where, however, *a* might represent the prepositions *at*[1] or *on*); *athirst* Matt. xxv. 44, for which *thirsty* is substituted in vers. 35, 37, 42, where the connection with *an hungred* is not so close[2]. *An* is also made to precede *w* in three passages of the standard Bibles, *an whole* Num. x. 2 up to 1762 (but not in Num. xi. 20), *an whore* Prov. xxiii. 27 also up to 1762; 2 Esdr. xvi. 49 altered after 1638. *Such a one*, where the sound is cognate to that of *w*, should be of this form if we acquiesce in *a* before *whole*, &c., and is adopted by our Translators in Gen. xli. 38; Ruth iv. 1; Ps. l. 21 (*an* 1762); lxviii. 21 (*an* 1762); Ecclus. xxvi. 28 (*an* 1638); 1 Cor. v. 5 (*an* 1638), 11 (*an* both books of 1629); 2 Cor. x. 11 (*an* 1629 Camb.); xii. 2, 5 (*an* both books of 1629); Gal. vi. 1 (*an* 1629 Camb.); Philem. 9 (*an* 1762): but *such an one* Job xiv. 3; Ecclus. vi. 14; x. 9; xx. 15; 2 Macc. vi. 27.

My and *mine*, *thy* and *thine*, should of course be used respectively as *a* and *an* before a consonant, or vowel, or *h*; but neither the original Translators nor later editors have shown any knowledge of the fact: thus in Rom. xvi. 23

---

[1] As "a work," 2 Chr. ii. 18 (לְהַעֲבִיד): compare "await," Acts ix. 24 with Acts xx. 19.

[2] Dr Angus alleges Shakespeare's "Poor Tom's a cold," which seems exactly parallel. So "His greatness is a ripening" (*Henry VIII*. Act III. Scene 2).

mine host occurs in all our Bibles. The changes introduced in more recent books are apparently capricious or accidental, being as often wrong as right. Thus if *my* of 1611 is turned into *mine* before *integrity* Job xxvii. 5 in 1762, and *mine* correctly changed into *my* before *head* by the same, Luke vii. 46; the opposite alterations of *my* for *mine* before *eyelids* Job xvi. 16 in 1617, of *thy* for *thine* before *eyes* Job xv. 12 in 1769, and of *thine* for *thy* before *hands* 1 Macc. xv. 7 in 1629, prove clearly that they had no principle to guide them in the matter. Mutations of these forms made for the better in later Bibles will be seen in Deut. xvi. 15 and xviii. 4 (1769); Isai. lxiv. 8 (1629 Camb.); Ezek. xvi. 11 (1762); Zech. viii. 6 (1629 Camb.); Tobit. ii. 13 and v. 14 (1629); Wisd. viii. 17 (1629); 1 Macc. ii. 18 (1629); Luke xiii. 12 (1616); 2 Cor. xi. 26 (1629, both books). Those changed for the worse are Deut. ii. 24 and xv. 7 (1769); Ruth ii. 13 (2nd) and 1 Sam. ii. 35 (1629, both books); Job xxxi. 7 (1762); xl. 4 (1629 Camb.); Ps. cxvi. 16 (later than 1638); Eccles. iii. 18 (1629 Lond.); 2 Esdr. x. 55 and Ecclus. v. 8 (1629); Ecclus. li. 2 (1629, 1630).

The apparent solecisms also and unusual grammatical constructions of our standard of 1611 should be scrupulously retained, without any attempt to amend them. Such as they are, they comprise an integral part of the Translation, and preserve phrases once legitimate enough, which have since grown obsolete. Thus "riches," which is plural in Ps. lxxii. 10, retains its old use as singular in Col. i. 27; Rev. xviii. 17. Later editors have but ill spent their pains in partial attempts to remove or conceal such peculiarities. Some, indeed, violate the concord of the verb with its subject, as Ex. ix. 31 "the flax and the barley was smitten," as in the Hebrew: "tidings is brought" 2 Sam. xviii. 31 *marg.*: "thou *wast* he that leddest" 1 Chr. xi. 2: "earth and water was wont" Judith ii. 7 *marg.*: "the number of names together were" Acts i. 15[1]: "a great company...were obedient" Acts vi. 7, as in the Greek. In 1 Cor. vii. 32, however, we acquiesce in "the things that belong" (see Appendix A), "belong" being substituted for "belongeth" as early as 1612: compare also 1 Cor. xiv. 10, below p. 191. These faults may be imputed to venial carelessness, to the momentary relaxing of close attention which every one is sensible of in the course of a long task. At other times our version reminds the reader of some racy idiomatic expression which once formed a part of the spoken or even of the written language of our ancestors. A good example of this kind of archaism, which the best grammarians even now hesitate to condemn, is the double genitive in such cases as Gen. xxxi. 1 and the rest, given in Appendix C, p. 216 note 1. The opposite practice of suppressing the sign of the possessive altogether, which survives in modern Bibles, Judg. iii. 16 "of a cubit length," is found in 1611 in Lev. vii. 23; xiv. 54 (Appendix C, p. 216); xxv. 5 "it[2] own accord"; and in one issue at Esther i. 13 "the king manner[3]" (Appendix B below, pp. 207, 210): it was never removed from Rev. xviii. 12 (*bis*). It may be stated here that the habit of placing the apostrophe before or after *s* to indicate the possessive case, singular or plural respectively, was first adopted by the editor of 1762 in part, more consistently by Blayney, yet with so little care that not very few errors in the placing of the apostrophe, such as one glance at the original would have detected, have

---

[1] Thus also Rev. ix. 16 (and viii. 9) in all. In 1 Esdr. viii. 49 a similar oversight should be corrected, as also in Acts xxv. 23 "was" amended into "were." See Appendix A. In Tobit iv. 10 (see Appendix C), the text of 1611 is correct. Compare also Cant. iv. 2 with ch. vi. 6; Ecclus. xxxv. 15.

[2] The only place in our version where "it" occurs in the possessive case, although much wanted in Zech. iv. 2. See Mr Aldis Wright's full note on "It" in his *Bible Word-Book*, and Bain, *English Grammar*, p. 87.

[3] So take Shakespeare's " Even daughter welcome", (*As You Like It*, Act v. Scene 4).

clung to our common Bibles to this day. These are all noted in Appendix A (see below, p. 152 note), and, being of modern date, ought to be distinguished by being placed within brackets: e.g. 1 Sam. ii. 13; 1 Chr. vii. 2, 40. Since there exists no doubt that this *s* represents the Old English possessive ending *-es* or *-is*, it is manifest that the pronoun *his* standing after the possessive noun is a mere error. We should accordingly adopt the changes of 1762, "Asa's heart" 1 Kin. xv. 14 for "Asa his heart" (Bishops'); "Mordecai's matters" Esther iii. 4 for "Mordecai his matters," even though we elsewhere retain the original form in 1 Esdr. ii. 30; iii. 7, 8; Judith xiii. 9; xv. 11; 2 Macc. i. 33 *marg.*; iv. 38; xii. 22 (Bishops'), all in the debased style of the Apocrypha. The antiquated singular for plural with the word "year" may be kept in 2 Kin. xxiii. 36; Jer. lii. 1; Dan. v. 31; Amos i. 1; 1 Esdr. i. 39; 1 Macc. ix. 57; 2 Macc. iv. 23; Rom. iv. 19 (see App. C. *in locis citatis*). In like manner we have in 1611 "two mile" John xi. 18 *marg.* (App. C): "three pound" 1 Kin. x. 17; Ezra ii. 69; Neh. vii. 71, 72; 1 Macc. xiv. 24; xv. 18; John xix. 39: "thirty change" Judg. xiv. 12, 13: "thirty foot" Ezek. xli. 6 *marg.*: so "an eight days" Luke ix. 28: these last have never been altered. The use of the cardinal for the ordinal number we would suppress only four times, the earliest being Gen. viii. 13, on which passage in Appendix A the case is stated. Nor need we meddle with a few manifest inaccuracies of other kinds, most of which the hands even of Dr Blayney have spared. Such are the pronouns pleonastic in "which pains...they slack not" 2 Esdr. xvi. 38; "Onias...he went" 2 Macc. iv. 4, 5; "the keeper...he drew" Acts xvi. 27[1]: as also the double negatives in "shall not leave...neither name

---

[1] In Heb. ix. 12, though "he" before "entered" may be technically wrong, it could not well be dispensed with. The pleonastic *it* in Isai. xxviii. 4 (see Appendix A) might very well have been retained.

nor..." 2 Sam. xiv. 7; "Give none offence, neither...nor... nor" 1 Cor. x. 32: but see Lev. xvii. 14 below, p. 203, note 2. The objective in the place of the nominative in "him that soweth" Prov. vi. 19 was corrected in 1769; it is less clear that "whom" is wrong in Matt. xvi. 13, 15; Acts xiii. 25. The use of the adjective for the adverb is not unfrequent in the Authorized Version (Eph. iv. 1; 1 Thess. ii. 12; 2 Pet. ii. 6), and may not be disturbed even in so extreme a case as "wonderful great" 2 Chr. ii. 9. Double superlatives, "most straitest" Acts xxvi. 5; "chiefest" Mark x. 44, have ceased to displease by reason of their very familiarity. Verbs transitive and intransitive are sometimes confounded; e.g. "lying in wait" Acts xx. 19 compared with "laying await" Acts ix. 24; "to be heat" Dan. iii. 19; "shall ripe" 2 Esdr. xvi. 26; "will fat" Ecclus. xxvi. 13 (see Appendix C for the last three); "can white" Mark ix. 3; compare "did fear" Wisd. xvii. 9. The following errors of 1611 have not yet been touched, the first three being imported from the Bishops' Version: "that we should live still in wickedness and to suffer, and not to know wherefore" 2 Esdr. iv. 12; "if any man knew where he were" John xi. 57; "or ever he come near" Acts xxiii. 15; "to have gained" (with "should" preceding), *ibid.* xxvii. 21, after Tyndale and all the rest, only that 1762 (not 1769) omits "to"; "if we know that he hear us" 1 John v. 15 (Bishops', after Tyndale). The next instance seems to have been influenced by the Greek (like Acts vii. 39), "she took *it*, and laid *it* on her mule; and made ready her carts, and laid them (αὐτὰ) thereon" Judith xv. 11.

A few miscellaneous observations may close this branch of the subject.

The more English prefix *un-* in the place of *im-* or *in-* may be restored in all the eleven passages where it was given in 1611; even modern Bibles keep *unperfect*, Ps. cxxxix. 16.

The Orthography.

This form comes chiefly from the Bishops' Version; and except in those cases cited on Matt. xvii. 20 in Appendix C (below, p. 233), it is found only in Wisdom and Ecclesiasticus. To set *s* after the Hebrew termination *-im* (Gen. iii. 24; Ex. xxv. 18; xxvi. 1, &c.) is a manifest inaccuracy, and if the American rule (*Report*, &c. p. 22) had been adopted of rejecting the *s* throughout, no valid objection could be raised. The middle course taken in recent English editions, that of sometimes making the required change and sometimes not, admits of no reasonable defence. We have simply to abide by the standard of 1611 in every instance, not caring to adopt even such changes as that set down in Appendix C on Gen. xxvi. 1. In regard to the interjection *O* or *Oh*, the American plan (see above, p. 37) looks tempting from its simplicity, since it limits *O* to the pure vocative, and employs *Oh* for the optative, which practically introduces the latter into the great majority of places. But *Oh* in English is neither dignified nor pleasing enough for constant repetition, and after having vainly attempted to discover the law observed by our Translators, it may be judged advisable to limit *Oh* to passages where the optative sense is very decided, as when it answers to the Hebrew נָא Gen. xix. 18, 20, or אִם 1 Chr. iv. 10, or אָנָּה Ps. cxvi. 16, or הוֹי Isai. xxix. 1 *marg.*: unless it be deemed better to banish *Oh* altogether. The intensive forms of certain words are occasionally put for the weaker, and *vice versâ*, perhaps for euphony: thus *bide* Rom. xi. 23 becomes *abide*, *ware* in Matt. xxiv. 50 becomes *aware* (see App. C *in loco*), both in 1762: *rise* becomes *arise* 1 Sam. xxiv. 8 (both books of 1629, 1630); xxv. 42 (1629 Camb., which makes the opposite change in ch. xxviii. 25); 2 Sam. xix. 8 (1629 Lond.); Tobit xii. 21 (1638); 1 Macc. ix. 23 (1769); Mark x. 1 (1629 Camb.); Luke viii. 24 (1616). In Gen. xi. 3 *thoroughly* best represents *thorowly* of 1611, though the latter has *throughly* in Ex. xxi. 19 (where *thoroughly* is found in 1762); 2 Kin. xi. 18; Job vi. 2. Lastly, it ought to be stated that the diphthongs *æ* and *œ* occur only in that small Roman type which in the Bibles of 1611 answers to our italic, and have no corresponding characters in the black letter in which the text is printed. In this way we mark *Cæsars* Phil. i. 13 *marg.*, *chœnix* Rev. vi. 9 *marg.*, the same character being set up in both places. In fact, a simple *e* represented both these diphthongs in the ordinary Bibles until after Blayney's time, when they gradually came into use, though they are wanting in the latest copies for *Nagge* Luke iii. 25, *Menan* ver. 31, *Colosse* Col. i. 2, nor do they exist at all in the American book, except in *chœnix*. In 1611 indeed they found more favour than afterwards, for beside the margins afore-mentioned, we meet with *Coelosyria* in 1 Esdr. ii. 17, &c., *Aenon* John iii. 23, which double vowels, after having been made real diphthongs in 1630, and partly in both books of 1629, were converted into simple *e* in the influential edition of 1638.

The employment of capital letters was much more free in the seventeenth century than at present, and in the Authorized Version whole classes of words that seem little entitled to that distinction are constantly so represented. Such are *Altar*, *Ark*, *Court*, *Hanging*, *Mercy-seat*, *Noble*, *Priest*, *Sabbath*, *Statutes*, *Tabernacle;* even *Cedar-wood*, *Shittim-wood*, &c. The tendency of later times has been to diminish such capitals very considerably, and in a few instances the moderns may have gone a little too far. *Cherubims* has a capital now only in Gen. iii. 24, and the Americans seem right in removing it thence. Archbishop Trench would restore the lost capital in "Vengeance" Acts xxviii. 4, which is not in the Bishops' Bible, and was withdrawn as early as 1629 (both editions); but then we must treat Wisd. xi. 20 in the same way, for the personification is just as strongly marked, though the initial *v* is small in 1611. Ordinary words also, when pregnant with sacred associations, may wisely be distinguished by a capital. Such are *Testimony* Ex. xvi. 34, &c., *Witness* Num. xvii. 7, 8, &c., especially in Acts vii. 44, where in 1611 the *w* is small. But indeed the practice of our Translators in this matter is little more consistent than in certain others. Thus we have "the city of Salt" Josh. xv. 62, but "the valley of salt" 2 Sam viii. 13, in all our books from 1611 downwards. With Mr Gorle (see above, p. 79 note 2) we prefer no capital, where the character rather than the name of the region is designated. Sometimes an initial capital is useful to intimate a change of speaker, as in John iv. 9, where "For" of 1611 ("for" 1629 Camb., &c.) shews that the woman's speech is already ended[1].

But what in most instances is only a matter of taste or propriety, becomes of real importance where the Divine Persons are spoken of. The familiar rule that *Spirit* should have a capital when the Holy Ghost or Spirit Himself is indicated, while *spirit* ought to be used in other cases, even when His power or influence is referred to, may be as safe as any, yet in application it gives rise to occasional perplexity, which the inconsistencies of the standard and other editions do little to remove. Thus in Gen. xli. 38 the Bible of 1611 has *spirit* (changed as early as 1613, though *Spirit* was not finally adopted before 176?), while in the precise parallel (Ex. xxxi. 3) it reads *Spirit*. The original edition is right also in 2 Chr. xxiv. 20 (*s*); Ps. cxxxix. 7 (*s*); Isai. xi. 2 (*S* once, and *s* three times); xxx. 1 (*S*); lix. 19 (*s*); Matt. iv. 1 (*S*); Mark i. 12 (*S*); Acts x. 19 (*s*, as in ch. xi. 12, 28); Rom. i. 4 (*S*); 1 John v. 8 (*S*, as all in ver. 6), against

---

[1] James iv. 5 is less easy to deal with. In 1611 we have "the spirit," but from 1629 (both editions) "The spirit" has prevailed, as if a quotation began at this point, which is hardly true.

some or many later Bibles, but it wrongly has *S* in Num. xi. 17, 25 (*bis*), 29. In 2 Esdr. vi. 39 *Spiritus* calls for the capital, when the verse is compared with Gen. i. 2, though none hitherto have so printed it, whereas *spiramen* 2 Esdr. xvi. 62 requires the opposite. Thus every case must be considered on its own merits. So again, while we admit that "Son of God" or "Son of man," wheresoever the word refers to the Lord Christ, should invariably have a capital letter[1], we may legitimately question its propriety in Dan. iii. 25; vii. 13, where it does not appear in 1611: only that the analogy of Rev. i. 13 persuades us to receive *S* from the books of 1629 (Lond.), 1630. Appellations derived from the Divine attributes should be indicated by capitals, whatever the variations of editions; and we ought to be more studious of uniformity in such matters than of following the inconsistencies of editors that have preceded us. Thus, when relating to God, we adopt *Author* (Wisd. xiii. 3), *Father, the Most High, the Holy One, Maker*[2], *Mighty One, Redeemer*[3], *Saviour*[4]. As regards *Scripture*, we may safely abide by the ordinary rule of using the capital where the whole body of Holy Writ is meant (e.g. John v. 39; Acts xviii. 24; 2 Tim. iii. 15, 16), the small *s* where some particular portion is referred to[5].

Section VI.

On the references to parallel texts of Scripture which are set in the margin.

A large proportion of the time and labour bestowed on

---

[1] Hence "Son" should stand in John viii. 36, but not in ver. 35, where the reference is general.

[2] As in 1611: but "maker" has no capital in Isai. xlv. 9, 11, where a contrast is intended with the "makers" of idols.

[3] So (against the standard of 1611) we will read in Prov. xxiii. 11, comparing Job xix. 25.

[4] Yet not so with 1611 in Ps. cvi. 21, since temporal deliverance seems to be intended: cf. Judg. iii. 9 *marg.*

[5] For the small capitals, by which our Translation represents the Hebrew JEHOVAH, see Appendix A.

Parallel References. 117

the Cambridge Paragraph Bible has been spent upon the references to parallel texts which are set in the margin. The Authorized Version only followed the example of earlier English translations in providing these materials for the exact study of Holy Scripture by means of comparing one portion of it with others. In fact, more than half the references contained in the edition of 1611 are derived from manuscript and printed copies of the Vulgate Latin Bible, and thus present to us the fruits of the researches of mediæval scholars and the traditional expositions of the Western Church. The references found in the standard of 1611, however, scarcely amount to a seventh part of those printed in modern Bibles, and have been computed not to exceed nine thousand[1]; the whole of which, inasmuch as they must be regarded as an integral portion of the Translators' work, have been scrupulously retained in all later Bibles; except only a few where the reference given is hopelessly wrong. Such are ch. xvi. 15 in the margin of 2 Sam. xix. 19: Eccles. v. 12 in that of Job xx. 19: Judg. xiii. 21 in that of Ps. cvi. 2: Judg. vii. 19 in that of Ps. cvi. 6. Sometimes they appear to have mistaken the drift or meaning of the passage; e.g. 1 Chr. ix. set over against Neh. xii. 23, where our existing books of the Chronicles are scarcely meant at all: Prov. xv. 30 as parallel to Eccles. vii. 1: Ps. cxxxii. 6 as parallel to Jer. vii. 14: and 2 Macc. iii. 4 referred to in Ecclus. l. 1, although quite a different person is meant: the last two have disappeared from modern Bibles. Occasionally, indeed, the original reference has been preserved, where it

---

[1] In the Old Testament 6588, in the Apocrypha 885, in the New Testament 1517. Comparatively few additions have been made to the original parallel texts in the Apocrypha—Blayney has only 1772 in all—and many more in proportion in the New Testament than in the Old. These figures are taken from Hewlett's *Commentary*, Vol. I. p. 45, 4to., cited by Hartwell Horne (*Introduction*, Vol. II. Part II. p. 81, 1834), who computes Blayney's additions alone at 30,495 (p. 80), which is probably too high a sum.

would hardly have been accepted on its own merits: such is the case of Ex. xxxiv. 6 in the margin of Neh. ix. 32: Deut. vii. 1, (2) in that of Ps. cxlix. 9: Ps. l. 9 in that of Prov. xxi. 27: Isai. liii. 3 in that of Wisd. ii. 15: 2 Cor. iii. 17 in that of John iv. 24: Matt. xxviii. 19 in that of John xv. 16: Mark ix. 12 (from the Vulgate) in Isai. liii. 3: Rom. vii. 9 in 1 Thess. iii. 8[1]. As we cannot praise very highly the typographical correctness of the Bibles of 1611 in other particulars (see p. 8), so it must be stated that no other portion of the work is so carelessly printed as these parallel texts, each issue exhibiting errors peculiar to itself[2], but few leaves indeed being exempt from some gross fault common to them both. The references to the Psalms direct us constantly to the wrong verse; namely, that of the Latin Vulgate from which they were first derived, not to that of the English Bible on whose pages they stand. The marks of reference from the text to the margin are so often misplaced, that it would be endless to enumerate glaring errors in regard to them which have long since been removed.

One of the main services rendered by the revisers of the Cambridge folios of 1629 and 1638 was the setting right these vexatious inaccuracies of the earlier books, which toilsome duty they performed very thoroughly, leaving to their successors the more congenial employment of adding largely to the original texts, a liberty which seems to have been taken by almost every one who prepared a

---

[1] In Amos ii. 1 the reference of 1611 to 2 Kin. iii. 27 may be retained, because the heading to the latter chapter renders it plain that our Translators supposed (wrongly, as it would seem) that the king of Edom's son was sacrificed.

[2] Thus the copy from which the Oxford reprint was taken corrects Synd. A. 3. 14 in 1 Kin. ii. 11; 2 Chr. xxxiv. 4; xxxvi. 10; Ezra viii. 20: while the latter is right and the former wrong in Ps. xxxii. 5; xliii. 5; lxxviii. 60, where it should be stated that the first and third examples are from the revised sheets of Synd. A. 3. 14 (p. 6). But these are exceptional cases. The two issues ordinarily coincide in most manifest errors.

special edition. Whensoever a reference had once found its way into the margin, there it was allowed to remain, unchallenged and even unexamined, however frivolous or mistaken it might be. Moreover, in recent Bibles which do not contain the Apocryphal books, all references drawn from them by our Translators have been summarily rejected, through the same unwarrantable license that led certain of them to expunge altogether the marginal note in 1 Chr. vii. 28 ("‖ *Or*, *Adassa*, 1 Macc. vii. 45": see below, p. 195 note 2), and to mutilate that on Acts xiii. 18 by striking out the reference to 2 Macc. vii. 27. All such texts from the Apocrypha, together with a few others dropped through apparent inadvertence, ought to be restored to their rightful places. The parallel references in the Apocrypha require to be largely increased, as well for other purposes, as with a view to illustrate the style of the Greek New Testament.

The textual references which have been gradually accumulating in the margins of our modern Bibles have been received or expunged in the Cambridge Paragraph Bible solely on their own merits: they have no such general reception to plead in their favour as those in the standard of 1611. Many of them are excellent, and help much for the right understanding of Scripture: these, after having been verified more than once, as well in the original tongues as in the Authorized version, have of course been retained. Of the rest, a larger portion than might have been anticipated have been judged irrelevant, questionable, or even untrue. No editions are more open to criticism in this particular than those of Dr Paris (1762) and of Dr Blayney (1769), who between them added at least half as many references as they found already existing. The worst errors, because unlearned readers cannot discover or so much as suspect them, relate to parallelisms which are true in the English, false in the Hebrew or Greek.

Such are Judg. ix. 27 cited at Judg. xvi. 25 (1769): 1 Chr. v. 26 cited at 1 Kin. xi. 14 (1769): 1 Sam. xii. 21 (1762) and Isai. xli. 29 (1769) cited at 1 Kin. xvi. 13: 1 Sam. ix. 9 cited at 1 Chr. xxi. 9 (1762): Ruth i. 21 cited at Job x. 17 (1769): Hos. xi. 12 cited at Ps. cxxxii. 16 (1762): Ex. xxviii. 36; xxix. 6; Lev. viii. 9 cited at Zech. vi. 11 (1769): John xix. 40 cited at Acts v. 6 and *vice versâ* (1762). Even in the Bible of 1611 we have Gen. iv. 4 made to illustrate Num. xvi. 15, although the resemblance is far less exact than the English might make it appear. References objectionable on more general grounds, some few being scarcely intelligible, are Num. ii. 3, 10, 18, 25 to illustrate Ezek. i. 10 (1762): the marvellous comment implied by citing John i. 14; Col. ii. 9 in Rev. xiii. 6, and 2 Kin. xx. 7 in Rev. xiii. 14 (both due to 1762): the allusions to the Great Day of Atonement in Jer. xxxvi. 6 (1762 and 1769), whereas some special fast is obviously meant (ver. 9): the hopeless confusion arising from connecting Acts xx. 1, 3 with 1 Tim. i. 3 (1762): the tasteless quotation of 1 Sam. xxiv. 3 in Jonah i. 5 (1762). Hardly less false are John x. 23 and Acts iii. 11 cited at 1 Kin. vii. 12 (1762): 1 Chr. xxiv. 10 and Luke i. 5 made parallel to Neh. xii. 4, 17 (1762): Josh. xiv. 10 to Matt. iii. 1 (1762): while Ex. xxiii. 2 employed to explain Job xxxi. 34 (1769); Esther vii. 8 compared with Prov. x. 6 (1769); 1 Kin. v. 17, 18 with Prov. xxiv. 27 (1769); Ps. lxviii. 4 with Isai. xl. 3 (1762); Dan. iv. 27 with Ecclus. xxxv. 3 (1762), will be regarded as but slender helps to the student of Scripture. In 2 Macc. ii. 8 the allusion surely is to Ex. xl. 38, not (as in 1762) to Ex. xxxiv. 5. Finally, the note of interrogation should in fairness be annexed to some over bold, though not impossible, suggestions of the more recent editors, as when in Ps. cxxxiii. 3 the reference to Deut. iv. 48 would identify עִיוֹן with שְׂנִיר.

We can only conjecture that the "Scotch edition" of

which Dr Blayney speaks so vaguely in his Report to the Delegates (see Appendix D), was that of Brown of Haddington, then just published. The parallel texts of Canne (1664, 1682), though often surprisingly wide of the mark, are said by those who have patiently used them to be at times very suggestive, and to contain more truth than might appear on the surface[1]. The editor of Bagster's Miniature Quarto Bible 1846, while "admitting without examination the references of Blayney, Scott [1822], Clarke [1810, &c.], and the English Version of Bagster's Polyglot..., from their acknowledged accuracy," held himself obliged "to verify all that were found in Canne, Brown, and Wilson [i.e. Crutwell, 1785]; the aggregate number, it is believed, being nearly half a million" (*Preface*, p. i.). It is plain that so numerous a host can prove little else than an encumbrance to the private Christian, by positively discouraging him from resorting to the margin at all, and that even earnest students will often be sensible of the danger incurred by such burdensome and minute commentaries, lest, "after all, the design

[1] "Canne's references are very different in character from those of the edition of 1611, being more for the purpose of comment and explanation, and less for that of scholarlike illustration. He refers scarcely at all to quotations. His references are more suggestive than immediately striking. They are not numerous, but evidently carefully selected. In the edition I have seen (Edin. 1747) they are most incorrectly printed." *Grote MS.* p. 13 (see above, p. 23 note). John Canne was a Baptist, and a prolific writer in the interest of that sect. His own small octavo editions bear no mark of place or printer's name, but came from Amsterdam, whither he went into exile after the Restoration. He had prepared a larger work, which was never published, on the principle of making the Bible its own Interpreter. In his edition of 1682 he says, "The sweetness and great content that I have had all along in this Scripture work, hath caused me to account other studies and readings (which I formerly used) very low in comparison of it. It is said of Jacob, that *he served seven years for Rachel, and they seemed but a few days, for the love he had to her.* I can truly speak it, I have served the Lord in this work more than thrice seven years, and the time hath not seemed long, neither hath the work been any way a burden to me, for the love I have had to it" (*Preface*, p. 2). His book was often reprinted in the former half of the eighteenth century.

and scope of the whole may not be understood, while the reader's mind stays so long in the several parts" (Bp. Patrick, *Dedication to Paraphrase of Job*). Bagster's publications have been so perpetually consulted in cases of difficulty for my purposes, that I may fairly express my regret that what is intrinsically valuable in them should be buried under a heap of irrelevant matter. Less full, but on the whole more profitable for study, is the collection of texts in the Religious Tract Society's "Annotated Paragraph Bible" of 1861, but here too, as in Bagster's books, nearly all the old matter is adopted without any attempt at revision, or apparent consciousness of the need of it. That the additions made in the Cambridge Paragraph Bible to the store of already existing references will by many be deemed too copious, their compiler is painfully aware. He can only plead in self-defence that he has aimed at brevity throughout; that no single text has been accepted as parallel which did not seem to him really illustrative either of the sense or language of Scripture; and that all the materials, whether new or old, have been digested into such a shape as, it is hoped, will prove convenient for practical use; while the form in which they are given will afford some indication as to their respective characters and relative values. With this last end in view, the reader's attention is directed to the following simple rules, on which the collection of textual references in the margin of that volume has been constructed and arranged.

(1) When the parallel between the passage in the text and that in the margin, whether it be verbal or relate to the general sense, is as exact as the subject allows, the Scripture text stands in the margin with no prefix: e.g. 2 Cor. iv. 6 cited in the margin of Gen. i. 3.

(2) If "So" stand before the Scripture text, it indicates

that the parallel, although real, is less complete, or that the language is more or less varied in the two places: e.g. 2 Chr. xiii. 9 "ᵃno gods" being exactly like Jer. v. 7, but less closely akin to Deut. xxxii. 21, the marginal note is thus expressed "ᵃJer. 5. 7. So Deut. 32. 21." Again, Job xi. 10 "ᶠshut up," being precisely identical with Lev. xiii. 4, while in Job xii. 14 the Hebrew verb is of a different conjugation, the margin runs "ᶠLev. 13. 4, &c. So ch. 12. 14."[1]

(3) If instead of "So," the word "Compare" or "Comp." be prefixed, it is intimated that the resemblance is slighter and less direct, or even that there is a seeming inconsistency between the two places: e.g. 2 Kin. ii. 11 in the margin of Gen. v. 24, where the events recorded are not in all respects analogous. So also "ᶠComp. 2 Kin. 8. 26 and ch. 21. 20" annexed to 2 Chr. xxii. 2, draws attention to the numerical difficulty. Such phrases as "Supplied from" in the margin of 2 Sam. xxi. 19; "Expressed in" Ex. xxiii. 2; "Expressed" Judg. vii. 18 will be understood at once by consulting the passages alleged.

(4) Much space has been economised and the constant repetition of a body of texts, all bearing on the same point, has been avoided, by setting them down once for all in full, and elsewhere referring the reader to that place by means of the word "See." Thus "See 1 Chr. 29. 14" in the margin of 2 Chr. ii. 6, directs the reader to a place where all extant examples of a certain idiom had already been brought together. In Num. ix. 15, "See Ex. 13. 21" shews that the latter place contains a collection of the texts relating to the pillars of cloud and of fire. This method has been much

---

[1] Occasionally the reference assumes the character of a brief exposition: e.g. Heb. ix. 27 cited at Job xxi. 33 (after 1769); Ex. xvi. 12 at Job xxxi. 31; Luke v. 7, 10 at Job xli. 6. But this liberty has been taken very sparingly.

employed in regard to Proper Names both of places and persons. It should also be stated that where passages of the New Testament are noticed as "Cited from" the Old, it has been judged needless to repeat the textual references previously set down in the corresponding places from which the citation is made: e.g. Matt. xxii. 37, 39, 44.

(5) When the parallelism extends to a whole paragraph, or indeed to any portion of the sacred text exceeding a single verse, the fact is carefully indicated by a peculiar notation. Thus in the margin of Ex. xxi. 1, "To ver. 17, *Deut.* 5. 6—21" (the name of the book being printed in italic type), intimates that Ex. xx. 1—17 is in substance identical with Deut. v. 6—21. Such instances occur very frequently, especially in the books of Samuel and Kings compared with Chronicles, and in the first three or Synoptic Gospels. Here again it has not been thought advisable to repeat in a later passage the textual references already given in an earlier passage in great measure resembling it. Such as are found in the second passage either belong to it alone, or are intended to direct attention to its divergencies from the first one: e.g. "Compare 2 Sam. 10. 18" in the margin of 1 Chr. xix. 18.

(6) The parallel is frequently a real one in the original tongues, although it appears faintly or not at all in the Authorized Version. In this case (Heb.), (Chald.), or (Gk.), as the case may be, is annexed to the citation, to give notice of the fact: e.g. Lev. xi. 17. Where several texts are cited, and this is true of two or more of them, the expression is varied to "in the Heb.", "in the Gk.": e.g. Deut. xxxiii. 27, where the notation happens to relate to all the three places in the Psalms. Whensoever, in the margin of the New Testament, (Gk.) is set after a quotation from the Old, it is intimated that the Septuagint version agrees with the

Parallel References. 125

New Testament: e.g. Matt. xxvi. 12. In a few instances, and for special reasons, the word (Septuagint) has been printed at length.

(7) If, on the contrary, the resemblance between two or more passages belong only to the English, and have no respect to the original, (Eng.) or (English) is added to the quotation. Such notices are designed to gather in one view words nearly obsolete, or otherwise to throw light upon the phraseology of the Authorized Version: e.g. Gen. xlv. 6; 1 Sam. ix. 5; 1 Kin. xx. 11; 2 Chr. xxvi. 14; Dan. vi. 3; 2 Esdr. xvi. 49; Tobit iv. 14; vi. 12; Matt. x. 10; xiii. 20; xiv. 8; xvii. 12, 25; xx. 11; xxiv. 48; xxvi. 67; xxvii. 39; Mark x. 44; Luke i. 54; vi. 32; vii. 4; viii. 23; xiv. 32; 1 Tim. ii. 9. Compare Judg. xii. 14.

(8) Lastly, as a note of interrogation (?) has been employed to bring into question the references both of the standard of 1611 and of its more recent editors (p. 120), so it has been occasionally employed for the same purpose with certain that appear in the Paragraph Bible either alone, or with little countenance elsewhere: e.g. "1 Chr. 27.21" cited for "Iddo" in 1 Kin. iv. 14. Names of places and persons are frequently so marked, if the orthography be somewhat varied: e.g. "Ramah", Josh. xviii. 24. In Judg. xviii. 30, by illustrating "Gershom" from "Ex. 2. 22 ? & 18. 3 ?" attention is directed to the proposed substitution of "Moses" instead of "Manasseh", a reading both probable in itself, and supported by weighty and varied authorities. In the same spirit, an attempt has frequently been made to convey some notion of the relative value of the marginal renderings (see above, pp. 41—59) as compared with those in the text, by means of passages cited to illustrate one or both of them: e.g. Esther vi. 1: Ps. vi. 6.

Advantage has also been taken of the same opportunity to insert in the margin a great number of passages tending to illustrate the internal connection and relative dates of the several books of the Old Testament, which have been the most subjected in modern times to criticism more or less sober and profound. Such references as are made to the Pentateuch in Judg. xix. 7, 8; 2 Sam. xiv. 7, are so many additional proofs that the diction of the oldest books of the Bible clave to the memory, and was wrought into the literary style even of the earliest surviving writers after the conquest of Canaan. Nothing short of actual collation of parallel texts, undertaken by the student for himself, can cause him to realize the extent to which the peculiar language of the book of Job has influenced those which followed it, or can do justice to its claim to the most venerable antiquity. Thus too the resemblances between Zech. i.—viii. and ix.—xiv. have been diligently recorded: while in regard to the prophecies of Isaiah it may be confidently affirmed that no unprejudiced scholar, who shall but faithfully examine the numberless coincidences both in thought and expression between the first thirty-nine and last twenty-seven chapters of his book (coincidences which are all the more instructive by reason of their often being very minute and sometimes even lying below the surface), will ever again admit into his mind the faintest doubt, whether the two several portions of that inspired volume are the production of one author or of more.

The compilation of this virtually new body of textual references has been greatly aided by Wetstein's only too copious collections from the Septuagint in the notes to his Greek Testament (1751—2), and yet more by two laborious volumes, to which the editor has been more largely indebted than he knows how to express;—Canon Wilson's accurate and exhaustive "English, Hebrew and Chaldee Lexicon and Concordance" (*Second edition* 1866: he died 1873, æt. 90) especially valuable for the attention paid therein to the marginal notes; and Wigram's "Hebraist's Vade Mecum" (1867), which, answering as it does many of the purposes of that great *desideratum* of sacred literature, a real Hebrew Concordance, has been his hourly companion ever since it was published. He has also enjoyed the benefit of using for the Poetical and Prophetic books, that glory of the Clarendon Press, the "Origenis Hexaplorum quæ supersunt" (1867—1871) of Dr Field; whose Latin version of the Hebrew passages cited throughout the work, by reason of its elegance and precision no less than from an almost instinctive perception of the true sense of the original in cases of difficulty, leaves us nothing to regret save its fragmentary character, and begets in the student an earnest longing for a continuous translation, at least of these harder portions of the Old Testament, from the same able and accomplished hand.

SECTION VII.

Miscellaneous observations relating to the present work, and general Conclusion.

It is obvious that the practice of printing the English Bible in sections or paragraphs accommodated to the sense (the notation of the chapters and verses being set in the margin), which Mr Reeves the King's Printer introduced early in the present century, and in which he has found so many imitators, is in substance only a return to the fashion that prevailed in our early versions, before the Genevan New Testament of 1557 unfortunately broke up the text into divisions at once so minute and so arbitrary as the verses invented by Robert Stephen. "The subdivision of the books of Sacred Scripture into chapters and verses, without regard to the sense, and frequently to its great injury, has thrown a most serious obstacle in the way of common readers." It has given rise to "a very erroneous impression, that the Bible is rather a collection of apophthegms, or disconnected sentences, than composed of regular histories and treatises on religion, which have their separate topics and connexions." "It is a method peculiar to the Bible, and confined to translations alone. Yet the word of God is not deserving of such an injurious peculiarity as this[1]." Thus clearly is the case stated by an editor who seems to have been the first to introduce this simple plan into the United States of America, and who has certainly carried it out with singular skill and discretion.

For indeed the division of the sacred text into sections suitable for general use will not be deemed an easy matter by any one who has essayed it. If we look only to the broad and prominent breaks in a Bible narrative or discourse, they will usually be found too far apart for the reader's convenience: if the subordinate members be separated from each other, the result will often be a virtual return to the discarded verse divisions. Something between these two extremes is to be aimed at, and in this effort there is room as well for much honest difference of opinion, as for the exercise of careful discrimination and a subtil faculty of analysis. From the marks of paragraph division (¶) employed for the first time in the Authorized Version, little help can be derived. They are unequally and capriciously distributed, and in both issues of 1611 and in the Bible of 1613 they cease altogether after Acts xx. 36: nor have they any perceptible connection with the headings of the chapters, hereafter to be mentioned. The editor of the Cambridge Paragraph Bible would have been glad, in the prosecution of this portion of his task, if he could have followed rather

---

[1] *The Holy Bible with the text of the common Translation arranged in Paragraphs*, &c. By James Nourse. Boston and Philadelphia, 1836. Preface, pp. 1, 2.

than preceded the publication of the new Church Lectionary of 1871. It is, however, with great satisfaction that on comparing the paragraphs in this volume with the beginnings and endings of the Lessons as appointed by the Royal Commissioners, he has been able to note a resemblance between the two which is quite remarkable, due allowance being always made for the motives which sometimes cause a Church Lesson to commence or leave off at a certain place, irrespective of considerations suggested by the sense.

The poetical portions of the Old Testament and Apocrypha, as well as a very few passages of the New Testament[1], have been arranged in the Paragraph Bible according to the principles first enunciated by Bishop Lowth, and modified and improved upon by his successors. The series of couplets or triplets of parallel lines is furthermore broken everywhere by divisions (similar to those in the prose books) suggested by the sense, which throughout Job (as represented by Delitzsch), and in some of the Psalms (e.g. xlii., xliii.; lxxxix.; cvii.) may be regarded as stanzas, often though by no means always of uniform length. The thirteen alphabetical poems[2] are distinguished by Hebrew letters at the proper places, so that an English reader may form some notion of the grounds on which the Lowthian system of Hebrew parallelism ultimately rests. Here again a difficulty often occurs which is at times unavoidable in a version made before the true laws of the poetry were ascertained, in that

---

[1] Luke i. 46—55; 68—79; ii. 14; 29—32. Rev. xviii. 2—24. Also, in imitation of some of the earliest Greek manuscripts, the Beatitudes (Matt. v. 3—12; Luke vi. 20—26), the short parables of Matt. xiii., and the eight woes of Matt. xxiii. (compare Luke xi.), have been set each in a separate paragraph.

[2] Ps. ix.; x. (imperfect); xxv.; xxxiv.; xxxvii.; cxi.; cxii.; cxix.; cxlv. Prov. xxxi. 10—31. Lam. i.; ii.; iii.; iv.

the order of the English, departing for good reasons from that of the original, forbids a correct distribution of the verse into its proper members. Instances may be noticed in Job xxxvii. 13, 21. Ps. xxxi. 18; lxviii. 23; lxxiv. 6; lxxv. 8; xci. 9; xcviii. 1; cxix. 4; cxx. 1; cxxix. 5; cxxxii. 12; cxxxiv. 3; cxxxvii. 2. Prov. viii. 2, 3; xxiv. 11. Isai. xxviii. 4. Mic. iv. 8. Nah. iii. 3. Zeph. iii. 17. Zech. ix. 1. Mal. i. 3. Ecclus. i. 2, 3; xviii. 6; xxvi. 9; xxxiii. 19; xl. 29; xlviii. 22. Not that we should be over anxious to maintain an equable length for the lines, as Nourse too often does, dividing (for example) Mal. iv. 5 at the word "coming" instead of "prophet," in violation of the sense, and against the Masoretic points, which, through some happy instinct of their authors, seldom lead us wrong. More considerable is the perplexity, in dealing with writers that pass gradually from what might well be deemed poetry into rhetorical prose, and so back again, to determine the precise point at which the poetical structure should begin or terminate. This was found especially the case in Jeremiah and the earlier chapters of Zechariah, wherein another mind might easily arrive at a different result. Portions also of Ecclesiastes (ch. vii. 1—14; x. 1—xii. 7) and 2 Esdras xvi., are imperfectly metrical, though printed as prose; while on the other hand the tone of Zephaniah is less elevated than is usual in poetry. We notice a burst of poetic fervour in so prosaic a book as Daniel (ch. ii. 20—23), while the last prayer of David (1 Chr. xxix. 10—19), which began in the same high strain, gradually sinks to a lower level. Passages of the hymn in Neh. ix. 5 &c., are among the latest breathings of an expiring literature of holy song. The opening of Wisdom again is quite as capable of being thrown into parallel lines as Ecclesiasticus, yet as the book proceeds (though it is the work of a single writer and composed on a regular plan), it insensibly swells into the ornate periods of the later Greek style[1]. How wholly unsuitable some parts of it are for reduction into parallel lines may be seen in the edition of O. T. Fritzsche (*Libri Apocryphi V. T.* 1871), yet both he and W. J. Deane, in his valuable edition of the Book of Wisdom (1881), mostly follow the line divisions of Codex Alexandrinus.

We are very little concerned with the chapters and verses of ordinary Bibles, though they should not be interfered with needlessly. In the Apocryphal additions to Esther, nothing can be more confused or preposterous than the order of the matter and the numbering of the chapters in our own Version, and to some extent in the Clementine Vulgate and earlier English Bibles. By adopting Jerome's arrangement, and omitting his explanatory notes, we have as a result, among other inconsistencies, the interpretation of Mardocheus' dream before the dream itself[2]. In other cases the divisions of chapters may be disregarded without scruple, whensoever they appear erroneous or unnecessary. Thus with the Hebrew we should join Lev. vi. 1—7 with ch. v. Connect also Josh. v. 15 with ch. vi.; Isai. ii. 22 with ch. iii.; Isai. x. 1—4 with ch. ix.; Jer. xix. 14, 15 with ch. xx.; Ezek. xx. 45—50 with ch. xxi. (the parable with its solution), as in the Hebrew (which also rightly joins Hos. xi. 12 with ch. xii.; and Nah. i. 15 with ch. ii.); Amos ii. 1—3, or 1—5 with ch. i.; Ecclus. vi. 1 with ch. v. 15; Matt. xv. 39 with ch. xvi.; xix. 30 with ch. xx.; Mark ix. 1 with ch. viii.; the first clause of Acts viii. with ch. vii.; 1 Cor. xi. 1 with ch. x.; 2 Cor. v. 1 with ch. iv.; vii. 1 with ch. vi.; Col. iv. 1 with ch. iii.; Rev. viii. 1 with ch. vii. Nor can anything be worse than the verse divisions at times, especially in the Old Testament, e.g. Ps.

---

[1] "Grandiloquus, cothurnatus, tumidus" are Lowth's expressive epithets. *De Sacra Poesi.* Prælect. XXIV.

[2] Bp. Lord A. C. Hervey in *Smith's Dictionary of the Bible.* Coverdale and the Bishops' Bible get rid of the difficulty by omitting ch. x. 4—xi. 1 altogether.

lxxviii. 30, 31; xcv. 7, 8; Isai. i. 16, 17. We may also notice that in the Song of the Three Holy Children the modern verses are from the beginning one in advance of those of 1611 (see Appendix A), and that the English verses in Luke i. 74, 75; vii. 18, 19; John i. 38, 39; Acts ix. 28, 29; xi. 25, 26; xiii. 32, 33; xix. 40, 41; xxiv. 2, 3; 2 Cor. ii. 12, 13; v. 14, 15; xi. 8, 9; xiii. 12, 13; Eph. i. 10, 11; iii. 17, 18; Phil. iii. 13, 14; 1 Thess. ii. 11, 12; Heb. vii. 20, 21 (where Elzevir 1624 agrees with the Engl.); x. 22, 23 (with Beza); 1 John ii. 13, 14 (in some editions); 3 John 13, 14; Apoc. xii. 18 or xiii. 1 (but Tomson's Geneva 1606 and the Bishops' of 1602 are said by Dr Hort to agree with the Greek); xviii. 16, 17 differ slightly from those in ordinary Greek Testaments[1].

As regards the headings of the chapters, as also those set over the several columns of the text, nothing considerable would be lost by their omission. The column headings of necessity varied more or less for every edition which did not (like the black-letter books of 1617, 1634, and that of 1640 very nearly) correspond with the standard of 1611 page for page. The headings summing up the contents of each chapter do not much resemble those previously given either in the Genevan or in the Great and Bishops' Bibles (which two in this particular are almost identical), but seem to be quite original. In the early chapters of the Acts of the Apostles they are inordinately long. The variations between our present headings and those of 1611, other than mere corrections of the press, are but twelve in number, that prefixed to Ps. cxlix. being the only one of importance[2]. Dr

---

[1] We hardly know how to recognise the claim set up by Robert Stephen, in his Greek Testament of 1551, of being the earliest to divide the sacred text into verses: "Quod autem per quosdam, ut vocant, versiculos, opus distinximus, id, vetustissima Græca Latinaque ipsius N.T. exemplaria secuti, fecimus."

[2] Where "that power which he hath given to the Church to rule

Blayney, however, for his edition of 1769, gave what may be called "a New Version of these headings, bearing somewhat of the same relation to the Old that Tate and Brady does to Sternhold and Hopkins. It has been stigmatized by some as a doctrinal depravation of them, and praised by others as an improvement. It is in fact a modernization or dilation of them, with little systematic difference of doctrine, but with less force of it, giving however in many cases a better account of the real contents of the chapters than the old[1]." This portion of his labours Blayney speaks of with complacency in his *Report to the Delegates of the Clarendon Press* (see below, Appendix D); but whatever might be its merits, it met with no sort of acceptance. Oxford Bibles have returned long since to the headings of 1611; his changes were never adopted at Cambridge. It was felt, perhaps, that there is much comment of this kind in the original edition which long prescription alone has persuaded men to tolerate, and his work was rejected not because it was bad, but because it was new.

The chronological dates placed in the margin of our modern Bibles are derived from that of Bishop Lloyd in 1701 (see above, p. 26, 27) without any pretence on the part of any one of vouching for their correctness. They are in substance taken from Archbishop Ussher's *Annales V. et N. Testamenti* (1650—4), and are beyond doubt sufficiently

---

the consciences of men" is discreetly curtailed in the edition of 1762 by the omission of the last six words, that of 1769 further amending by substituting "his saints" for "the Church," which latter some modern Bibles still retain. D'Oyly and Mant stand to the words of 1611. Observe also (with Bp. Charles Wordsworth) that in the heading of Ecclus. xxxiv. 18 the words ran "The offering of the ancient," until Blayney substituted "unjust" for "ancient." On this subject the editor is much indebted to an obliging communication from the Rev. C. K. Paul, of Bailie, Wimborne.

[1] Grote MS. (see above, p. 23 note), p. 18.

exact to be a real help to the reader, the *data* on which they are constructed being always assumed as true. In the history of the later kings of Judah modern researches have not been able to suggest a variation from them of more than two years. The dates according to the Greek reckoning, set in the Paragraph Bible under those of the Hebrew in the first six books of the Bible, are grounded upon the well-known differences in respect to numerals between the text of the Hebrew and that of the Septuagint, in the fifth and eleventh chapters of Genesis. Bp. Lloyd's dates have not been materially tampered with since they were first brought into our Bibles, though in some copies they are repeated more frequently than in others. Lloyd, and after him the books of 1762 and 1769, had assigned to the ninth chapter of Zechariah the date of B.C. 587 (being 67 years earlier than that of his first chapter), in accordance with an opinion, more plausible than solid, to which Joseph Mede first lent the weight of his profound learning, that the last six chapters of that prophecy are the composition of some earlier writer, who flourished about the period of the Captivity. Modern Bibles later than 1835 have substituted in ch. ix. the date of B.C. 517; in Bagster's edition of 1846 it is reduced to B.C. 510, in the American of 1867 to B.C. 487, which is much too low. A mark of interrogation may simply be placed after this and some other questionable dates. The year B.C. 791, alleged for the eclipse referred to in Amos viii. 9, being now known to be incorrect, other more possible dates have been substituted within brackets. In Jer. xxvii. 1, "B.C. 598" is omitted altogether, as it rests on the needless supposition that for "Jehoiakim" in the text we ought to read "Zedekiah." The like remedy has been applied to Isai. ix. 8 and x. 1, which obviously belong to the same idyl or ode, and are connected by the same refrain: yet the one part of it is assigned to B.C. 738, the other to B.C. 713. It would be well to set a query after the date (B.C. 862) of the prophecy of Jonah, inasmuch as it is nearly certain that the Twelve Minor Prophets stand in the Canon in chronological order: and certainly on comparing Mic. vi. 16, the third chapter of that book must have been written before the fall of Samaria, not eleven years after it (B.C. 710). In the Second Prologue to Ecclesiasticus "the eight and thirtieth year" being seemingly that of the writer's life, not of the reign of Euergetes, instead of B.C. 133 we should probably read some earlier time. The few dates added in the Paragraph Bible are included in brackets, and may perhaps be regarded as at once convenient and certain: such as that on Esther xi. 1. It is not easy to approve of the boldness of the editor of 1762, who affixes to Ps. cxx. "cir. 1058," apparently on the authority of the chapter heading which assumes that Doeg is the enemy referred to, as indeed a comparison of ver. 4 with Ps. lii. 1, renders not improbable.

The present is scarcely a fit opportunity for discussing at length the merits and faults of the Authorized Version, which "so laborious, so generally accurate, so close, so abhorrent of paraphrase, so grave and weighty in word and rhythm, so intimately bound up with the religious convictions and associations of the English people'" will never yield its hard earned supremacy, save to some reverential and well-considered Revision of which it has been adopted as the basis, that shall be happy enough to retain its characteristic excellencies, while amending its venial errors and

---

[1] Preface to *The Gospel of S. John revised by Five Clergymen*, p. vi. In regard to the rhythm it may be said that those can best appreciate the Translators' happy skill, who have tried to improve upon their version. Even such an expression as "that that" Ezek. xxxvi. 36; Dan. xi. 36; Jonah. ii. 9; Zech. xi. 9 (*bis*), 16—all the work of one Company—is common in so musical a contemporary writer as Fletcher.

supplying its unavoidable defects. Yet it may not be improper to touch briefly on one or two particulars, which have not been prominently noted by others, but have impressed the writer's mind in the prosecution of his laborious, yet most interesting task.

First then we mark great inequality in the execution of the several portions of this version. The limits of life and human patience would forbid the whole Bible (including the Apocrypha), from being committed to the care of a single Company, but it was surely a mistake to divide the whole body of Translators into six parties. The Bishops' Bible indeed seems to have had a fresh translator for almost every book[1], and the inconsistencies which such a plan must needs engender may have been one of the causes which hindered that version from obtaining general acceptance. No doubt it had been wisely provided by the King's ninth and tenth *Instructions* that "As any one Company hath despatched any book..., they shall send it to the rest to be considered of seriously and judiciously; for His Majesty is very careful in this point": as also that "If any Company doubt or differ upon any place...the difference to be compounded at the general meeting, which is to be of the chief persons of each company at the end of the work." But our very meagre information respecting

---

[1] Fourteen of the sacred books have appended to them the initials of their translators, eight of these being Bishops, so far as they can be identified; but "they do not indicate all the contributors." Westcott, *General View of the History of the English Bible*, p. 135. This last statement is plainly true both from the manner in which the initials are distributed, and because the names of some persons known to have been employed nowhere appear. But even in regard to the present Authorized Translation, tradition has assigned a share in the final revision to Dr Thomas Bilson, Bishop of Winchester, whose name appears in no list of the six Companies. Observe what is said of him and of Miles Smith (see above, pp. 12 note 4, 39) in the Decrees of the Synod of Dort (below, p. 264). William Eyre's review has been mentioned above, p. 13 note 2.

the progress of the Translators gives us no great reason to believe that this wholesome device was carried out in practice (see above, p. 13), while internal evidence points decidedly to a contrary conclusion[1]. Certain it is that the six or twelve who met at Stationers' Hall during the nine months which immediately preceded publication had mechanical work enough on their hands in carrying the sheets through the press, without troubling themselves much about higher matters. The first Westminster Company undertook the historical books from Genesis down to the end of 2 Kings, and included the great names of Andrewes then Dean of Westminster, of Overall then Dean of S. Paul's, and of Adrian de Saravia, by birth a Fleming, at that time Prebendary of Westminster, but best known as the bosom friend and spiritual counsellor of saintlike Richard Hooker. Compared with other portions of Holy Scripture their share in the work may seem an easy one, yet the eminent success of the whole enterprise is largely due to the simple dignity of their style, and to the mingled prudence and boldness wherewith they so blended together the idioms of two very diverse languages, that the reader is almost tempted to believe that the genius of his native tongue must have some subtil affinity with the Hebrew. Not inferior to theirs in merit, but far surpassing it in difficulty, is the work of the third, or first Oxford Company, the Prophets from

---

[1] One instance of this lack of consistency observable in the different parts of our Translation, the more minute the better for our purpose, will serve to illustrate a statement which is notoriously true. The Oxford Company, which revised the Prophets, was careful to render the Niphal conjugation of דבר with some intensity of meaning, whether wrongly or rightly matters not. In Ezek. xxxiii. 30 we find "still are talking;" in Mal. iii. 16 "spake often;" three verses before "spoken so much," where 1629 so little understands what is intended as to put "*so much*" in italics. This Niphal form occurs only once elsewhere, Ps. cxix. 23, where the second Company simply has "speak."

Isaiah to Malachi inclusive. This body was presided over by Dr John Harding, Regius Professor of Hebrew [1591—8; 1604—10], in the room of the great Puritan John Rainolds[1], President of Corpus Christi College [d. 1607], who is reputed to have first suggested the new translation at the Hampton Court Conference (1603—4), full three years before it was actually commenced. This party included Dr Richard Kilbye, Rector of Lincoln College [1590—1620], afterwards Regius Professor of Hebrew [1610—1620], whose testimony to the anxious pains devoted to the version is preserved by Isaac Walton, and will be most readily credited by those whose privilege it has been to bear a part in similar conferences, directed to the same great end[2]. It needs but the comparison of a single chapter of Isaiah, for instance, as rendered by the Authorized Translation, with that in the Bishops' Bible which was adopted as the ground of their labours, to estimate very highly the improvements effected by this third Company. The common notion that the Minor Prophets are less felicitously rendered than the four Greater, must be modified by the consideration that three or four of the twelve, as well from their pregnant brevity as from the

---

[1] So spelt, as Dr Newth tells me, on the title pages of his books, and on his monument in his College Chapel.

[2] "The Doctor going to a Parish Church in Derbyshire...found the young preacher to have no more discretion than to waste a great part of the hour allotted for his sermon in exceptions against the late translation of several words (not expecting such a hearer as Dr Kilbye), and shewed three reasons why a particular word should have been otherwise translated. When Evening Prayer was ended, the preacher was invited to the Doctor's friend's house, where after some other conference the Doctor told him, he "might have preached more useful doctrine, and not have filled his auditors' ears with needless exceptions against the late translation; and for that word for which he offered to that poor congregation three reasons why it ought to have been translated as he said, he and others had considered all of them, and found thirteen more considerable reasons why it was translated as printed." Walton, *Life of Sanderson*, p. 367 (Zouch, 1807).

obscurity of their allusions, are among the very hardest books of the Bible in the original, whose difficulties no faithful translator would wish to dissemble or conceal. Respecting the second, or first Cambridge Company, which sustained irreparable loss by the death of Edward Lively, Regius Professor of Hebrew [1580—1606], before their task was fairly begun, his successor also, R. Spalding, apparently dying a year after, it may be confessed that its version of Job is very unsatisfactory, nor indeed could it well be otherwise before the breaking forth of that flood of light which Albert Schultens long afterwards (1737) shed upon it from the cognate languages. A more legitimate subject of complaint is the prosaic tone of its translation of the Psalms, which, however exact and elaborate, is so spiritless as to be willingly used by but few that are familiar with the version in the Book of Common Prayer; a recension which, though derived immediately from the Great Bible, is in substance the work of that consummate master of rhythmical prose, Bishop Miles Coverdale[1]. Of the other three Companies it will suffice to re-echo the general verdict, that the Epistles, entrusted to persons sitting at Westminster of whom little is now known, are worse done than any other part of the Canonical Scriptures, and bear no comparison with the Gospels, the Acts (which book is especially good, as indeed is its prototype in the preceding version, from the hand of Bishop Cox of Ely), and the Apocalypse,

---

[1] Burnet (*History of the Reformation*, Part III. Book 5) knows so little about Coverdale and his English style as to assert that "On the 19th of February [1554—5], some small regard was had to Miles Coverdale, as being a foreigner; for he was a Dane: he had a passport to go to Denmark, with two servants, without any unlawful let or search." We learn from Dr Eadie (*English Bible*, Vol. I. p. 432) that Queen Mary released Coverdale at the earnest and renewed entreaty of Christian II., king of Denmark, whose chaplain, J. M. Macalpine, was married to the sister of Coverdale's wife.

as revised by the second Oxford Company, on which served Sir Henry Savile, then the most famous Greek scholar in England. In the New Testament, as was both right and almost necessary, the renderings of the older English versions were more closely adhered to than in the Old. Of the performance of the fourth, or second Cambridge Company, to which the Apocrypha was consigned, little favourable can be said. It was the earliest party to complete its share, as appears from the fact that John Bois (see above, pp. 12, 22) was transferred to the first Cambridge Company after his proper task herein was completed[1]. A formal correction of the text, often so obviously corrupt, might have been impossible with the means within their reach; yet it required very little critical discrimination to perceive the vast superiority of that which they perpetually appeal to as the "Roman edition" (see above, p. 47) over the older recensions of the Complutensian and of Aldus. For the rest, they are contented to leave many a rendering of the Bishops' Bible as they found it, when nearly any change must have been for the better; even where their predecessor sets them a better example they resort to undignified, mean, almost vulgar words and phrases[2]; and on the

---

[1] Yet John Selden, who was twenty-seven years old in 1611, and must have had means of information not open to us, is represented in his *Table Talk* (p. 6) as speaking thus: "The translation in King James' time took an excellent way. That part of the Bible was given to him who was most excellent in such a tongue—as the Apocrypha to Andrew Downes" [Regius Professor of Greek, 1585—1625]. He adds moreover this interesting piece of information, to whatever part of the work it may apply: "Then they met together, and one read the translation, the rest holding in their hands some Bible, either of the learned tongues, or French [*Olivetan* 1535, *The Pastors* 1588], Spanish [*Pinel* 1553, *De Reyna* 1569, the Valencia Bible of 1478 revised by *De Valera* 1602], Italian [*Bruccioli* 1532?, or more probably *Diodati* 1607], &c. If they found any fault, they spoke; if not, he read on." We hear nothing from him of Luther's German [1522, &c.], which, however, is no doubt the "Dutch" of the *Translators*' Preface, a passage that Selden probably had in his mind.

[2] Such are the colloquial forms,

whole they convey to the reader's mind the painful impression of having disparaged the importance of their own work, or of having imperfectly realised the truth that what is worth doing at all is worth doing well[1].

Nor can the attentive student of the Authorized version fail to marvel at the perfect and easy command over the English language exhibited by its authors on every page. The fulness and variety of their diction, the raciness of their idiomatic resources, seem almost to defy imitation, while they claim our just and cheerful admiration. We need not extenuate that great error of judgment which is acknowledged to be the capital defect of the Translation, especially in the New Testament, in that the same foreign word is perpetually translated by several English ones, while on the other hand a single English word is made to represent two or three in the original, and that too in the same context, where the cogency of the argument or the perspicuity of the narrative absolutely depends on identity in the rendering. But in avoiding this conspicuous fault of the men of 1611, some modern revisers whose efforts are already before the public have fallen into the opposite mistake of forcing the same English word to stand for the same Hebrew

---

"He sticks not" 1 Esdr. iv. 21; "Cocker thy child" Ecclus. xxx. 9; "a shrewd turn" Ecclus. viii. 19; "get the day" (yet the verbal play of the Greek is thus kept up) 2 Macc. v. 6; "he is not for our turn" Wisd. ii. 12; "sour behaviour" 2 Macc. xiv. 30. Add the mere archaisms "brickle" Wisd. xv. 13; "the party" Tobit vi. 7; "pensions" (κλήρους) 1 Esdr. iv. 56 (Bp.); "liberties" (ὁρίοις) 1 Macc. x. 43 (Bp.). We find nothing like this elsewhere in our version.

[1] The foregoing estimate of the relative merits of the several portions of our version differs only in one particular from that of its sturdy opponent Dr Robert Gell: "The further we proceed in survey of the Scripture, the Translation is the more faulty, as the Hagiographa more than the Historical Scripture, and the Prophets more than the Hagiographa [?], and the Apocrypha most of all; and generally the New more than the Old Testament." (*An Essay toward the Amendment of the last English Translation of the Bible*, 1659. Preface, pp. 38, 39.)

or Greek one where there is no real need for preserving such slavish uniformity, thus at once impoverishing our native tongue which is so much more copious than either of the others, and casting over the version an air of baldness very painful to a cultivated taste. Let us take for an example of the beautiful flexibility of their English style the numberless devices our Translators resort to while endeavouring to convey the intensive force of the Hebrew gerundial infinitive when used with some finite form of the selfsame verb, of which the earliest example occurs in Gen. iii. 4, "Ye shall not surely die." The passages are cited almost at random and might be multiplied indefinitely.

> 1 Sam. ii. 16, Let them not fail to burn the fat. 2 Sam. xiv. 14, we must needs die (after the Bishops'); xvii. 10, shall utterly melt; 16, speedily pass over; xviii. 2, I will surely go forth; 3, if we flee away (with the Bishops'); 25, came apace (Bishops'); xx. 18, They were wont to speak (margin, *They plainly spake*). 1 Kin. ii. 37, (42), thou shalt know for certain that thou shalt surely die; iii. 26, 27, in no wise slay it (Bishops'); ix. 6, If ye shall at all turn. 1 Chr. iv. 10, Oh that thou wouldest bless me indeed (Bishops'). Neh. i. 7, We have dealt very corruptly against thee ("grievously sinned," Bishops'). Esther iv. 14, If thou altogether holdest thy peace. Job vi. 2, Oh that my grief were throughly weighed ("truly weighed" Bishops'); xiii. 17 and xxi. 2, Hear diligently (Bishops'); xxvii. 22, he would fain flee. Jer. xxiii. 17, They say still; 32, profit at all; 39, utterly forget; xxv. 30, mightily roar; xxxi. 20, earnestly remember; xli. 6, weeping all along; l. 34, throughly plead. Ezek. i. 3, came expressly. Thus too both versions even in translating the Latin of 2 Esdr. iii. 33; iv. 2, 26; vii. 21, &c. In Isai. xxiv. 19 the Hebrew idiom assumes three different English forms: "the earth is utterly broken down, the earth is clean dissolved, the earth is moved exceedingly."

Yet it has been said by one who ought to know, that "our Translators of the Bible, in their attempt to maintain idiom, have sometimes sacrificed vigour[1]."

[1] Dean Goulburn, *Thoughts on Personal Religion*, Part III. ch. viii. p. 232. His example is Prov. iv. 23, where he prefers the marginal rendering to the text.

The editor earnestly trusts that no apology is necessary for the labour bestowed in the Cambridge Paragraph Bible on the English text and marginal references of the Apocrypha. So long as that very miscellaneous collection of books shall comprise a part of the Holy Bible in its largest form, or lessons shall be selected from it for the course of Divine service, it deserves far more regard than has been paid to it in recent times, even by those who have undertaken to reprint it. But the frequent and exact study of a large portion of the Apocryphal writings may be vindicated on higher grounds by such as most loyally accept the rule that "the Church doth read them for example of life and instruction of manners; but yet doth it not apply them to establish any doctrine." Few more conspicuous instances can be alleged of the tendency in man's nature to rush into extremes than the strong reaction to their prejudice which has set in since the Reformation, by way of protest against the error that had placed the greater part of them on a level in point of authority with the Canonical books of the Old Testament. Add to this that by some untoward accident those portions of the Apocrypha which deserve the least esteem had until recently become the best known, as in the case of the History of Susanna (unfit for public reading, for all its delicate touches of natural beauty), and of the grotesque story of Bel and the Dragon. Yet Ecclesiasticus and the first book of the Maccabees, written in the second century before the Christian era, are among the noblest of uninspired compositions; if indeed their authors, so full of faith and holy fear, can be regarded as entirely uninspired. The second book of the Maccabees also, though greatly inferior to the first in respect of energy, judgment, veracity, and correct taste, abounds in passages fraught with encouragement to those who in every age shall be called upon to suffer for the truth's sake; not to add that it powerfully illustrates the eleventh chapter and other parts of Daniel's prophecies. The Wisdom of Solomon (which was not seriously intended to be ascribed to the king of Israel) approximates in tone to the spirit of Christ more nearly than any book without the Canon; the Epistle of S. James is full of allusions to it, and to the first five chapters of Ecclesiasticus. Judith too is a fine work; grave, elevated, pious, chaste in thought and expression, exquisitely finished. Were it not buried where it is, it would long since have attracted the admiration it deserves; but it is not history, and does not claim to be such. It is fable constructed with a moral purpose; and must have stirred up the heart of many a Jewish patriot in that heroic struggle for liberty and religion whose details fill the histories of the Maccabees. For the remaining books less can be said. Tobit, probably the oldest of them all, exhibits a pleasing picture of the prosperity of a religious household in the land of their captivity: the main outlines seem correct, though sadly deformed by childish superstitions, which are more visible in the Old Latin version followed by the Bishops' Bible, than in our own which adhered to the Greek. Baruch, though of course a pseudonym, contains some excellent poetry: the Prayer of Manasses and the Song of the Three Children need no praise. It is difficult to determine the precise relation of 1 Esdras to the Canonical books of Ezra and Nehemiah: after all the trouble bestowed upon it, we can but conclude that it contains not much intrinsically valuable. "The rest of the book of Esther" seems worth little for any purpose, since it is founded on a radically false conception of the character of two of the most worldly-minded persons God ever employed in the dispensations of His Providence, and rewarded for their obedience with blessings purely temporal. The remaining book, the second of Esdras, is a curious composition, not very fitly placed in the same volume as the rest, and never accounted Canonical by any branch of the Church. Though extant only in Latin, it betrays on every page its Hebrew original; but since no considerable portion of it can be earlier than the second century after Christ, what it has in common with the Revelation and other books of the New Testament is drawn from them, not they from it. It can hardly be questioned that the fortunes of the Roman emperors during the first century are herein figuratively depicted. The celebrated passage ch. vii. 26—35 bears every appearance of interpolation.

The reader is now referred to the subjoined Appendices, in which, under their proper heads, the numerous variations found in later Bibles from the model of 1611 have been carefully arranged. All the more pains have been bestowed upon this portion of the work from the conviction that the task essayed in the present volume would have been accomplished long since thoroughly and once for all, had Dr Blayney and those who preceded him been aware of the necessity of avoiding undue haste in carrying out an enterprise whose difficulty they much under-rated, and which, being intimately concerned with our best and highest interests, demands to be brought as near to perfection as human infirmity will allow.

APPENDIX A.

(See above, pp. 3, 4.)

Catalogue of the variations from the original edition of the Authorized Version of the Holy Bible (1611), which, being found in all modern editions, have been retained in the Cambridge Paragraph Bible. Obvious misprints and the peculiar orthography of the original are excluded, and the dates annexed are those of the editions in which the several variations originated, so far as these can be ascertained.

Genesis	Reading of the Authorized Bible.	Variation of later editions.
v. 32; vi. 10; vii. 13	Sem	Shem, 1629.
vi. 5	God	GOD[1], 1629.
viii. 13	six hundredth and one	six hundredth and first[2], 1629.
ix. 18, 23, 27; x. 1, 2, 21	Japhet	Japheth, 1629.
x. 14	Philistiim	Philistim, 1612 (not 1613), 1629.
x. 19	Sodoma and Gomorah (Gomorrah, 1612)	Sodom and Gomorrah, 1629.
xiv. 15	Hoba	Hobah, 1638.
xv. 7	Caldees (Chaldees, ch. xi. 31)	Chaldees, 1629.

[1] Heb. JEHOVAH. The words "Lord" and "God" are always intended to be printed in small capitals in the Authorized Version, when they are employed to translate that Holy Name. *Adonai Jehovah* is represented by "Lord GOD" about a hundred times in Ezekiel alone, and *Jehovah Adonai* by "LORD God" only in Hab. iii. 19, itself corrected (perhaps wrongly) in the Cambridge folio of 1629. See Appendix B II. on Ps. xliv. 23.

[2] In some places this bold archaism (see above, p. 111) is retained in the text of the Cambridge Paragraph Bible, e.g. Ezek. xliii. 27; 2 Esdr. vii. 68; 1 Macc. xiii. 15; 2 Macc. xi. 21; but not in 1 Kin. vi. 1; xvi. 8, 23.

148 *Appendix A.] Wrong readings of the Bible*

Genesis	Reading of the Authorized Bible.	Variation of later editions.
xv. 19	Kenizites	Kenizzites, 1629.
xvi. 14; xx. 1	Cadesh (Kadesh, ch. xiv. 7)	Kadesh, 1638.
xix. 21	this thing	this thing also, 1638.
xxii. 7	and wood	and the wood, 1616 (not 1617).
xxiii. 10	gates	gate, 1762.
xxxiv. 3 *marg.*	to her heart	to the heart of the damsel, 1744.
xxxvi. 33	Bozra	Bozrah, 1613.
xxxix. 16	her lord	his lord, 1638.
xlii. 40 *marg.*	armed	be armed, 1629.

Exodus

xiv. 25 *marg.*	made	and made, 1629.
xv. 25	made a statute	made for them a statute, 1638.
xxi. 19 *marg.*	ceasing	his ceasing, 1638.
xxi. 32	shekels	shekels of silver, 1638.
xxiii. 13	names	name, 1769.
xxiii. 27 *marg.*	necks (so all in Josh. vii. 8)	neck, 1629.
xxvi. 8	and the eleven	and the eleven curtains, 1629.
xxx. 3 *marg.*	† Hebr. *the roof...and the walls*	† Heb. *roof,* 1629.
xxxiv. 25	of Passover	of the passover, 1762.
xxxv. 11	and his bars	and his boards, his bars, 1638.
xxxv. 29	hands of Moses	hand of Moses, 1629.
xxxvii. 19	Three bowls made he after	Three bowls made after, 1629.

Leviticus

i. 8	in the fire	on the fire, 1638.
i. 9	the inwards	his inwards, 1638.
ii. 4	an unleavened cake	unleavened cakes, 1638.
vi. 2	in ‖ fellowship ... †violence	‖ in †fellowship ... violence, 1629 (nearly).
vi. 5 *marg.*	†Heb. *the day*	†Heb. *in the day*, 1629.
x. 14	the sacrifice	the sacrifices, 1629.
xviii. 20 *marg.*	Moloc	*Moloch*, 1629.
xix. 34	shall be	shall be unto you, 1638.
xx. 11	be put	surely be put, 1638.
xxiii. 10 *marg.*	an Omer	*omer*, 1638.

of 1611 *amended in later editions.*

Leviticus	Reading of the Authorized Bible.	Variation of later editions.
xxiii. 20	for the priests	for the priest, 1638.
xxiii. 22	the field	thy field, 1638.
xxv. 5 *marg.*	*separations*	*separation*, 1629 C.¹, 1630.
xxv. 6	the stranger	thy stranger, 1638.
xxv. 31	walls	wall, 1769.
xxvi. 23	reformed	reformed by me, 1638.
xxvi. 40	the iniquity (the iniquities, 1613)	their iniquity and the iniquity, 1616.

Numbers

i. 2, 18, 20	poll	polls, 1769 (so all in ver. 22).
iv. 40	houses	house, 1769 (so all in ver. 42).
vi. 2	‖ prefixed to first "separate."	‖ prefixed to second "separate," 1744 (not 1762), 1769.
vi. 14	and one lamb	and one ram, 1638.
vii. 31, 55	charger	charger of the weight, 1762 (so all in ver. 43).
vii. 48, 53 & x. 22	Ammiud	Ammihud, 1638 (so all in ch. i. 10).
vii. 54, 59 & x. 23	Pedazur	Pedahzur, 1638 (so all in ch. i. 10).
vii. 61	a silver bowl	one silver bowl, 1638 (so all in ver. 55, &c.).
xix. 11 *marg.*	*soul*	*soul of man*, 1638.
xxi. 20 *marg.*	*hill*	*the hill*, 1638 (Cf. Deut. xxxiv. 1).
xxi. 24	Jabok	Jabbok, 1629, C. and L.¹ (so all in Gen. xxxii. 22, &c.).
xxii. 31 *marg.*	‖ *Bowed*	‖ Or, *bowed*, 1629.
xxiv. 3 *marg.*	open	opened.
xxvi. 6	Hesron...Hesronites	Hezron ... Hezronites, Bagster 1846.
xxvi. 21	Hesron...Hesronites²	Hezron ... Hezronites, 1769.

¹ By 1629, with or without C. annexed, we indicate the Cambridge folio of that year (see above, pp. 19—21), but by 1629 L., the London quarto (*ibid.*).

² Cambr. Synd. A. 3. 14 (see above, p. 14), Brit. Mus. 1276. l. 4 (not

Deuteronomy	Reading of the Authorized Bible.	Variation of later editions.
iv. 25	shalt have remained	ye shall have remained, 1762.
iv. 32	upon earth	upon the earth, 1629.
iv. 49	of this side	on this side, 1617 (not 1629 L., 1630), 1629 C.
v. 29	my commandments	all my commandments, 1629.
ix. 10	of fire	of the fire, 1762.
x. 10 *marg.*	*fortie*	*former*, 1629.
xv. 11 *fin.*	the land	thy land, 1629.
xvi. 4	coasts	coast, 1762.
xvi. 5	the gates	thy gates, 1616 (not 1617, 1629 L., 1630), 1629 C.
xix. 6 *marg.*	*third day*	the third day, 1612, 1613 (not 1629 C. and L., 1630), 1638. Cf. ver. 4, &c.
xx. 7	in battle	in the battle, 1769. Cf. vers. 5, 6.
xxvi. 1	the LORD	the LORD thy God, 1629, 1637.
xxviii. 5 *marg.*	*kneading troughs*	*kneading trough*, 1762. Cf. Ex. viii. 3.
xxviii. 23	the heaven	thy heaven, 1638.
xxviii. 42	locusts	locust, 1612 (not 1613 &c.), 1629.
xxix. 26 *text*	†*whom* he had not given	‖ *whom* he had not †given.
marg.	†*Hebr. divided: Or, who had not given to them any* portion	‖ Or, *who had not given to them* any portion. †Heb. *divided*, 1629.
xxxii. 15 & xxxiii. 5, 26	Jesurun	Jeshurun, 1638 [1].
xxxiv. 1 *marg.*	*Hill*	*the hill*, 1638. Cf. Num. xxi. 20.

30:50. g. 2 or g. 3) have "Hezronites" in ver. 21, but "Hesron" in the same verse. Comp. also 1 Chr. v. 3.

[1] In Deut. xxxiii. 5 alone "Jeshurun" is read also in 1629 C and L, 1630. In Isaiah xliv. 2 the same form is found in 1616 alone of all our editions.

of 1611 amended in later editions.

Joshua	Reading of the Authorized Bible.	Variation of later editions.
iii. 10	Girgashites	the Girgashites, 1612 (not 1613), 1629.
iii. 15	at the time	all the time, 1638.
vii. 14	and the households	and the household, 1616, 1617, 1629 C. (not 1629 L., 1630).
vii. 26	the place	that place, 1629.
x. 10 & xvi. 3, 5	Bethoron	Beth-horon, 1629. Cf. ch. xviii. 13, &c.
xi. 8 *marg.*	*burning of waters*	*burnings of waters*, 1629[1].
xi. 17	unto Baal-Gad	even unto Baal-Gad, 1638.
xii. 6	and Gadites	and the Gadites, 1762.
xii. 11	Lachis	Lachish, 1613 (not 1616, 1617), 1629 C. and L.
xii. 18 *marg.*	*Saron*	*Sharon*, 1629
xiii. 27	Cinneroth	Cinnereth, 1629—1762 (Chinnereth, 1769 mod.). Cf. ch. xix. 35.
xiii. 29	Manasseh, by	the children of Manasseh, by, 1638.
xv. 33	Esthaol	Eshtaol, 1629 (Esthahol, 1630).
xv. 38	Dileam (Diieam 1612, Diliam 1617)	Dilean, 1629.
xv. 42	Lebnah (Lebanah, 1630)	Libnah, 1638.
xv. 43	Jiphta	Jiphtah, 1638.
xv. 49	Kirjath-Sannath	Kirjath-sannah, 1629.
xv. 50	Ashtemoth, Camb. Synd. A. 3. 14, but Ashtemoh, Oxf. 1611, 1612, 1613, &c.	Eshtemoh 1638
xv. 57	Gibbeah	Gibeah, 1629 C. and L., 1630.
xv. 59	Maarah	Maarath, 1629.
xix. 18	Izreel	Jezreel, 1629. Cf. ch. xvii. 16, &c.
xix. 22	Shahazimath	Shahazimah, 1617.
xix. 35	Cinnereth	Chinnereth, 1769.
xix. 38	Bethanah	Beth-anath, 1629.

[1] Modern editions follow 1762, 1769 in omitting "*of waters*."

152 *Appendix A.*] *Wrong readings of the Bible*

Joshua	Reading of the Authorized Bible.	Variation of later editions.
xix. 44	Baalah	Baalath, 1629.
xxi. 23	Gibethon	Gibbethon, 1629.
xxi. 31	Helkah	Helkath, 1629.
Judges		
i. 31	Achzib, nor Helbath, nor Aphik	of Achzib, nor of Helbah, nor of Aphik, 1762 (Helbah, 1629, &c.).
i. 36 *marg.*	*Maale-*	*Maaleh-*, 1629.
iv. 21	†took (first)	†took (second), 1629.
v. 26 *text*	†smote (first)	†with the hammer.
marg.	†*Heb. hammered*	†*Heb. she hammered*, 1629.
v. 29 *marg.*	*words*	*her words*, 1638.
v. 30 *marg.*	†*Heb. for the necks of the spoil*	Delet 1638.
xi. 1 *marg.*	*Jephte* (Jephthah Heb. xi. 32)	*Jephthae*, 1629.
xi. 2	his wives sons	his wife's sons, 1762 [1] (wifes, 1744).
xi. 31 *marg.*	shall come forth	*which shall come forth*, 1629.
ibid.	Or, *I will offer*	Or, *or I will offer*, 1638.
xiv. 17	while the feast	while their feast, 1638.
xxi. 19	Lebanon	Lebonah, 1629.
Ruth		
ii. 3 *marg.*	‖*Called Math.* i. 5, *Booz*	Brought up to ver. 1 *marg.* in 1762.

---

[1] The apostrophe does not appear in our Bibles (see, however, below, p. 235 note 1) before 1762, nor constantly before 1769 (e.g. not in 1762, Ezra ii. 59. Neh. vii. 61. Ps. vi. 4; xxxi. 16; xliv. 26; lxxxi. 12; cvii. 27; cxl. 3, &c.). Through the errors of these books, it is sometimes misplaced, as is noted in this list within brackets. Cf. 1 Sam. ii. 13. 1 Chr. vii. 2, 40. Ezra ii. 59. Ps. lxxxi. 12. Matt. xiv. 9. Mark vi. 26, in which places, unless the contrary be stated, the apostrophe is placed right for the first time in the Cambridge Paragraph Bible.

of 1611 *amended in later editions.* 153

1 Samuel	Reading of the Authorized Bible.	Variation of later editions.
i. 20 *text*	†time	†when, 1638.
marg.	*revelation* (so 1612, 1613, 1629 L)	*revolution*, 1616, 1617, 1629, 1630: *in revolution*, 1638.
[ii. 13	priest's custom, 1762, 1769	priests' custom]. See p. 152 note.
iv. 21 *text*	‖Ichabod, saying, ‖The glory	‖ Ichabod, saying, The glory.
marg.	‖ *That is, where is the glory?* ‖ *Or, there is no glory*	‖ *That is, where is the glory?* or, there is no glory, 1629.
v. 4 *marg.*	*the filthy part*[1]	*the fishy part*, 1616, 1617.
vi. 7	the calves	their calves, 1629.
x. 10	a company of the prophets	a company of prophets, 1629.
x. 23	the shoulders	his shoulders, 1638.
xiii. 18	Bethoron	Beth-horon, 1629.
xvii. 38 *marg.*	*clothed*	*clothed David*, 1638.
xviii. 27	David arose	David arose and went, 1629.
xxv. 16	keeping sheep	keeping the sheep, 1629.
xxviii. 7	And his servant said	And his servants said, 1629.

2 Samuel

iii. 26	Siriah	Sirah, 1629.
vi. 12	*pertained*	*pertaineth*, 1638.
viii. 11	he had dedicate[2]	he had dedicated, 1612 (not 1613).
xi. 1	that after the year (*that* 1638)	after the year, 1762.
xi. 3 [*marg.*]	*Bath-shuah*, 1762, 1769	*Bath-shua*, Bagster 1846, American 1867. Cf. 1 Ch. iii. 5.
xi. 21	Jerubesheth	Jerubbesheth, 1629.

[1] That this marginal rendering of 1611, 1612, 1613 cannot be designed appears from the version of Tremellius and Junius, which, especially in the margin (see above, p. 44), our Translators closely follow; —*quod referebat piscem*. See Cardwell, *Oxford Bibles*, p. 16.
[2] But these archaisms we have elsewhere retained: e.g. 2 Kin. xii. 18. See above, p. 102. Compare 1 Chr. xxvi. 20, Appendix C pp. 220, 221.

2 Samuel	Reading of the Authorized Bible.	Variation of later editions.
xiii. 20 *marg.*	set not thine heart	set not thine heart upon, So Bagster 1846. Cf. ch. xviii. 3 *marg.*
xv. 3 *marg.*	none will hear you	none will hear thee, 1638.
xvi. 12	requite good	require me good, 1629.
xix. 34 *marg.*	† *How many*	† Heb. *How many*, 1616, 1617.
xxi. 4 *marg.*	silver or gold	silver nor gold, 1616, 1617.
xxiii. 32	Elihaba	Eliahba, 1629.
xxiii. 37	Berothite	Beerothite, 1629.

1 Kings

iv. 10	Heseb, *marg. Ben-Heseb*	Hesed, *marg. Ben-Hesed*, 1629.
vi. 1	fourscore[1]...Cf. ch. xvi. 8, 23	eightieth, 1762.
vii. 42 *marg.*	upon the face Cf. 2 Chr. iv. 13 *marg.*	upon the face of the pillars, 1638.
vii. 51 *marg.*	things of David	holy things of David, 1629.
viii. 61	the LORD your God	the LORD our God, 1629.
ix. 11	that then Solomon	that then king Solomon, 1638.
ibid.	Galile (Tobit i. 2)	Galilee, 1629. Cf. C. and L., 1630.
xi. 1	Sydonians Camb. Synd. A 3. 14 but Sidonians Oxf. 1611, 1612—1638	Zidonians, 1629. Cf. vers. 5, 33.
xi. 5	Amorites (Ammorites 1612)	Ammonites, 1629.
xi. 33	Ashtaroth (pl. Cf. Judg. x. 6)	Ashtoreth, 1629. Cf. ver. 5.
xiii. 6	was restored again	was restored him again, 1638.
xiv. 4 *marg.*	stood for hoariness	stood for his hoariness, 1638.

---

[1] But these archaisms we have elsewhere retained. See above, p. 111.

of 1611 *amended in later editions.* 155

1 Kings	Reading of the Authorized Bible.	Variation of later editions.
xv. 2 [*marg.*]	Michaia, 1769	Michaiah, Bagster 1846, Camb. 1858, American 1867. Cf. 2 Chr. xiii. 2.
xv. 10 *marg.*	grandmother	grandmothers, 1638, 's, 1762.
xv. 14	Asa his heart[1]	Asa's heart, 1762.
xv. 19	break the league	break thy league, 1629 C. and L., 1630.
xvi. 8	twentieth and sixt (sixth 1613)	twenty and sixth, 1629. Cf. vers. 10, 15.
xvi. 23	the thirty and one year[1]	the thirty and first year, 1769.
2 Kings		
v. 11 *marg.*	†Heb. *said*	†Heb. *I said*, 1617 (not 1629 C. and L., 1630), 1638.
viii. 19	promised	promised him, 1629.
ix. 23	turned his hand (Vulgate)	turned his hands (Heb., LXX.) 1629.
xi. 10	the Temple	the temple of the Lord, 1638.
xii. 19, 20	Jehoash	Joash, 1629.
xiii. 24	Hazael the king of Syria	Hazael king of Syria, 1612 (not 1613), 1629.
xv. 15	the conspiracy	his conspiracy, 1638.
xviii. 8	fenced cities	fenced city, 1629.
xviii. 18	Helkiah (so ver. 37 Camb. Synd. A. 3. 14 alone, not being a reprint: see above, p. 6)	Hilkiah, 1629.
xix. 37	Adramelech	Adrammelech, 1638. Cf. ch. xvii. 31.
xx. 1	Amos	Amoz, 1629. Cf. ch. xix. 2, 20.
xx. 13	shewed them the house	shewed them all the house, 1638.
xxi. 21 & xxii. 2	all the ways	all the way, 1629.
xxiii. 13	Milchom	Milcom, 1638.

---

[1] For these archaisms see above, p. 111.

2 Kings	Reading of the Authorized Bible.	Variation of later editions.
xxiii. 21	this book of the Covenant	the book of this covenant, 1629[1].
xxiii. 31	Hamital	Hamutal, 1629.
xxiv. 13	and the treasure	and the treasures, 1629.
xxiv. 19	Jehoiachin (Cf. LXX.)	Jehoiakim, 1629.
xxv. 4, 5, 10, 13, 24, 25, 26	Caldees	Chaldees, 1744.

1 Chronicles

i. 9	Siba	Seba, 1629.
i. 20	Hazermaveth	Hazermaveth, 1634, 1638.
i. 33	Ephar	Epher, 1638.
i. 39 *marg.*	*Heman* 1611—1769[2] (*Hemah* 1617)	*Hemam*, Bagster 1846, Camb. 1858, American 1867.
i. 40 *marg.*	*Sepho*	*Shepho*, 1629. Cf. Gen. xxxvi. 23.
i. 42	Bilham...Dishon	Bilhan, 1629 ... Dishan, 1638.
i. 44	Bosrah	Bozrah, 1638. Cf. Isai. lxiii. 1, &c.
ii. 10	Aminadab *bis*	Amminadab *bis*, 1629.
ii. 13 *marg.*	*Shamma*	*Shammah*, 1629. Cf. 1 Sam. xvi. 9.
ii. 14	Nathanael	Nethaneel, 1638.
ii. 18	Shobab	and Shobab, 1629.
ii. 25	Ozen	Ozem, 1629.
ii. 27	Ekar	Eker, 1638.
ii. 42	Maresha	Mareshah, 1638. Cf. ch. iv. 21.
ii. 48	Maacha. Cf. ch. ix. 35	Maachah, 1638.
ii. 52 & iv. 2 *marg.*	Haroe	Haroeh, 1638.
ii. 54	Salmah	Salma, 1638. Cf. ver. 51.
iii. 2	Maacha...Adoniah	Maacha, 1638 ... Adonijah, 1629. Cf. 1 Kin. i. 5, &c.

---

[1] The rendering of 1611 is quite justifiable, but the LXX. and Vulgate translate as in 1629.

[2] The editions of 1629—1769 correct the discrepancy with Gen. xxxvi. 22 in the wrong way, by putting "Heman" in the earlier place. The latter error is corrected by some (e.g. D'Oyly and Mant 1817, Oxford 1835) that retain *Heman* in 1 Chr. i. 39 *marg.*

of 1611 *amended in later editions.* 157

1 Chronicles	Reading of the Authorized Bible.	Variation of later editions.
iii. 3	Shephatia	Shephatiah, 1629.
iii. 5 *marg.*	Bethsabe	Bath-sheba, 1629.
iii. 7	Noga	Nogah, 1638.
iii. 8 *marg.*	Beliada	Beeliada, 1769 (Beeliada, 1762).
iii. 10 *marg.*	Abiam	Abijam, 1629.
iii. 11 *marg.*	and	or, *Jehoahaz*, 2 Chr., 1762.
iii. 15, 16	Joakim	Jehoiakim, 1629.
iii. 15 *marg.*	*Joachaz*	*Jehoahaz*, 1629.
ibid.	Mathania	Mattaniah, 1638 (Mattania, 1629).
iii. 15	Sallum	Shallum, 1629.
iii. 16	‖Zedekiah his son	Zedekiah* his son[1], 1629.
iii. 18	Hosanna, Camb. Synd. A. 3. 14, B. M. 1276. l. 4 only. Hosama, Oxf. 1611, 1612—1630	Hoshama, 1638.
iii. 20	Hazubah	Hashubah, 1629.
iii. 22	Semaiah, *bis*	Shemaiah, *bis*, 1629.
iv. 6	Ahusam...Ahashtari	Ahuzam, 1629...Haahashtari, 1638.
iv. 7	Zoar	Jezoar, 1638.
iv. 13	Saraia (Saraiah, 1616)	Seraiah, 1629. Cf.ver.14.
iv. 14	Charasim	Charashim, 1629.
iv. 20	Simeon	Shimon, 1629. Cf. ver. 24.
iv. 29	Bilha, *marg.* Bela	Bilhah, 1638, *marg.* Balah, 1629.
iv. 31 *marg.*	Hazar-Susa	Hazar-susah, 1629.
iv. 34	Amashiah	Amaziah, 1629.
iv. 35	Josibia...Seraia	Josibiah, 1629...Seraiah, 1638.
iv. 36	Jehohaiah,Camb. Synd. A. 3. 14 alone, but Jesohaiah, Oxf. 1611, 1612—1630	Jeshohaiah, 1638.

[1] The references to the margin, up to 1629 L., 1630, are in hopeless confusion; "‖ Or *Coniah*, Jer. 22. 24" being made a marginal note to "Zedekiah," instead of to "Jeconiah," and "* 2 Kin. 24. 17 *being his uncle*," which is the proper note on "his son," being misplaced so as to stand after † Heb. *Shealtiel*, ver. 17.

1 Chronicles	Reading of the Authorized Bible.	Variation of later editions.
iv. 37	Jedaia	Jedaiah, 1638.
v. 2	chief ‖ rulers	‖chief ruler, 1629 (place of ‖ changed by Bagster 1846).
v. 3	Ezron	Hezron, 1629.
v. 6 *marg.*	*Tiglath-pilneser*	*Tiglath-pileser*, 1629.
v. 8	Azah (Aza, 1630)	Azaz, 1629.
vi. 2, 22 *marg.*	Izahar	Izhar, 1629. Cf. vers. 18, 38.
vi. 21 *marg.*	*Adaia*	*Adaiah*, 1629. Cf. ver. 41.
vi. 40	Baasiah...Melchiah	Baaseiah...Malchiah, 1638.
vi. 57	Libna	Libnah, 1638[1].
vi. 60	Anathoth (Anathoch, 1617)	and Anathoth, 1629.
vi. 69 & viii. 13	Aialon	Aijalon, 1629[2].
vi. 78 *marg.*	‖ *Or, Bozor, Josh.* xxi. 35	Delet 1629.
[vii. 2, 40	father's house, 1762, 1769	fathers' house], see p. 152 note.
vii. 18	Ishad	Ishod, 1638.
vii. 18 [*marg.*]	*Jezer*, 1762, 1769	*Jeezer*, Bagster 1846, Camb. 1858, Amer. 1867. Cf. Num. xxvi. 30.
vii. 24	Bethoron	Beth-horon, 1629.
vii. 25	Rezeph	Resheph, 1638.
vii. 26 & ix. 4	Amihud	Ammihud, 1629.
vii. 32	Shuah	Shua, 1638.
viii. 11	Ahitub	Abitub, 1629.
viii. 14	Jerimoth	Jeremoth, 1638.
viii. 31	Gidor	Gedor, 1638. Cf. ch. ix. 37.
viii. 31 *marg.*	*Zachariah*	*Zechariah*, 1629. Cf. ch. xxiv. 25, &c.
viii. 36	Asmaveth	Azmaveth, 1638. Cf. ch. ix. 42.

---

[1] *He* final is usually represented by *h*: yet not so by any edition in 1 Chr. iii. 10; v. 5 (Reaia); vi. 29.

[2] All editions retain the false form "Ajalon" Josh. x. 12. 2 Chr. xxviii. 18: all have the true form "Aijalon" Josh. xxi. 24. Judg. i. 35. 1 Sam. xiv. 31. In Josh. xix. 42 and 2 Chr. xi. 10, 1629 makes the same change as here.

of 1611 *amended in later editions.* 159

1 Chronicles	Reading of the Authorized Bible.	Variation of later editions.
viii. 37	Elasa	Eleasah, 1638. Cf. ch. ix. 43.
ix. 12	Maasia	Maasiai, 1629.
ix. 35	Maacha. Cf. ch. ii. 48	Maachah, 1629.
ix. 44	Ismael	Ishmael, 1638. Cf. ch. viii. 38.
x. 2 *marg.*	Ieshui	Ishui, 1629. Cf. 1 Sam. xiv. 49.
xi. 15	to the rock of David	to the rock to David, 1629.
xi. 33	Elihaba	Eliahba, 1629.
xi. 34	Shageh	Shage, 1629.
xi. 43	Maacah	Maachah, 1638.
xi. 45	Zimri, *marg. Zimrite*	Shimri, *marg.* Shimrite, 1629.
xi. 46	Elnaan	Elnaam, 1629.
xii. 3 *marg.*	Hasmaa	Hasmaah, 1629.
xii. 5	Bealiath	Bealiah, 1638.
xii. 6	Azariel	Azareel, 1638.
xii. 7	Jeroam	Jeroham, 1613 (not 1612, 1616, 1617, 1629 L., 1630), 1629 C.
xii. 10	Mashmannah	Mishmannah, 1638.
xii. 11	Atthai	Attai, 1629.
xii. 20	Jediel	Jediael, 1638.
xiii. 11 *marg.*	Heb.	That is, 1629.
xiv. 6	Noga	Nogah, 1638.
xiv. 7	Elpalet	Eliphalet, 1629.
xv. 18, 20	Zachariah	Zechariah, 1639.
xv. 18	Jaziel	Jaaziel, 1638.
xv. 18, 20	Maasiah	Maaseiah, 1638. See 2 Chr. xxiii. 1.
xv. 18, 21	Eliphaleh (Eliphaleb, 1612, ver. 18) ... Mikniah	Elipheleh...Mikneiah, 1638.
xv. 18	Jehiel (*second*)	Jeiel, 1629 [1].
xv. 21	Azzaziah	Azaziah, 1638.
xv. 24	Nathaneel...Zachariah (so ch. xvi. 5)	Nethaneel ... Zechariah (so ch. xvi. 5), 1638.

---

[1] To distinguish יְעִיאֵל (Jeiel) from יְחִיאֵל (Jehiel) of ver. 20. In this verse and ch. xvi. 5 both names occur, and are thus distinguished in 1611. "Jeiel" is right in ver. 21 and in ch. v. 7; "Jehiel" in ch. xxiii. 8; 2 Chr. xxi. 2; xxix. 14; xxxi. 13; xxxv. 8; Ezra viii. 9; x. 2, 21, 26. See also 2 Chr. xx. 14; xxix. 13.

1 Chronicles	Reading of the Authorized Bible.	Variation of later editions.
xviii. 8 *marg.*	Beta	Betah, 1769. Cf. 2 Sam. viii. 8.
xviii. 16 *marg.*	Saraia...Sisa	Seraiah ... Shisha, 1629. Cf. 2 Sam. viii. 17; 1 Kin. iv. 3.
xxi. 7 *marg.*	† *And it was*	† Heb. *And it was*, 1616, 1617.
xxiii. 10 *marg.* & ver. 11	Ziza	Zizah, 1638.
xxiii. 19	Jekamiam	Jekameam, 1629.
xxiii. 23	Jerimoth	Jeremoth, 1629.
xxiv. 6	Nathanael	Nethaneel, 1638. Cf. ch. xxvi. 4.
xxiv. 20	Jedeiah	Jehdeiah, 1629.
xxv. 2 *marg.*	by the hand	by the hands, 1629. Cf. ver. 6.
xxv. 4	Eliatha	Eliathah, 1638. Cf. ver. 27.
xxv. 22	Jerimoth [1]	Jeremoth, 1638.
xxvi. 1 *marg.*	*Abiasaph*	*Ebiasaph*, 1629.
xxvi. 16	Hosa	Hosah, 1629. Cf. ver. 10, ch. xvi. 38.
xxvi. 18 *init.*	And Parbar	At Parbar, 1638.
xxvii. 6	Amizabad	Ammizabad, 1638.
xxvii. 20	Azazziah	Azaziah, 1629.
xxvii. 22	Azariel	Azareel, 1629.
xxvii. 27	Sabdi (Zabdi 1612) the Ziphmite	Zabdi the Shiphmite, 1629.
xxvii. 29	Shetrai	Shitrai, 1638.
xxvii. 33, 34	Ahitophel	Ahithophel, 1638. Cf. 2 Sam. xv. 12, 31, &c.
xxix. 2	the silver for *things*	and the silver for *things*, 1629.
xxix. 29	‖ book of Samuel... † book of Nathan	‖ book of Samuel...book of Nathan, 1629.

2 Chronicles

iii. 10	most holy place	most holy house, 1629.
iv. 13 *marg.*	*upon the face*	add *of the pillars*. So Bagster 1846, also 1638 mod. in 1 Kin. vii. 42.

---

[1] In ver. 4 the vowel points are different, and "Jerimoth" correct.

of 1611 *amended in later editions.*

2 Chronicles	Reading of the Authorized Bible.	Variation of later editions.
vi. 27	the land	thy land, 1638.
xi. 8	Maresha	Mareshah, 1638.
xi. 10	Aialon	Aijalon, 1629. See p. 158 note 2.
xi. 20	Atthai	Attai, 1616 (not 1617, 1629 L., 1630), 1629 C.
xi. 20—22	Maacah	Maachah, 1629.
xiii. 2	Gibea	Gibeah, 1629.
xiii. 6	his LORD[1]	his lord, 1629.
xvii. 18	Jehoshabad	Jehozabad, 1629.
xviii. 7, 8	Jimla (Jimlah, 1630)	Imla, 1612, 1638. But cf. 1 Kin. xxii. 8, 9.
xx. 14 & xxix. 13	Jehiel	Jeiel, 1638[2].
xxiii. 1 & xxvi. 11 & xxxiv. 8	Maasiah	Maaseiah, 1638. Cf. ch. xxviii. 7. See also 1 Chr. xv. 18, 20; Ezra x. 18.
xxiv. 26	Shimeah	Shimeath, 1629.
xxv. 1	Jehoadan (Jehoiadan 1612)	Jehoaddan, 1638.
xxv. 23	Joahaz	Jehoahaz, 1629. Cf. ver. 25.
xxvii. 5 *marg.*	†*Heb. much*	† Heb. *this*, 1629.
xxviii. 11	wrath of God	wrath of the LORD, 1638.
xxviii. 22	this distress	his distress, 1638.
xxix. 12	Amashai...Jahalelel	Amasai, 1629, Jehalelel, 1638.
xxix. 15 *marg.*	*of the Lord*[1]	*of the LORD*, 1629.
xxix. 27	with the †instruments	with † the instruments, Bagster 1846.
xxxi. 5 *marg.*	*brought forth*	*brake forth*, 1629.
xxxi. 6	tithes of oxen	tithe of oxen, 1638.
xxxi. 14	Immah (Immath 1612)	Imnah, 1629.
xxxii. 5	prepared Millo	repaired Millo, 1616, 1617.

---

[1] A strange oversight (retained up to 1630) in a matter about which our Translators are usually more careful than later editors, viz. in representing יְהֹוָה by LORD (or GOD, see p. 147 note 1) but אֲדֹנָי by "Lord" or "lord." In ch. xxix. 15 *marg.* "Lord" is a misprint, the text being correct. Compare also Neh. i. 11; iii. 5; viii. 10. Ps. ii. 4, and Append. C, p. 223 note 3.

[2] See above, p. 159 note.

S.

2 Chronicles	Reading of the Authorized Bible.	Variation of later editions.
xxxii. 20	For this *cause*	And for this *cause*, 1638.
xxxiv. 12	Sechariah	Zechariah, 1612 (not 1613), 1629.
xxxv. 8	Zachariah	Zechariah, 1638.
xxxv. 9	Jehiel...Joshabad	Jeiel [1], 1638 ... Jozabad, 1629.
xxxvi. 17	Caldees	Chaldees, 1638.

Ezra		
ii. 2	Saraiah (Saraioh, 1617)	Seraiah, 1629. Cf. Neh. vii. 7 *marg.*
ii. 22	The children of Netophah	The men of Netophah, 1638.
ii. 24 *marg.*	Beth-Asmaveth	Beth-azmaveth, 1629. Cf. Neh. vii. 28.
ii. 40	Hodavia, *marg. Juda*	Hodaviah, *marg. Judah*, 1629. Cf. Neh. vii. 43 *marg.*
ii. 50	Nephushim	Nephusim, 1629.
[ii. 59	father's, 1769	fathers']. See above, p. 152 note.
iii. 2 *marg.*	*Josua* (but Josuah, Hagg. i. 1)	*Joshua*, 1613 (but Josuah, Hagg. i. 1).
iii. 5	that willingly offered, offered	that willingly offered, 1613.
iv. 9	Apharsathkites	Apharsathchites, 1629.
v. 12	Caldean	Chaldean, 1638.
vii. 4	Zeraiah	Zerahiah, 1638. Cf. ch. viii. 4.
vii. 9 *marg.*	† *He* (*Hee*, 1616) *was the foundation*, 1611, 1612, 1613, 1616, 1617	† Heb. was *the foundation*, 1629 C.: *was the f.*, 1629 L., 1630.
vii. 23 *marg.*	†Heb. *Whatsoever*	† Chald. *Whatsoever*, Bagster 1846.
viii. 13 & x. 43	Jehiel	Jeiel [1], 1638.
viii. 16	and for Jarib	also for Joiarib, 1638.
x. 18, 21, 22, 30	Maasiah	Maaseiah, 1638. So Neh. iii. 23; viii. 4, 7; x. 25; xi. 5, 7; xii. 41, 42 in 1611. See 2 Chr. xxiii. 1.

---

[1] See above, p. 159 note.

of 1611 amended in later editions.

Ezra	Reading of the Authorized Bible.	Variation of later editions.
x. 23	Kelitah	Kelita (אָ֖), 1638.
x. 25	Jesiah	Jeziah, 1638.
x. 33	Mattatha	Mattathah (הָ֖), 1638.
x. 35	Bedaiah	Bedeiah, 1638.
x. 38	Bennui (Benui, 1612)	Binnui, 1638.

Nehemiah

i. 11	O LORD (1611—1769)	O Lord, Oxf. 1835, Camb. 1858, Amer. 1867. See above, p. 147 note 1.
ii. 12	what God had put	what my God had put, 1638.
iii. 4, 21 & x. 5 & xii. 3	Merimoth	Meremoth.
iii. 5, & viii. 10 prim.	LORD	Lord, 1629. See above, p. 147 note 1.
iii. 6	Besodaiah	Besodeiah, 1638
iii. 15	Shallum	Shallun, 1629.
vi. 10	Mehetable, Camb. Synd. A. 3. 14, B.M. 1276. l. 4 only, but Mehetabel, Oxf. 1611—1630	Mehetabeel, 1638.
vi. 17 *marg.*	*multiplied letters*	*multiplied their letters*, 1629.
vii. 7	Nahum	Nehum, 1638.
vii. 24 *marg.*	*Jora*	*Jorah*. Bagster 1846. Cf. Ezra ii. 18.
vii. 31	Michmash	Michmas, 1638.
vii. 38	Senaa	Senaah, 1629. Cf. Ezra ii. 35.
vii. 39	Jedaia	Jedaiah, 1629. Cf. Ezra ii. 36.
vii. 46	Tabaoth	Tabbaoth, 1638. Cf. Ezra ii. 43.
vii. 54	Baslith	Bazlith, 1629.
[vii. 61	father's, 1769	fathers']. See above, p. 152 note.
ix. 7	Caldees	Chaldees, 1638.
ix. 17	the wonders	thy wonders, 1638.
x. 11	Micah	Micha, 1629. Cf. ch. xi. 17, 22.

11—2

Nehemiah	Reading of the Authorized Bible.	Variation of later editions.
x. 18	Hodiah (Hodaiah, 1616)	Hodijah, 1638. Cf. ver. 13.
xi. 8	Gabai	Gabbai, 1638.
xi. 13	Meshilemoth	Meshillemoth, 1638.
xi. 24	Meshezabel	Meshezabeel, 1612 (not 1613, &c.), 1638.
xi. 27	Hazer-Shual	Hazar-shual, 1638.
xi. 28	Ziglag	Ziklag, 1612, 1613 (not 1629 L., 1630).
xii. 3 *marg*.	*Sebaniah*	*Shebaniah*, 1629 (not 1638), 1744. Cf. ver. 14.
xii. 5	Madiah	Maadiah, 1638.
xii. 21, 36	Nethanael	Nethaneel, 1629.
xii. 36	Asarael	Azarael, 1629.
xii. 41	Zachariah	Zechariah, 1638.
Esther		
i. 8	for the king had appointed	for so the king had appointed, 1629.
i. 9, 11, 12, 15—17, 19; ii. 1, 4, 17	Vasthi (Vulg.)	Vashti, 1629.
i. 14	Tarshis	Tarshish, 1629.
iii. 1	Amedatha (Amm. 1629 C.)	Hammedatha, 1638. Cf. ch. viii. 5; ix. 10, 24.
iii. 10	Ammedatha	
iii. 4	Mordecai his matters	Mordecai's matters, 1762. See above, p. 111.
iv. 4	the sackcloth	his sackcloth, 1629.
Job		
i. 17	Caldeans	Chaldeans, 1638.
iv. 6	; the uprightness of thy ways (, 1616, 1617) and thy hope?	, thy hope, and the uprightness of thy ways?[1] 1638.

[1] In 1629, 1637 we find "; and the uprightness of thy ways, thy hope?" Though this has been noted as a mere error, the changes both of 1629 and 1638 (which all later editions have followed) are plainly intentional, and unique for their boldness. In the Paragraph Bible we have changed the comma after "hope" into a semicolon, although the Hebrew has only *Rebia* and *Athnakh* in the word before. Cf. Grote MS. pp. 130, 131.

of 1611 *amended in later editions.*

Job	Reading of the Authorized Bible.	Variation of later editions.
iv. 19	on them that	in them that, 1762. Cf. ver. 18.
xx. 21 *marg.*	*meats*	*meat*, 1629.
xxiv. 19 *marg.*	*take it*	*take*, 1629.
xxiv. 22	‖ and no *man*	and ‖ no *man*, Bagster 1846.
xxxiii. 22	His soul draweth	Yea, his soul draweth, 1638.
xxxix. 30	there *is* he	there *is* she, 1616, 1617[1].
xli. 5	wilt thou bind	or wilt thou bind, 1638.
xlii. 10 *marg.*	*added to Job*	*added all that* had been *to Job*, 1638.
Psalms		
ii. 6 & *marg.*	Sion	Zion, 1638[2]. Cf. Ps. lxix. 35.
xxix. 8, 9	‖ shaketh...to calve	shaketh ...... ‖ to calve, 1629.
xxxiv. 5	‖ They looked ... were lightened	They looked ... ‖ were lightened, 1629, 1638, Bagster 1846 only.
xxxvii. 3 *marg.*	*in truth and stableness*	*in truth*, or *stableness* (1629), 1638.
xxxix. 6 *marg.*	*image*	*an image*, 1629.
xlii. 6	Missar	Mizar, 1629.
xlii. 9	God, My (my 1612, 1630) rock, why	God my rock, Why (1629), 1638.
xliv. title	of Korah	of Korah, Maschil, 1629.
liii. 6	Jaakob (Jakob, 1630)	Jacob, 1629, 1638.
lix. title *marg.*	‖ *Or, to the chief Musician, destroy*	‖ *Destroy*, 1638. Cf. Ps. lviii. & lxxv. titles *marg.*
lxii. 10	become not vain	and become not vain, 1629.
lxv. 1	Sion	Zion, Amer. 1867 only. See below, note 2.
lxv. 9	and ‖ waterest it	‖ and waterest it. Bagster 1846.

[1] The "eagle" should have been masculine throughout vers. 27—30, but after having regarded it as feminine thus far, it is too late to change here.

[2] So Ps. ix. 11, 14; xiv. 7; xx. 2; xlviii. 2, 11, 12; l. 2; li. 18; liii. 6; lxxiv. 2; lxxvi. 2; lxxviii. 68; xcvii. 8. Elsewhere 1611 has "Zion," except in Ps. lxv. 1, where all have "Sion" except Amer. 1867. Cf. Ps. lxix. 35.

166   *Appendix A.*]   *Wrong readings of the Bible*

Psalms	Reading of the Authorized Bible.	Variation of later editions.
lxix. 32	seek good	seek God, 1617.
lxix. 35	Sion	Zion, 1762. Cf. p. 165 note 2.
lxxv. title *marg.*	‖ *Or, to the chief musician destroy not* (Altaschith, 1616, 1617 for [*destroy not*]) *a psalm or song for Asaph.*	‖ Or, *Destroy not.* ‖ Or, *for Asaph*, 1638.
[lxxxi. 12	hearts', 1769	heart's]. See p. 152 note.
lxxxix. 4 *marg.*	to generation and generation	Deest (ver. 4 being cited in ver. 1 *marg.*) 1762.
xcix. 2	all people	all the people, 1612 (not 1613, &c.), 1769.
cv. 30	The land	Their land, 1638.
cvii. 43	those things	these things, 1762.
cxix. 101	that I may keep	that I might keep, 1638.
cxxvii. 1 *text*	that† (‖ Camb. Synd. A. 3. 14; B. M. 1276. l. 4 only; 1613) build'	†that build.
marg.	†Heb. *are builders*	† Heb. that are *builders*, 1638.
cxxxii. 6	Ephrata	Ephratah, 1629. Cf. Ruth iv. 11; Mic. v. 2.
cxxxix. 7	fly, Camb. Synd. A. 3. 14, & B. M. 1276. l. 4 only, 1612, 1630; flie, Oxf. 1611, 1613—1629 L.	flee, 1629 C. Cf. Prov. xxviii. 17. See 2 Esdr. xiv. 15.
[cxl. 3	adders', 1769	adder's]. Cf. Isai. lix. 5 *marg.*
cxliii. 9	flie	flee, 1616 (not 1617), 1629.
Proverbs		
vi. 19	and him that soweth	and he that soweth, 1769.
vii. 21	With much fair speech	With her much fair speech, 1638.
x. 23	as a sport (a sport, 1629 C.)	as sport, 1638.
xi. 1	A †false	† A false, Bagster 1846. (So read.)
xx. 14	nought *bis*	naught *bis*, 1638.

of 1611 amended in later editions.

Proverbs	Reading of the Authorized Bible.	Variation of later editions.
[xxvi. 3	the fool's, 1762	the fools']. See p. 152 note.
xxvii. 26	thy field	the field, 1638.
xxviii. 17	flie	flee, 1617 (not 1629 L., 1630), 1629. Cf. Ps. cxxxix. 7.
[xxxi. 14	merchants', 1769 (merchant, 1762)	merchant's]. Cf. ch. xxx. 28. See p. 152 note.
Eccles.		
i. 5	the place	his place, 1638.
ii. 16	shall be forgotten	shall all be forgotten, 1629.
vii. 26 *marg.*	†*He* (*Hee*, 1613) *that is*, († Heb. *that is*, 1612, 1629 L., 1630)	† Heb. *he that is*, 1616 (not 1617), 1629.
viii. 17	seek *it* out	seek *it* out, yet he shall not find *it*; 1629.
Canticles		
iv. 6	mountains of myrrh	mountain of myrrh, 1629.
v. 12	rivers of water	rivers of waters, 1616 (not 1617, 1629 L., 1630), 1629.
vi. 5	*is* a flock	*is* as a flock, 1616, 1617. Cf. ch. iv. 1.
vi. 12 *marg.*	*the chariot*	*the chariots*, 1629.
Isaiah		
viii. 8 *marg.*	*stretching*	*stretchings*, 1629.
ix. 1	Galile. See Tobit i. 2.	Galilee, 1629.
x. 34	forests	forest, 1769.
xxiii. 13 & xliii. 14 & xlvii. 1, 5 & xlviii. 14, 20	Caldeans	Chaldeans, 1638 (1630, ch. xlvii. 5).
xxviii. 4	seeth it (*it*, 1638, 1744)	seeth, 1683 (Grote MS. p. 93), 1762.
xxviii. 26 *marg.*	as God	as *his* God, 1629.
xxix. 1 *text*	Woe...‖ the city	‖ Woe...‖ the city.
marg.	God: Or, *of the city*	God.‖ Or, *of the city*, 1629.

168   *Appendix A.]   Wrong readings of the Bible*

Isaiah	Reading of the Authorized Bible.	Variation of later editions.
xxxi. 9 *text*	he shall...‖ his strong (‖†his strong, 1629)	† he shall...‖ his strong.
marg.	‖ Or, *his strength:* Heb. *rocke*	† Heb. *his rock,* &c. Or, *his strength,* 1638.
xxxiv. 11	The cormorant	But the cormorant, 1629.
xxxviii. 17 *marg.*	me	*my soul,* 1638.
xliv. 2	Jesurun	Jeshurun 1616, Amer. 1867, only. See p. 150 note.
xliv. 20	feedeth of ashes	feedeth on ashes, 1762.
xlvii. 6	the yoke	thy yoke, 1629.
xlix. 13	heaven...God	heavens, 1629 ... the LORD, 1638.
liii. 6 *marg.*	he hath made	*hath made,* 1629.
lvii. 8	made a covenant	made thee *a covenant,* 1638[1].
[lix. 5 *marg.*	*adders',* 1769	*adder's,* Bagster 1846, Amer. 1867]. Cf. Ps. cxl. 3.
lxii. 8 *marg.*	*if he give*	*If I give,* 1629.
lxiv. 1	rent the heavens (see p. 102)	rend the heavens, 1762.
lxvi. 9	[bring...cause to bring	bring ... [cause to bring, 1629.
Jeremiah		
i. 13	the face thereof *was*	the face thereof *is,* 1762.
iv. 6	standards	standard, 1629.
xii. 15	will bring again	will bring them again, 1629.
xv. 4 *marg.*	*a moving*	*a removing,* 1629.
xix. 11	no place else to bury	no place to bury, 1629 C., 1638.
xxi. 4, 9	Caldeans	Chaldeans, 1638[2].
xxiii. 30	my word	my words, 1638.
xxiv. 5 *marg.*	*captivity*	*the captivity,* 1629.

[1] Cardwell (*Oxford Bibles,* p. 16) imputes this change to Bp. Lloyd in 1701. But he knew no more of Camb. 1638 than Bp. Turton did of Camb. 1629. See above, p. 41 note.

[2] So ch. xxii. 25; xxiv. 5; xxv. 12; xxxii. 4, 5, 24, 25, 28, 29, 43; xxxiii. 5; xxxv. 11; xxxvii. 5, 8—11, 13, 14; xxxviii. 2, 18, 19, 23; xl. 9, 10; xli. 3, 18; xliii. 3; l. 1, 8, 25, 35, 45; li. 4, 54; lii. 7, 8, 14, 17.

of 1611 amended in later editions.

Jeremiah	Reading of the Authorized Bible.	Variation of later editions.
xxvi. 18	Morashite	Morasthite, 1629. Cf. Micah i. 1.
ibid.	the high places	as the high places, 1629. Cf. Micah iii. 12.
xxviii. 6	the words	thy words, 1629.
xxxi. 14	goodness	my goodness, 1629.
xxxi. 18	thou *art* the Lord	for thou *art* the Lord, 1629.
xxxiii. 16 *marg.*	*Jehova*	*Jehovah*, 1629.
xxxv. 13	and inhabitants	and the inhabitants, 1616 (not 1617), 1629.
xxxv. 19 *text*	Jonadab...†want(†shall not want, 1629)	† Jonadab...want.
marg.	†Heb. *there shall not a man be cut off from*, &c.	† Heb. *There shall not be cut off from Jonadab the son of Rechab to stand*, &c., 1638.
xxxvii. 14 *marg.*	*or, lie*	*, or a lie*, 1638.
xxxviii. 16	So the king	So Zedekiah the king, 1638.
xl. 1	Ramath	Ramah, 1629 C. and L. (not 1630), 1638.
xl. 5	all the cities	the cities, 1638.
9, 10 *text*	ver. 9 † to serve	ver. 10. † to serve.
marg.	† Heb. *to stand before. And so verse 10*[1]	† Heb. *to stand before*, 1629—1769, Bagster 1846, American 1867.
xli. 1	Elishamah	Elishama, 1638.
xlii. 16	after you in Egypt	after you there in Egypt, 1629.
xlviii. 36	is perished	are perished, 1762.
xlix. 1	inherit God (so 1612, 1613)	inherit Gad, 1616, 1617 ...1629 C. and L.
l. 10 & li. 24, 35	Caldea	Chaldea, 1638.
li. 12	watchman	watchmen, 1629.
li. 27	her horses	the horses, 1638.
li. 30	their dwelling places	her dwelling places, 1629.
lii. 31	Jehoiakim *bis*	Jehoiachin *bis* (Jehoiakin 1616), 1629.

---

[1] This gross error of 1611—1630, though corrected long ago, is revived in most modern Bibles, e.g. D'Oyly & Mant 1817, Oxford 1835, Camb. 1858.

Lament.	Reading of the Authorized Bible.	Variation of later editions.
ii. 2 *marg.*	*made to couch*[1]	*made to touch*, 1629.
Ezekiel		
i. 2	Jehoiakins	Jehoiachins, 1629 C. and L. (Jehoiakims 1617, 1630), 1638.
i. 3 & xii. 13 & xxiii. 14, 23	Caldeans	Chaldeans, 1638 (1612, ch. i. 3).
i. 17	returned	turned, 1769. Cf. vers. 9, 12.
iii. 5 *marg.*	*deep of lips*	*deep of lip*, 1629.
iii. 6 *marg.*	*heavy language*	*heavy of language*, 1629.
iii. 11	thy people	the children of thy people, 1638.
iii. 26 *marg.*	‖ *A man*	† Heb. *a man*, 1629.
v. i.	take the balances	take thee balances, 1638.
vi. 8	that he may have	that ye may have, 1613.
xi. 24 & xvi. 29 & xxiii. 15, 16	Caldea	Chaldea, 1638 (1630, ch. xvi. 29).
xii. 19	of them that dwell	of all them that dwell, 1629.
xxi. 30 *marg.*	*cause to it to return*	*cause it to return*, 1629 C. and L.
[xxii. 10	fathers', 1769	father's]. See above, p. 152 note.
xxiii. 23	Shoah	Shoa, 1629.
xxiii. 43 *marg.*	‖ ‖ *Her whoredoms*	† † Heb. *her whoredoms*, 1629 C. & L. († † Heb. *whordomes*, 1617).
xxiv. 5	let him seethe	let them seethe, 1638.
xxiv. 7	poured it	poured it not, 1613.
xxiv. 25 *marg.*	*of the soul*	*of their soul*, 1638.
xxvi. 14	they shall be a place	thou shalt be a *place*, 1638.
xxvii. 6 *marg.*	*made hatches*	*made thy hatches*, 1629.
xxvii. 16 *marg.*	*works*	*thy works*, 1638.
xxvii. 22, 23	Shebah	Sheba, 1638.
xxvii. 27 *marg.*	*withall*, 1611 — 1630 (*withal*, 1744)	*with all*, 1629, 1638, 1762.

[1] This rendering might possibly stand, but that Tremellius, from whose version our Translators mostly derived their margin in the Old Testament (see above, p. 44), has Heb. *facit ut pertineat*. Hence "*couch*" is a mere misprint.

of 1611 *amended in later editions.* 171

Ezekiel	Reading of the Authorized Bible.	Variation of later editions.
xxxi. 4	† Heb. *conduits*	‖ Or, *conduits*, 1638. Cf. Job xxxviii. 25.
xxxii. 22	Ashur	Asshur, 1638.
xxxii. 25	all her multitudes	all her multitude, 1629.
xxxiv. 28	beasts of the land	beast of the land, 1762.
xxxiv. 31	my flock of my pasture	my flock the flock of my pasture, 1629.
xxxvi. 2	the enemy had said	the enemy hath said, 1630 (not 1629 C. & L., 1638, 1744), 1762.
xxxvi. 15	the nations	thy nations, 1629.
xxxix. 11	at that day	in that day, 1638.
xlii. 17	a measuring reed	the measuring reed, 1638. Cf. vers. 16, 18, 19.
xliii. 3 *marg.*	See chap. 9. 2, 5	See ch. 9. 1, 5, 1769.
xliv. 23	cause men	cause them, 1629.
[xliv. 30	the priest's, 1769	the priests'], Gorle. See above, p. 79 note 2, and p. 152 note.
xlvi. 13 *marg.*	*of his year*	*a son of his year*, 1638.
xlvi. 23	a new *building*	a row *of building*, 1638.
xlviii. 8	they shall offer	ye shall offer, 1638.

Daniel		
i. 4	Caldeans	Chaldeans, 1638[1].
i. 12	give † pulse	give us † pulse, 1629.
ii. 5 *marg.*	Cal. (² Camb. Synd. A. 3. 14)	Chald., 1638 (*Chal.* ch. ii. 14, in Camb. Synd. A. 3. 14: so 1616 in ch. v.).
ii. 8 *marg.* also	Cald.²	Chald., 1638.
v. 7, 9, 12, 16 *marg.*	Calde	Chaldee, 1638.
[ii. 41	potters', 1769	potter's]. See p. 152 note.
ii. 45 *marg.*	*in hand*, 1611—1769, Oxf. 1835, 1857, Lond. 1859	*in hands*, Bagster 1846, Camb. 1858, Amer. 1867. Cf. ver. 34 *marg.*

---

[1] So Dan. ii. 2, 4, 5, 10 (*bis*); iii. 8; iv. 7; v. 7, 11, 30; ix. 1.
[2] So *Cal.* or *Cald.* (the two issues of 1611 sometimes varying between these forms) Dan. ii. 8, 14, 18, 25 (*bis*), 28, 29, 31, 43, 44 (*bis*), 45; ch. iii. 4 (*bis*), 12, 19, 20, 22, 25, 26, 29 (*ter*), 30; iv. 2, 10, 14; v. 2, 6 (*ter*), 20, 31; vi. 8; vii. 1, 12, 15, 18, 19.

172 *Appendix A.*] *Wrong readings of the Bible*

Daniel	Reading of the Authorized Bible.	Variation of later editions.
iii. 15	a fiery furnace	a burning fiery furnace, 1638.
iii. 18	thy golden image	the golden image, 1629.
iii. 21 *marg.*	mantle...turbant	mantles...turbants, 1629.
v. 17 *marg.*	fee, as	fee, Bagster 1846.
vi. 13	the captivity of the children	the children of the captivity, 1629 C. (not L., 1630).
vi. 27 *marg.*	Heb.	Chald. Bagster 1846 only.
vii. 18 *marg.*	i. things (in things, 1630)	that is, things 1613 (not 1629 L.), 1629 C.
viii. 13 *marg.*	‖ The numberer	‖ Or, the numberer, 1744.
ix. 13 *marg.*	† Heb. intreated the face	† Heb. intreated we not the face of the, &c., 1638.
ix. 26 *marg.*	‖ Or, shall have nothing	‖ Or, and shall have nothing, 1629.
ix. 27 *marg.*	‖ Or, with the abominable armies¹	‖ Or, and upon the battlements shall be the idols of the desolator, 1762.
xi. 13 *marg.*	of times [, 1744] of years	of times [, 1769] even years, 1762.
xi. 24 *marg.*	peaceable or fat	peaceable and fat, 1629.
ibid.	think thoughts	think his thoughts, 1629.
xi. 38 *text*	But in his estate ... ‖ forces	But † in his estate ... ‖ † forces.
marg.	‖ Or, munitions. Heb. Mauzzim, or, as for the Almighty (Almightie 1617) God	† Heb. (*potius*, ‖ Or) as for the Almighty God ...‖ Or, munitions. † Heb. Mauzzim, 1638 (so 1744, but in the same order as 1611). To Mauzzim 1744, 1762, 1769 add "or, Gods (God's 1744, 1762) protectors."

---

¹ This rendering of the margin in 1611 comes, as usual, from Tremellius (above, p. 44), "*legiones detestationum desolantes.* Heb. *alam detestationum desolantem: ala pro copiis metaphoricè, ut Isai.* viii. 8." Whatever may be its value, it ought not to have been displaced by 1762 (which 1769 and the moderns have servilely followed) for something not so very good of its own. In the Paragraph Bible, we have retained both. See above, p. 46.

of 1611 amended in later editions.

Daniel	Reading of the Authorized Bible.	Variation of later editions.
xii. 8	O my Lord (so all before 1629 in ch. x. 16, 17, 19. Zech. iv. 4, 5, 13; vi. 4)	O my lord (אֲדֹנִי), 1744 only here.
xii. 13	in the lot	in thy lot, 1638.
Hosea		
iv. 4	this people	thy people, 1629.
vi. 9 *marg.*	*Sichem* (*Sychem*, 1630)	*Shechem*, 1629, C. (not L.).
ix. 11	flee away	fly (flie 1629, 1638) away, 1744.
x. 5 *marg.*	‖ *Chemarims*	‖ Or, *Chemarim* (*Chemarims*, 1629 C. and L., 1630), 1629, 1638.
xiii. 3	dew it passeth	dew that passeth, 1638 (but not in ch. vi. 4).
10 [*marg.*]	Hosea, 1762, 1769	Hoshea, Oxf. 1835, &c.
Joel		
i. 16	your eyes	our eyes, 1629.
iii. 13	the wickedness	their wickedness, 1629.
Amos		
i. 3 *marg.*	*he,* (*hee* 1616, 1617) *for four*	*yea for four*, 1629.
i. 11	and kept	and he kept, 1762.
viii. 3	songs of the Temples (temples, 1629)	songs of the temple, 1638.
ix. 5	all that dwelleth [1]	all that dwell, 1629.
Jonah		
i. 16 *marg.*	*a sacrifice*	*a sacrifice unto the* LORD, 1638.

---

[1] So in Amos vi. 7 Camb. Synd. A. 3. 14 alone has "first that goeth" for "first that go" of Oxf. 1611, 1612, 1613, 1616, 1617, &c. See Appendix B, p. 212.

174 Appendix A.] Wrong readings of the Bible

Micah	Reading of the Authorized Bible.	Variation of later editions.
v. 2	Beth-leem	Beth-lehem, 1629 C. and L.
vii. 3 *marg.*	*the soul*	*his soul,* 1629.
Nahum		
i. 1 *marg.*	Lord	LORD, 1638. See above, p. 147 note 1.
i. 4	floure	flower, 1629. See 2 Esdr. xv. 50.
ii. 2 *marg.*	*and the pride*	*as the pride,* 1629.
ii. 3 *marg.*	† † Heb. *fiery*	‖ ‖ Or, *fiery,* 1629.
iii. 17	The crowned	Thy crowned, 1629.
Habakkuk		
i. 9 *marg.*	*init.* † Heb.	‖ Or, († *before the following* Heb.), 1638.
iii. 1 *text*	Sigionoth	Shigionoth, 1762.
marg.	*Shigianoth*	*Shigionoth,* 1629.
iii. 13	†by discovering	by †discovering, 1629 —1762, Bagster 1846 (not 1769, mod.).
iii. 19	LORD God 1611— 1630, 1762, 1769, moderns	Lord GOD, 1629 C., 1638, 1744. Cf. Zeph. i. 7. See p. 147 note 1.
Zephaniah		
iii. 11	mine holy	my holy, 1629 C. & L., 1630. Cf. *marg.*
Haggai		
i. 1, 12, 14 & ii. 2	Josuah. Cf. Ezra iii. 2 *marg.*	Joshua, 1629 (ver. 12, 1629 L.).
Zechariah		
i. 1, 7	Barachiah	Berechiah, 1762[1].
iv. 12 *marg.*	*by the hand*	*by the hand of,* Bagster 1846: cf. ch. vii. 7, 12 *marg.*

[1] Thus 1611 reads in all the other nine places where the name occurs, except in 1 Chr. vi. 39, "Berachiah."

Zechariah	Reading of the Authorized Bible.	Variation of later editions.
vii. 7	of the plain	and the plain, 1638.
viii. 19 *marg.*	††Heb. *solemn*	‖ ‖ Or, *solemn*, 1762.
viii. 21 *marg.*	*the face*	*the face of the LORD*, 1638.
xi. 2	all the mighty	the mighty, 1638.
xiv. 10	Hananiel	'Hananeel, 1762.
Malachi		
iii. 4	offerings	offering, 1638.
iv. 2	and shall go forth	and ye shall go forth, 1617, 1629, &c.
1 Esdras		
i. 6, 11	Moyses	Moses, 1629.
i. 8	Siclus	Syelus, 1638.
i. 9, 12 *marg.*		Or, *prefixed to marginal note*, 1638. So 1629, ch. v. 73; vi. 31; viii. 16, 50, 61, 63.
i. 25	Pharao	Pharaoh, 1629.
[i. 31	father's, 1762, 1769	fathers' (πατρικῷ)]. Cf. 2 Chr. xxvi. 24.
i. 52	Caldees	Chaldees, 1638. So ch. iv. 45; vi. 15, 1611, 1612, 1613: not 1629, 1630.
ii. 8	tribes of Benjamin	tribe of Benjamin, 1769.
ii. 9	very free	very many free, 1629.
iii. 15 *marg.*	*counsel*	*council*, 1744 (*councel*, 1638)[1].
iv. 43	the kingdom	thy kingdom, 1629.
v. 5	Joachim...Juda...*marg.* *Juda*, Oxf. 1611	Joacim, 1629, 1630... Judah, 1629...*marg. Judah*, Camb. Synd. A. 3. 14, 1616, &c.
v. 9 *marg.*	*Shephatia*	*Shephatiah*, 1638.
v. 15 *marg.*	*Ater-*	*Ater-*, 1629 (not 1630), 1638.
v. 18 *marg.*	*Asmaveth*	*Azmaveth*, 1629, 1630.
v. 19 *marg.*	*Kiriashiarim*	*Kiriathjarim*, 1629 (not 1630), 1638.

[1] Gk. χρηματιστηρίῳ : Vulg. *concilio;* Junius *consilio.* Similar confusion between the words occurs in Matt. v. 22; Mark xiv. 55.

176   *Appendix A.*]   *Wrong readings of the Bible*

1 Esdras	Reading of the Authorized Bible.	Variation of later editions.
v. 19	Pyra[1]	Pira, 1629 (not 1630). Aldus πίρας.
v. 20	Cyrama	Cirama, 1629. Aldus κιραμά.
v. 20 *marg.*	Rama	*Ramah*, 1613 only. Cf. Ezra ii. 26.
v. 20 *marg.*	Gabah	*Gaba*, 1613 (not 1616, 1617, 1630), 1629. Cf. Neh. vii. 30.
v. 26 *marg.*	Hodoviah	*Hodaviah*, 1629. Cf. Ezra ii. 40.
v. 30 *marg.*	Giddes	*Giddel*, 1629. Cf. Ezra ii. 47.
v. 31 *marg.* & 31	Neumin...Asipha	*Meunim*, 1629 (*Mehunim*, Ezra ii. 50)... Acipha, 1629. Aldus ἀκιφά.
v. 32	Chareus	Charcus, 1629. Aldus χαρκούς.
v. 33	Jocli	Jecli, 1629. Aldus ἰεηλί.
v. 37	the sons of Ban	the son of Ban, 1629.
v. 38	*marg. note* Barz- *referred to* Addus	*marg. note* Barz- *referred to* Berzelus, 1630 only.
v. 66	Juda	Judah, 1612 (not 1613), 1629. Cf. ver. 5.
v. 69 *marg.*	Asar-haddon, ch. iv. 3	Esar-haddon, Ezra iv. 2, 1744.
vi. 3 *marg.*	Shether-	Shethar-, 1638. Cf. Ezra v. 3.
vii. 9 *marg.*	Esdr.	Ezra, 1629.
viii. 2	Eleasar	Eleazar, 1629, 1630. Cf. vers. 43, 63.
viii. 6	of king Artaxerxes (Bishops' Bible)	of Artaxerxes, 1629.
viii. 29, 32 *marg.*	Shecheniah	Shechaniah, 1638 (1629 in ver. 32).

---

[1] This word is wanting in the Roman edition (1586—7), the Alexandrian MS., the Vulgate, and Junius. Our Translators (after the Bishops' Bible) followed the text of Aldus (1518) in this book, as plainly appears above, p. 47. 1 Esdras is not contained in the Complutensian (1517—22). Yet how could Junius say, in his Preface to the Apocryphal books (1592) "Hezrae libros duos me tacente evincit veritas: quos neque Hebraicè neque Graecè vidi, aut fuisse visos memini legere"? See above, p. 44.

of 1611 *amended in later editions.* 177

1 Esdras	Reading of the Authorized Bible.	Variation of later editions.
viii. 40	†Bago *in text, but no marg.*	*marg.* †Heb. *Bogvai,* 1613, 1616, 1617. †Heb. *Bogua,* 1630. †Heb. *Bigvai,* 1629, 1638, &c. Cf. Ezra viii. 14.
viii. 41 *marg.*	*Ahave*	*Ahava,* 1629. Cf. Ezra viii. 15.
viii. 44 *marg.*	‖ *Or, these mens names*	These men's names, 1629 (not 1630).
viii. 45	Saddeus...who was... the treasury	‖Saddeus...‖who was... ‖the treasury, 1629.
viii. 47 *marg.*	*Sherebia*	*Sherebiah,* 1613 (not 1616, 1617, 1630), 1629, &c. Cf. Ezra viii. 18.
viii. 48 *marg.*	*Hashabia* (referred to ver. 47)	*Hashabiah,* 1630 (not 1629, which sets the reference right). Cf. Ezra viii. 19.
viii. 69	Chanaanites	Canaanites, 1629. See Judith v. 9.
ix. 4 *marg.*	‖ *utterly destroyed*	Or, *utterly destroyed,* 1744 only.
ix. 5	Juda	Judah 1769. Cf. ch. v. 5.
ix. 21	Hierel	Hiereel, 1629. LXX. ἱερεήλ.
ix. 22	Ellionas (ἑλλίονας Ald.)	Elionas, 1629, 1630. LXX. (*Fritzsche,* 1871), ἐλιωναῖς.
ix. 22 *marg.*, 23	Josabad	Jozabad, 1629 (1630, 1762, &c., ver. 23 only), 1638, 1744. Cf. ver. 29.
ix. 26 *marg.*	*Malchuah* (*Malchiath,* 1744)	*Malchiah,* 1629. Cf. Ezra x. 25.
ix. 28 *marg.*	*Sabad*	*Zabad,* 1629. Cf. Ezra x. 27.
ix. 30	Many	Mani, 1629.
ix. 31	Balunus	Balnuus, 1629. Aldus βάλνουος.
ix. 32	Milchias	Melchias, 1629. Cf. ver. 44.
ix. 34	Selenias...Azailus	Selemias...Azaelus, 1629. So Aldus.
ibid.	Josiphus (Ἰώσιφος Ald.)	Josephus, 1769.
ix. 49 *marg.*	*the priest and scribe*	*the priest the scribe,* 1762. Cf. Neh. viii. 9.

S.   12

2 Esdras	Reading of the Authorized Bible.	Variation of later editions.
i. 10	Pharao	Pharaoh, 1629.
i. 13	Moyses	Moses, 1629, 1630.
i. 31	new moon	new moons, 1629 (Vulg., Bishops' Bible).
ii. 7 *marg.*	‖ *Sacrament*	‖Or, *Sacrament*, 1612, 1613 (not 1616—1630), 1638.
ii. 8	Gomorrhe	Gomorrha, 1630 (Gomorah, 1612. Gomorrah, 1629).
ii. 10 & x. 47	Hierusalem. See Matt. ii. 1	Jerusalem, 1629 (1616, in ch. x. 47).
iii. 16	Isahac (*bis*)	Isaac (*bis*), 1638. See Mark xii. 26.
iii. 18	depth	depths, 1629 (Vulg.).
iii. 19 *marg.*	‖ *And to all*	‖ Or, *and to all*, 1744.
iii. 27	the city	thy city, 1629.
iv. 21 *marg.*	‖ *The land*	‖Or, *the land.*
iv. 36 *marg.*	‖ *Jeremiel*	‖Or, *Jeremiel*, 1629.
iv. 47	unto you	unto thee, 1638 (*tibi*, Vulg.).
v. 1 *marg.*	‖ *Shall be*	‖Or, *shall be*, 1638.
v. 12 *marg.*	rejected	directed, 1629 (*dirigentur*, Vulg.).
vi. 49 *marg.*	‖ *Behemoth*	‖Or, *Behemoth*, Cambr. 1863.[1]
vii. 37 *marg.*	Achor	Achor, 1616, 1617, &c.
viii. 31, 32 *marg.*	‖ *Are sick* ‖ *Be willing*	‖Or, *are sick.* ‖Or, *be willing*, 1638.
viii. 43	the rain	thy rain, 1629.
viii. 53 *marg.*	‖ Or, *grave*	‖Or, *the grave*, 1638.
x. 2 *marg.*	countrymen [, 1630] citizens	countrymen, Lat. *citizens*, 1629.
xiii. 14	wonders	these wonders, 1629.
xiv. 15	flie. But cf. ch. xv. 32; xvi. 41	flee, 1629[2] (*transmigrare*).
xv. 41	fleeing. Cf. Rev. xii. 14	flying, 1629 (*volantes*).
xv. 50	as floure (*sicut flos*), so 1612	as a floure, 1613, 1617: as a flowre, 1616, 1630: as a flower, 1629, 1638. See Nah. i. 4.

---

[1] See above, p. 38.
[2] A like variation is found in Ps. cxxxix. 7. Prov. xxviii. 17. Wisd. i. 5. Ecclus. xi. 10. Baruch vi. 55. 1 Macc. i. 53. 2 Macc. ix. 4. 1 Tim. vi. 11.

of 1611 *amended in later editions.* 179

2 Esdras	Reading of the Authorized Bible.	Variation of later editions.
xvi. 28	clefts of rocks	clefts of the rocks, 1629.
xvi. 42	as he that had (*qui... capiat*)	as he that hath, 1769.
xvi. 52	yet a little iniquity	yet a little, and iniquity, 1616, 1617.
Tobit		
i. 2	Galile[1]	Galilee, 1638.
iv. 12	Isaak	Isaac, 1616 (not 1617), 1629, 1630.
v. 15	the wages	thy wages, 1629 (σοι ἐπὶ τὸν μισθόν).
vi. 3 *marg.*	‖ *Cast*	‖ Or, *cast*, 1616.
viii. 10	lest he	lest he also, 1629.
xiii. 18	Halleluiah	Alleluia, 1638. Cf. Rev. xix. 1, 3, 4, 6.
xiv. 10 *marg.*	*Nitsban*	*Nitzba*, 1629 (*sic* Junius). See p. 51 note.
Judith		
Judith, title, ch. viii. 1, *passim*	Judeth	Judith, 1744.
i. 6	Elimeans	Elymeans, 1629.
i. 8 & xv. 5	Galile[1]	Galilee, 1638.
i. 8	Esdrelon (Vulg.)	Esdrelom, 1638. Cf. ch. iii. 9 *marg.*; iv. 6 *marg.*
ii. 7 *marg.*	‖ *Or, after the manner*	‖ After the manner, 1629.
ii. 28	Aschalon	Ascalon, 1629.
v. 6, 7	Caldeans...Caldea	Chaldeans ... Chaldea, 1638.
v. 9, 10, 16	Channan...Chanaanite	Canaan ...... Canaanite, 1629 only (ver. 3, Canaan, 1611). Cf. 1 Esdr. viii. 69.
v. 16	Pheresite	Pherezite, 1638.
vii. 7	fountain	fountains, 1629.
vii. 18	Dotha-em	Dothaim, 1638. Cf. ch. viii. 3.
viii. 5	on sackcloth on	on sackcloth upon, 1629.

[1] So 1 Kin. ix. 11. Isa. ix. 1. Judith i. 8; xv. 5. 1 Macc. x. 30; xii. 47 (*bis*); 49. Mark xv. 41; xvi. 7. Luke iv. 44. Acts xiii. 31 (Camb. Synd. A. 3. 14). Yet 1611 often has "Galilee," e.g. seven times in 1 Macc. v.

180 Appendix A.] Wrong readings of the Bible

Judith	Reading of the Authorized Bible.	Variation of later editions.
viii. 29	all thy people	all the people, 1629.
x. 5 *marg.*	‖ *Wrapped*	‖ Or, *wrapped*, 1638.
xii. 11	Ebrewe (Ebrew 1612, 1616, 1629)	Hebrew, 1630, 1638.
xiv. 10	the foreskin of his flesh	the flesh of his foreskin, 1629.
xv. 4	Bethomasthem	Betomasthem, 1638 (Βαιτ-).
xv. 13	before the people	before all the people, 1629.
xvi. 8 *marg.*	† Gr. *or miter*	† Gr. *mitre*, 1629.
xvi. 24	to all them that are nearest	to all them that were nearest, 1612, 1616, 1617, &c.
Esther		
Esther, title,	Calde	Chaldee, 1638.
xi. 1	Ptolomeus (*ter*). Cf. 1 Macc. i. 18	Ptolemeus (*ter*), 1638.
Wisdom		
i. 5	flie (φεύξεται)	flee, 1629[1].
xii. 12	to be ‖ revenged[2]	‖ to be revenged, 1629 (not 1630), 1638 (not 1744), 1762, 1769, Oxf. 1835, not D'Oyly and Mant 1817, Camb. 1863.
[xv. 4	painter's 1762	painters' (σκιαγράφων)].
xvi. 11 *marg.*	† *Hebr.* († Heb. 1616—1630)	† Gr., 1638.
xvi. 29	unfaithful (ἀχαρίστου)[3]	unthankful, 1629 (not 1630), 1638.

---

[1] See p. 178 note 2.

[2] The errors of 1611 and its earlier reprints in regard to these marginal marks are numberless. We note only the most important, or those remarkable for other causes, adopting in silence the corrections made in other places, chiefly in the editions of 1629 C. and 1638.

[3] Evidently an oversight. Vulg. and Junius have "ingrati," the Bishops' Bible "unthankful." Cf. Luke vi. 35. 2 Tim. iii. 2.

of 1611 *amended in later editions.* 181

Ecclus.	Reading of the Authorized Bible.	Variation of later editions.
iv. 16	his generation 1611—1769	his generations, Camb. 1863.
xi. 10	flying (διαδράς)	fleeing, 1629[1].
[xiii. 19	lion's 1762, 1769	lions' (λεόντων)[2]].
xx. 13	‖ *Lost*	‖ Or, *lost*, 1638.
xxiii. 27	commandment	commandments, 1629.
xxiv. 25	Physon	Phison, 1629.
xxv. 9	of him that will hear	of them that will hear, 1629.
xxvii. 5	vessel	vessels, 1629.
xxix. 6	If he prevail	‖ If he prevail, 1613, 1616 (not 1617), 1629.
xxxv. 15	Doeth not the tears (p. 110 note 1)	Do not the tears, 1638.
xxxv. 18	till he hath smitten	till he have smitten, 1629, 1640.
xliii. 5 *marg.*	†Gr. *he stayed*	‖ Or, *he stayed*, 1629.
xlv. 15	Moises (Moyses 1616, 1617, 1630)	Moses, 1613, 1629, 1638.
xlvii. 4	Goliah	Goliath, 1629 (Γολιάθ).
xlviii. 12	Elizeus	Eliseus, 1638.
xlix. 4	Ezechias	Ezekias, 1613, 1616 (not 1617, 1630, 1634), 1629, 1640. Cf. ch. xlviii. 17, 22.
xlix. 8	Ezechiel	Ezekiel, 1612 (not 1613, 1634), 1629, 1640.
li. 12	deliverest (ἐξεῖλου)	deliveredst, 1616 (not 1617, 1634, 1640), 1629, 1630.
Baruch		
i. 2 & Song ver. 25	Caldeans	Chaldeans, 1638.
[Baruch i. 4	king's sons 1762, 1769	kings' sons (βασιλέων)]. Cf. 1 Macc. x. 89.
i. 10 *marg.*	*a meat offering*	that is, *a meat offering*, 1744.
iv. 2	take heed	take hold, 1629 (ἐπιλαβοῦ).
vi. 45	workman	workmen, 1762.
vi. 55	fly (flie 1613—1630)	flee, 1629 (φεύξονται)[1].

[1] See p. 178 note 2.
[2] Ecclus. xxxviii. 33 judges' (1769) may stand, since Cod. 248 and the Complutensian edition read δικαστῶν, against δικαστοῦ of Codd. א B. Vulg., δυνάστου of Cod. A.

Song	Reading of the Authorized Bible.	Variation of later editions.
Title and ver. 1	[And they walked in the midst of the fire, praising God and blessing the Lord]... [Then Azarias (Azaria 1617) stood up] ...[And Nabuchadonosor (Nabuchodonosor, Oxf. 1611, 1612, 1616, 1630)]	—fell down bound into the midst of the burning fiery furnace [1769 *adds* ver. 23] — ... And they walked ... Then Nebuchadnezzar, ver. 24. 1638.
ver. 23 *marg.*	*naptha...c.* (*ca.* 1616) 105	*naphtha* .... cap. 105, 1629.
ver. 66 *marg.*	grave	the grave, 1744 (not 1762), 1769.
Hist. of Susanna		
ver. 56	Chanaan	Canaan, 1629, Ostervald 1808 only. See Judith v. 9.
Bel and Dragon		
ver. 27	fat	and fat, 1629.
Prayer of Manasseh		
line 36	iniquity	iniquities, 1762.
1 Maccab.		
i. 18	Ptolomee (*bis*) [Camb. Synd. A. 3. 14, Potlomee *secundo loco*]	Ptolemee, 1629. Cf. Esther xi. 1; ch. iii. 38; x. 51, 55, 57; xi. 3; xv. 16. 2 Macc. i. 10; iv. 45, 46.
i. 53	flie	flee, 1629^1 ($\phi\epsilon\upsilon\gamma\alpha\delta\epsilon\upsilon\tau\eta\rho\iota\psi$). Cf. ch. iv. 5.
ii. 26, 54	Phineas (Phinchas 1616, & 1630 ver. 26)	Phinees, 1638. Cf. 2 Esdr. i. 2.

[1] See p. 178 note 2.

1 Maccab.	Reading of the Authorized Bible.	Variation of later editions.
ii. 29 *marg.*	*sit, abide*	*sit*, or *abide*, 1638.
ii. 70	sepulchre	sepulchres, 1629 (τάφοις).
iii. 28 *marg.*	† *Gr. or at*	† Gk. *at*, 1629.
iii. 38	Ptoleme (Ptolomee 1616, 1630)	Ptolemee, 1629.
iv. 9	Pharao	Pharaoh, 1629.
iv. 18	your enemies	our enemies, 1629.
iv. 29	met with them	met them with, 1613, &c.
v. 3 *marg.*	‖ Or, *Arabathene*	‖ Or, *Arabathane*, 1629, Vulg., Bishops' Bible (-tthane, 1638, mod.).
	fin. Arabettine	*Akrabattine*, 1629.
v. 9	Galead	Galaad, 1612. Cf. vers. 17, 20, &c.
v. 65	townes thereof (πύργους)	towers (towres, 1638) thereof, 1629.
vi. 1	Elimais	Elymais, 1638.
vi. 5	brought in tidings (ἀπαγγέλλων αὐτῷ)	brought him tidings, 1629.
vii. 24	the coast	the coasts, 1629.
vii. 45	Gasera (Aldus Γάσηρα)	Gazera, 1638. Cf. ch. iv. 15.
viii. 4	that place	the place, 1629.
viii. 8	Lidia	Lydia, 1616 (not 1617), 1629.
viii. 17	Accas	Accos, 1629.
viii. 26	covenant	covenants, 1769.
ix. 4 & 35 *marg.* & x. 1 & 81 *marg.*	Jos. (*Josep.* 1611, ch. xi. 34)	Joseph. (1613, 1616, 1630), 1629.
ix. 35	Nabbathites	Nabathites, 1616 (not 1617), 1629. Cf. ch. v. 25.
ix. 49 *marg.*	*ant.* (*anti.* 1617)	Antiq., 1762. Cf. ch. xi. 34.
ix. 50 *marg.*	*Techea*, Camb. Synd. A. 3. 14, &c., 1617, *Techoa*, Oxf. 1611, 1612, 1613, 1616	Tecoa, 1629.
ix. 68	travail	travel, 1629—1762, not 1769 or moderns (ἔφοδος). See above, p. 97
x. 25	unto him	unto them, 1629, 1630.
x. 30 & xii. 47 (*bis*), 49	Galile	Galilee, 1638. See Tobit i. 2.

1 Maccab.	Reading of the Authorized Bible.	Variation of later editions.
x. 51, 55	Ptoleme (Ptolome ver. 55, 1630)	Ptolemee, 1616 (not 1629), 1638. See ch. i. 18.
x. 57	Ptolome	Ptolemee, 1638 (Ptoleme, 1629).
x. 58	gave unto him (1612 — 1762), Camb. 1863	he gave unto him, 1630, 1769, Ostervald 1808, D'Oyly and Mant 1817, Oxf. 1835.
[x. 89	the king's blood, 1762, 1769	the kings' blood]. Cf. Baruch i. 4.
xi. 3, 8, 13, 15—18	Ptolomee (Ptololmee ver. 8, 1612, Ptolmee ver. 13, 1616)	Ptolemee, 1629, 1617, ver. 4 (Oxf. 1611, ver. 18).
xi. 34	Lidda	Lydda, 1616 (not 1617 —1630), 1638.
xi. 56	Triphon	Tryphon, 1616 (not 1617), 1629.
xi. 62	the chief men	their chief men, 1629.
xi. 70	Absolon (Absalon 1630)	Absalom, 1629 ('Αψαλώμου). Cf. ch. xiii. 11.
xii. 7 *marg.*	look...Ant.	See, 1744 ... Antiq., 1613.
xii. 8 *marg.*	Jos. Ant.	Joseph. (1613 &c.). Antiq. (1638).
xii. 19 *marg.* xii. 31 *marg.*	} Jos.	Joseph., 1629.
xii. 19	Omiares	Oniares, 1629.
xii. 28 *marg.*	lib. ant. 13. 9 (Ant. lib. 1616, &c.)	Antiq. lib. 13. cap. 9, 1762.
xiii. 11	Absolom (Vulg.)	Absalom, 1613, 1629.
xiii. 15 *marg.*	officers	offices, 1629, 1630.
xv. 16	Ptolome, Camb. Synd. A. 3. 14, &c., 1617, -omee, Oxf. 1611, 1612,1613, 1616, also Ptolomeus	Ptolemee, 1638 (Ptoleme, 1629).
xvi. 11	Ptolomeus	Ptolemeus, 1629.
xvi. 16, 18, 21	Ptolome	Ptolemee, 1638 (Ptoleme, 1629). Cf. ch. i. 18.
xv. 22	The same thing	The same things, 1629.
xv. 23	Sycion ... Phaseilis ... Sidee...Gortina	Sicyon (1629) ... Phaselis (1638) ... Side (1638) ..... Gortyna, 1616, 1629 (not 1617).
xvi. 10 *marg.*	set fire	set on fire, 1629.
xvi. 14	seventh year	seventeenth year, 1769.

of 1611 *amended in later editions.* 185

2 Maccab.	Reading of the Authorized Bible.	Variation of later editions.
i. 10	hundreth[1]...eight	hundred...eight, 1629.
i. 10 & iv. 21 & ix. 29 & x. 12	Ptolomeus	Ptolemeus, 1629 (except ch. i. 10), 1638. So 1611 in ch. viii. 8, 1630 in ch. iv. 21. See 1 Macc. i. 18.
i. 29 & ii. 4, 8, 10 & vii. 6	Moises (Moyses 1613 —1630 *ferè*)	Moses, 1629. So 1611 in ch. vii. 30 and 1612 in ch. i. 29 & vii. 6.
iv. 4	Appolonius	Apollonius, 1612, 1613, 1616 (not 1617), &c.
iv. 21	Manastheus (Monastheus 1630)	Menestheus, 1629.
iv. 30	Tharsus (Tharsos 1629)	Tarsus, 1638.
iv. 40	on Auranus	one Auranus, 1629 (not 1630), 1638.
iv. 45, 46 & vi. 8	Ptolomee (Ptolome 1630, ch. vi. 8)	Ptolemee, 1629.
vi. 2 *marg.*	*Jos....c.*	Joseph., 1744 ... cap. 1613.
viii. 33	Calisthenes	Callisthenes, 1638.
ix. 4	flie (πεφυγαδευκότων)	flee, 1629, 1630. See 2 Esdr. xiv. 15 note.
xi. 4	thousand (*bis*)	thousands of (*bis*), 1629.
xi. 9	altogether	all together, 1629 (ὁμοῦ δὲ πάντες).
xii. 15	Josua	Joshua, 1629.
xii. 26 *marg.*	*i.* (Or, 1613)	That is, 1629, 1630.
xii. 35 *marg.*	‖ *Put by his army*	‖ Or (1638) *put by his arm:* or, 1629 (not 1630), 1638.
xiv. 16	Dessaro	Dessau, 1629 (Δεσσαού).
xv. 3	this most ungracious	the most ungracious, 1629.

---

[1] See p. 147 note 2. But "hundreth" is only an old way of spelling "hundred" and is often found in 1611, as in Esther xvi. 1; Ecclus. xvi. 10: especially in these reckonings by the Greek era, 1 Macc. i. 10, 20, 54; ii. 70; iii. 37; iv. 52; vi. 16 (not vi. 20); vii. 1; x. 67; xi. 19. 2 Macc. xiii. 1; xiv. 4.

S. Matthew	Reading of the Authorized Bible.	Variation of later editions.
i. 5	Boos (*bis*)	Booz (*bis*), 1629.
i. 9	Achas (*bis*)	Achaz (*bis*), 1629.
ii. 1	Hierusalem *passim* [1]	Jerusalem, 1629 (not 1629 L., 1630), 1638.
iv. 13, 15	Nephthali	Nephthalim, 1638.
v. 22	Racha	Raca, 1638.
v. 22	counsell (counsel 1744)	council, 1629 L., 1630 (councel 1612, 1629, 1638). See 1 Esdr. iii. 15 note.
vi. 3	thy right doeth	thy right hand doeth, ✓ 1613 (not 1616, 1617), 1629, 1630.
xii. 41	Nineve (Ninive 1616)	Nineveh, 1629 (not Luke xi. 32).
[xiv. 9 & Mark vi. 26	oath's, 1762 &c.	oaths']. See p. 152 note.
xiv. 34	Genesaret	Gennesaret, 1629 C., 1638. Cf. Mark vi. 53; Luke v. 1.
xvi. 16	Thou art Christ	Thou art the Christ, 1762. Cf. ver. 20.
xvi. 19	whatsoever thou shalt loose	and whatsoever thou shalt loose, 1616 (1617), 1629.
xviii. 28 *marg.*	7. *d. ob.* Cf. ch. xx. 2	seven pence halfpenny, 1616 (not 1617), 1629.
xx. 29	Hiericho	Jericho, 1616 (not 1617), 1629.
xxvi. 75	the words of Jesus	the word of Jesus, 1762.
xxvii. 22	Pilate said	Pilate saith, 1629.
xxvii. 46	Lamasabachthani (Lamm-, 1613)	lama sabachthani, 1629.
S. Mark		
ii. 4	for press	for the press, 1743. Cf. Luke viii. 19.
v. 6	he came	he ran, 1638.
vii. 3 *marg.*	*Theophilact*	Theophylact, 1629.

[1] "Hierusalem" is the constant form in the N. T. except in Acts xxv. 1 (Camb. Synd. A. 3. 14, &c., 1612, 1613, 1617; not Oxf. 1611, 1616). 1 Cor. xvi. 3. Gal. i. 17, 18; ii. 1; iv. 25, 26. Heb. xii. 22. See 2 Esdr. ii. 10.

of 1611 *amended in later editions.*

S. Mark	Reading of the Authorized Bible.	Variation of later editions.
x. 18	there is no man good, but one	there is none good but one, 1638[1].
x. 46	high ways side	high-way side, 1629. Cf. Matt. xiii. 4.
xi. 8	branches of the trees	branches off the trees, 1638 (ἐκ).
xii. 26 & Luke xx. 37	Isahac	Isaac, 1612 & 1617 (Mark), 1629. So 2 Esdr. iii. 16.
xiv. 32	Gethsemani (Clementine Vulg.)	Gethsemane, 1616 (not 1617, 1630), 1638. Cf. Matt. xxvi. 36.
xiv. 55	counsel	councell, 1630, councel, 1629 C. (not L.), 1638, council, 1743. See 1 Esdr. iii. 15 note.
xv. 34	lamasabachthani	lama sabachthani, 1629.
xv. 41 & xvi. 7 & Luke iv. 44 & Acts xiii. 31 (Camb. Synd. A. 3. 14, &c.)	Galile	Galilee, 1629 (1612 *ter*). See Tobit i. 2 note.
S. Luke		
i. 3	understanding of things	understanding of all things, 1629.
i. 5, 7, 13, 24, 36, 40, 41 (*bis*), 57	Elizabeth	Elisabeth, 1638.
i. 74	out of the hands	out of the hand, 1762.
ii. 25, 34	Simeon	Symeon.
iii. 21	and it came to pass	it came to pass, 1629.
iii. 25, 26	Matthathias	Mattathias, 1629.
iii. 30	Simeon	Symeon. Cf. Appendix E § 1, p. 244 and Acts xv. 14.
iii. 31	Menam (Μενὰμ Erasmus 1516, Aldus 1518, Tyndale, Great Bible)[2]. See Appendix E, p. 244.	Menan, 1629 (Geneva N. T., 1557).

---

[1] A variation taken from Matt. xix. 17. A like change might well be made in some other places, e.g. Matt. xi. 27; ch. xiii. 32. In John x. 28 "any," 29 "none" of 1638—1762, are rejected by 1769 and later Bibles for "any man," "no man," of 1611—1630; "*man*" however being printed in italic type.

[2] In the same way all our books from Tyndale downwards (excep

S. Luke	Reading of the Authorized Bible.	Variation of later editions.
iii. 35	Phaleg (Clementine Vulg.)	Phalec, 1629.
iv. 27	Elizeus	Eliseus[1], 1638.
v. 1	Genesareth (Genn— 1638—1743)	Gennesaret, 1762. Cf. Matt. xiv. 34.
vii. 11	Naim (Ναΰμ Erasmus 1516, Aldus, Vulg. All Early English versions Naim, except Tynd. 1526 Naym)	Nain, 1638 (Ναεὶν Erasm. 1519).
viii. 5	the wayes side	the way side, 1743. Cf. ver. 12. Matt. xiii. 4; Mark iv. 4.
xi. 32	Nineve. Cf. Matt. xii. 41	Nineveh, 1699, American 1867.
xiii. 4	Siloe (Silo, 1629 L., 1630), Tynd., Coverdale, Great and Bishops' Bibles	Siloam, 1629 (Geneva, 1557).
xvii. 34	the other shall be left	and the other shall be left, 1638. Cf. vers. 35, 36.
xix. 2, 5, 8	Zacheus	Zaccheus 1638—1769[1].
xix. 9	the son of Abraham	a son of Abraham, 1762.
xx. 12	sent the third	sent a third, 1762.
xxiii. 11	at naught	at nought, 1638. Cf. Acts xix. 27.
xxiii. 19	cast in prison	cast into prison, 1616 (not 1617—1638), 1743.
xxiv. 13	Emaus	Emmaus, 1613.
xxiv. 18	Cleophas	Cleopas, 1629.

Coverdale and the Genevan version) read "Heber" ver. 35 from Erasmus's Ἐβὲρ (retained in Beza 1589, 1598), though "Eber" is the form used in the O. T. See Appendix E, p. 249.

[1] *Elissæus* might be preferable here, as *Zacchæus* is spelt in Oxf. 1835, Camb. 1858, and some recent Bibles. An English reader can hardly fail to confound the three separate terminations in -*eus*, (1) *eu* diphthong, as Menestheus, 2 Macc. iv. 21, Nereus, Rom. xvi. 15: (2) the dissyllable ĕ-us, e being short, as Timothĕus, 1 Thess. i. 1, &c.: (3) the more usual dissyllable -ē-us, e being long, as here. Such are Aggēus, 1 Esdr. vi. 1; 2 Esdr. i. 40: Asmodēus, Tobit iii. 8: Cendebēus, 1 Macc. xv. 38: Channunēus, 1 Esdr. viii. 48: Elisēus, here: Hymenēus, 1 Tim. i. 20: Maccabēus, 1 Macc. iii. 1, &c.: Mardochēus, Esther x. 4, &c.: Ptolemēus, Esther xi. 1, &c.: Sabbathēus, 1 Esdr. ix. 14: Sabatēus, *ibid.* ver. 48: Timēus, Mark x. 46: Zacchēus, Luke xix.

of 1611 *amended in later editions.*

S. John	Reading of the Authorized Bible.	Variation of later editions.
i. 45 — 49 & xxi. 2	Nathaneel	Nathanael, 1629 (1612, ver. 47).
v. 18	not only because he	because he not only, 1629.
vii. 16	Jesus answered them,	Jesus answered them, and said, 1634, 1638.
viii. 30	those words	these words, 1629.
xi. 3	his sister	his sisters, 1629.
xii. 22	told Jesus	tell Jesus, 1762.
xv. 20	than the Lord (lord 1629—1743)	than his lord, 1762.
xvi. 25	the time	but the time, 1756, 1762, 1769.
xxi. 17 *init.*	He said unto him	He saith unto him, 1638.
Acts		
ii. 22	miracles, wonders	miracles and wonders, 1638.
iv. 17	no farther	no further, 1616 (not 1617, 1634), 1629, 1640. Cf. ver. 21; ch. xxi. 28.
vi. 5, 8 & vii. 59 & viii. 2 & xi. 19 & xxii. 20	Steven	Stephen, 1629.
vi. 5	Permenas	Parmenas, 1629.
vii. 10, 13	Pharao	Pharaoh, 1629, 1630 (1640, ver. 10). Cf. ver. 21.
vii. 16	Sichem (*bis*) ... Emor ('Εμὸρ Erasmus, Ald., Tynd., Great and Bishops' Bibles, &c.)	Sychem (*bis*) 1638... Emmor, 1629.
vii. 35	by the hands	by the hand, 1762.
viii. 32	the shearer	his shearer, 1629.
xiii. 18 *marg.*	ἐτροφοφόρησεν	ἐτροφοφόρησεν *bore, or fed them*, 1743[1].
xiii. 42 *marg.*	‖ *Or, in the week*	†Gr. *in the week*, 1629.

2, 5, 8. So also in 1 Esdr. ix. 21, 23, 30, 32 (*bis*), 33. These all represent the termination -αῖος. In 1 Macc. xii. 7 *marg.*, 20, Ἄρειος should be rendered Arīus, not Areus.

[1] After Deut. i. 31 in this marginal note modern Bibles which do not contain the Apocrypha (e.g. Camb. 1858) unwarrantably omit the reference to 2 Macc. vii. 27. See above, p. 119.

Appendix A.] Wrong readings of the Bible

Acts	Reading of the Authorized Bible.	Variation of later editions.
xv. 14	Simeon	Symeon. Cf. Luke iii. 30.
xvii. 22 *marg*.	‖ *Or, court*	‖ *Or, the court*, 1638.
xxi. 28 & xxiv. 4	farther. Cf. ch. iv. 17	further, 1699, 1762 (ch. xxiv. 4, 1629—1743).
xxiv. 24	which was a Jew	which was a Jewess, 1629. Cf. ch. xvi. 1.
xxiv. 27	Portius	Porcius, 1638.
xxvii. 5	Lysia	Lycia, 1629. Cf. 1 Macc. xv. 23.
xxvii. 7	Gnidus	Cnidus, 1638.
xxvii. 18	And being exceedingly tossed with a tempest the next day,	And we being exceedingly tossed with a tempest, the next *day* 1638[1].
Romans		
iii. 24	Jesus Christ (So Beza's Latin only)	Christ Jesus, 1762.
iv. 12	but also walk	but who also walk, 1762.
vi. 12	reign therefore	therefore reign, 1616 (not 1617), 1629.
vii. 13	Was that then	Was then that, 1616 (not 1617), 1629.
ix. 29	Sabboth (Sabbath 1629 L., 1630)	sabaoth, 1629—1762 (Sabaoth[2], 1769).
x. 16 *text* *marg*.	our ‖ † report ‖ *Or*, before † *Gr*.	†our ‖report. †*Gr*. before ‖*Or*, 1629 (not 1629 L., 1630), 1638.
xi. 28	for your sake	for your sakes, 1762.
xii. 2	that acceptable	and acceptable, 1629.
xiv. 6	regardeth a day	regardeth the day, 1629.
xiv. 10	we shall all stand	for we shall all stand, 1638.
xvi. 10	Appelles	Apelles, 1616 (not 1617, 1630), 1629 C. and L.

---

[1] In 1616 (not 1617)—1630 the stop is transferred, but ἡμῶν is still overlooked.

[2] In James v. 4 Sabbaoth, Camb. Synd. A. 3. 14, &c., 1613, 1617, 1629 L., 1630; Sabaoth, Oxf. 1611, 1612, 1616; sabaoth, 1629 C., 1638, &c.

of 1611 *amended in later editions.*

1 Cor.	Reading of the Authorized Bible.	Variation of later editions.
i. 12 & iii. 4—6, 22 & iv. 6	Apollo	Apollos, 1638.
vii. 32	things that belongeth	things that belong, 1612 (not 1613), 1616, &c. See p. 110.
ix. 9 & x. 2	Moyses	Moses, 1629 (1612, ch. ix. 9).
x. 28	The earth is	For the earth is, 1638.
xii. 28	helps in governments	helps, governments, 1629.
xiv. 10	none of them are	none of them *is*, 1638. Cf. pp. 109, 110.
xiv. 23	some place	one place, 1629.
xv. 6	And that	After that, 1616 (not 1617), 1629 C. & L. Cf. ver. 7.
xv. 41	another of the moon	and another glory of the moon, 1629.
xv. 48	such are they that are earthy	such *are* they also that are earthy, 1638.
xvi. 22	Anathema Maranatha	anathema, Maranatha, 1629—1743[1].
2 Cor.		
i. 19	Sylvanus	Silvanus, 1613 (not 1616, 1617), 1629 C. (not 1629 L., 1630). Cf. 1 Peter v. 12.
v. 2	earnestly, desiring	, earnestly desiring, 1769 (ἐπιποθοῦντες)[2].
v. 20	that ye be (that be ye Oxf. 1611) reconciled	be ye reconciled, 1612, 1616 (not 1613), 1617, 1629.
viii. 21	but in the sight	but also in the sight, 1638.
ix. 5	not of covetousness	and not as of covetousness, 1638.
ix. 6	sparingly...bountifully	also sparingly ... also bountifully, 1638.
xi. 26	journeying	journeyings, 1762.

---

[1] But 1762 and American 1867 have Anathema, Maran-atha, and 1769 even removes the necessary comma between the words; and so D'Oyly and Mant 1817, Oxf. 1835, Camb. 1858, and other moderns.

[2] Professor Grote (MS. p. 16. See above, p. 23 note) states that this punctuation was adopted in a small 8vo. Bible by Field in 1660, but that in Field's 12mo. N. T. of the same year, and in all later editions of that period, the change was revoked. See above, p. 91.

2 Cor.	Reading of the Authorized Bible.	Variation of later editions.
xi. 32	the city	the city of the Damascenes, 1629.
Subscription	Philippos	Philippi, 1629.
Galatians		
iii. 13	on tree (Tynd.—Bishops')	on a tree, 1629.
Ephesians		
iv. 24	that new man	the new man, 1616 (not 1617), 1629 C.
vi. 24	sincerity VULG	sincerity. Amen, 1616, 1617 (not 1629 L.), 1629, 1630. See Appendix E, p. 263.
Phil.		
iv. 2	Syntiche	Syntyche, 1629, 1638 (not 1699), &c.
iv. 6	request	requests, 1629.
2 Thess.		
ii. 14	the Lord Jesus Christ	our Lord Jesus Christ, 1629.
ii. 15	or our epistle	or by our epistle, 1613 only.
1 Tim.		
i. 4	edifying	godly edifying, 1638 (Tynd.—Bps').
vi. 11	flie (φεῦγε)	flee, 1613 (not 1616, 1617), 1629 C. & L. Cf. 2 Esdr. xiv. 15 note.
Subscription	Pacaciana (Bishops' Bible)	Pacatiana, 1629.
2 Tim.		
i. 7	of love	and of love, 1638.
ii. 19	the seal	this seal, 1617, 1629 C. & L., 1630.

2 Tim.	Reading of the Authorized Bible.	Variation of later editions.
iv. 8	unto them also	unto all them also, 1629.
iv. 13	bring *with thee*,	bring *with thee*, and the books, 1616, 1617, 1629 C. & L., 1630.
Heb.		
iii. 10	their hearts	their heart, 1638.
iv. 8 *marg.*	*Josuah*	*Joshua*, 1638.
viii. 8	and the house of Judah	and with the house of Judah, 1638.
xi. 4	Kain	Cain, 1638. Cf. 1 John iii. 12; Jude 11.
xi. 23	and they (thy, 1617) not afraid	and they were not afraid, 1638.
xi. 32	Gideon...Jephthah	Gedeon ... Iephthae, 1629. Cf. Judg. xi. 1 *marg.*
xii. 1	unto the race	the race, 1629 C. & L., 1630.
James		
v. 2	motheaten	are motheaten, 1638.
1 Peter		
ii. 1	evil speakings	all evil speakings, 1629 C.
ii. 5	sacrifice	sacrifices, 1629.
ii. 6	Wherefore	Wherefore also, 1638.
v. 12	Sylvanus	Silvanus, 1629 C. & L. (not 1630), 1638. Cf. 2 Cor. i. 19.
1 John		
ii. 16	the lust of the eyes	and the lust of the eyes, 1638.
v. 12	hath not the Son [1]	hath not the Son of God, 1629 C. (not 1629 L., 1630), 1638 [2].

[1] The Book of Common Prayer (Epistle for the First Sunday after Easter) follows the reading of 1611, as does the Gospel for Palm Sunday in Matt. xxvii. 52, "of saints which slept," not "the saints," as in 1762 and later Bibles. See Cardwell, *Oxford Bibles*, p. 14.

[2] Even after 1638 this variation continued: "of God" is omitted

Jude	Reading of the Authorized Bible.	Variation of later editions.
ver. 11	Kain	Cain, 1630, 1638. See Heb. xi. 4.
ver. 25	now and ever	both now and ever, 1638.
Revelation		
i. 4	Churches in Asia	Churches which are in Asia, 1638.
i. 11	Philadelphia	unto Philadelphia, 1638.
v. 13	honour, glory,	and honour, and glory, 1638.
vii. 5	Ruben	Reuben, 1616 (not 1617), 1629 C. & L., 1630.
vii. 6	Nepthali (Nephthali, 1629 C.)	Nephthalim, 1638 — 1762, Amer. 1867[1]. Cf. Matt. iv. 13, 15.
ix. 17 & xxi. 20	jacinct	jacinth, 1762.
xii. 14	flee (πέτηται). Cf. 2 Esdr. xv. 41	fly (flie, 1629—1699), 1743, 1762.
xiii. 6	them that dwelt	them that dwell, 1629.
xiii. 16 *marg.*	*to give*	*to give them*, 1769.
xviii. 12	Thine (Thyne 1629 L.)	thyine, 1629 C.
xx. 13 *marg.*	‖ *Or, hell* (‖ *Or, well*, 1612)	‖ *Or, grave*, 1613 — 1630 : ‖ Or, *the grave*, 1638.
xxi. 19	saphir[2]	sapphire, 1638.
xxi. 20	sardonix (even 1699)... topas	sardonyx 1634, 1640 ....topaz, 1629.
Colophon	FINIS	THE END, 1762.

by 1640—39, 1659 (fol.), 1677 (Camb.), 1678, 1679 (fol.), 1681; the words are retained by 1658 (Field) and its Dutch counterfeit (see above, p. 25 note 2), 1674, 1677 (4°), 1682, 1701, and by all later Bibles.

[1] 1769, followed by our standard (Camb. 1858) and all other moderns we know of, reads "Nepthalim."

[2] Elsewhere the forms employed in 1611 are *saphire* and *saphyre*. See above, p. 97.

N.B. All variations in the foregoing list, except those relating to the apostrophe, have been introduced into at least one previous edition. The changes described in the subjoined list (which relates chiefly to the Apocrypha) are peculiar to the Cambridge Paragraph Bible, and must justify themselves.

of 1611 *amended in later editions.*

Genesis	Reading of 1611 and later editions.	Correction made in the Paragraph Bible.
i. 20 x. 16	creature that hath †life Girgasite (Gergasite 1630)	† creature that hath life. Girgashite, *passim*.
Numbers		
xxvi. 58	Korathites	Korahites. Cf. 1 Chr. ix. 19[1]. (Gorle.)
2 Samuel		
xvii. 25 [*marg.*]	*Ismaelite*, 1762	*Ishmeelite.* Cf. 1 Chr. ii. 17.
2 Kings		
iii. 9 xvi. 7 [*marg.*]	†that followed † Heb. *Tilgath-pileser*, 1762	that † followed. † Heb. *Tiglath-peleser.*
1 Chronicles		
vii. 28	unto ‖ Gaza	‖ unto Gaza[2].
Ezra		
ix. 8	a † little space	a little † space. Cf. Isai. xxvi. 20.
Nehemiah		
iii. 12	Halloesh, 1611—1630 (Haloesh, 1616; Halohesh, 1638, &c.)	Hallohesh. Cf. ch. x. 24.

---

[1] Less palpable is the error in 1 Chr. xxvi. 19 (cf. ver. 1), where *Kore* (קֹרֵא) is put for *Korhite* (קָרְחִי).

[2] The annexed marginal note (omitted in Bibles which do not contain the Apocrypha, see above, p. 119) is almost unintelligible as it stands in 1611, &c. Inasmuch as the border of Ephraim did not reach to Gaza (Josh. xv. 47), our Translators suggest that עַד־עַזָּה may possibly mean *Adassa*, the Ἀδασά of 1 Macc. vii. 40, 45.

Appendix A.] Wrong readings of the Bible

Esther	Reading of 1611 and later editions.	Correction made in the Paragraph Bible.
viii. 5	† the letters devised (the † l. d. Bagster 1846; in 1630 *marg. devised* for *the device*)	the letters †devised.
Job		
xxxii. 6 *marg.*	*I feared* (*feared*, 1638, &c.)	*I feared to.*
Psalms		
vi. 4 & xxxi. 16 & xliv. 26	for thy mercies (mercies', 1769)	for thy mercy's (: חַסְדֶּךָ)[1].
cxxxvi. 8 *marg.*	*rulings*	*ruling.* Compare ver. 9 (Heb.).
Canticles		
iv. 2	every one bear (bare, 1629 L., 1630)	every one beareth. Cf. ch. vi. 6.
Isaiah		
vi. 9	Hear ye ‖ indeed (‖† 1629)	† Hear ye ‖ indeed.
marg.	‖ Or, *without ceasing, &c.* Heb. *hear ye in hearing, &c.*	† Heb. precedes ‖ Or, *Aliter sanat* Bagster 1846.
xi. 14	†and the children	and † the children.
xxvii. 8 *marg.*	*removeth it*	*removeth it with.*
xxix. 1 *marg.*	*cut off the heads*	*cut off the heads of.*
xliv. 14	he ‖ strengtheneth	‖ he strengtheneth (*marg.* from Tremellius, *quæ fortifical se*).
Ezekiel		
iii.' 20	† righteousness *primo loco*	† righteousness *secundo loco.*
xxxviii. 17 *marg.*	*by the hands* (Bagster 1846 adds *of*)	*by the hand of.* Cf. 1 Kin. xvi. 12.

---

[1] The noun *in pausâ* is no doubt singular, and so LXX., Vulg. have it in Ps. vi. 4; xxxi. 16. Our translators may have meant "mercies"

of 1611 *amended in later editions.*

Daniel	Reading of 1611 and later editions.	Correction made in the Paragraph Bible.
ix. 26 *text* [*marg.*]	but not for himself: ‖ and the people ‖ Or, *and [the Jews] they shall be no more his people,* ch. 11. 17, or, *and the prince's [Messiah's,* ver. 25] *future people,* 1762	* but not for himself: ‖ and the people. * Or, *and [the Jews]...* ch. 11. 17. ‖ Or, *and the prince's [Messiah's* ver. 25] *future people.*
Malachi		
i. 7	‖ ye offer	Ye ‖ offer[1].
1 Esdras		
ii. 12 *marg.*	*Shash-bazar, Greek* (Gr. *Shashbazar:* 1638), &c.	† *Sheshbazzar,* Ezra i. 8. *Greek,* (Ezra i. 8, being brought up from the end of the marginal note).
iv. 14 *marg.*	† Heb. *is of force*	† Gk. *is of force* (ἰσχύει).
v. 5 *marg.*	*Joachim ... Joachim ... Josedech*	*Joacim ...* Joacim *...* Jeshua.
v. 8	Reesaias (ῥεησαίου, Ald.)	Resaias ('Ρησαίου, LXX.)
v. 13 *marg.*	*Asgad (Asgar,* 1769, mod.)	*Azgad* (Ezra ii. 12 ; Neh. vii. 17).
v. 21 *marg.*	*Maghbis (Magbis,* 1744 only)	*Magbish* (Ezra ii. 30).
v. 24 *marg.*	*Immar*	*Immer* (Ezra ii. 37; Neh. vii. 40).
v. 26 *marg.*	Cadmeel (Cadmiel, 1638)	*Kadmiel* (Ezra ii. 40; Neh. vii. 43).
v. 29 *marg.*	Zich	*Ziha* (Ezra ii. 43; Neh. vii. 46).
v. 31 *marg.*	*Necodah ... Gazam ... Nephusin...Hacupa*	*Nekoda ... Gazzam ... Nephusim ... Hakupha* (Ezra ii. 48, 50, 51; Neh. vii. 62).
v. 32 *marg.*	*Barcos...Thamai*	*Barkos...Thamah* (Ezra ii. 53).

to be singular, as they so spell "mercy" about four times out of ten. In that case 1769 would be the first to go wrong. See p. 152 note.

[1] The marginal "bring unto" (b not B, 1611—1638) cannot be meant for the imperative, but renders *differentes super* of Tremellius.

1 Esdras	Reading of 1611 and later editions.	Correction made in the Paragraph Bible.
v. 33 *marg.*	*Darcon*	*Darkon* (Ezra ii. 56; Neh. vii. 58).
v. 34 *marg.*	*Hatti...Phoceroth* (*-eth*, 1629)	*Hattil...Pochereth* (Ezra ii. 57; Neh. vii. 59).
v. 37 *marg.*	*Necodah.* Cf. ver. 31 *marg.*	*Nekoda* (Ezra ii. 60; Neh. vii. 62)
v. 38 *marg.*	*Hobaiah* (*Hoboiah* 1612)... *Cos* ... *Barzelai*	*Habaiah* ... *Koz* ... *Barzillai* (Ezra ii. 61; Neh. vii. 63).
v. 47	of the ‖ first gate (first ‖ gate, 1629, &c.)	‖ of the first gate[1].
vii. 9 *marg.* & viii. 23 *marg.*	† *Hebr.* † *Heb.*	† Chald.
viii. 2	‖ Ozias (*text*), ‖ Azarias (*marg.*), [‖ Ezias (*text*), ‖ Ozias (*marg.*) 1629, ‖ Oziaz (*marg.*) 1744]	† Ozias (*text*) † Ezias (*marg.*): ἐζίου Aldus and Bishops' Bible.
viii. 20 *text* *marg.*	‖ cors...other things ‖ *Or, measures or salt*	‖ cors...‖ other *things.* ‖ *Or, measures.* ‖ *Or, salt.*
viii. 23 *marg.*	of those that	of all those that (Ezra vii. 25).
viii. 29 *marg.*	Parosh	*Pharosh* (Ezra viii. 3).
viii. 39 *marg.*	Shemaia	*Shemaiah* (Ezra viii. 13).
viii. 44	Joribas...Mosollamon	Joribus (ch. ix. 19)...Mosollamus. Cf. ch. ix. 14.
viii. 49	catalogue of whose names were. (See above, p. 110 note 1)	catalogue of whose names was. Cf. Acts xxv. 23.
viii. 54 *marg.*	*Serebias and Hassibias*[2]	‖ *Or, Sherebiah and Hashabiah* (Ezra viii. 24).
viii. 62 *marg.*	*Merimoth*	*Meremoth* (Ezra viii. 33).
ix. 19 *marg.*	*Maasias*	*Maaseiah* (Ezra x. 18, 21).
ix. 21 *marg.* & 43 *marg.*	*Maasiah*	*Maaseiah.*
ix. 23 *marg.*	*Kelitah*	*Kelita* (Ezra x. 23).
ix. 26 *marg.*	*Jesaiah* (*Jesiah*, 1629)	*Jeziah* (Ezra x. 25).
ix. 29	Josabad	Jozabad. (Ἰωξ.-LXX.).

[1] The margin notes the various reading upheld by Vulg. and Junius, πρὸ τοῦ for τοῦ πρώτου.

[2] So Camb. Synd. A. 3. 14, &c., 1613, 1617, &c.: but *Serenias*, Oxf. 1611, 1612, 1616. See below, p. 205.

of 1611 *amended in later editions.*

1 Esdras	Reading of 1611 and later editions.	Correction made in the Paragraph Bible.
ix. 33 *marg.*	*Mattithiah* (*Mati-* Camb. Synd. A. 3. 14, 1617)	*Mattathah.* Cf. Ezra x. 33: above, p. 163.
2 Esdras		
ii. 23 *marg.*	† *Signing*	† Lat. *signing.*
iii. 31 *text*	‖ I do not remember	I do not ‖remember[1].
marg.	‖ Or, *I conceive*	‖ Or, *conceive.*
ix. 17, 18 *text*	: for it was the time of the world. ‖ And	: ‖for it was the time of the world. And
marg.	‖ *And now...*	‖Or, *And now...*
ix. 19 *marg.*	‖ *But when*	‖Or, *but when*
x. 13 *marg.*	‖ *But the earth...*	‖Or, *but the earth....*
Tobit		
i. 14	‖ at Rages a city of Media	at Rages ‖*a city* of Media[2].
v. 18 *marg.*	‖ *Let not* (*no* Camb. Synd. A. 3. 14) *money*	‖Gk. *Let not money.*
Judith		
xiv. 16 *marg.*	‖ *Then*	‖Or, *Then* (καί).
xvi. 11 *marg.*	‖ *The Assyrians*	‖That is, *the Assyrians.*
Esther		
xiii. 18	most † earnestly	† most earnestly (ἐξ ἰσχύος αὐτῶν).
xv. 5	and very ‖ amiable (and ‖ very amiable, 1629)	‖and very amiable (ὡς προσφιλὲς).
Wisdom		
v. 14	a thin froth ... the ‖ smoke	‖a thin froth (πάχνη)... the smoke.

[1] This must be the intention of the Translators, since Vulg. has *Nihil memini* of the text, Junius *Nihil venit in mentem* of the margin, the Bishops' Bible "I cannot perceive."

[2] So Fritzsche's text of the LXX.: Vulg. has *civitatem.* But the arrangement of 1611 might very well stand, as the margin exactly represents the reading of Aldus, ἐν ἀγροῖς τῆς Μηδείας. See above, p. 51.

Wisdom	Reading of 1611 and later editions.	Correction made in the Paragraph Bible.
xii. 12	to ‖ stand against thee (to stand ‖ against thee, 1629)	‖ to stand against thee (εἰs κατάστασίν σοι).
xiv. 2 *marg.*	‖ Or, *vessel*	‖ That is, *vessel* (ἐκεῖνο).
xiv. 21 *marg.*	‖ *of God* (‖ Or, *of God*, 1612, 1629, &c., not D'Oyly and Mant 1817)	‖ That is, *of God* (*i. nomen Dei*, Junius).
xvi. 5 *marg.*	‖ Or, *thy people*	‖ That is, *thy people*.
xvi. 21 *marg.*	‖ Or, *manna*	‖ That is, *manna*.
Ecclus.		
viii. 11	to ‖ entrap thee in thy words (‖ to entrap, 1629, &c.)	to entrap thee ‖in thy words.
x. 21	‖ the obtaining of authority	the obtaining of ‖authority[1].
xlv. 8	†rich garments	rich †garments.
xlvii. 11	of kings...‖ of glory	‖ of kings...of glory.
xlix. 9 *marg.*	‖ *did good*	‖*did good unto* (Bps' Bible).
li. 20	‖ I directed my soul... I have had my heart	I directed my soul... ‖I have had my heart.
Baruch		
iii. 2	Chanaan	Canaan. Cf. Judith v. 9: above, p. 179.
Song		
Title	in the Hebrew	in the Chaldee.
1 Maccabees		
ii. 2 *marg.*	‖ *Gaddis*	‖Or, *Gaddis*.
ii. 35 *marg.*	‖ Gr. *the Jews* (‖ Or, *the Jews*, 1629)	‖That is, *the Jews*. Cf. Wisd. xvi. 5, 21.
ii. 42 & vii. 13	Assideans	Asideans (1630, ch. vii. 13; 1611, 2 Macc. xiv. 6).

---

[1] This must be the proper arrangement even if for πρὸ λήψεως ἀρχῆς be read πρὸ λήξεως ἀρχή with the Complutensian, or προλήψεως ἀρχή with Cod. 106, or πρὸ λήξεως ἀρχῆς with Grabe. The verse is wanting in the best manuscripts and the Aldine edition.

1 Maccabees	Reading of 1611 and later editions.	Correction made in the Paragraph Bible.
v. 4 *marg.*	Haran (Haron, 1630; Hakan, 1629, 1638)	Akan. Cf. Gen. xxxvi. 27.
v. 23 *marg.*	‖ Or, *captive Jews*	‖That is, *captive Jews*.
v. 26	Bosora, cf. ver. 28	Bossora, LXX. (Complut., Fritzsche). See above, p. 53.
v. 27 *marg.*	‖ Or, *the heathen*, (D'Oyly and Mant omit 1817 Or)	‖That is, *the heathen*.
v. 30 *marg.*	‖ *The heathen* (‖ Or, *the heathen*, 1629, &c., not D'Oyly and Mant 1817)	‖That is, *the heathen*.
v. 44 *marg.*	‖ *Judas and*	‖That is, *Judas and*.
v. 54 *marg.*	Antiq. 12. 12	Antiq. lib. 12, cap. 12. Cf. ch. vii. 1, &c.
vi. 49	‖ peace......city, (1638 and the moderns set ‖ after "peace," inserting *they* before *yielded* in the margin)	peace......city ‖.
vi. 52 & vii. 45 & ix. 11	‖ Or, *the Jews*	‖That is, *the Jews*.
ix. 24 *marg.*	*Bacchides and*	‖That is, *Bacchides and*.
ix. 63 *marg.*	‖ Or, *to such of*	‖That is, *to such of*.
xiii. 15 *marg.*	*that he had...for* (*that he had*, or, 1629, &c.)	*that he had*, or, *for*.
2 Maccabees		
ii. 17 *marg.*	*heritage*	*heritage to all.*
iv. 14	the game of ‖ Discus	‖the game of Discus.
v. 8	an open ‖ enemy	an ‖open enemy.
xi. 6 *marg.*	‖ *Maccabeus*	‖Or, *Maccabeus*.
xii. 20 *marg.*	‖ *Dositheus and...*	‖ That is, *Dositheus, and*.
xiii. 23	confounded (συνεχύθη)	was confounded [i.e. Eupator, Cotton].
S. Matthew		
xxiii. 24	strain at a gnat	strain out a gnat[1].

[1] So all the early versions from Tyndale to the Bishops' Bible, and even T. Baskett's 8vo. edition of the Authorized, London, 8vo. 1754, Brit. Mus. 1411. f. 5.

S. Mark	Reading of 1611 and later editions.	Correction made in the Paragraph Bible.
vi. 53	Genesareth (Gennesaret, 1638—1769)	Genesaret. Cf. Matt. xiv. 34; Luke v. 1.
S. Luke		
i. 78 *marg.*	Malach. iv. 2; *follows* Isai. xi. 1	Mal. iv. 1, follows *sunrising*.
S. John		
x. 25	and ye believed not	and ye believe not.
Acts		
vii. 11 & xiii. 19	Chanaan	Canaan (1612 only, ch. xiii. 19). See Judith v. 9.
xxi. 1	Choos (Coos, 1638, &c.)	Cos. Cf. 1 Macc. xv. 23.
xxv. 23	was entered (Bishops' Bible). Cf. 1 Esdr. viii. 49	were entered (Tyndale, Great Bible, Geneva 1557). See above, p. 110 note 1.
Romans		
xvi. 9	Urbane	Urban.
Philippians		
ii. 7, 8	‖ likeness of men... fashion as a man	likeness of men...... ‖ fashion as a man[1].
Hebrews		
i. 6	‖ And again, 1762, whose margin it is	And ‖ again.
viii. 8	Judah	Juda. Cf. Matt. ii. 6; ch. vii. 14; Rev. v. 5. So Camb. 1863 in Ecclus. xlix. 4.
x. 23	faith	hope. See Appendix E, p. 247.

---

[1] That the margin, "Or, *habit*" refers to σχήματι, not to ὁμοιώματι, is plain enough in itself, not to add that for σχήματι the Vulg. has *habitu*, Tyndale, Coverdale, and the Great Bible *apparel*.

APPENDIX B.

(See above, pp. 5—7.)

Catalogue of variations (not being very manifest misprints[1]) between the two issues of the Authorized version of 1611, represented by Camb. Synd. A. 3. 14 and the Oxford reprint of 1833 respectively. Wheresoever the contrary is not stated, the British Museum copies, 3050. g. 2, 3050. g. 3, and 1276. l. 4, have been ascertained to agree with Camb. Synd. A. 3. 14.

N.B. *Bp.* denotes the Bishops' Bible (1572), *Synd.* our Cambridge, *Oxf.* our Oxford model, *Amer.* the New York Bible, diamond, 24mo. 1867[2].

§ I. The readings of Camb. Synd. A. 3. 14 have been preferred in forming the text of the Cambridge Paragraph Bible in the following places:

GEN. x. 16 Amorite 1617, 1634, 1640, 1769, moderns,

---

[1] Such, and nothing more, are the following errors, noticed by Dr Schaff (*Companion to the Greek Testament*, p. 324). Ex. ix. 13 "serve thee" *Synd.*, B. M. 1276. l. 4, 3050. g. 2 and 3 for "serve me" *Oxf.*, B. M. 3050. g. 1. On the other hand *Oxf.*, 3050. g. 1 are wrong and *Synd.*, B. M. 1276. l. 4, 3050. g. 2 and 3 are right in Lev. xiii. 56 "plaine" for "plague" and in Lev. xvii. 14 "ye shall not" for "ye shall": but see above, p. 112, for this last.

[2] The readings of the Bishops' Bible are added in some places, in case that any should think that light may be thrown upon the origin of these variations by the Bible from which, as it would seem, our own version was set up for the press. Inferences thus drawn seem to the Editor for the most part too slight to be relied on.

Amer. (Emorite [*Bp.*] *Oxf.* 1612, 1613, 1616, 1629 L. & C., 1630, 1638, 1744, 1762, here only). xlvi. 17 Ishui 1617 (Isui *Oxf.* 1612, 1613, &c.). xlvii. 27 possessions [with B. M. 1276. l. 4 only] (possessions *Bp. Oxf.* 1612, 1613, &c.). EXOD. xxxviii. 11 the hooks (hoopes *Oxf.* 1612, but not ver. 10) of the pillars 1613, &c., cf. *Bp.* vers. 10, 11[1]. LEV. xviii. 30 ye shall 1630 (shall ye *Bp. Oxf.* 1612, 1613, 1629 L. & C., &c.). NUM. x. 2 thou shalt (shalt thou *Bp. Oxf.* 1612, 1613, &c.). xxvi. 21 Hezronites [with B. M. 1276. l. 4 only] (Hesronites *Bp. Oxf.* 1612, 1613, &c.). DEUT. viii. 7 the valleys (valleys *Bp. Oxf.* 1612, 1613, &c.). xvii. 4 it *is* true[2] (it *be* true *Bp. Oxf.* 1612, 1613, &c.). xxxii. 15 Thou art waxed 1617 (Thou art waxen *Oxf.* 1612, 1613, &c.). 2 SAM. xvii. 25 Abigal[3] 1612, 1613, 1616, 1617 (Abigail *Bp. Oxf.* 1629 C. and L., &c., as in 1 Chr. ii. 16). 1 KIN. iii. 20 rose [with B. M. 1276. l. 4 only] 1613 (arose *Bp. Oxf.* 1612, 1616, 1617, &c.). ix. 22 bondman 1613 (bondmen *Bp. Oxf.*, B. M. 3050. g. 3, 1612, 1616, 1617, &c.). JOB xix. 15 maidens *Bp.* 1613 (maides *Oxf.* 1612, 1616, &c.). PROV. xi. 20 unto the Lord 1613 (to the Lord *Oxf.*, B. M. 3050. g. 3, 1612, 1616, 1617, &c.). CANT. ii. 7 till he please (*so all known editions except Oxf.*[4] till she please, *here only, not in* ch. iii. 5; viii. 4). ISAI. xlix. 1 from afar 1613,

---

[1] Since *Bp.* has "hoops" in both verses (10, 11), though for the word rendered "fillets" in 1611, it is not unlikely that *Oxf.* was set up from a copy of *Bp.*, and the same inference might be drawn from other places where *Bp.* and *Oxf.* minutely coincide.

[2] The copy in S. John's College, Cambridge (T. 6. 26) and B. M. 3050. g. 3 must be earlier on this leaf, since they read "it *it* true". See above, p. 8.

[3] Thus dispensing with the marginal note of 1762 "†Heb. *Abigal.*" But B. M. 3050. g. 1 and 466. i. 6 have Abigal, against *Oxf.*

[4] So B.M. 466. i. 6 "she," but not 3050. g. 1 which is almost identical with it. *Bp.* has "till she be content her self" in all these places. The original American revise of 1851 (see above, p. 36) reads "she" uniformly in all, but Amer. 1867 returned to "he."

1617 (from far *Oxf.* 1612, 1616, 1629 C. and L., &c.).
ver. 20 strait 1613, 1617 (straight *Oxf.* 1612, 1616).
lix. 21 thy seed 1612, 1613, 1616, 1617 (the seed *Oxf.*).
JER. v. 24 latter 1612, 1613, 1617 (later *Oxf.* 1616, *not in* ch.
iii. 3). EZEK. xx. 37 *marg. delivering* 1613, 1630 (*a deliring
Oxf.*: so 1612, 1616, 1617, 1629 C. & L., &c.). xxxi. 18
with the sword *Bp.* 1617 (by the sword *Oxf.* 1612, 1613,
1616). Cf. ver. 17; ch. xxxii. 28, or ch. xxxii. 20, 21, 25,
26, 29, 30. xxxix. 9 *marg. for them*[1], 1617 (*of them Oxf.*
1612, 1613, 1616, &c.). DAN. ii. 14 *marg. Chald.* (*Cald.
Oxf.* 1612—1630). ver. 34 in pieces 1617, 1630 (to pieces
Bp. Oxf. 1612, 1613, 1616, &c.), cf. ver. 40 *bis*, 44, 45, or
ver. 35. HOS. vi. 5 hewed 1612, 1613, 1617, &c. (shewed
Oxf. 1616). NAH. i. 10 while they be drunken 1617 (while
they are drunken *Oxf.* 1612, 1613, 1616, &c.).

1 ESDR. v. 5 *marg. Judah* 1612, 1616, 1617, &c. (*Juda
Oxf.* 1613). ver. 15 *marg. hezekiah* 1617, 1629, &c. (*hezekia
Oxf.* 1612, 1613, 1616, 1630). ver. 16 *marg. Bezai* 1617,
1629 (*Besai Oxf.* 1612, 1613, 1616, 1630). ver. 26 Bannas
[Βάννου] (Banua *Bp.*, Banuas *Oxf.* 1612, 1613, moderns).
vi. 23 Ecbatane *Bp.* 1617 (Ecbatana *Oxf.* 1612, 1613, 1616,
moderns). Cf. Tobit iii. 7, &c. viii. 54 *marg. Serebias*, 1613,
1617, &c. (*Serenias, Oxf.* 1612, *Sereuias* 1616). See Appendix A, p. 198. TOBIT xi. 14 thy holy 1617 (thine holy *Oxf.*
1612, 1613, 1616, &c.). See above, p. 108. JUDITH iii. 5—vii.
16 Olofernes 1612, 1613, 1617, 1629, 1630, &c., *passim*, 1616
in ch. vii. 16 (Holophernes *Bp. Oxf.* 1616). See App. C, p.
229. WISD. iii. 14 *text* ‖in the Temple: *marg. Or, amongst
the people* 1612, 1613, &c. (*text* in the Temple: *marg.*, *or
amongst the people* after *chosen*, in the previous note, *Oxf.*).
ECCLUS. xxi. 24 with disgrace (with the disgrace *Oxf.* 1612,

---

[1] בָּהֶם: *of them*, is no alternative rendering to the text.

1613, &c.). xxiii. 4 *marg.* ‖Or, *giant like* 1612, 1617 (‖Or, *a giant like* in *Oxf.* 1613, 1616, 1630: *aliter sanat* 1629). xliv. 5 recited 1612, 1613, &c. (rejected *Oxf.*). SONG ver. 4 are (rather *are*) truth (truth *Oxf.* 1612, 1613, &c.). 1 MACC. vii. 1 *marg.*, *lib.* 12. 1617, 1630, &c. (*lib.* 10, 12. *Oxf.* 1612, 1613, 1616). x. 47 true peace 1612, 1613, 1616, 1617, &c. (*text* ‖peace, *marg.* ‖*true*, *Oxf.*). See above, p. 7 note 2. 2 MACC. iv. 13 not high priest 1612, 1616, 1617, 1629— 1762 (no high priest *Oxf.* 1613, 1630, 1769 moderns).

S. MATT. xiii. 4 way side 1613, 1617, 1743 [way-side 1762], 1769 (wayes side *Oxf.* 1612, 1616, 1629 C. & L., 1630, &c.), as all in ver. 19; Mark iv. 4; Luke viii. 12; xviii. 35. Cf. Mark x. 46; Luke viii. 5 (see Appendix A, p. 188), where *Synd. Oxf.* 1612, 1613, 1616, 1617, have "ways," but 1629 C. & L., 1630, 1638 vary between the two: 1744, 1762, 1769 have "way" consistently throughout. xiii. 31 like unto a grain 1613, 1617, 1629 L., 1630 (like to a grain *Bp. Oxf.* 1612, 1616, 1629 C., &c.), as all (including *Bp.*) in ver. 33, 44, 45, 47, 52. S. MARK vii. 4 *Oxf.* alone transposes the marginal notes, placing ‖*Or beds.* before ‖*Sextarius.* ACTS xxi. 2 Phenicia 1617, 1629, &c. (Phenicea *Oxf.* 1612, 1613, 1616, 1629 L., 1630). xxv. 1 Jerusalem 1612, 1613, 1617, 1629 C., &c. (Hierusalem *Oxf.* 1616, 1629 L., 1630): cf. ver. 3, and Appendix A, p. 186 and note. ROM. vi. 21 had you 1617 (had ye *Oxf.* 1612, 1613, 1616, &c.). x. 21 have I stretched *Bp.* 1613, 1617, 1629 L. (I have stretched *Oxf.* 1612, 1616, 1629 C., 1630, &c.). xi. 22 toward 1613, 1769 (towards *Bp. Oxf.* 1612, 1616—1762). 1 PET. ii. 7 *marg.* ‖he is precious 1617 (he is ‖precious *Oxf.* 1612, 1613, 1616, 1629 L. & C., 1630: but 1638, &c. retain ‖ before "precious," and omit "he is" in the margin).

§ II. List of variations between the two issues of 1611, wherein the readings of the Oxford reprint have been preferred in the Cambridge Paragraph Bible.

GEN. xvi. 6 But Abram *Bp.* 1612, 1613 (And Abram *Synd.*). xxvi. 34 Bashemath 1612, 1613 (Bashemah *Synd.*). xxxi. 30 longedst 1612, 1629 C. & L., 1630 (longest *Bp. Synd.* 1613, 1617, 1634, 1640). xxxvi. 10 Bashemath 1612, 1613 (Bashamath *Synd.*). xlvi. 34 an abomination *Bp.* 1612, 1613 (abomination *Synd.*). Ex. xi. 8 all these 1612, 1613 (also these *Synd.*). xix. 4 eagles wings *Bp.* 1612, 1613 (eagle wings *Synd.*)[1]. xxi. 26, 27 let him go 1629 C. (let them go *Bp. Synd.* [1612, 1613, 1629 L., 1630 in ver. 26], 1616, 1617)[2]. xxxvi. 29 *marg., twinned* 1629 C. & L.[3] (*twined, Synd.* 1612, 1613, 1616, 1617, 1630, 1634, 1640). LEV. i. 16 *marg., thereof* 1612, 1613 (*there Synd.*). xxv. 28 until the year *Bp.* 1612, 1613 (unto the year *Synd.*). NUM. i. 47 tribe 1612, 1613, 1629 C. & L. (tribes *Bp. Synd.* 1617). xvi. 34 said *Bp.* 1612, 1613 (say *Synd.*). xxi. 18 *direction* 1612, 1613 (*directions, Synd.* with B. M. 1276. l. 4 only). xxxiv. 2 this *is* the land *Bp.* 1612, 1613 (that *is* the land *Synd.*). Cf. ver. 13. ver. 11 go down *Bp.* 1612, 1613 (come down *Synd.*). Cf. ver. 12. DEUT. i. 18 all the things *Bp.* 1612, 1613 (all things *Synd* 1617). ix. 10 spake with you 1612,

---

[1] Yet "eagle wings" though antiquated is not incorrect. Marsh (*English Language*, p. 278) cites from Wyclif "unkil doughter" Gen. xxix. 10. So Num. xxiv. 6 (1611); Esther i. 13 (*Synd.*). Even modern Bibles retain "a cubit length" Judg. iii. 16. See above, p. 110.

[2] Several copies of the issue represented by *Oxf.*, agreeing with 1612, 1613, 1629 and 1630, have "let them go" in ver. 26. Such are Brit. Mus. 466. i. 6 (not 3050. g. 1): Camb. University Libr. 1. 15: Emmanuel Coll. B. 1. 23: and one belonging to Mr James North of Liverpool.

[3] So *Synd.* ch. xxvi. 24 *marg.*, though 1612, 1613, 1630 have "*twined*" there also, and so even 1629 L. in the earlier place. After the error was corrected in 1629—1744, the Bibles of 1762, 1769 went wrong again, misleading moderns (even Bagster 1846), till *twinned* was restored in Camb. 1858, Amer. 1867.

1613 (spake unto you *Synd.* 1617). xii. 26 thy holy things *Bp.* 1612, 1613 (the holy things *Synd.* 1640). xiv. 29 widow *Bp.* 1612, 1613 (widows *Synd.*). xvi. 14 thy maidservant 1612, 1613 (the maidservant *Synd.*). xxxiv. 1 plains 1612, 1613 (plain *Bp. Synd.*). JOSH. v. 8 they abode *Bp.* 1612, 1613 (all abode *Synd.*). viii. 32 the stones 1612, 1613 (the stone *Synd.*). xv. 50. See Appendix A, p. 151. xvi. 6 Taanath [so also B. M. 3050. g. 3], 1613 (Taanah *Synd.* 1612). xviii. 22 Betharabah *Bp.* 1612, 1613 (Bethabarah *Synd.*). xix. 5 Hazar- 1612, 1613, 1629 C. & L., 1630 (Hasar- *Synd.* 1616, 1617, 1634, 1640). Cf. 1 Chr. iv. 31 *marg.* RUTH ii. 11 thou knewest *Bp.* [B. M. 3050. g. 2], 1612, 1613 (thou knowest *Synd.*). iii. 8 *marg.* took hold on [B. M. 3050. g. 2], 1612 (*Synd.* 1613 add *him*). ver. 15 he went[1] (she went *Synd.* 1612, 1613, 1616, 1617, 1629 C. & L., 1630, 1634, 1638, 1640, 1744, 1762, 1769, all moderns). 1 SAM. vii. 1 Kirjath- [B. M. 3050. g. 2], 1612, 1613, &c. (Kiriah- *Synd.*). 2 SAM. vi. 9 ark of the LORD *Bp.* 1612, 1613, &c. (ark of God *Synd.*, with B. M. 1276. l. 4 only). ver. 16 city of David *Bp.* 1612, 1613, &c. (house of David *Synd.*, with B. M. 1276. l. 4 only). xviii. 31 all them that rose *Bp.* 1612, 1613, &c. (all that rose *Synd.*). Cf. ver. 32 (Heb.). xxiii. 20 a valiant man, of Kabzeel, 1612, 1616, 1629 C. & L., &c. (a valiant man of Kabzeel *Synd.* 1613, 1617). Cf. Heb. 1 KIN. xi. 1. See Appendix A, p. 154. xx. 3 the goodliest 1612, 1616, 1629 L. & C. (thy goodliest *Synd.* 1613, 1617, 1630). xxi. 2 my house *Bp.* 1612, 1613, 1616 (mine house *Synd.* 1617). 2 KIN. v. 12 turned *Bp.* 1612, 1616, 1617 (returned *Synd.*, with B. M. 1276. l. 4 only, 1613). xvii. 6 Halah 1612, 1613, 1616, 1629 (Halath [ה׳] *Synd.* 1617, 1629 L., 1630). ver. 35 commandment *Bp.* [B. M. 3050.

---

[1] American Report, p. 19. Yet *Amer.* restored "she" of the Vulgate in 1867. See above, p. 37 and note 2.

g. 3], 1612, 1613, 1616, &c. (commandments *Synd.* 1617).
xix. 15 before the LORD *Bp.* [B. M. 3050. g. 3], 1612, 1613,
&c. (unto the LORD *Synd.*). xxiv. 2 Chaldees *Bp.* 1612,
1630, 1744 (Caldees *Synd.* 1613—1638). 1 CHR. i. 5
Meshech 1612, 1613, 1616, &c. (Mesech *Bp. Synd.* 1617).
vers. 47, 48 Samlah [B. M. 3050. g. 3], 1612, 1616 *semel*,
1629, &c. (Shamlah *Synd.* 1613, 1616 *semel*, 1617). ii. 49
Sheua 1612, 1613, &c. (Shua *Synd.*, with B. M. 1276. l. 4
only). iii. 18 Hosama *Bp.* 1612, 1613, &c. (Hosanna *Synd.*,
with B. M. 1276. l. 4 only). Cf. Appendix A, p. 157. ver.
23 *marg. Hiskijah* [*Hiskijahu* Amer.], 1612, 1613, &c. (*Hiskiah Synd.*, with B. M. 1276. l. 4 only). iv. 30 and at
Hormah *Bp.* 1612, 1616, 1617, &c. (and Hormah *Synd.*,
with B. M. 1276. l. 4 only, 1613). ver. 36 Jesohaiah 1612,
1613, &c. (Jehohaiah *Synd.*). Cf. Appendix A, p. 157. vi. 74
Mashal 1612, 1613, &c. (Machal *Synd.*, with B. M. 1276. l. 4
only). vii. 13 Jezer *Bp.* 1612, 1616, &c. (Gezer *Synd.*, with
B. M. 1276. l. 4 only, 1613, 1617). ver. 36 Suah *Bp.*
1612, 1629 C. & L. (Shuah *Synd.*, with B. M. 1276. l. 4 only,
1613, 1616, 1617). xxvi. 5 Issachar *Bp.* 1612, 1616 (Isachar
Synd. 1613, 1617). ver. 25 Jeshaiah 1612, 1613 (Jeshiaiah
Synd.). Cf. ch. xxv. 3. xxvii. 33 Hushai [B. M. 3050. g.
3], 1612, 1616 (Hushi *Synd.* 1613, 1617). 2 CHR. vi. 5 my
people Israel *Bp.* 1612, 1616, 1617 (my people of Israel *Synd.*
1613). xvi. 1 *fin.* Judah [B. M. 3050. g. 3], 1612, 1616,
1617 (Juda *Bp. Synd.* 1613). xxi. 15 disease of thy bowels
Bp. 1612, 1613 (diseases of the bowels *Synd.*, with B. M.
1276. l. 4 only). xxx. 6 his princes 1612, 1616, 1629 C.,
1630 (the princes *Synd.* 1613, 1617). xxxii. 20 Amoz 1612,
1616 (Amos *Bp. Synd.* 1613, 1617). Cf. ver. 32. xxxiv.
21 for them that are left *Bp.* 1612, 1613, &c. (of them that
are left *Synd.*). EZRA ii. 28 two hundred, twenty *Bp.* 1612,
1613, 1616 (two hundred and twenty *Synd.* 1617). ver. 33
Hadid 1612, 1613, &c. (Haddid *Synd.*). ix. 2 hath been

chief 1612, 1616, 1617 (have been chief *Synd.* 1613).
NEHEM. vi. 10 Mehetabel 1612, 1613 (Mehetable *Synd.*,
with B. M. 1276. l. 4 only). Cf. Appendix A, p. 163. viii.
10 unto our LORD *Bp.* 1612, 1616 (unto the LORD *Synd.*
1613, 1617). ix. 14 thy holy sabbath *Bp.* 1612, 1613, &c.
(the holy sabbath *Synd.*, with B. M. 1276. l. 4 only). x. 1
those that sealed 1612, 1613, 1616, &c. (these that sealed
Synd. 1617). ver. 16 Biguai *Bp.* 1612, 1613, &c. (Bigui
Synd., with B. M. 1276. l. 4 only). xi. 11 Hilkiah 1612,
1613 (Helkiah *Synd.*, with B. M. 1276. l. 4 only). Cf. ch.
xii. 7, 21. ESTHER i. 13 king's manner *Bp.* 1612, 1613,
&c. (king manner *Synd.*, with B. M. 1276. l. 4 only). See
above, p. 110. ix. 6, 11 Shushan 1612, 1613 (Sushan *Synd.*
here only). JOB ix. 9 *marg. Cesil* [B. M. 3050. g. 2], 1612,
1616, 1617, &c. (*Cecil Synd.* 1613). xi. 16 *thy* misery *Bp.*
[B. M. 3050. g. 2], 1612, 1616, 1617, &c. (*the* misery *Synd.*
1613). PSALM xxiv. 8 Who is this king 1612, 1613, 1617
(Who is the king *Bp. Synd.*, with B. M. 1276. l. 4 only,
1616, so 1630 even in ver. 10). xxxiii. 7 gathereth *Bp.*
1612, 1613, &c. (gathered *Synd.*, with B. M. 1276. l. 4
only). xxxv. 27 yea let them say *Bp.* 1612, 1613, &c. (yet
let them say *Synd.*, with B. M. 1276. l. 4 only). xliv. 23 O
Lord 1612, 1616—1744, Oxf. 1835, Camb. 1858, Amer.
1867 (O LORD *Synd.* 1613, 1762, 1769, even D'Oyly and
Mant 1817, Bagster 1846). See above, p. 147 note 1. lvi.
6 gather [B. M. 3050. g. 3], 1612, 1613, &c. (gathered
Synd.). lxxiv. 23 rise up 1612, 1616, &c. (arise up *Synd.*,
with B. M. 1276. l. 4 only, 1613, 1617). lxxx. 9 preparedst
1612, 1613, &c. (preparest *Synd.*, with B. M. 1276. l. 4 only).
civ. 4 his angels *Bp.* 1612, 1613, &c. (the angels *Synd.*,
with B. M. 1276. l. 4 only). PROV. viii. 27 *marg. a circle*
1612, 1616, &c. (*circle Synd.* 1613). xxiii. 31 upon the
wine *Bp.* [B. M. 3050. g. 3], 1612, 1613, &c. (among the
wine *Synd.*). ECCLES. i. 17 spirit 1612, 1613, 1616, &c.

(the spirit *Synd.* 1617, here only). xii. 1 thy Creator 1612, 1613, &c. (the Creator *Synd.*, with B. M. 1276. l. 4 only). ISAIAH i. 9 Gomorrah 1613, 1616, 1617 (Gomorah *Synd.*, with B. M. 1276. l. 4 only, not in ver. 10: 1612 in both). ix. 18 smoke 1612, 1616, 1617 (the smoke *Synd.*, with B. M. 1276. l. 4 only, 1613). x. 15 *as if it were* 1612, 1613, 1616, 1617 (*as it were Synd.*, with B. M. 1276. l. 4 only). ver. 19 ¹*with* few 1612, 1616, 1617 (¹*with* write *Synd.*, with B. M. 1276. l. 4 only, 1613). xiii. 1 Amoz 1612, 1629 C., 1630 (Amos *Synd.* 1613, 1616, 1617, 1629 L.). xix. 5 the river 1612, 1616, 1629 C. & L., 1630 (the rivers *Bp. Synd.*, with B. M. 1276. l. 4 only, 1613, 1617). xxiii. 12 have no rest *Bp.* 1612, 1613, 1616, 1617 (take no rest *Synd.*, with B. M. 1276. l. 4 only). ver. 13 founded 1612, 1613, 1616, 1617 (found *Synd.* with B. M. 1276. l. 4 only). lvii. 10 wearied [B. M. 3050. g. 3], 1612, 1616, 1617, 1629 C. & L. (weary *Bp. Synd.* 1613). lix. 14 afar off [B. M. 3050. g. 3], 1612, 1613, 1616, 1617 (far off *Bp. Synd.*). lx. 4 from far *Bp.* [B. M. 3050. g. 3], 1612 (from afar *Synd.* 1613). Cf. ver. 9. lxi. 10 and as a bride *Bp.* 1612, 1616, 1617, 1629 C. & L. (as a bride *Synd.* 1613). lxv. 2 my hands *Oxf.* 1612, 1613, 1616 (mine hands *Synd.* 1617). See Jer. xxv. 15. JEREM. v. 15 upon you *Bp.* 1612, 1613, 1616, 1617 (upon thee *Synd.*). xii. 7 hand 1612, 1613, 1616 (hands *Synd.* 1617). xxv. 15 my hand *Bp. Oxf.* 1612, 1616, 1617, 1629, &c. (mine hand *Synd.* 1613). See above, p. 108 and Isai. lxv. 2 ; Ezek. vi. 14. xxvi. 20 Kiriath- 1612, 1613, 1616 (Kiriah- *Synd.* 1617). xl. 12 of all places *Bp.* 1612, 1613, 1616, 1617 (of the places *Synd.*). xlviii. 34 Elealeh 1612, 1613, 1616, 1617 (Elealeth *Synd.*, with B. M. 1276. l. 4 only). EZEK. v. 5 This *is* Jerusalem 1612, 1616, 1617, 1629 C. & L. (Thus *is* Jerusalem *Synd.*, with B. M. 3050. g. 3, 1613). vi. 14 my hand *Oxf.* 1612, 1616, 1617, 1629, &c. (mine hand *Bp. Synd.*, 3050. g. 3 only). See Jer.

xxv. 15. xvi. 16 And of thy garments 1612, 1616, 1617, 1629 C. & L. (And thy garments *Synd.*, Of thy garments 1613). ver. 59 hast despised *Bp.* 1612, 1613, 1616, 1617, 1629 C. & L. (hath despised *Synd.* 1630). xxvii. 10 thy men of war 1612, 1613, 1616, 1617 (the men of war *Synd.*). xxix. 18, 19 Nebuchadrezzar 1612, 1613, 1616, 1617 (Nebuchadnezzar *Synd.*). xxxi. 4 the field *Bp.* 1612, 1613, 1616, 1617 (the fields *Synd.*). xxxv. 10 mine *Bp.* 1612, 1613, 1616, 1617 (thine *Synd.*). xxxvi. 10 the wastes 1612, 1613, 1616 (the waste *Synd.* 1617). xlii. 12 directly *Bp.* 1612, 1613, 1616, 1617 (directed *Synd.*). xliv. 29 the trespass offering 1612, 1613, 1616, 1617 (their trespass offering *Synd.*). DAN. xi. 6 she shall be given up 1612, 1613, 1616, 1617 (he...*Synd.*). ver. 10 sons 1612, 1613, 1616, 1617 (son *Synd.*). HOSEA xiv. 3 Asshur *Bp.* 1612, 1613, 1616 (Ashur *Synd.* 1617). AMOS vi. 7 that go captive *Bp.* 1612, 1613, 1616, 1617 (that goeth captive *Synd.*). OBAD. ver. 7 thy confederacy *Bp.* 1612, 1613, 1616 (the confederacy *Synd.* 1617). MICAH i. 5 for the sins 1612, 1613, 1616, 1617 (the sins *Bp. Synd.*). HAB. ii. 15 that puttest 1612, 1613, 1616, 1617 (thou puttest *Synd.*). ZEPH. i. 7 hath bid 1612, 1613, 1616, 1617 (had bid *Synd.*). ZECH. iii. 7 *marg., walks* 1612, 1613, 1616 (*walk, Synd.* 1617). x. 3 his goodly 1612, 1613, 1616, 1617 (the goodly *Synd.*).

1 ESDRAS i. 23 his Lord 1612, 1613 (the Lord *Synd.*). ver. 29 king Josias 1612, 1613 (Josias *Synd.*). 2 ESDR. ii. 33 at nought 1612, 1616, 1629, 1630 (at naught *Synd.* 1613, 1617). Cf. ch. iv. 23. vii. 40 Sennacherib *Bp.* 1612, 1613, 1616 (Sannacherib *Synd.* 1617). xiv. 12 the tenth *Bp.* 1612, 1613, 1616 (a tenth *Synd.* 1617). TOBIT v. 18 *marg. Let not* 1612, 1613 (*Let no, Synd.*). JUDITH xvi. 4 stopped 1612, 1613, 1616, &c. (stoppeth *Synd.* 1617). ECCLUS. xxiii. 19 eyes of men *Bp.* 1612, 1613 (eyes of man *Synd.*). BARUCH vi. 40 Chaldeans 1612, 1616, 1630 (Caldeans

1613, 1617, 1629 C.). PRAYER OF MANASSES l. 3 their righteous 1612, 1613, 1616, 1629 (the righteous *Bp. Synd.* 1617). 1 MACC. xii. 47 *marg.*, *left* 1612, 1613 (*let, Synd.*).

MATT. xiii. 45 goodly pearls *Bp.* 1612, 1613, 1616, &c. (good pearls *Synd.* 1617). xviii. 30 went *Bp.* 1612, 1616, 1617, &c. (went out *Synd.* 1613). Cf. ver. 28 (Gk.). xxii. 24 a man *Bp.* 1612, 1616, 1629 C. & L. (any man *Synd.* 1613, 1617, 1630)[1]. MARK xv. 46 unto the door *Bp.* 1612, 1613, &c. (upon the door *Synd.*). LUKE ii. 24 offer a sacrifice 1612, 1613, &c. (offer sacrifice *Synd.*). x. 36 among the thieves *Bp.* 1612, 1613, &c. (among thieves *Synd.*). JOHN xiv. 23 a man *Bp.* 1612, 1616, &c. (any man *Synd.* 1613)[1]. ACTS iv. 27 thy holy child *Bp.* 1612, 1613, &c. (the holy child *Synd.*). vi. 12 came upon *Bp.* 1612, 1616, &c. (came unto *Synd.* 1613). Cf. Luke xx. 1; ch. iv. 1. xv. 11 the Lord *Bp.* 1612, 1616, 1629 C. & L. (our Lord *Synd.* 1613, 1617). xvi. 7 suffered them *Bp.* 1612, 1613 (suffered him *Synd.*). ver. 19 drew them into *Bp.* 1612, 1613, &c. (drew them unto *Synd.*). ROM. xvi. *Subscription*, of the Church *Bp.* 1612, 1616, &c. (to the Church *Synd.* 1613). EPH. vi. 21 ye also may *Bp.* 1612, 1613, 1616, 1629 C. & L. (ye may also *Synd.* 1617, 1630). 1 THESS. *Title*, Paul the Apostle 1612, 1613, 1616, 1617, &c. (the Apostle Paul *Synd.* here only). ch. i. 9 turned *Bp.* 1612, 1613, 1616, 1617, 1630, &c. (returned *Synd.* 1629 L.). JAMES v. 4 Sabaoth 1612, 1616, 1629 C. (Sabbaoth *Synd.* 1613, 1617, 1630). 1 PET. i. 22 your souls *Bp.* 1612, 1616, 1629, &c. (your selves *Synd.* 1613, 1617). 2 PET. ii. 6 Gomorrha 1612, 1616, 1629 L., 1630, 1638 (Gomorrah *Synd.* 1617, 1630; Gomorra 1629 C.).

---

[1] The context must decide which form is preferable, since the practice varies in rendering τις: e.g. John xv. 13 "a man;" John xvi. 30 "any man."

NOTE. Between the two copies in the British Museum which resemble the Oxford reprint (3050. g. 1 and 466. i. 6) the only differences in any of the passages cited in the foregoing lists § I. and § II. occur in Ex. xxi. 26; Cant. ii. 7. Of the other issue, B. M. 3050. g. 2 being regarded as the standard, and 3050. g. 3, 1276. l. 4, and Synd. A. 3. 14 mixed copies, the Syndics' nowhere agrees with 3050. g. 2 against the other two, but with 3050. g. 3 alone in Ezek. v. 5; with 3050. g. 2 and 1276. l. 4 against 3050. g. 3 in 15 places; with 3050. g. 3 and 1276. l. 4 against 3050. g. 1 in 5 places; with 1276. l. 4 alone (which is a fine tall volume, once the property of Lea Wilson) in no less than 34 places. Not one of the four is ever left without one of the other copies to countenance it, except Synd. in 2 Kin. xviii. 37; 1 Chr. iv. 36. Hence it is plain that Synd. A. 3. 14 and B. M. 1276. l. 4 were among the earliest and least revised of the copies printed off. See Sect. I. pp. 5—13.

APPENDIX C.

(See above, p. 14.)

List of passages in which the readings of the edition of the Authorized Bible of 1611 have been restored in the Cambridge Paragraph Bible. The date annexed is that of the later edition in which each change is supposed to have originated.

N.B. Variations relating only to English orthography or grammatical inflexions are not often admitted into the following list, since they have been sufficiently described in Section v. pp. 93—105.

Genesis	Reading of 1611 restored.	Variation of later Bibles.
v. 26	*marg.* † Heb. *Lemech*	omitted 1629, transferred to ver. 25, 1638.
vii. 2	† by sevens	by † sevens, 1629.
x. 7	Sabtecha	Sabtecah, 1762, Sabtechah, 1769.
xix. 21	concerning this thing	concerning this thing also, 1638[1].
xxv. 4	Abida	Abidah, 1629[2].
xxvi. 1, 8, 14, 15, 18	Philistims	Philistines, 1629 C. (1613 *bis*, 1629 L. *ter*).

[1] This change, however, might have been acquiesced in: cf. Hebrew.
[2] So all have the word in 1 Chr. i. 33, and the final *Ain* is not usually represented by *h*: cf. 2 Sam. v. 14. 1 Chr. xxiv. 11. See however *h* final in Gen. xxxv. 27; xxxviii. 2 (but not 1 Chr. ii. 3); Josh. xxi. 11.

Genesis	Reading of 1611 restored.	Variation of later Bibles.
xxxi. 1	which was of our father's	which was our fathers, 1616[1].
xxxvi. 14	daughter of Zibeon	the daughter of Zibeon, 1629.
xxxvii. 36	Medanites, 1612—1630	Midianites, 1616, 1629 C. Cf. ch. xxv. 2.
xxxix. 1	hand	hands, 1629 C. and L., 1630, 1637.
xlvi. 12	Zerah	Zarah, 1769 (Serah, 1630)[2].
xlvii. 6	any man [better than "*any* man"]	any men, 1762: *any* men, 1769.
xlvii. 18	also had our herds. Cf. ver. 22	also hath our herds, 1629 C. (had also…1630).
Exodus		
vi. 21	Zichri	Zithri, 1769[3].
xxiii. 23	the Hivites, 1612, 1613, 1617, 1629 L., 1769[4]	and the Hivites, 1616, 1629 C.—1762 (*and*, 1638—1762).
xxix. 26	consecrations (as ver. 34; Lev. viii. 28, 31), Heb.	consecration, 1762 (as vers. 22, 27, 31; Lev. viii. 33).
Leviticus		
v. 10	had sinned	hath sinned, 1762. Cf. ver. 6.
vii. 23 & xiv. 54[5]	manner	manner of, 1762 (as ch. vii. 26, 27, &c.).
xi. 3	cheweth cud	cheweth the cud, 1629 (as vers. 4—6).
xi. 10	nor scales (as ver. 12)	and scales, 1769.

[1] Cf. Lev. xxii. 10. Deut. xxiii. 25. 1 Cor. x. 29. This double possessive is sometimes retained even in modern Bibles: e.g. 2 Kin. xxii. 12. 2 Chr. ii. 13; xxxiv. 20. Matt. xxvi. 51 (not so Mark xiv. 47; Luke xxii. 50). Luke xv. 17. See above, p. 110.

[2] Yet so even 1611 in ch. xxxviii. 30 on account of the Hebrew pause.

[3] Corrected in the Scotch and American (1867) Bibles only.

[4] The re-correction of 1769 is followed by D'Oyly and Mant 1817, Oxford 8vo. 1835, Bagster 1846, Oxford 4to. 1857, London 8vo. 1859, American 1867, but not by our standard (Cambr. 8vo. 1858) and some modern Bibles.

[5] See above, p. 110.

restored, later corrections being withdrawn. 217

Leviticus	Reading of 1611 restored.	Variation of later Bibles.
xii. 6 *marg.*	son of his year	a son of his year, 1629. Cf. Gen. xvii. 12.
xiii. 29	hath a plague	have a plague, 1769. Cf. ver. 38.
xv. 33	which is unclean	that is unclean, 1769.
xxii. 10	a sojourner of the priest's	a sojourner of the priest, 1638[1].
xxv. 5	it own accord	its own accord, 1744[2].
xxv. 23	were strangers, 1613, 1617	are strangers, 1616, 1629 C. and L., 1630.
Numbers		
iii. 13	they shall be	shall they be, 1769.
iii. 35	northwards	northward, 1629. Cf. vers. 23, 29, 38.
v. 19, 20	hath lien[3] (lain, 1762), 1613—1762	have lien, 1629 L. (lain, 1769).
ix. 18	in the tents	in their tents, 1769 (as in vers. 17, 20, 22).
xx. 5	or vines	or of vines, 1769.
xxiv. 6	the river side, 1613, 1617[4]	the rivers (river's, 1762) side, 1616, 1629 C. and L., 1630.
xxiv. 20 *marg.*	‖ *The first of the nations*	‖ Or, *the first of the nations*, 1744.
xxx. 8	disallow	disallowed, 1769.
xxxvi. 3	whereinto. Cf. ch. xiv. 24	whereunto, 1629.
Deuteronomy		
xxii. 9 *marg.*	*the seed*	*thy seed*, 1629.
xxiii. 25	the standing corn of thy neighbours	the standing corn of thy neighbour, 1769[1].
xxiv. 15 *marg.*	he lifteth	lifteth, 1638.
xxvii. 12	Gerizzim	Gerizim, 1769. Cf. ch. xi. 29.
xxviii. 29	noon days	noon-day, 1762.

[1] See note 1 p. 216.
[2] See above, p. 110 note 2. Mr Aldis Wright finds "its" in Bibles of about 1681, but only to be dropped again. In Ben Jonson's *Silent Woman*, acted in 1609, the expression "it knighthood" several times occurs as an affected archaism, as though it had already grown obsolete in common speech.
[3] On this participial form see above, p. 103.
[4] See Appendix B, p. 207, note on Ex. xix. 4.

Joshua	Reading of 1611 restored.	Variation of later Bibles.
iii. 11	even the Lord, 1612—1630	of the Lord, 1629 (LXX., Vulg.).
x. 1, 3	Adoni-zedek (-ck, 1629 L., ver. 1)	Adoni-zedec, 1769.
xi. 2 & xii. 3	Cinneroth	Chinneroth, 1769. Cf. ch. xiii. 27 (Appendix A, p. 151); xix. 35.
xii. 2	river of Arnon (*of*, 1629)	river Arnon, 1638.
xiii. 18	Jahazah. Cf. ch. xxi. 36	Jahaza, 1629 C. and L., 1630.
xiii. 23	villages, 1612, 1613, 1616, 1629 L., 1630	the villages, 1617, 1629 C.
xix. 2	or Sheba, 1612, 1613. Cf. Gen. xxvi. 33	and Sheba, 1616—1762, Sheba, 1769[1].
xix. 19	Hapharaim	Haphraim, 1769.
ibid.	Shion, 1612, 1613, 1616, 1629 C. and L., 1630	Shihon, 1617, 1638.
xix. 42	Aijalon	Ajalon, 1629 C. (not L.). See p. 158 note 2.
xxi. 11 *text* & *marg.*	Arbah, 1612 — 1630 (*text*). Cf. Gen. xxxv. 27	Arba, 1638.

Judges

iii. 15 *marg.*	*Jemini.* Cf. 1 Sam. ix. 1	*Gemini*, 1762[2].
vi. 15 & ix. 9	‖ ‖ Or, 1612—1630	††Heb. (1629 C., ch. vi. 15), 1638.
xix. 29	coasts	coast, 1769, Bagster 1846: not Oxf. 1857, Lond. 1859, American 1867.

1 Samuel

ii. 20 *marg.*	*he asked*	*she asked*, 1638.
iv. 7 *marg.*	or *the third*, 1612, 1613, 1617, 1629 C., 1638, 1769[3]	or *the third*, 1616, 1629 L., 1630: or, *the third*, 1744, 1762, moderns.
xvii. 20 *marg.*	battle ray	battle array, 1744.

---

[1] Modern Bibles are divided between the two wrong renderings of 1616, 1769. The American alone follows 1611.
[2] This gross error is corrected in Bagster 1846, Camb. 1858, Speaker's Commentary 1872.
[3] So Oxf. 1835, Bagster 1846, Speaker's Commentary 1872.

restored, later corrections being withdrawn.

1 Samuel	Reading of 1611 restored.	Variation of later Bibles.
xviii. 1	when he made	when he had made, 1629.
xx. 5	in the fields	in the field, 1638.
xxxi. 2	Malchishua. Cf. 1 Chr. viii. 33; ix. 39; x. 2	Melchishua, 1769. Cf. ch. xiv. 49.
2 Samuel		
ii. 9	he made him	made him, 1762.
iv. 4	feet, *and* was	feet. He was, 1762.
v. 14	Shammua[1]	Shammuah, 1638.
vii. 7 *marg.*	‖ In the 1 Chr. xvii. 6, *any of the judges*	‖ 1 Chr. xvii. 6, *any of the judges*, 1638.
xvi. 8	to thy mischief[2]	in thy mischief, 1629.
xxi. 21	Shimea[3]	Shimeah, 1769.
xxiii. 20 *marg.*	lion. Cf. *marg.* of Isai. xxix. 1; Ezek. xliii. 15	*lions*, 1638.
xxiii. 37	Naharai	Nahari, 1769.
1 Kings		
iii. 4	offer up on, 1613, 1617	offer on, 1612: offer upon, 1616, 1629 C. and L., &c.
iii. 12	thy word (LXX.)	thy words (Vulg.), 1629 C.
xiii. 11	his son came	his sons came[4], 1616, 1617, &c.
xv. 5	Urijah (as 1638, &c. Neh. iii. 4)	Uriah, 1629 C. (not L.), as 1611 in Ezra viii. 33; Neh. iii. 4.
xv. 27	belongeth	*belonged*, 1762.

---

[1] See p. 215 note 2, Gen. xxv. 4. *Ain* is not represented in ver. 15 *bis*, 16 *bis*.

[2] Vulg. has *premunt te mala tua*. The Translators give what they hold to be the general sense in the text, reserving a more literal rendering for the margin.

[3] The reading of the *K'eri* and of 1 Chr. xx. 7. The correction of 1769 will not suit the form in the *Chetiv* and the Vatican Septuagint (Cεμεεί). Yet "Shimeah" is correct in ch. xiii. 3.

[4] A very needless change, though upheld by LXX. and Vulg. Cf. Cardwell, *Oxford Bibles*, p. 16. In 1762, &c. we find the marginal note † Heb. *son*.

1 Kings	Reading of 1611 restored.	Variation of later Bibles.
xvi. 19	to make Israel sin	to make Israel to sin, 1762.
xviii. 28	cried loud, 1612, 1613, 1617, 1630	cried aloud, 1616, 1629 C. and L.
xxii. 2	on the third year	in the third year, 1629 C.
xxii. 25 *marg.* & 2 Chr. xviii. 24 *marg.*	† Heb. *chamber in*	† Heb. *a chamber in*, 1638.

2 Kings		
iv. 35	neesed. Cf. Job xli. 18	sneezed, 1762.
viii. 19	to give to him	to give him, 1629 C.
xii. 18	had dedicate	had dedicated, 1762. Cf. App. A, p. 153.
xix. 2	Esai, 1612, 1613, 1617 (Esay, 1616, 1629 L., 1630)	Isaiah (transferring to ver. 2 the marginal note of 1611 on ver. 6), 1629 C.
xx. 17	unto Babylon	into Babylon, 1629 C.
xxiii. 36	twenty and five year old. Cf. 1 Esdr. i. 39	twenty and five years old, 1629 C. See above, p. 111.

1 Chronicles		
i. 25	Rehu	Reu, 1638. Cf. Gen. xi. 18, 19[1].
i. 38	Ezer. Cf. ver. 42. Gen. xxxvi. 21, 27	Ezar, 1629 C. and L. (not 1630).
ii. 47	Geshan	Gesham, 1769.
ii. 49	Achsah. Cf. Josh. xv. 17; Judg. i. 13	Achsa, 1638.
iii. 19	and the son of Zerubbabel[2]	and the sons of Zerubbabel, 1629 C. and L., 1630.
iii. 23 *marg.*	*Hiskijah.* Cf. Appendix B, p. 209.	*Hizkijahu*, 1629—1744, *Hiskijahu*, 1762, &c.
v. 11	Salchah. Cf. Deut. iii. 10	Salcah, 1629.

---

[1] *Ain* final is usually mute (see p. 215 note 2), but in the middle of a word the practice is less fixed.

[2] In ver. 21 the first "sons" is also singular in Hebrew, so that 1611 is inconsistent in the matter. Cf. ch. vii. 35.

restored, later corrections being withdrawn. 221

1 Chronicles	Reading of 1611 restored.	Variation of later Bibles.
v. 18	of † valiant men	† of valiant men, 1629[1].
vii. 1	Shimron	Shimrom, 1629 C. and L., 1630 (not 1638—1762), 1769.
vii. 5	men of might	valiant men of might, 1638. Cf. ver. 2.
vii. 19	Shemida[2]	Shemidah, 1762.
vii. 27	Jehoshua[2]. Cf. Num. xiii. 16	Jehoshuah, 1630, 1762.
vii. 35	And the son. Cf. ch. iii. 19	And the sons, 1744.
xii. 5	Eleuzai	Eluzai, 1629 C.
xiii. 9	‖ ‖ Or, *shook*	† (‖ 1762) † Heb. *shook*, 1762, &c.
xiii. 11 *marg.*	‖ *Hebr.* (That is, 1629) *breach*	‖ That is, *The breach*, 1638.
xviii. 3 *marg.* & ver. 16 *marg.*	*Hadadezer* in *Ahimelech* in ... *Saraia* in	*Hadadezer*, 1769. *Ahimelech* ... *Seraiah*, 1744. But cf. App. A, p. 160.
xxiii. 20	Michah. Cf. ch. xxiv. 24, 25	Micah, 1629.
xxiv. 11	Jeshua. Cf. Ezra ii. 36	Jeshuah, 1629 C. and L. (not 1630).
xxvi. 20, 26 & xxviii. 12. 2 Chr. xxiv. 7 & xxxi. 12. Ezek. xliv. 29	dedicate things	dedicated things, 1762. Compare App. A, p. 153 and note 2.
xxix. 6	rulers over the king's work	rulers of the king's work, 1762.
xxix. 17 *marg.*	† Heb. *found*. Cf. Judg. xx. 48	‖ Or, *found*, 1638.
2 Chronicles		
ix. 11 *marg.*	*stairs* (*staires*)	(*staies*, 1629 C., *stayes*, 1638), *stays*, 1744—1769[3].

---

[1] Corrected only in Bagster 1846 of the moderns.
[2] See note 1 p. 219.
[3] This mere typographical error, whose adoption may have been helped by "stayes" ver. 18, remains in D'Oyly and Mant 1817, Bagster 1846, and some modern Bibles, but is corrected in Oxford 1835, Cambridge 1858, American 1867, Speaker's Commentary 1872.

2 Chronicles	Reading of 1611 restored.	Variation of later Bibles.
xvi. 6	was a building. See above, p. 108.	was building, 1769.
xx. 36	Ezion-geber (*sic legendum*). Cf. 1 Kin. xxii. 48	Ezion-gaber, 1638 (*in pausâ*). Cf. Num. xxxiii. 35, 36; Deut. ii. 8.
xxv. 18 *marg.*	*furre bush* (*fur*, 1612, 1613, 1630, 1744)	*furze-bush*, 1762: *furze bush*, 1769.
xxvi. 18	pertaineth, 1612, 1613, 1617, 1630	*app-rtaineth*, 1616, 1629 C. and L.
xxix. 23	and laid	and they laid, 1629.
xxxii. 6 *marg.*	*he spake*	*spake*, 1638.
xxxiii. 19	all his sin	all his sins, 1762.
xxxiv. 10	mend. Cf. ch. xxiv. 12	amend, 1769.
xxxv. 20	Carchemish. Cf. Isai. x. 9; Jer. xlvi. 2	Charchemish, 1762.
Ezra		
ii. 2	Mispar	Mizpar, 1744.
iii. 2 *marg.*	Matt. i. 12 and Luke iii. 27, *called Zorobabel*	Called *Zorobabel*, Matt. i. 12; Luke iii. 27, 1629.
iv. 10	Asnappar. 1612, 1613, 1616, 1629 C.—1744	Asnapper, 1617, 1629 L., 1630, 1762, 1769, &c.
iv. 24	house of the God which	house of God which, 1616, &c.[1]
vii. 18	the silver and gold	the silver and the gold, 1762.
viii. 21	the river Ahava (Heb. not as ver. 31)	Ahava, the river of, 1762.
Nehemiah		
vii. 30	Geba (Gaba, Ezra ii. 26)	Gaba, 1638 (*in pausâ*).
vii. 59	Pochereth (, 1629 L.) Zebaim	Pochereth of Zebaim, 1629 C. Cf. Ezra ii. 57.[2]

---

[1] This seems to be an attempt on the part of the Translators (afterwards given over, as in ch. vii. 18) to represent, whensoever it might be possible, the *status emphaticus* of the Chaldee.

[2] The passage is too obscure to be worth altering. The Vulgate has *filii Phochereth, qui erat ortus ex Sabaim filio Amon.*

restored, later corrections being withdrawn. 223

Job	Reading of 1611 restored.	Variation of later Bibles.
iii. 8 *marg.*	*leviathan*	*a leviathan* 1659 (Field), 1674, 1677, 1679, 1701—69.
x. 10	cruddled (crudled, 1613)	curdled, 1762.
xviii. 9	grinne, 1612 — 1630 : grin, 1629 C.	gin, 1762. See Ps. cxl. 5, and above, p. 100.
xx. 25	glistering	glittering, 1762. Cf. Deut. xxxii. 41.
xxviii. 17 *marg.*	*vessel*	*vessels*, 1744.
xxviii. 27 *marg.*	*did number*	*number*, 1638.
xxix. 17 *marg.*	*I cast*	*cast*, 1638.
xxx. 3	flying	fleeing, 1629 (LXX.).
xxx. 6	clifts[1]	cliffs, 1762.
xli. 6	the companions[2]	thy companions, 1769.
xli. 30 *marg.*	*of the potsherd*	*of potsherd*, 1762.
Psalm		
ii. 4	the LORD, 1612—1630, 1762, 1769	the Lord, 1629 C.— 1744[3].
xxiv. 3	and who shall stand	or who shall stand, 1769.
xlv. 11	thy Lord. Cf. Isai. li. 22	thy lord, Camb. 8vo. 1858 (our standard) only. See above, p. 38.
lxxxi. 12 *marg.*	*imagination*	*imaginations*, 1762.
cvii. 19	he saveth	*and* he saveth, 1762. So
cxiii. 9	to be a joyful	*and to be* a joyful, 1629.
cxv. 3	whatsoever he pleased	whatsoever he hath pleased, 1769.
cxix. 42 *marg.*	*reproveth*	*reproacheth*, 1638.
cxxxii. 12	also shall sit [Cf. Heb.]	shall also sit, 1762.

---

[1] In 2 Chr. xx. 16 "cliffe" of 1611 represents another Hebrew word. "Clift" in Ex. xxxiii. 22; Isai. lvii. 5 is left unaltered in 1762 and the moderns, the general sense, though not the Hebrew words, being the same as here.

[2] That is, the partners in the fishery (Luke v. 7, 10). Blayney's variation hardly looks accidental, and lingers in many later Bibles, e.g. Ostervald 1808, Oxford 8vo. 1813, D'Oyly and Mant 1817, even in Bagster 1846.

[3] The present text is *Adonai*, but *Jehovah* is read in at least 85 Hebrew manuscripts and five early editions, so that the Translators (who seldom err in this matter) probably intended to use capitals. Since Oxf. 8vo. 1835, as also by Bp Turton's direction (Sect. 1., above, p. 36), the capitals have been again withdrawn, but not in Bagster 1846.

224   Appendix C.]   Original readings of 1611

Psalm	Reading of 1611 restored.	Variation of later Bibles.
cxl. 5 & cxli. 9	grinnes (grins, 1613 *semel*, 1638, &c. *bis*). See Job xviii. 9, p. 223	gins, 1762.
cxli. 9	from the snare	from the snares, 1769.
cxliii. 9 *marg.*	*hid me*, 1613—1744	*hide me*, 1612, 1630, 1762, 1769
cxlviii. 8	vapour (so American, 1867)	vapours, 1769.
Proverbs		
xxv. 24	a corner. Cf. ch. xxi. 9	the corner, 1769.
Ecclesiastes		
viii. 8 *marg.*	*casting of*	*casting off*[1], 1629 C., 1638 (not 1744), 1762, &c.
viii. 17	further. Cf. ch. xii. 12	farther, 1762.
Canticles		
viii. 4 *marg.*	*stir up, or* (, 1612) *why*	*stir up*, or, *why*, 1744.
Isaiah		
vi. 8	I said	said I, 1629.
viii. 6	For so much (Forsomuch, 1629)	Forasmuch, 1762.
x. 26	rock Oreb. Cf. Judg. vii. 25	rock of Oreb, 1629 C. and L. (not 1630), 1638.
xiv. 9 *text marg.*	† chief ones † Heb. *leaders*, or *great goats*	† ‖ chief ones. † Heb. *leaders*. ‖ Or, *great goats*, 1629.
xiv. 17 *marg.*	*homeward*	*homewards*, 1762.
xviii. 7 *marg.*	*polished*. &c. (*polished*, &c. 1612, 1616, 1629 L., 1630)	*polished*. 1613, 1629 C., 1638, 1744; but *polished*: 1762, &c.
xix. 14 *marg.*	*perversities*	*perverseness*, 1762.
xxii. 17 *marg.*	*v*. 18. shall surely, &c.	shall surely, &c. ver. 18, 1629.

---

[1] *Nec est dimissio in bello*, Field. The sense given by 1629 C. and the moderns may be as good as that of 1611, but is not identical with it. For "off" see 1611 in Gen. xxxviii. 14; Ex. iii. 5.

restored, later corrections being withdrawn.

Isaiah	Reading of 1611 restored.	Variation of later Bibles.
xxviii. 11 *marg.*	*lip*	*lips*, 1638.
li. 16	and have covered	and I have covered, 1769.
lxiii. 19 *marg.*	† † Heb.	†(|| 1744). ‖ Or, 1638.
Jeremiah		
xvi. 2	nor daughters	or daughters, 1769.
xxxiv. 11 & xlvi. 26	afterwards	afterward, 1769.
xxxiv. 16	whom ye had set	whom he had set, 1629 C., 1638, moderns.
xxxvii. 9	your † selves	†yourselves, 1762.
xl. 1	The word which	The word that, 1762.
xliv. 28 *marg.*	*or from them* (*men* 1616)	*or them*, 1762.
lii. 1	one and twenty year, 1612 — 1638. See above, p. 111	one and twenty years, 1630, 1744.
Ezekiel		
vii. 11 *text*	‖ theirs (‖ their multitude, 1611)[1]	their ‖multitude.......... ‖ theirs.
marg.	‖ *Or, their tumultuous persons. Heb. tumult*	‖ Or, *tumult*. ‖Or, *their tumultuous persons*, 1629.
x. 5	utter court	outer court, 1762[2]. Cf. 2 Macc. xiv. 41.
xi. 24	in vision	in a vision, 1769.
xiii. 9 *marg.*	*counsel*	*council*, 1762.
xviii. 1	And the word	The word, 1638.
xxiii. 23	all the Assyrians	and (*and*, 1638) all the Assyrians, 1616 (not 1617), 1629.
xxvii. 16 *marg.*	‖ ‖ *Or, chrysoprase* (*Chrysophrase* 1616). Cf. ch. xxviii. 13	†‖(† 1744) †Heb. *chrysoprase*, 1638, 1744.
xxx. 17	Phi-beseth	Pi-beseth, 1762.

---

[1] The error of 1611, &c., which misplaces the reference mark in the text (as it so often does), led to the hopeless confusion of 1629 and the moderns. Our Translators merely wish to give, as an alternative rendering for "theirs," Tremellius' *ex Thrasonibus ipsorum*.

[2] In 14 other places in Ezekiel "utter" is left unchanged.

226   *Appendix C.*]   *Original readings of* 1611

Ezekiel	Reading of 1611 restored.	Variation of later Bibles.
xxxi. 14	‖ their trees	their trees ‖, 1629[1].
xxxvi. 3 *marg.*	*come up on*	*come upon*, 1612, 1616 (not 1613, 1617), 1629.
xliii. 27	eight day. See above, p. 111	eighth day, 1629 C., 1630.
xlvii. 3	† the waters	the † waters, 1629.
xlviii. 28	‖ ‖ Or, *Meribah*	†† Heb. *Meribah*, 1638.
Daniel		
ii. 27	astrologians	astrologers, 1638.
iii. 19	to be heat. See above, p. 112	to be heated, 1762.
v. 31	two year. See above, p. 111	two years, 1612 (not 1613, 1616, 1617), 1629 L., 1630 (not 1629 C., 1638), 1744.
xi. 38 *marg.*	*or, as for the Almighty* (or, *as for the Almighty*, 1629 C., 1744)	† Heb. *as for the Almighty*, 1638, 1762, mod. Cf. Appendix A, p. 172.
Hosea		
xiii. 3	a whirlwind	the whirlwind, 1638.
Amos		
i. 1	two year. See above, p. 111	two years, 1616, 1630 (not 1612, 1613, 1617, &c., 1629 C. and L., 1638), 1744.
ii. 2	Kerioth. Cf. Jer. xlviii. 24	Kirioth, 1629 C. and L., 1630. Kerioh, 1612.
Jonah		
i. 4	† was like	was † like, Bagster 1846, Camb. 8vo. 1858, American 1867.

---

[1] The correctors of 1629 failed to perceive that the margin (following Tremellius, *conquiescant in se ipsis altitudine suâ*) translates by "upon themselves" the word rendered "their trees" by the Bishops' and Authorized versions.

restored, later corrections being withdrawn.

Nahum	Reading of 1611 restored.	Variation of later Bibles.
iii. 16	flieth. Cf. Hab. i. 8	fleeth, 1762.
Zechariah		
iv. 2	which were (*were*, 1629) upon	which *are* upon, 1762.
Malachi		
i. 14 *marg.* ii. 2	† † Heb. and will curse	‖ ‖ Or, 1629. and I will curse, 1616 (not 1617), 1629.
1 Esdras		
i. 9	Jechonias	Jeconias, 1629.
i. 28, 32, 47, 57 & ii. 1	Jeremie. Cf. 2 Esdr. ii. 18; Ecclus. xlix. 6; 2 Macc. ii. 1, 5, 7; Matt. ii. 17	Jeremy, 1762 (1612, 1613, 1616, 1629, &c. partially).
i. 39	twenty year old. See above, p. 111	twenty years old, 1612 (not 1613, &c.), 1629, 1630. Cf. 2 Kin. xxiii. 36.
i. 55	brake down...set fire	and break down, 1769... and set fire, 1762.
iii. 11	strongest, 1612—1630, 1769	the strongest, 1629—1762[1].
iv. 21	He sticks. See above, p. 140 note 2	He sticketh, 1769. Cf. Ecclus. xliv. 12.
iv. 29 *marg.*	*Themasius*	*Themasus*, 1769[2].
v. 14	Adonican (Aldus), 1612, 1630	Adonicam, *Bp.*, 1613—1744: -kam, 1762, 1769, moderns. Cf. ch. viii. 39.
v. 29 *marg.*	*Agabah*	*Agaba*, 1629. Cf. Neh. vii. 48.
v. 34 v. 55	Sabie (Σαβιή, LXX.) Sidon. Cf. 2 Esdr. i. 11; 1 Macc. v. 15	Saby, 1629; Sabi, 1744. Zidon, 1769.

---

[1] Most moderns here, with our standard (see above, p. 38), omit "the." Ostervald (1808) reads it consistently in vers. 11, 12.
[2] Blayney in the very same note corrects the false reference to Josephus of 1611—1762 from *cap.* 4. to *cap.* 3.

228   *Appendix C.] Original readings of* 1611

1 Esdras	Reading of 1611 restored.	Variation of later Bibles.
v. 69	Asbazareth (1630)	Azbazareth, 1629.
vii. 6	and other that were	and others that were, 1762[1].
viii. 2	Memeroth (Aldus)	Meremoth, 1762.
viii. 39	Adonicam (Aldus *here*)	Adonican, 1612: Adonikam, 1762. Cf.ch.v.14.
viii. 75 *marg.*	† † *Greek*	† † (‖ ‖ 1638) Or, 1629.
viii. 96 *marg.*	*and of all Israel*	*and all Israel*[2], 1629.
ix. 19 *marg.*	*Maas-... Jarib ... Gedaliah*	1629 prefixes "Or," to each.
ix. 48	Sabateus, 1612, 1613, 1630 (Σαβραῖος, Vat. MS. [*Vercellone*], Σαβαταῖος, Rom. edit.)	Sabatteas, 1629—1762: Sabateas, 1769 (Σαβαrraίas, Aldus).
2 Esdras		
i. 40	Zacharie...Malachie	Zachary..........Malachy, 1762 (1616, &c. partially).
ii. 18	I will send...Jeremie	will I send, 1629...Jeremy, 1744.
iii. 17	Sina. Cf. Acts vii. 30, 38	Sinai, 1762. Cf. ch. xiv. 4; Gal. iv. 24, 25.
iii. 35	hath so kept	have so kept, 1769.
vii. 68	the ten thousand part (Bishops')	the ten thousandth part, 1638.
xiii. 12	saw I, 1612—1630, 1769, D'Oyly and Mant 1817, Oxf. 1835	I saw, 1629—1762, Ostervald 1808, Camb. 4to. 1863. See above, p. 38.
xiv. 43	and held	and I held, 1629.
xiv. 47	fountains	fountain, 1629, Vulg., Bishops', Junius.
xv. 22	upon earth. Cf. ver. 29	upon the earth, 1629.
xv. 53	alway. Cf. ch. xvi. 20	(alwaies, 1629), always, 1744.
xvi. 26	shall ripe. See above, p. 112	shall ripen, 1638.
xvi. 30	or, when as	or as when, 1638.

[1] See above, p. 87 and note.
[2] The correction of 1629 represents *et omnem Israel* (πάντα τὸν 'Ισραήλ) of the Vulgate and (virtually) of Junius. Our Translators seem to have read somewhere Καὶ παντὸς τοῦ 'Ισραήλ, but Aldus, with the Vatican and Alexandrian MSS., has no καί.

restored, later corrections being withdrawn. 229

Tobit	Reading of 1611 restored.	Variation of later Bibles.
ii. 4	I start (ἀναπηδήσας)	I started, 1762.
iii. 17	belongeth (ἐπιβάλλει)	belonged, 1629.
iv. 10	alms doth deliver... suffereth	alms do deliver, 1629 ...suffer, Camb. 4to. 1863, after Bp Turton (see above, p. 36)[1].
vii. 1	after that they had	after they had, 1629.
vii. 3	Nephthali. Cf. ch. i. 1, 2, &c.	Nephthalim, 1638 (not 1744), 1762, &c.

Judith

ii. 4, *passim*	Olofernes. See Appendix B, p. 205	Holofernes, 1638, Vulg.; Holophernes, Junius, Bishops'.
ii. 20	A great multitude	A great number, 1769.
v. 3	Canaan. Cf. Appendix A (p. 179) 1629, in vers. 9, 10, 16	Chanaan, 1638.
vii. 3	Esdraelon, Bishops', Aldus (*ferè*), LXX. (Fritzsche), Vulg.	Esdraelom,1638.Compl., Ald. (*hic*), LXX. (Rom., &c.).
viii. 6	the eves of the sabbath	the eves of the sabbaths, 1629.
xv. 5	Choba	Chobai, 1638. Cf. ver. 4[2].

Wisdom

iv. 5	unperfect, Bishops'. See above, p. 112	imperfect, 1762.
v. 16 *marg.*	unproperly	improperly, 1744.
vii. 25 *marg.*	*stream* (ἀπόρροια)	*dream*, Oxf. 1835, Camb. 1863, not D'Oyly and Mant 1817.
x. 10	travails. Cf. ch. vi. 14	travels, 1612 (not 1613), 1629 (not 1630), 1638, &c. See above, p. 97.

---

[1] Yet "alms" is left as a singular noun in ver. 11; ch. xii. 9; Ecclus. xvii. 22; Acts iii. 3, as in Shakespeare and the purest later writers.

[2] Both the Aldine and Roman editions of the Septuagint, which our Translators much used (see above, pp. 47, 48) have the same variation in vers. 4, 5.

Wisdom	Reading of 1611 restored.	Variation of later Bibles.
xii. 1	uncorruptible, Bishops'	incorruptible, 1762. Cf. ch. xviii. 4 *marg.*
xv. 13	brickle. See p. 140 note 2	brittle, 1762.
xvi. 18	sometimes (ποτέ)	sometime, 1629. See Col. i. 21 (below, p. 236 note).
xviii. 9	alike (ὁμοίως)	like, 1629 (not 1630, 1744), 1638, 1762, &c.
xviii. 18	here, another	here, and another, 1638.
Ecclus.		
vi. 15	unvaluable	invaluable, 1762.
vii. 24	have care	have a care, 1629.
xi. 25	no remembrance	no more remembrance, 1629.
xvii. 23	Afterward	Afterwards, 1629.
xvii. 24	those that fail (ἐκλείπονταs)	those that failed, 1629.
xix. 8	to friend, 1612—1630, 1744, D'Oyly and Mant 1817, Camb. 1863	to a friend, 1629, 1638, 1762, &c., Ostervald 1808, Oxf. 1835.
xxiii. 13	untemperate (unhonest, Bishops')	intemperate, 1744.
xxv. 22	impudencie (impudency, 1638)	impudence, 1762.
xxvi. 13	will fat. See above, p. 112	will fatten, 1762.
xxvi. 15, 25 & xxxii. 10 & xli. 16, 24	shamefast	shamefaced, 1744.
xxvii. 12	undiscreet, Bishops'	indiscreet, 1744.
xxx. 15	state of body (εὐεξία)	estate of body, 1629.
xxxii. 1	(of the feast)	(of a feast), 1629 (not 1630), 1638.
xli. 16	shamefastness. See ch. xxvi. 15	shamefacedness, 1744. Cf. 1 Tim. ii. 9.
xlii. 24	unperfect (unperfit, 1611)	imperfect, 1744.
xliii. 5 *marg.*	stayed	stayeth, 1769[1].
xliv. 12	stands fast	standeth fast, 1769.

---

[1] Blayney wishes to render the Complutensian reading κατέπαυσε, which the margin represents, in the same tense as κατέσπευσεν is translated in the text, without perceiving that the marginal sense refers to Josh. x. 13.

restored, later corrections being withdrawn. 231

Ecclus.	Reading of 1611 restored.	Variation of later Bibles.
xlv. 8 *marg.*	Gr.	Heb. 1769, Oxf. 1835, Camb.1863, not D'Oyly and Mant 1817.
xlvii. 23	Nabat, LXX., Bishops'	Nebat, 1629, 1630.
xlviii. 8	anointed	anointedst, 1762. Cf. vers. 7, 9, and ver. 8 [*marg.*].
xlix. 6 *marg.* & Baruch vi. *Title*, *bis*	Jeremie. See 1 Esdr. i. 28	Jeremy, 1744 (1629, *semel*).
Baruch		
iii. 23	Merran	Meran[1], 1638 (not 1744), 1762.
vi. 9, 21	loves...comes	loveth...cometh, 1769.
Song		
ver. 17	burnt offering	burnt offerings[2], 1629.
Hist. of Susanna		
Title	in Hebrew	in the Hebrew, 1638.
ver. 22	I am straited	I am straitened (straitned, 1744), 1762.
Bel & Dragon		
33—35, 37, 39	Habacuc	Habbacuc, 1629 (Ἀμβακούμ, LXX.).
1 Macc.		
iii. 16, 24 & vii. 39 & ix. 50	Bethoron (Βαιθωρῶν)	Bethhoron, 1769 (Beth-h., 1762 *bis*).
v. 25	in peaceable manner. Cf. ver. 48	in a peaceable manner, 1769.
v. 26	in Alema (*et in*, Vulg.)	and Alema, 1629 (not 1630), 1638.
ix. 37	Canaan	Chanaan, 1638.

[1] Μέρραν Aldine and Roman editions, Μέραν Complutensian.
[2] ὁλοκαυτώσει Vulg., Bishops', Roman edition: ὁλοκαυτώμασι Ald., Compl., Fritzsche.

1 Macc.	Reading of 1611 restored.	Variation of later Bibles.
ix. 57	two year. See above, p. 111	two years, 1629 (not 1630), 1638.
x. 29	I do free	do I free, 1629, &c. (I free, 1744.)
x. 45	for building (*second*)	for the building, 1629 (not 1630), 1638. Cf. vers. 44, 45.
x. 52 & xiv. 29	Forsomuch	Forasmuch, 1629 (ch. xiv. 29, 1744).
xi. 6	Joppa	Joppe, 1638 (as elsewhere).
xiii. 51	seventy and one year	seventy and first year, 1769.
xiii. 53	, and dwelt [1]	, and he dwelt, 1762 (; 1769).
2 Macc.		
i. 36	as much to say as	as much as (1629 om. as) to say, 1638.
ii. 1, 5, 7	Jeremie	Jeremy, 1744 (ver. 7, 1613). See 1 Esdr. i. 28 (above, p. 227).
iii. 12	such wrong	such wrongs, 1629 (not 1630), 1638.
iv. 2	tendred (κηδεμόνα)	tendered, 1638.
iv. 21	unto Egypt. Cf. ver. 22	into Egypt, 1638.
iv. 23	Three year ... foresaid. See above, p. 111	Three years, 1630 (not 1629, 1638) ... aforesaid, 1629 (not 1630), 1638.
iv. 50	in power	of power, 1629 (not 1630, 1744), 1638, 1762.
v. 20	the adversities	the adversity, 1629 (not 1630), 1638.
viii. 33	who was fled (πεφευγότα)	who had fled, 1769.
ix. 3	Ecbatana	Ecbatane, 1762. Cf. Tobit iii. 7.

---

[1] The comma is from Synd. A. 3. 14 (only) and 1613, not Oxf. 1611 and 1612. Notwithstanding ch. xvi. 1, Simon, not John, is intended by the Translators to be the subject of "dwelt."

restored, later corrections being withdrawn. 233

2 Macc.	Reading of 1611 restored.	Variation of later Bibles.
ix. 18	the letter, 1612—1630, Camb. 1863	the letters, 1629, 1638, moderns.
xi. 21	eight[1] and forty year, the four and twenty day	eight and fortieth year, the four and twentieth day, 1638.
xi. 21 *marg.*	*Dioscores*	(*Dioscores*, 1630), *Dioscorus*, 1762.
xii. 42	for the sin, LXX.	for the sins, Vulg., 1629 (not 1630), 1638.
xiv. 6	Asideans. Cf. 1 Macc. ii. 42 (above, p. 200).	Assideans, 1629 (not 1630), 1638.
xiv. 41	utter door	outer door, 1762. See Ezek. x. 5.
Colophon	The end of Apocrypha	The end of the Apocrypha, 1638.

S. Matthew

ii. 17 & xxvii. 9	Jeremie	Jeremy, 1699 (1629, in ch. xxvii. 9). See 1 Esdr. i. 28.
iii. 12	but will burn up	but he will burn up, 1629.
ix. 34	casteth out the devils	casteth out devils, 1762.
xii. 23	Is this the son	Is not this the son, 1638[2].
xiii. 6	had not root. Cf. ver. 21	had no root, 1762.
xvii. 20 & xix. 26 & Luke i. 37; xviii. 27	unpossible (Bishops'). See above, p. 112	impossible, 1743. Cf. Mark x. 27.
Matt. xxiv. 50 & Luke xii. 46	ware. Cf. Acts xiv. 6; 2 Tim. iv. 15	aware, 1762. See above, p. 113.
Matt. xxvi. 39 & Mark i. 19	further	farther, 1762, moderns (not American 1867).
Matt. xxvii. 52	bodies of saints which slept	bodies of the saints which slept, 1762[3].

[1] In ver. 33 "eight" of 1611—1630 (not 1629) may be regarded as another mode of spelling the ordinal, as 1611 has it in Lev. xiv. 10, 23; Luke xv. 8 *marg.* Compare also 2 Kin. xv. 8 and Ezek. xliii. 27, p. 226.

[2] So, though wrongly, nearly all the moderns, but not Scholefield, in the Cambridge Greek and English N.T. (above, p. 79 note 1), and the Tract Society's Bible 1868. Archbishop Trench contrasts the insertion of "not" in John iv. 29 with its omission in John viii. 22; xviii. 35; Acts vii. 42; x. 47. Compare also John vii. 26, 31.

[3] This change has not been imported into the Gospel for Palm Sunday in the Book of Common Prayer. Cf. 1 John v. 12 in Appendix A (p. 193), and 1 Cor. xiii. 2 below, where in modern Prayer-Books we

234   *Appendix C.*]   *Original readings of* 1611

S. Mark	Reading of 1611 restored.	Variation of later Bibles.
vi. 7	he calleth	he called, 1769.
xiv. 36	not that I will, but what	not what I will, but what, 1629.
S. Luke		
viii. 8	when he said (λέγων)	when he had said, 1629.
xi. 16 & xviii. 9	other. Cf. ver. 42; ch. xxiii. 32. See above, p. 87 note	others, 1744 (ch. xviii. 9 in 1629).
xii. 20 *marg.*	††Gr.	‖ ‖ Or, 1629.
xix. 13 *marg.*	*two shillings sixpence*	*two shillings and sixpence*, 1769.
S. John		
xi. 18 *marg.*	*two mile*, 1613, 1617, 1629 L. See above, p. 111	*two miles*, 1612, 1616, 1629 C., 1630.
xi. 34	They say unto him	They said unto him, 1769, moderns (not American 1867).
Acts		
v. 34	a doctor of law	a doctor of the law, 1762. Cf. Luke v. 17.
x. 9	upon the house (δῶμα)	upon the house top, 1629. Cf. Matt. xxiv. 17[1].
xvii. 31	‖ hath given	hath ‖ given, 1629 C. (not L., 1630), 1638.
xviii. 5	pressed in spirit	pressed in the spirit, 1769. Cf. ver. 25.
xix. 19	also of them	of them also, 1769.
xxiv. 14	and the prophets, Bishops'	and in the prophets, 1762. See Appendix E, p. 259.
xxv. 6	sitting in the judgment seat, Bishops' (but both read "on," ver. 17)	sitting on the judgment seat, 1762.
xxviii. 8	flixe (flix, 1629)	flux, 1699. See above, p. 103.
Fin.	The end of the Acts of the Apostles	omitted, 1629.

read "not" in the Epistle for Quinquagesima Sunday. So in John iii. 13, in the Gospel for Trinity Sunday, "which" of 1611 and the rest is changed into "who."

[1] In Acts xv. 14 some modern editions have "Symeon," "Simeon" is the form used from 1611 to 1769 and its imitators. Appendix A (p. 187), Luke iii. 30.

Romans	Reading of 1611 restored.	Variation of later Bibles.
iv. 19	an hundred year, 1612—1699. See above, p. 111	an hundred years, 1630, 1743. &c.
ib. & ix. 9	Saras[1], 1629, 1638, 1743 (chap. iv. 19, Saraes, 1611-1630). Cf. Heb. xi. 11; 1 Pet. iii. 6	Sarah's, 1762 (so 1743 in 1 Pet. iii. 6 only).
vii. 2	law of the husband	law of her husband, 1616 (not 1617, 1629 L., 1630), 1629 C., &c.
xi. 23	bide	abide, 1762. See above, p. 113.
1 Cor.		
iv. 9	approved to death, 1612, 1613	appointed to death[2], 1616, 1617, 1629 C. and L., &c.
x. 29	of the other's (others, 1611 — 1743), τοῦ ἑτέρου	of the other, 1762, 1769. See above, p. 216 note 1.
xiii. 2	have no charity	have not charity, 1762. See p. 233 note 3.
xiv. 15	and will pray	and I will pray, 1638.
xiv. 18	than [then: see above, p. 97] you all	than ye all.
2 Cor.		
v. 1	made with hand	made with hands, 1612 (not 1613, 1616, 1617), 1629.
Galatians		
v. 15	take heed ye be not	take heed that ye be not, 1629.
Ephesians		
i. 9	had purposed	hath purposed, 1629.

---

[1] So always in the Apocrypha. In Rom. iv. 19, and not elsewhere, so far as we know, 1701 has "Sara's". See above, p. 152 note.

[2] A deliberate but needless correction, derived from Tyndale's, Coverdale's, the Great, and the Bishops' Bibles. The Geneva (1557), has "destinate to death."

236   Appendix C.]   Original readings of 1611

Colossians	Reading of 1611 restored.	Variation of later Bibles.
i. 21	sometimes	sometime, *Bp.*, 1629[1].
1 Timothy		
ii. 9	shamefastness	shamefacedness, 1743 (shamefac'dness, 1674, 1683, 1699). Cf. Ecclus. xli. 16.
iv. 16	the doctrine, 1611— 1630, 1769, moderns	thy doctrine, 1629 C., 1638, 1699, 1743, 1762. See above, p. 4 note.
2 Timothy		
i. 12	and I am persuaded	and am persuaded, 1762.
James		
v. 4	which have reaped down	who have reaped down, 1762.
1 Peter		
v. 10	called us into	called us unto, 1638.
2 Peter		
i. 9	see far off	see afar off, 1769.
1 John		
ii. 29	which doeth (doth, 1612, 1613, 1616, 1630)	that doeth (doth, 1629 C.), 1629 C. and L.., 1638.
iii. 17	hath need	have need, 1629 C. (not 1629 L., 1630), 1638.

---

[1] So Wisd. xvi. 18, where the Bishops' renders ποτὲ "sometimes" and "sometime" in consecutive verses. The modern distinction between the two words did not exist when these versions were made. Hence all our Bibles have "sometimes" Eph. ii.13; v. 8; Titus iii. 3: all "sometime" Col. iii. 7; 1 Pet. iii. 20, the Greek being always ποτέ.

Revelation	Reading of 1611 restored.	Variation of later Bibles.
ii. 6, 15	Nicolaitans	Nicolaitanes, 1638 (not 1743), 1762.
vii. 7	Isachar	Issachar, 1629 C. and L., 1630 (not 1638—1743), 1762.
xvii. 2	inhabiters. Cf. ch. viii. 13; xii. 12	inhabitants, 1762.
xvii. 4	precious stone	precious stones, 1630 (not 1629 C. and L., 1743), 1762. Cf. ch. xviii. 12, 16; xxi. 19.
xxi. 20	chrysolite. Cf. Ezek. xxviii. 13 *marg.*	chrysolyte, 1762.
xxii. 2	of either side	on either side, 1762.

APPENDIX D.

(See above, p. 28).

To the Rev. the Vice-Chancellor, and the other Delegates of the Clarendon Press.

THE Editor of the two editions of the Bible lately printed at the Clarendon Press thinks it his duty, now that he has completed the whole in a course of between three and four years' close application, to make his report to the Delegates of the manner in which that work has been executed; and hopes for their approbation.

In the first place, according to the instructions he received, the folio edition of 1611, that of 1701, published under the direction of Bishop Lloyd [see above, p. 26], and two Cambridge editions of a late date, one in quarto, the other in octavo, have been carefully collated, whereby many errors that were found in former editions have been corrected, and the text reformed to such a standard of purity, as, it is presumed, is not to be met with in any other edition hitherto extant.

The punctuation has been carefully attended to, not only with a view to preserve the true sense, but also to uniformity, as far as was possible.

Frequent recourse has been had to the Hebrew and Greek Originals; and as on other occasions, so with a special regard to the words not expressed in the Original Language, but which our Translators have thought fit to insert in Italics, in order to make out the sense after the English idiom, or to preserve the connexion. And though Dr Paris [see above, p. 28] made large corrections in this particular in an edition published at Cambridge, there still remained many necessary alterations, which escaped the Doctor's notice; in making which the Editor chose not to rely on his own judgment singly, but submitted them all to the previous examination of the Select Committee, and particularly of the Principal of Hertford College[1], and Mr Professor Wheeler. A list of the above alterations was intended to have been given in to the Vice-Chancellor at this time, but the Editor has not yet found time to make it completely out.

Considerable alterations have been made in the Heads or Contents prefixed to the Chapters, as will appear on inspection; and though the Editor is unwilling to enlarge upon the labour bestowed by himself in this particular, he cannot avoid taking notice of the peculiar obligations, which both himself and the public lie under to the Principal of Hertford College, Mr Griffith of Pembroke College, Mr Wheeler, Poetry Professor[2], and the late Warden of New College[3], so long as he lived to bear a part in it; who with a prodigious expence of time, and inexpressible fatigue to themselves, judiciously corrected and improved the rude and imperfect Draughts of the Editor.

The running titles at the top of the columns in each page, how trifling a circumstance soever it may appear, required no small degree of thought and attention.

Many of the proper names being left untranslated, whose etymology was necessary to be known, in order to a more perfect comprehension of the allusions in the text, the translation of them, under the inspection of the above named Committee, has been for the benefit of the unlearned supplied in the margin.

---

[1] David Durell, D.D., 1757—1775.
[2] 1766—1776; Regius Professor of Divinity, 1776—1783.
[3] Thomas Bayward, 1764—1768.

Some obvious and material errors in the chronology have been considered and rectified.

The marginal references, even in Bishop Lloyd's Bible, had in many places suffered by the inaccuracy of the Press; subsequent editions had copied those *Errata*, and added many others of their own; so that it became absolutely necessary to turn to and compare the several passages; which has been done in every single instance, and by this precaution several false references brought to light, which would otherwise have passed unsuspected. It has been the care of the Editor to rectify these, as far as he could, by critical conjecture, where the copies universally failed him, as they did in most of the errors discovered in Bishop Lloyd's edition. In some few instances he confesses himself to have been at a loss in finding out the true reference, though the corruption was manifest in the want of any the most distant resemblance between the passages compared together. Cases of this sort indeed did not often occur; so that a very small number only of the old references are, with the sanction of the Committee, omitted, and their places more usefully supplied.

It had been suggested by the late Archbishop of Canterbury[1], that an improvement might be made in the present editions of the Bible, by taking in a number of additional references, of which many useful ones, as he supposed, might be furnished from other editions referred to by him, and particularly from a Scotch edition[2], of which the present Vice-Chancellor was kind enough to lend a

---

[1] Thomas Secker, born 1693; Bishop of Bristol, 1735; of Oxford, 1737; Archbishop of Canterbury, 1758—1768.

[2] In the absence of a date it seems impossible to identify this "Scotch edition," unless it be Brown's or one of Canne's (see above, p. 121 note). Dr Eadie (*English Bible*, Vol. II. p. 320) names one printed at Edinburgh in 1760 which omits "not," Heb. ii. 16.

Dr Blayney's Report, 1769. 241

Copy. The references found in it, which were indeed very numerous, having been severally turned to and examined, such of them were selected as the Editor judged most pertinent, together with others that occurred from his own reading and observation. In doing this he has endeavoured to keep clear of mere fanciful allusions, of which too many presented themselves in the before named Scotch edition; and to adhere as near as possible to the plan marked out in the former collection made by Bishop Lloyd; pointing out such passages chiefly, where the same history or the same name was introduced, the same matter treated of, or sentiment expressed, or at least where parallels might fairly be drawn; and sometimes where a similar use of a particular word or expression tended to illustrate the application of it on another occasion. The number of References being thus augmented considerably, the Collection upon the whole will, it is hoped, be regarded as useful in the light of a Concordance, material as well as verbal, always at hand.

In this state the quarto Copy was sent to press; and the first proofs carefully collated with the Copy both text and margin; after which the second proofs were again read, and generally speaking, the third likewise; not to mention the frequent revisions of proofs besides, which are common in correcting the press. This proved indeed a very tiresome and tedious task; but was not more than was absolutely necessary in order to attain the degree of accuracy that was wished. A particular attention was required with respect to the figures belonging to the marginal References, where errors were continually creeping in after a manner that would appear highly astonishing to those, who have never been concerned in correcting multitudes of figures, as they came from the press.

When the quarto Sheets were printed off, the Forms
S. 16

were lengthened out in order to make up the folio edition; in doing which the parts were often so jumbled together, and such Confusion introduced by misplacing the References and mistaking the Chronology, that nothing else would suffice than a fresh Collation of the whole with the quarto Copy, and a repetition of almost the same trouble and care in the revisal, and in making up the running Titles anew, as had been used before. But the Editor thinks he has just reason to congratulate himself on the opportunity hereby given him of discovering and correcting some few trivial inaccuracies, which in spite of all his vigilance had escaped his notice in the quarto edition. So that the folio edition is rendered by this somewhat the more perfect of the two, and therefore more fit to be recommended for a standard Copy.

The Editor humbly hopes this Account of his proceedings will not be unacceptable to the Board; and will think his time and pains not ill bestowed, if he shall have succeeded in his desire of giving satisfaction to those who honoured him with the employment, and of contributing in any wise to God's honour, and the public utility.

B. BLAYNEY[1].

Hertford College,
Oct. 25, 1769.

[1] Benjamin Blayney, D.D., Regius Professor of Hebrew, 1787—1802.
This Report is reprinted from the *Gentleman's Magazine* for 1769 (Vol. XXXIX. p. 517), to which periodical the writer seems to have sent it. Crutwell republished it in 1785 in his edition of the Holy Bible with Bp Wilson's notes.

APPENDIX E.

(See above, pp. 59—60.)

The Greek text adopted by the Translators of the Authorized Version of the New Testament.

N.B. In forming this list, that of Scrivener (*Supplement to English Version*, 1845, pp. 7, 8), that of Canon Westcott (*Smith's Dictionary of the Bible*, Vol. II. p. 524 *note*), and that of Professor Abbot of Harvard University (1872) as given by Dr Philip Schaff (*Revision of English Version*, 1877, p. xxix), have been compared throughout, their errors corrected, and defects supplied. *Compl.* indicates the Complutensian Polyglott (1514—1522); *Erasm.* the editions of Erasmus (1516, 1519, 1522, 1527, 1535); *Ald.* that of Aldus (1518).

§ I. Passages wherein the text of the Authorized Version differs from those of Stephen (1550) and of Beza (1589 and 1598) jointly.

S. MATT. ii. 11. εἶδον (for εὗρον) Compl., Bishops'.

ix. 18. ἄρχων εἰς Compl., Vulg.

x. 10. ῥάβδους Compl., Stephen 1546, 1549.

x. 25. Βεελζεβούβ Compl. (*hic tantum*), Vulg.

xi. 21. Βηθσαϊδά Compl., Vulg.

xiii. 24. σπείραντι Compl., Colinæus 1534, Stephen 1549, Vulg.

S. MARK iv. 18. The second οὗτοί εἰσιν omitted in Compl.

v. 38. καὶ κλαίοντας Erasm., Ald., Vulg.

vi. 45 and viii. 22. Βηθσαϊδά Compl., Vulg.

S. Mark vi. 53. Γεννησαρὲθ Erasm., Vulg. (Clementine).

ix. 42. τῶν μικρῶν τούτων Compl., Vulg. ("these" 1611, *these* 1638).

xiii. 9. ἀχθήσεσθε Erasm., Ald., Col., Tynd.

xv. 3. To the end αὐτὸς δὲ οὐδὲν ἀπεκρίνατο added by Compl., Stephen 1546, 1549, Bishops'.

S. Luke iii. 30. Σιμεών Erasm. : but Συμεών Stephen, Beza, Vulg. Cf. 2 Pet. i. 1.

iii. 31. Μενάμ Erasm., Ald., Tyndale, Coverdale, Great Bible, Bishops', Authorized before 1629 (Cambridge). See Appendix A, p. 187.

vi. 37. *init.* καὶ omitted by Erasm., Ald., Col., Vulg., Tynd.

viii. 37. παρεκάλουν Erasm., Vulg., Beza's Latin, Tynd.

xii. 56. τοῦ οὐρανοῦ καὶ τῆς γῆς Compl., Vulg. (Clementine), Coverdale, Great Bible, Bishops': but the reverse order is found in Erasm., Tyndale, Geneva 1557, &c.

xvii. 35. Erasm., Ald., Col., Tynd. and all English prefix ἡ to μία.

xx. 31. καὶ is inserted before οὐ κατέλιπον by Erasm. and all English.

xxii. 42. Ald., Vulg., Tynd., all English read παρένεγκε.

S. John viii. 6. To the end μὴ προσποιούμενος added by Compl., Stephen 1546, 1549, Bishops' ("as though he heard them not" italicised not earlier than 1769).

viii. 42. Erasm., Ald., Col., Stephen 1546, 1549, Tynd. omit οὖν.

xvi. 25. Erasm., Ald., Vulg., Tynd. all English except Coverdale up to 1762 omit ἀλλά.

xviii. 1. τοῦ Κέδρων apparently. (Vulg. *Cedron*.)

xviii. 15. Erasm., Ald., Col., Tynd. prefix ὁ to ἄλλος.

xix. 31. Erasm., Ald., Col., Vulg., Tynd., all English set ἐπεὶ παρασκευὴ ἦν after Ἰουδαῖοι, not after σαββάτῳ.

Acts iii. 3. Compl., Erasm. 1516, Ald., Stephen 1546, 1549 omit λαβεῖν.

vii. 16. 'Εμὸρ Erasm., Ald., Tyndale, Great Bible, Geneva, Bishops', Authorized before 1629 (Camb.). See Appendix A, p. 189.

vii. 44. Erasm., Ald., Col., Vulg., Tyndale omit the first ἐν.

viii. 13. δυνάμεις καὶ σημεῖα γινόμενα Erasm., Ald., (δυνάμεις καὶ σημεῖα μεγάλα γινόμενα Compl.), Tyndale, (Coverdale), Great Bible, Bishops'. The marginal reading is due to 1762.

xxi. 4. τοὺς before μαθητὰς is omitted by Complut., Erasm., Ald., Col., Stephen 1546, 1549, Tynd.

xxi. 8. ἤλθομεν Compl., Vulg., Beza's Latin.

xxvi. 20. ἀπήγγελλον Compl., Vulg.

xxvii. 3. τοὺς set before φίλους Compl., Erasm., Ald., Col. is perhaps a little refined.

xxvii. 29. ἐκπέσωμεν Compl., Stephen 1546, 1549, Vulg., Tyndale, Bishops'.

1 Cor. xi. 27. It does not appear whence Coverdale and Geneva 1557 render ἢ πίνῃ as though it were καὶ πίνῃ.

xiv. 10. Col., Vulg. omit αὐτῶν. See above, p. 68 and below, p. 251.

Phil. iv. 12. καὶ (not δὲ) before ταπεινοῦσθαι Compl., Erasm., Ald., Col., Stephen 1546, 1549, Vulg., Tynd.

1 Thess. i. 9. Compl., Erasm., Col., Stephen 1546, Vulg., Tynd. read ἐσχομεν.

1 Tim. i. 2. Ἰησοῦ Χριστοῦ Erasm., Ald., Tynd. The same inversion is made by Tyndale and the Authorized Version, apparently through inadvertence, in Rom. vi. 3 (but not in Tynd. 1526), 11; 1 Cor. i. 4; Gal. ii. 16 (second); iii. 14.

Philem. 7. χαρὰν Compl., Vulg., all English: χάριν Erasm., Stephen, Beza.

Heb. xii. 24. τὸ Ἄβελ Erasm. (not his Latin), Ald. (*quam sanguis Abel* Erasm. Lat., and English versions up to the Bishops': "that of" 1611, not italicised before 1638).

James ii. 24. Ald., Col., Tynd. end the verse with a full stop, not with the interrogative mark.

iv. 15. ζήσομεν Stephen 1546 only. See below, p. 253.

v. 9. Compl., Erasm., Ald., Col., Stephen 1546, 1549, prefix ὁ to κριτής.

2 Peter i. 1. Σίμων Compl., Vulg., all English except Tyndale 1526, Geneva 1557 ("Simeon"): but Συμεὼν Erasm., &c.

i. 21. Compl. ἅγιοι without οἱ.

ii. 9. Compl. πειρασμῶν.

1 John i. 5. ἀγγελία Col., Vulg., all English ("tidings").

Jude 12. ὑμῖν added after συνευωχούμενοι by Compl., Geneva 1557, Beza's Latin, Bishops'.

Rev. i. 11. Compl., Col., Vulg., Beza's Latin, prefix ἑπτὰ to ἐκκλησίαις.

vii. 2. ἀναβαίνοντα Compl., Vulg.

vii. 14. Compl., Vulg., Tynd. have αὐτὰς for στολὰς αὐτῶν.

viii. 6. Compl., Vulg., Tynd. prefix οἱ to ἔχοντες.

ix. 19. ἡ γὰρ ἐξουσία αὐτῶν (τῶν ἵππων Compl., Vulg.) ἐν τῷ στόματι αὐτῶν ἐστί, καὶ ἐν ταῖς οὐραῖς αὐτῶν Compl., Vulg., Tynd., against Erasm., &c.

ix. 20. οὐ μετενόησαν (not οὔτε) Compl., Erasm. 1516, Tynd.

xi. 4. αἱ prefixed to δύο λυχνίαι Compl. [So perhaps vi. 14 ὁ οὐρανὸς; ix. 16 τῶν στρατευμάτων; x. 8 τοῦ ἀγγέλου; xi. 8 τῆς πόλεως; xiii. 8 τοῦ ἐσφαγμένου; xv. 3 τοῦ δούλου; xvi. 14 τὸν πόλεμον; xvii. 8 τὸ θηρίον, all with Compl.]

Rev. xvii. 4. ἦν (for ἡ) περιβεβλημένη Compl., Vulg., all English.

xviii. 1. ἄλλον prefixed to ἄγγελον Compl., Erasm., Ald., Vulg., all English.

xviii. 5. ἐκολλήθησαν (for ἠκολούθησαν) Compl. ("pervenerunt" Vulg., "are gone up" Tyndale, Coverdale, Great Bible, Bishops': "are commen" Geneva 1557; "have reached" Authorized).

xix. 14. τὰ prefixed to ἐν τῷ οὐρανῷ Compl., Vulg., Tynd.

xix. 16. τὸ omitted before ὄνομα Compl., Tynd. 1534.

xix. 18. τε added after ἐλευθέρων Compl. ("both" italicised 1769).

xx. 4. Compl., Erasm., Ald., Col., Stephen 1546, 1549 omit τὰ before χίλια.

xxi. 13 is perhaps doubtful: καὶ ἀπὸ βορρᾶ...καὶ ἀπὸ νότου...καὶ ἀπὸ δυσμῶν Compl., Vulg., Tyndale, Coverdale, Great Bible, Bishops': καὶ ἀπὸ βορρᾶ Geneva 1557: καὶ ἀπὸ δυσμῶν Geneva 1557, Authorized. Total 80.

The variation in Heb. x. 23 "faith" for "hope" is not included, since it is a mere oversight of our Translators (*Tregelles' Horne*, Vol. IV. p. 227 note). Too precarious to be insisted on are Mark ix. 38 where ἐν of Erasm., Ald., Col., Steph. 1546, 1549, Vulg., Tyndale, and the Authorized is omitted by Compl., Steph. 1550, 1551, Beza, Geneva 1557 ("by"). Luke ii. 39 ἑαυτῶν Compl., Vulg. xx. 32 where Erasm., Tynd. and all English omit δέ. xxii. 45 Erasm., (Ald.), Col., and all English add αὐτοῦ to μαθητάς. John v. 5 καὶ ὀκτὼ Erasm., Ald., Vulg. vii. 12 Compl., Tynd., all English omit δέ. In Acts ix. 29 ἐλάλει τε might seem omitted, but "spake boldly" is adopted after "spake frankly" of Geneva 1557, as adequately rendering παρρησιαζόμενος...ἐλάλει τε.

§ II. Passages wherein the text of the Authorized version agrees with Beza (1589 and 1598)[1] against Stephen (1550).

S. Matt. ix. 33. ὅτι omitted[2] Compl., Erasm.
xxi. 7. ἐπεκάθισαν.
xxiii. 13, 14 are transposed by Compl., Stephen.

S. Mark vi. 9. ἐνδύσασθαι Erasm.
vi. 29. ἐν [τῷ Steph.] μνημείῳ[3].
viii. 14. οἱ μαθηταὶ inserted after ἐπελάθοντο. The italics of modern Bibles are not earlier than 1638.
viii. 24. ὅτι and ὁρῶ omitted in Compl., against Erasm. and the earlier English versions.
ix. 40. ἡμῶν [ὑμῶν Compl., Steph., Beza 1565, Vulg.] *twice*, Erasm., Ald., all English except Tyndale.
x. 25. διελθεῖν (after ῥαφίδος) with Vulg.
xii. 20. οὖν added after ἑπτά; so Coverdale, Geneva 1557.
xiii. 28. ἐκφύῃ, not ἐκφυῇ.

S. Luke i. 35. ἐκ σοῦ added after γεννώμενον in Compl., Erasm. (1516 only), Ald., Vulg. (editions), with Coverdale "(of the)," Geneva 1557.
ii. 22. αὐτῆς (for αὐτῶν) Compl.

---

[1] Although Beza, late in life, reckoned the edition of 1556, wherein his Latin version first appeared, as the earliest in which he revised the Greek text, and so calls that of 1565 his *second*, it is evident that the Greek text of 1556 is nearly identical with that of Stephen 1551, and that (excluding reprints, some without authority) his principal editions are but four, those of 1565, 1582, 1589, and 1598.

[2] This is one of Canon Westcott's examples, but he sees how precarious it is. In fact ὅτι is untranslated in ver. 18; ch. vi. 5, 16; x. 7, and numberless other places.

[3] All the English have "a tomb," or "a grave," but they are so careless in respect of the definite article, that, but for Canon Westcott's authority, this instance too would have been withheld. Luke vii. 12; x. 6; xvi. 8; xvii. 35; xx. 47; Rev. xiii. 3 (all given below) are also not a little doubtful.

S. LUKE ii. 25, 34. Σιμεών Erasm. (not in ver. 34, Beza 1565).
iii. 23. 'Ηλί Erasm., Vulg., not 'Ηλί: Ηλί Beza 1565.
iii. 35. ῎Εβερ Erasm., Beza 1589, 1598, Tyndale, Great Bible, Bishops'. See Appendix A, p. 187 note 2.
vii. 12. ἱκανὸς ἦν.
viii. 24. παρήγγειλε Erasm.
x. 6. ὁ inserted before υἱὸς (*quispiam* Beza's Latin).
x. 22. καὶ στραφεὶς πρὸς τοὺς μαθητὰς εἶπε omitted.
xv. 26. παίδων (without αὐτοῦ) Compl., Vulg., Coverdale, Geneva 1557. Erasm. reads αὐτοῦ.
xvi. 8. Beza alone omits the second τὴν.
xvii. 35. ἡ μία Erasm., all English.
xvii. 36. This verse, extant in Compl., the Great Bible (though within brackets and in another type), and the Bishops', is omitted by Erasm., Vulg., and the other English versions.
xx. 47. μακρὰ, not μακρᾷ with Erasm., Stephen.

S. JOHN iv. 37. The second ὁ is omitted with Vulg., Tynd., English, and Erasmus' Latin, against Compl. and Erasmus' Greek.
vi. 28. ποιῶμεν Compl., Vulg., Tynd.: ποιοῦμεν Erasm.
viii. 25. ὅ τι (ὅτι Compl., Erasm., Steph.).
xiii. 30, 31. ἦν δὲ νύξ· ὅτε οὖν (ἦν δὲ νὺξ ὅτε Compl., Steph.) Erasm., Ald., Vulg., Engl.[1]
xvi. 33. ἕξετε, for which there is very little authority, is a false correction by Beza of a typographical error of Stephen 1550[2]. Even Tyndale (not Coverdale), the Great Bible, and Geneva 1557 have the future, after Vulg.

---

[1] But οὖν is not rendered by Tyndale or Coverdale, though they pause after νύξ.
[2] ἔξετε, which Stephen himself corrects into ἔχετε at the end of his volume. Erasm., Stephen 1546, 1549 have ἔχετε.

S. JOHN xviii. 24. οὖν added after ἀπέστειλεν, so Geneva 1557, Bishops' Bible: "And Annas" Tyndale, Coverdale, Great Bible, after Vulg.

ACTS i. 4. In Beza's editions of 1582, 1589, 1598 (not 1565) μετ' αὐτῶν follows συναλιζόμενος, being doubtless derived from his own celebrated manuscript, Codex D. The italics in "with *them*" belong to 1769: no other English have "with."

i. 24. ὃν ἕνα (see Beza's note) for ἕνα ὃν. Compare Erasm., Tynd.; though the order of the other words is different.

vii. 16. Σιχὲμ twice with the Clementine Vulgate. See above, p. 189.

ix. 35. σάρωνα with Geneva 1557 for ἀσσάρωνα of Erasm., σαρωνᾶν of Compl., Stephen.

xvii. 25. καὶ τὰ πάντα Vulg. So Geneva alone of preceding English versions, which have "every where."

xix. 33. προβαλλόντων Compl., Vulg., Erasmus' Latin and all English except Wicklif and Coverdale: προβαλόντων Erasmus' Greek, Stephen.

xxii. 25. προέτειναν Compl., Beza 1589, 1598 (not 1565, 1582), Vulg., the other English; against Erasm., Stephen, Coverdale προέτεινεν.

xxiv. 13. παραστῆσαι (Erasm., Steph. add με) Compl.

xxiv. 18. τινες (Erasm., Steph., Vulg., Tyndale, Coverdale, Great Bible, Bishops' add δὲ) Compl.

xxiv. 19. ἔδει Vulg., Geneva 1557: but δεῖ Compl., Erasm., Steph., Tyndale, Coverdale, Great Bible, Bishops'.

xxv. 5. The Authorized is rather loose, but seems to read ἄτοπον after ἐστὶν, as do Compl., Bishops' after τούτῳ, and Vulg., Tynd., Great Bible, Geneva for τούτῳ.

xxvi. 3. Beza 1598 (not 1565) adds εἰδὼς after σὲ: "because I know" was not italicised in the Authorized before 1769.

Acts xxvi. 18. καὶ for τοῦ after ἐπιστρέψαι Beza only. In the Authorized "and" was not italicised before 1769.

xxvii. 12. Beza stands alone in omitting κατὰ before χῶρον.

xxvii. 13. ἆσσον Erasm. (but his Latin *Asson*, as Steph. 1550, 1551, Vulg., Tyndale, Coverdale, Great Bible, Bishops'), Steph. 1546: but ἆσσον Steph. 1549, Beza (*propius* Latin), "nearer" Geneva 1557.

Rom. vii. 6. ἀποθανόντος, on no known authority except Chrysostom as alleged by Erasmus. So Tomson 1576.

viii. 11. διὰ τοῦ ἐνοικοῦντος αὐτοῦ πνεύματος Compl.: but διὰ τὸ ἐνοικοῦν αὐτοῦ πνεῦμα Erasm., Ald., Steph., Vulg., all English.

xii. 11. κυρίῳ Compl. (Erasm. 1516 κυρίου), Vulg., Geneva 1557, Bishops': but καιρῷ Erasm. 1519 (and Latin of 1516), 1535, Steph., Tyndale, Coverdale, Great Bible.

xvi. 20. Ἀμὴν only in Bishops': omitted in other English, after Compl., Erasm., Steph., Vulg.

xvi. 27. Omits ᾧ with Compl. against Erasm.

1 Cor. v. 11. ᾖ πόρνος Erasm. (Latin), Vulg., all English. ἢ πόρνος Erasm. (Greek), Steph.

xiv. 10. *of them* is placed in the type representing italics in the Bishops' Bible and in ours of 1611, in deference to Beza, who, after Colinæus (1534) and Vulg., would fain omit αὐτῶν. See above, pp. 68, 245.

xv. 31. ὑμετέραν Compl., Beza 1598, Vulg., Geneva 1557: but ἡμετέραν Erasm. and his Latin, Steph. (even Beza 1565 against his own version), Tyndale, Coverdale, Great Bible, Bishops'.

2 Cor. iii. 1. ἢ μὴ χρῄζομεν Beza 1598, Vulg., Coverdale, Bishops', for εἰ μὴ χρ. of Compl., Erasm., Steph., Beza 1565.

2 COR. v. 4. ἐφ' ᾧ "for that" Compl., Vulg., Geneva 1557 ("wherein whiles we are"), but ἐπειδὴ Erasm., Steph.; "for" Tyndale, Coverdale; "because" Great Bible, Bishops'.

vi. 15. Βελίαλ Compl., Erasm. (Lat.), Vulg., all English: Βελίαρ Erasm. (Greek), Steph.

vii. 12. τὴν σπουδὴν ἡμῶν τὴν ὑπὲρ ὑμῶν Compl., Vulg., Tyndale, Geneva 1557: but τὴν σπουδὴν ὑμῶν τὴν ὑπὲρ ἡμῶν Erasm., Steph., Coverdale, Great Bible, Bishops'.

vii. 16. χαίρω οὖν Geneva 1557: οὖν is omitted by Compl., Erasm., Ald., Steph., Tyndale, Coverdale, Great Bible, Bishops'.

x. 10. φασὶ Beza 1582—98, Vulg., Dr Paris 1762, marg. φησὶ Compl., Erasm., Steph., Beza 1565.

xi. 10. σφραγίσεται (for φραγήσεται) is a mere error of Steph. only.

xiii. 4. καὶ γὰρ καὶ. The second καὶ only in Vulg., Wicklif, the Rhemish, but not in Tynd., Coverdale, Great Bible, Geneva 1557.

EPH. i. 3. ἐν Χριστῷ Compl., Vulg., Geneva 1557, Bishops': but Erasm., Ald., Steph. omit ἐν ("by Christ," Tyndale, Coverdale, Great Bible).

vi. 7. ὡς follows δουλεύοντες in Compl., Beza's three last editions, Vulg., Tyndale 1526 ("even as though ye served the lorde"), but not in Erasm., Steph., Beza 1565, Tyndale 1534 or the subsequent English versions.

COL. i. 2. Κολοσσαῖς in nearly all: Κολασσαῖς Erasm., Steph.

i. 24. ὅς is set before νῦν χαίρω in Beza's last three editions (not in 1565, though his Latin has *qui*), Vulg., and our Authorized version only among the English.

ii. 13. ὑμῖν Vulg., Geneva 1557 (Bishops'): but ἡμῖν Compl., Erasm., Steph., other English versions.

Authorized Bible agrees with Beza's against Stephen's. 253

COL. iv. 10. Βαρνάβᾳ Beza 1565, 1598, no English except the Authorized.

1 THESS. ii. 15. ἡμᾶς all except Steph., which has ὑμᾶς.

1 TIM. i. 4. οἰκοδομίαν Erasm., Ald., Vulg., all English, but οἰκονομίαν Compl., Steph.

TITUS ii. 10. ἡμῶν all except Steph., who reads ὑμῶν.

HEB. ix. 1. σκηνὴ omitted by Erasm., Ald., Beza (even in 1565), Vulg. ("Testament" Great Bible, "*covenant*" Geneva 1557, Bishops', Authorized), but Compl., Tyndale, Coverdale have it.

ix. 2. ἅγια Compl., Erasm. 1516, 1519, Geneva: ἁγία Erasm. 1522—1535, Steph., Vulg., Tynd., Great Bible. See above, p. 58.

x. 10. Compl., Erasm., Steph., but apparently no English version, prefix οἱ to διά.

xii. 22, 23. Compl., Erasm., Steph., Vulg., with all the English versions before the Authorized, and most modern editors, join πανηγύρει with ver. 22. See above, p. 86.

JAMES ii. 18. See above, p. 58.

iv. 13. ἢ αὔριον Compl., Vulg., Geneva 1557 : καὶ αὔριον Erasm., Steph., Tynd., Great Bible, Bishops'.

iv. 13, 15. The four verbs in ver. 13 and ποιήσομεν in ver. 15 are futures in Vulg., Geneva 1557 (the Authorized, as stated above, p. 246, stands alone in reading with Stephen 1549[1] ζήσομεν ver. 15), but they are aorists subjunctive in Compl., Erasm., Tyndale, Coverdale, Great Bible, Bishops'.

[1] Canon Westcott considers ζήσομεν a conjecture of our Translators: if so, it was a happy one, being the reading of the three great manuscripts אAB.

JAMES v. 12. εἰς ὑπόκρισιν of Compl., Erasm., Steph., Tyndale, Coverdale, Great Bible, was corrected into ὑπὸ κρίσιν by Beza 1565 &c., Geneva 1557, Bishops' ("sub judicio" Vulg.).

1 PET. i. 4. εἰς ὑμᾶς Compl., Erasm., Beza 1598, Vulg., but εἰς ἡμᾶς Steph., Beza 1565.

i. 8. ἰδόντες Beza 1589, 1598 (see his note), Vulg., but εἰδότες Compl., Erasm., Col., Steph., Beza 1565.

ii. 21. Beza (not 1565) after Compl. prefixes καὶ to ἐκλήθητε.

iii. 21. *init.* ᾧ Compl., Ald., Geneva 1557, Bishops': but ὃ Erasm., Steph., Vulg., Tyndale, Coverdale, Great Bible.

2 PET. i. 1. Beza 1565—98 adds ἡμῶν after σωτῆρος.

ii. 18. ἐν ἀσελγείαις of Beza is certainly the reading of the Authorized ("through" was not italicised before 1769), possibly of Tyndale, Coverdale, Great Bible, Geneva 1557: but the Bishops' ("they entice through lusts with the bait of wantonness of the flesh") after Compl., Erasm., Steph., rightly omits ἐν.

iii. 7. τῷ αὐτῷ λόγῳ Vulg., Tyndale, Geneva 1557, but αὐτοῦ λόγῳ Compl., Erasm., Steph., Coverdale, Great Bible, Bishops'.

1 JOHN i. 4. χαρὰ ὑμῶν after Erasm. is rendered in all English versions except Tyndale 1534, but ἡμῶν in Compl., Steph., Vulg.

ii. 23. ὁ ὁμολογῶν τὸν υἱὸν καὶ τὸν πατέρα ἔχει is the well-known clause inserted in italics in our own and the Bishops' versions, to indicate thereby a doubtful reading (see above, p. 68). Though not in Compl., Erasm., Steph., or even in Beza 1565, Tyndale, Coverdale, Geneva 1557, it was brought in within brackets and italicised in the Great Bible, doubtless from the Vulgate, and rightly forms a part of the text in Beza's last three editions. Wicklif alone prefaces the clause by "but."

1 JOHN iii. 16. After ἀγαπὴν Compl., Beza 1589, 1598 (not 1565) add τοῦ Θεοῦ: "of God" was italicised as late as 1769 in the Authorized Bible. See above, p. 69.

v. 14. ὑμῶν is a mere *erratum* of Stephen.

2 JOHN 1, 13. ἐκλεκτῇ, ἐκλεκτῆς Erasm., but Ἐκλεκτῇ, Ἐκλεκτῆς Steph., Vulg.

3. ὑμῶν Compl., all English except the Great Bible: ἡμῶν Erasm., Steph., Vulg. (manuscripts, not Clementine edition).

5. γράφω Erasm., Steph. only: γράφων Compl.

3 JOHN 7. αὐτοῦ after ὀνόματος of Compl., Vulg. (Clementine), English versions, is omitted in Erasm., Steph., Vulg. manuscripts.

JUDE 19. ἑαυτοὺς is added after ἀποδιορίζοντες in Vulg., Beza, and our own Version, against Compl., Erasm., and the other English ("makers of sects"): compare Beza's note.

24. ὑμᾶς Vulg., English versions, but αὐτοὺς Compl., Erasm., Steph.

REV. ii. 14. τὸν Βαλὰκ Compl., Vulg., but ἐν τῷ Βαλὰκ Erasm., Steph.[1]

ii. 24. καὶ τοῖς λοιποῖς Beza 1598, λοιποῖς Beza 1565 (see his note), καὶ λοιποῖς Steph.

iii. 1. ἑπτά is prefixed to πνεύματα in Compl., Vulg., all English except Tyndale ("the spirit"); but not in Erasm., Steph., Luther.

---

[1] The marked inferiority of Stephen's text in the Apocalypse will be seen to arise from his following Erasmus in preference to the Complutensian throughout that book.

Rev. v. 11. Erasm., Steph. omit καὶ ἦν ὁ ἀριθμὸς αὐτῶν μυριάδες μυριάδων with Tyndale, Coverdale, Great Bible, Bishops': μυριάδες μυριάδων is omitted in Vulg., Geneva 1557. But Compl. and the Authorized have the whole clause.

vii. 3. σφραγίσωμεν Compl., English versions: σφραγίζωμεν Erasm., Steph.

vii. 10. τῷ θεῷ ἡμῶν τῷ καθημένῳ ἐπὶ τοῦ θρόνου Compl., Vulg., Geneva 1557: but τῷ καθημένῳ ἐπὶ τοῦ θρόνου τοῦ θεοῦ ἡμῶν Erasm., Steph., Tyndale, Coverdale, Great Bible, Bishops'.

viii. 6. οἱ ἔχοντες Compl., Vulg., all English: but Erasm., Steph. omit οἱ.

viii. 11. τῶν ὑδάτων after τὸ τρίτον is omitted by Tyndale, Great Bible, Bishops'; but not by Compl., Vulg., Coverdale, Geneva 1557.

xi. 1. καὶ ὁ ἄγγελος εἱστήκει before λέγων is omitted by Erasm., Steph., Vulg., Tyndale, Coverdale, Great Bible: the words are found, less correctly, in Compl., Geneva 1557, Bishops'.

xi. 2. ἔξωθεν (before τοῦ ναοῦ) Compl., Vulg., Geneva 1557, Bishops'; but ἔσωθεν Erasm., Steph., Tyndale, Coverdale, Great Bible.

xi. 14. καὶ ἰδοὺ Beza 1598 (not 1565, see his note), Vulg. The italics in the Authorized are not earlier than 1638.

xiii. 3. ἐθαύμασεν ὅλη ἡ γῆ Compl., Vulg., all English: ἐθαυμάσθη ἐν ὅλῃ τῇ γῇ Erasm., Steph.

xiv. 18. τοὺς βότρυας τῆς ἀμπέλου Compl., Vulg., Geneva 1557, Bishops': but τῆς ἀμπέλου is omitted in Erasm. (yet not in his Latin of 1516), Steph., Tyndale, Coverdale, Great Bible.

xvi. 5. ἐσόμενος (for ὅσιος), a bold variation of Beza's

last three editions (not of that dated 1565: see his note), is adopted in the Authorized Version and the Elzevir text of 1633.

REV. xvi. 14. ἃ ἐκπορεύεται Compl., Vulg. (Clementine): but ἐκπορεύεσθαι of Erasm., Steph., all English versions before the Authorized, is perhaps preferable.

xix. 14. τὰ is prefixed to ἐν τῷ οὐρανῷ in Compl., Vulg., all English versions ("which were" not being italicised in the Authorized before 1769): but τὰ is omitted by Erasm., Steph. Total 113.

§ III. Passages in which the text of the Authorized version agrees with that of Stephen (1550) against Beza (1589 and 1598).

S. MATT. i. 23. καλέσουσι all English. Beza's καλέσεις must be derived from the edition of 1556 containing Beza's Latin version: it is countenanced by Codex D (Greek, but its Latin version *vocabit*), which in 1565 had been in his possession about three years, and has little other support.

xx. 15. εἰ ὁ ὀφθαλμός σου Compl., Erasm., Vulg., English versions, but ἢ (for εἰ) Beza.

S. MARK i. 21. Beza (1565—98) omits τὴν before συναγωγήν.

xvi. 14. Beza adds δὲ after ὕστερον.

xvi. 20 *fin.* Ἀμὴν of Compl., Vulg. (manuscripts), is omitted by Erasm., Vulg. (Clementine), and all English versions except the Authorized.

S. LUKE vii. 12. αὕτη ἦν χήρα Erasm., Ald., Vulg., all English except Geneva 1557: but αὐτῇ χήρᾳ Compl.

vii. 45. εἰσῆλθεν Beza 1589, 1598 (see his note), Vulg. only, with the Peshito, but not the Curetonian Syriac.

viii. 5. ὁ μὲν Beza, for ὃ μὲν.

ix. 15. ἅπαντες Beza 1589, 1598 only.

xii. 1. For πρῶτον, Προσέχετε of Compl., Erasm., Ald.,

Col., Steph. 1546—50, we have Πρῶτον προσέχετε in Steph. 1551, Beza, Tynd.

S. JOHN iv. 5. Συχάρ Compl., Erasm., Vulg., Bishops', but Σιχάρ other English.

ix. 10. σου Compl., Erasm., all English: σοι Vulg.

xii. 17. ὅτε Compl., Erasm., Ald., Col., Steph., Vulg., Tynd., but ὅτι Beza.

xviii. 20. πάντες of Erasm., Vulg., Tyndale, Coverdale, Great Bible, Geneva 1557, Bishops', is the true reading: our Authorized version derives πάντοτε from Compl., Steph.: πάντοθεν seems a mere conjecture of Beza.

xxi. 12. Χριστὸς for Κύριος Beza, but not his Latin version.

ACTS ii. 36. καὶ Κύριον Compl., Erasm., Vulg., Geneva 1557, Bishops': καὶ, not rendered by Tyndale, Coverdale, Great Bible, is omitted by Beza.

iv. 25. Beza (but not in 1565), Vulg., insert Πνεύματι Ἁγίῳ before διά.

iv. 27. ἐν τῇ πόλει ταύτῃ is added after ἐπ' ἀληθείας only in Stephen's 1546, 1549, Beza's last three editions (not 1565), the Vulgate, and Great Bible, but there in other type and within brackets.

iv. 36. Ἰωσήφ Beza (not 1565), Vulg.

vii. 2. ὑμῶν Beza 1565—98 (but not his Latin) for ἡμῶν.

xvi. 7. Beza (but not in 1565), Vulg., add Ἰησοῦ to Πνεῦμα, against Erasm., Compl., Steph.

xvi. 17. ἡμῖν Compl., Erasm., Beza 1565, all English: ὑμῖν Beza 1582—98, Vulg., &c.

xxi. 3. ἀναφάναντες Erasm., Steph. 1550, 1551, perhaps Vulg., but ἀναφανέντες Compl., Ald., (Col.), Steph. 1546, 1549, Beza.

xxi. 11. Beza alone in 1565—98 (not his Latin) omits τε αὐτοῦ.

Acts xxiv. 8. Beza similarly omits τούτων.
xxiv. 14. τοῖς προφήταις (without ἐν) Compl., Erasm., Vulg., all English except Coverdale. The word "in" before "the prophets" in modern Bibles is as late as 1762. See above, p. 234.
xxv. 6. Beza (1582—98, not 1565), Vulg., Geneva, with the margin of the Authorized, insert οὐ before πλείους.
xxvi. 8. τί ἄπιστον Compl., Erasm., all English, rather than τί; ἄπιστον of Beza.

Rom. i. 29. κακίᾳ, πορνείᾳ, πονηρίᾳ, πλεονεξίᾳ Beza (not 1565), also Vulg., Tynd. partly.
v. 17. τῷ ἑνὶ for τῷ τοῦ ἑνὸς Beza (not 1565), margin of Authorized.
viii. 20. ἐπ' ἐλπίδι· ὅτι Compl., Erasm. 1522—35, Ald., Col., Steph., Tynd., but . ἐπ' ἐλπίδι ὅτι Erasm. 1516, 1519, Beza. See above, p. 91.
xi. 28. Col., Beza 1582—98 (not 1565), Vulg. add οὖν to μὲν.

1 Cor. ii. 11. εἶδεν twice for οἶδεν Beza 1565, 1582, 1589, 1598.
iii. 3. ἡμῖν for ὑμῖν, Beza 1589, 1598 (not Beza's Latin).
vii. 29. ὁ καιρὸς συνεσταλμένος· τὸ λοιπόν ἐστιν (omitting ὅτι before ὁ καιρὸς) Compl., Erasm., Vulg., Tyndale, Coverdale, Great Bible (the Bishops' renders ὅτι "because"): but ὅτι ὁ καιρὸς συνεσταλμένος τὸ λοιπόν ἐστιν· Geneva 1557 with Beza.
xi. 22. ὑμᾶς ἐν τούτῳ; οὐκ ἐπαινῶ Compl., Geneva 1557: but ὑμᾶς; ἐν τούτῳ οὐκ ἐπαινῶ Erasm., Beza, Tyndale, Coverdale, Great Bible, Bishops'.

2 Cor. i. 6. Beza (not 1565) sets εἴτε παρακαλούμεθα, ὑπὲρ τῆς ὑμῶν παρακλήσεως (omitting the second καὶ σωτηρίας) before τῆς ἐνεργουμένης.

2 COR. ii. 5. Beza alone, and that not in his Latin, punctuates ἵνα μὴ ἐπιβαρῶ as if the clause were parenthetic.

iii. 14. ὅ τι Erasm. 1519, Beza 1565, all English: but ὅτι Compl., Erasm. 1516, Beza 1598, Vulg. (Compl., Erasm. have in their Latin *quòd*).

viii. 24. καὶ εἰς πρόσωπον Erasm., Beza 1565, Coverdale, with the Authorized: καὶ is omitted in Compl., Beza's last three editions, Vulg., and the other English versions.

x. 6. ἡ before ὑπακοὴ omitted by Steph. 1551, Beza.

xi. 1. τῇ ἀφροσύνῃ Compl., Erasm., Ald., all *our* English: τί τῆς ἀφροσύνης Beza, Vulg. ("some little of my folly" Rhemish).

GAL. iv. 17. The second ὑμᾶς becomes ἡμᾶς in Beza (see his note) and in the margin of the Authorized Bible.

PHIL. i. 23. πολλῷ Compl., Erasm., Vulg., all English: Beza, &c. add γάρ.

ii. 24. Beza (not 1565), Vulg., add πρὸς ὑμᾶς to ἐλεύσομαι.

iii. 20. Beza 1589, 1598 (not 1565, see his note), Vulg., Tynd. have δὲ for γὰρ with the Syriac.

COL. i. 2. Beza (not 1565), Vulg., add Ἰησοῦ to Χριστῷ.

1 THESS. i. 4. The comma stands after ἠγαπημένοι in the later editions of Erasm., in Stephen, and in Beza 1565, 1582 with the Authorized, but after Θεοῦ in Compl., Beza 1589, 1598, and Tynd.

1 TIM. vi. 15. Beza (not 1565) reads ὃν for ἥν.

2 TIM. ii. 22. Beza and his Latin version read Χριστὸν for Κύριον.

TITUS ii. 7. ἀφθαρσίαν of Compl., Bishops', Authorized, is omitted by Erasm., Ald., Vulg., and the other English versions.

HEB. ix. 28. Beza (not 1565) with Compl., Erasm., Ald., Col., Steph. 1546, 1549, Vulg., Tynd. adds καὶ to οὕτω.

HEB. x. 2. οὐκ ἂν ἐπαύσαντο προσφερόμεναι; Erasm., Ald., Col., Vulg. MSS., Tyndale, Great Bible, Geneva 1557, Beza 1565, Bishops': ἂν ἐπαύσαντο προσφερόμεναι, Compl., Beza, Clementine Vulg., Coverdale.

JAMES iii. 6. To τῆς γενέσεως Beza 1589, 1598, Vulg. add ἡμῶν.

1 PET. v. 10. Compl., Beza 1589, 1598 read ὑμᾶς after καλέσας, but Erasm., Ald., Col., Steph., Beza 1565, 1582, Vulg., have ἡμᾶς.

2 JOHN 9. Beza (1565—98) omits τῇ before διδαχῇ. Similarly

REV. ii. 23. Beza (1565—98) omits ὁ before ἐρευνῶν.
vi. 12. The same editions, after Vulg., add ὅλη to σελήνη.
xxii. 20. For the second ναί Beza has καὶ and his Latin *igitur* (see his note). Total 59.

The following variations of the Greek could scarcely be represented in our English versions:

Acts vii. 26 & xv. 32. τε Compl., Erasm., Steph. δέ Beza.

xix. 27. μέλλειν δέ Compl., Erasm. 1516, Steph., but μέλλειν τε Erasm. 1519, Beza.

1 Cor. vii. 5. συνέρχησθε Compl., Erasm., Steph., Beza 1565, 1589: συνέρχεσθε Beza 1598 (note and punctuation, not text), Vulg., Tyndale 1534 (perhaps also 1526), Great Bible, Geneva 1557, Bishops'.

2 Thess. ii. 4. "all that is called God" is the rendering of all our versions from Tyndale downwards, or it might be thought to represent Beza's conjectural reading πᾶν τὸ for πάντα.

Rev. iv. 10. Since all read πεσοῦνται, no stress can be laid in the variation between the present and future in the verbs that follow.

x. 7. τελεσθῇ Compl., Erasm., Steph., Beza 1565: "shall be finished" other English versions after Vulg. But Beza's last three editions have τελεσθήσεται, which ill suits "should be finished" of the Authorized.

It may be useful to subjoin a list, probably quite an incomplete one, of places in which the Translators of 1611 have apparently followed the Latin Vulgate, mostly after the example of Tyndale, sometimes of Versions later than his, especially of the Rhemish of 1582, whereof the Epistle of the Translators to the Reader speaks so contemptuously (see below, p. 302). It is probable that at least some of the passages collected in the first section of the present Appendix, wherein the text of the Authorized Version is supported by Compl., Vulg. only, were derived from the Vulgate rather than from the Complutensian. In 1 Cor. xiv. 10; 1 John i. 5, where Colinæus (1534) and the Vulgate alone favour the rendering of 1611, the Vulgate is almost certainly their authority, not Colinæus.

Matt. xii. 24, 27; Mark iii. 22; Luke xi. 15, 18, 19, *Beelzebub*. So Tynd. (So also Compl. in Matt. x. 25). Mark xiii. 37 ὃ *quod*. xiv. 43 *om*. ὦν. So Tynd. Luke i. 35 *nascetur*. So Tynd. i. 49 μεγάλα *magna*. So Tynd. xx. 35 *habebuntur*. So Tynd. xxiii. 34 *sortes:* but *sortem* Matt. xxvii. 35; Mark xv. 24; John xix. 24, the English versions having *lots* in all the four places, save that Wicklif alone keeps up the distinction of Vulg. xxiii. 46. παρατίθεμαι *commendo*. So Tynd. John vii. 9 *om*. δέ. So Tynd. x. 16 *unum ovile* Vulg. So Great Bible and Geneva 1557. xii. 26 *om*. καὶ after ἔσται. So Rhemish Version 1582. xviii. 1 τοῦ

Κεδρών, *Cedron.* So Tynd. Acts ii. 22 *approbatum.* So Tynd. iv. 32 *cor unum* Vulg. *Clementine.* So Tynd. vi. 3 καταστήσωμεν *constituamus.* So Tynd. vii. 26 συνήλλασσεν *reconciliabat.* So Tynd. vii. 44 *om.* ὁ: *loquens.* So Tynd. x. 20 *itaque* (ἀλλά). So Tynd. xiii. 1 *Simeon* (Σίμων Er.: *Simon* Vulg. in ch. xv. 14). xiii. 15 εἴ τις *si quis.* So Tynd. xvii. 30 *hujus ignorantiæ.* So Tynd. xix. 20 Θεοῦ *Dei* Vulg. *Clementine.* So Tynd. xxiii. 15 *aliquid certius (om.* τά). So Tynd. xxiv. 25 *tremefactus* Vulg. *Clementine.* So Tynd. xxvi. 6 πατέρας ἡμῶν *patres nostros.* So Tynd. Rom. xiv. 2 *alius enim.* So Rhemish 1582. xvi. 4 *suas cervices.* So Tynd. 1 Cor. xiii. 1 *velut æs sonans.* So Tynd. xvi. 23 *domini nostri.* So Geneva 1557. Gal. iv. 15 text: *ubi.* So Rhemish 1582. Eph. vi. 24 *om.* Ἀμήν. Vulg. MSS. (A. V. 1611): not Vulg. *Clementine* (A. V. 1616). Phil. ii. 21 Ἰησοῦ Χριστοῦ *Jesu Christi.* So Tynd. Col. i. 4 *quam habetis.* So Tynd. nearly. i. 24. *qui nunc.* So Rhemish 1582. 1 Thess. ii. 12 *qui vocavit.* So Tynd. ii. 13 οὐχ ὡς λόγον *non ut verbum.* So Tynd. ii. 16 *enim.* So Tynd. iv. 1 *ut quemadmodum.* So Rhemish 1582. 1 Tim. i. 17 *immortali.* So Tynd. iii. 15 *oporteat te.* So Tynd. iv. 15 *om.* ἐν: *manifestus sit omnibus* (A. V. marg. in all things). 2 Tim. i. 18 διηκόνησέ μοι *ministravit mihi* Vulg. *Clementine.* So Tynd. James iii. 14 *cordibus vestris.* So Tynd. 1 Pet. ii. 13 *om.* οὖν. So Tynd. 1 John iii. 20 *om.* ὅτι *secund.* So Tynd. v. 8 *hi tres* Vulg. *Clementine.* So Tynd. 2 John 3 ἔστω *sit.* So Tynd. Rev. xiii. 10 *qui in captivitatem duxerit, in captivitatem vadet.* Vulg. *Clementine.* So Tynd. xvi. 11 *om.* ἐκ *secund.* So Tynd. xvii. 9 *et hic.* So Tynd. xviii. 23 φάνῃ *lucebit.* So Geneva 1557.

NOTE ON THE SYNOD OF DORT

(See above, p. 12 note.)

In that dreary folio *Acta Synodi Nationalis...Dordecti habitae* (1620) we read (pp. 19, 20) that the seventh Session of the Synod was spent in considering a written Report from the English Delegates (Carleton, Bp of Llandaff, the illustrious Joseph Hall, afterwards Bp of Norwich, Dr Davenant, afterwards Bp of Salisbury, and Dr Ward, Master of Sidney Sussex College, 1609—43[1]) on the method employed in executing our Authorized Bible, wherein are made the following statements: "Post peractum a singulis pensum, ex hisce omnibus duodecim selecti viri in unum locum convocati integrum opus recognoverunt ac recensuerunt." "Postremo, Reverendissimus Episcopus Wintoniensis, Bilsonus, una cum Doctore Smitho, nunc Episcopo Glocestriensi, viro eximio et ab initio in toto hoc opere versatissimo, omnibus mature pensitatis et examinatis, extremam manum huic operi imposuerunt."

None of these Delegates had any share in the Translation of 1611, but as seven years had elapsed since its publication, it is wonderful that they had not found out by that time how very carelessly the last revise had been carried through the press.

[1] Dr Ward was one of the revisers of the Cambridge Bible of 1638: see above, p. 22.

THE
TRANSLATORS TO THE READER.

THE

TRANSLATORS TO THE READER[1].

(See above, p. 39.)

ZEAL to promote the common good, whether it be by devising any thing ourselves, or revising that which hath been laboured by others, deserveth certainly much respect and esteem, but yet findeth but cold entertainment in the world. It is welcomed with suspicion instead of love, and with emulation instead of thanks: and if there be any hole left for cavil to enter, (and cavil, if it do not find a hole, will make one) it is sure to be misconstrued, and in danger to be condemned. This will easily be granted by as many as know story, or have any experience. For was there ever any thing projected, that savoured any way of newness or renewing, but the same endured many a storm of gainsaying or opposition? A man would think that civility, wholesome laws, learning and eloquence, synods, and Church-main-

The best things have been calumniated.

---

[1] The text of the original edition has been restored, except where later books have corrected manifest errors. The marginal references set within brackets (chiefly derived from Migne's *Patrologia*), as also the short foot-notes, are added in the present work: the rest are in the Bible of 1611. The quotations from Scripture are somewhat too loosely given, but in test passages (e.g. 1 Kin. xii. 4; Neh. iv. 2, 3; 1 Cor. xiv. 11) the writer comes very near the Genevan version of 1560: sometimes he uses the Authorized, never the Bishops' Bible.

tenance, (that we speak of no more things of this kind) should be as safe as a sanctuary, and ||out of shot, as they say, that no man would lift up the heel, no, nor dog move his tongue against the motioners of them. For by the first we are distinguished from brute beasts led with sensuality: by the second we are bridled and restrained from outrageous behaviour, and from doing of injuries, whether by fraud or by violence : by the third we are enabled to inform and reform others by the light and feeling that we have attained unto ourselves : briefly, by the fourth, being brought together to a parle face to face, we sooner compose our differences than by writings, which are endless : and lastly, that the Church be sufficiently provided for is so agreeable to good reason and conscience, that those mothers are holden to be less cruel, that kill their children as soon as they are born, than those nursing fathers and mothers (wheresoever they be) that withdraw from them who hang upon their breasts (and upon whose breasts again themselves do hang to receive the spiritual and sincere milk of the word) livelihood and support fit for their estates. Thus it is apparent, that these things which we speak of are of most necessary use, and therefore that none, either without absurdity can speak against them, or without note of wickedness can spurn against them.

<small>¹ ἔξω βέλους. [Steph. Thesaur., Βέλος.]</small>

<small>Anacharsis [Herod. IV. 26], with others.</small>

<small>Locri.</small>

Yet for all that, the learned know that certain worthy men have been brought to untimely death for none other fault, but for seeking to reduce their countrymen to good order and discipline : and that in some Commonweals it was made a capital crime, once to motion the making of a new law for the abrogating of an old, though the same were most

pernicious: And that certain, which would be count- *Cato the elder.*
ed pillars of the State, and patterns of virtue and
prudence, could not be brought for a long time to
give way to good letters and refined speech; but
bare themselves as averse from them, as from rocks
or boxes of poison: And fourthly, that he was no *Gregory the Divine* [ὁ
babe, but a great clerk, that gave forth, (and in writing Θεόλογος,
to remain to posterity) in passion peradventure, but *of Nazianzus*: ἔχω μὲν
yet he gave forth, That he had not seen any profit οὕτως, εἰ δεῖ τἀληθὲς γρά-
to come by any synod or meeting of the Clergy, but φειν, ὥστε πάντα σύλ-
rather the contrary: And lastly, against Church- λογον φεύγειν ἐπισκόπων,
maintenance and allowance, in such sort as the am- ὅτι μηδεμιᾶς συνόδου
bassadors and messengers of the great King of kings τέλος εἶδον χρηστόν,
should be furnished, it is not unknown what a fiction μηδὲ λύσιν κακῶν μᾶλ-
or fable (so it is esteemed, and for no better by the λον ἔσχη-κυίαν ἢ
reporter himself, though superstitious) was devised: προσθήκην *Epist.* 130.
namely, That at such time as the professors and Compare
teachers of Christianity in the Church of Rome, then 124.]
a true Church, were liberally endowed, a voice for- *Nauclerus* [*Chronica*,
sooth was heard from heaven, saying, Now is poison Colon. 1579, p. 504].
poured down into the Church, &c. Thus not only
as oft as we speak, as one saith, but also as oft as we
do any thing of note or consequence, we subject ourselves to every one's censure, and happy is he that is
least tossed upon tongues; for utterly to escape the
snatch of them it is impossible. If any man conceit
that this is the lot and portion of the meaner sort
only, and that princes are privileged by their high
estate, he is deceived. As *the sword devoureth as well* 2 Sam. 11. 25.
one as another, as it is in *Samuel;* nay, as the great
commander charged his soldiers in a certain battle
to strike at no part of the enemy, but at the face;
and as the king of *Syria* commanded his chief captains
to fight neither with small nor great, save only against 1 Kin. 22. 31.

the king of Israel: so it is too true, that envy striketh most spitefully at the fairest, and at the chiefest. *David* was a worthy prince, and no man to be compared to him for his first deeds; and yet for as worthy an act as ever he did, even for bringing back the ark of God in solemnity, he was scorned and scoffed at by his own wife. *Solomon* was greater than *David*, though not in virtue, yet in power; and by his power and wisdom he built a temple to the Lord, such a one as was the glory of the land of Israel, and the wonder of the whole world. But was that his magnificence liked of by all? We doubt of it. Otherwise why do they lay it in his son's dish, and call unto him for †easing of the burden? *Make,* say they, *the grievous servitude of thy father, and his sore yoke, lighter.* Belike he had charged them with some levies, and troubled them with some carriages; hereupon they raise up a tragedy, and wish in their heart the temple had never been built. So hard a thing it is to please all, even when we please God best, and do seek to approve ourselves to every one's conscience.

<small>2 Sam. 6. 16.</small>

<small>† σεισάχ-θειαν [Steph. Thesaur., Tom. 1, p. 616].
1 Kin. 12. 4.</small>

If we will descend to later times, we shall find many the like examples of such kind, or rather unkind, acceptance. The first Roman Emperor did never do a more pleasing deed to the learned, nor more profitable to posterity, for conserving the record of times in true supputation, than when he corrected the Calendar, and ordered the year according to the course of the sun: and yet this was imputed to him for novelty and arrogancy, and procured to him great obloquy. So the first Christened Emperor, (at the leastwise, that openly professed the faith himself, and allowed others to do the like) for strengthening the empire at his great charges, and providing for the

<small>The highest personages have been calumniated. C. Cæsar. Plutarch [cap. 59].</small>

<small>Constantine [A.D. 306—35].</small>

Church, as he did, got for his labour the name *Pu-* [Aurel. Vict. *cap.* XLI. 16].
pillus, as who would say, a wasteful Prince, that had
need of a guardian or overseer. So the best Chris- [Theodosius A.D. 379 —95].
tened Emperor, for the love that he bare unto peace,
thereby to enrich both himself and his subjects, and
because he did not seek war, but find it, was judged [Zosimus [πολέμοις μὲν ἀπειπεῖν ἐγνώκει καὶ μάχαις, *lib.* IV. *cap.* 50].
to be no man at arms, (though in deed he excelled in
feats of chivalry, and shewed so much when he was
provoked) and condemned for giving himself to his
ease, and to his pleasure. To be short, the most
learned Emperor of former times, (at the least, the [Justinian A.D. 527 —65].
greatest politician) what thanks had he for cutting off
the superfluities of the laws, and digesting them into
some order and method? This, that he hath been
blotted by some to be an Epitomist, that is, one that
extinguished worthy whole volumes, to bring his
abridgments into request. This is the measure that
hath been rendered to excellent Princes in former
times, even, *cum bene facerent, male audire*, for their
good deeds to be evil spoken of. Neither is there
any likelihood that envy and malignity died and were
buried with the ancient. No, no, the reproof of *Moses*
taketh hold of most ages, *You are risen up in your* Numb. 32. 14.
fathers' stead, an increase of sinful men. What is that Eccles. 1. 9.
that hath been done? that which shall be done: and
there is no new thing under the sun, saith the wise
man. And St. *Stephen, As your fathers did, so do ye.* Acts 7. 51.
This, and more to this purpose, his Majesty that now His Majesty's constancy, notwithstanding calumniation, for the survey of the English translations.
reigneth (and long and long may he reign, and his
offspring for ever, *Himself and children and children's*
children always*) knew full well, according to the
singular wisdom given unto him by God, and the rare
learning and experience that he hath attained unto; * Αὐτὸς καὶ παῖδες καὶ παίδων παῖ- δων πάν- τοτε παῖδες.
namely, that whosoever attempteth any thing for the

[Compare *Homer, Iliad.* xx. 308.]

Suidas. Ὥσπερ τις ἀνδριὰς ἀπερίτρεπτος καὶ ἄκμων ἀνήλατος.

publick, (specially if it pertain to religion, and to the opening and clearing of the word of God) the same setteth himself upon a stage to be glouted upon by every evil eye; yea, he casteth himself headlong upon pikes, to be gored by every sharp tongue. For he that meddleth with men's religion in any part meddleth with their custom, nay, with their freehold; and though they find no content in that which they have, yet they cannot abide to hear of altering. Notwithstanding his royal heart was not daunted or discouraged for this or that colour, but stood resolute, *as a statue immoveable, and an anvil not easy to be beaten into plates,* as one saith; he knew who had chosen him to be a soldier, or rather a captain; and being assured that the course which he intended made much for the glory of God, and the building up of his Church, he would not suffer it to be broken off for whatsoever speeches or practices. It doth certainly belong unto kings, yea, it doth specially belong unto them, to have care of religion, yea, to know it aright, yea, to profess it zealously, yea, to promote it to the uttermost of their power. This is their glory before all nations which mean well, and this will bring unto them a far most excellent weight of glory in the day of the Lord Jesus. For the Scripture saith not in vain, *Them that honour me I will honour:* neither was it a vain word that *Eusebius* delivered long ago, That piety towards God was the weapon, and the only weapon, that both preserved *Constantine's* person, and avenged him of his enemies.

1 Sam. 2. 30.

θεοσέβεια. *Eusebius* [*Hist. Eccl.*] *lib.* 10. *cap.* 8.

The praise of the Holy Scriptures.

But now what piety without truth? What truth, what saving truth, without the word of God? What word of God, whereof we may be sure, without the Scripture? The Scriptures we are commanded to search. *John* 5. 39. *Isaiah* 8. 20. They are commended that searched and studied them. *Acts* 17. 11. and 8. 28, 29. They are reproved that were unskilful in them, or slow to believe them. *Matth.* 22. 29. *Luke* 24. 25. They can make us wise unto salvation. 2 *Tim.* 3. 15. If we be ignorant, they will instruct us; if out of the way, they will bring us home; if out of order, they will reform us; if in heaviness, comfort us; if dull, quicken us; if cold, inflame us. *Tolle, lege; tolle, lege;* Take up and read, take up and read the Scriptures, (for unto them was the direction) it was said unto S. *Augustine* by a supernatural voice. *Whatsoever is in the Scriptures, believe me,* saith the same S. *Augustine, is high and divine; there is verily truth, and a doctrine most fit for the refreshing and renewing of men's minds, and truly so tempered, that every one may draw from thence that which is sufficient for him, if he come to draw with a devout and pious mind, as true religion requireth.* Thus St. *Augustine.* And S. *Hierome, Ama Scripturas, et amabit te sapientia,* &c. Love the Scriptures, and wisdom will love thee. And S. *Cyrill* against *Julian, Even boys that are bred up in the Scriptures, become most religious,* &c. But what mention we three or four uses of the Scripture, whereas whatsoever is to be believed, or practised, or hoped for, is contained in them? or three or four sentences of the Fathers, since whosoever is worthy the name of a Father, from Christ's time downward, hath likewise written not only of the riches, but also of the perfection of the Scripture? *I adore the fulness of the Scripture,* saith *Tertullian* against *Hermogenes.* And again, to *Apelles* a heretick of the like stamp he saith, *I do not admit that which thou bringest in* (or concludest) *of thine own* (head or store, *de tuo*) with-

S. August. Confess. lib. 8. *cap.* 12.

S. August. De utilit. credendi, cap. 6.

S. Hieronym. ad Demetriad. [*cap.* 20].

S. Cyrill. 7⁰ [p. 234] contra *Julianum* [Παιδία γε μὴν τοῖς ἱεροῖς ἐν- τεθραμμένα γράμμασιν γένοιτο ἂν εὐθὺς τῶν ὅτι μάλιστα θεοφιλεστά- των].

Tertul. advers. Hermo. [*cap.* 22].

Tertul. De carne Christi. [*cap.* 7].

out Scripture. So Saint *Justin Martyr* before him; *We must know by all means* (saith he) *that it is not lawful* (or possible) *to learn* (any thing) *of God or of right piety, save only out of the Prophets, who teach us by divine inspiration.* So Saint *Basil* after *Tertullian*, *It is a manifest falling away from the faith, and a fault of presumption, either to reject any of those things that are written, or to bring in* (upon the head of them, ἐπεισάγειν) *any of those things that* are not written. We omit to cite to the same effect S. *Cyrill*, Bishop of *Jerusalem* in his 4. *Cateches.* Saint *Hierome* against *Helvidius*, Saint *Augustine* in his third book against the letters of *Petilian*, and in very many other places of his works. Also we forbear to descend to latter Fathers, because we will not weary the reader. The Scriptures then being acknowledged to be so full and so perfect, how can we excuse ourselves of negligence, if we do not study them? of curiosity, if we be not content with them? Men talk much of εἰρεσιώνη, how many sweet and goodly things it had hanging on it; of the Philosopher's stone, that it turneth copper into gold; of *Cornu-copia*, that it had all things necessary for food in it; of *Panaces* the herb, that it was good for all diseases; of *Catholicon* the drug, that it is instead of all 'purges; of *Vulcan's* armour, that it was an armour of proof against all thrusts and all blows, *&c.* Well, that which they falsely or vainly attributed to these things for bodily good, we may justly and with full measure ascribe unto the Scripture for spiritual. It is not only an armour, but also a whole armoury of weapons, both offensive and defensive; whereby we may save ourselves, and put the enemy to flight. It is not an herb, but a tree, or rather a whole paradise of trees of life, which bring forth fruit every month, and the fruit thereof is for meat, and the leaves for medicine. It is not a pot of *Manna* or a cruse of oil, which were for memory only, or for a meal's meat or two; but as it were a shower of heavenly bread sufficient for a whole host, be it never so great, and as it were a whole cellar full of oil vessels; whereby all our necessities may be provided for, and our debts discharged. In a word, it is a panary of wholesome food against fenowed[1] traditions; a physician's shop (Saint *Basil* calleth it) of preservatives against poisoned heresies; a pandect of profitable laws against rebellious spirits; a treasury of most costly jewels against beggarly rudiments; finally, a fountain of most pure water springing up unto everlasting life. And what marvel? the original thereof being from heaven, not from earth; the author being God, not man; the inditer, the Holy Spirit, not the wit of the Apostles or Prophets; the penmen, such as were sanctified from the womb, and endued with a principal portion of God's Spirit; the matter, verity, piety, purity, uprightness; the form, God's word, God's testimony, God's oracles, the word of truth, the word of salvation, *&c.*: the effects, light of understanding, stableness of persuasion, repentance from dead works, newness of life, holiness, peace, joy in the Holy Ghost; lastly, the end and reward of the study thereof, fellowship with the saints, participation of the heavenly nature, fruition of an inheritance immortal, undefiled, and that never shall fade away: Happy is the man that delighteth in the

Κοινὸν ἰα- τρεῖον. *S. Basil. in Psal. pri- mum* [*initio*].

---

[1] "Fenowed," i.e. mouldy. Richardson quotes Dr Favour, *Triumph over Novelty* (1619), "The foisty and fenowed festival," the word being chosen perhaps for the sake of alliteration.

Scripture, and thrice happy that meditateth in it day and night.

Translation necessary.

But how shall men meditate in that which they cannot understand? How shall they understand that which is kept close in an unknown tongue? as it is written, *Except I know the power of the voice, I shall be to him that speaketh a barbarian, and he that speaketh shall be a barbarian to me.* The Apostle excepteth no tongue; not *Hebrew* the ancientest, not *Greek* the most copious, not *Latin* the finest. Nature taught a natural man to confess, that all of us in those tongues which we do not understand are plainly deaf; we may turn the deaf ear unto them. The *Scythian* counted the *Athenian,* whom he did not understand, barbarous: so the *Roman* did the *Syrian* and the *Jew:* (even S. *Hierome* himself calleth the *Hebrew* tongue barbarous; belike, because it was strange to so many:) so the Emperor of *Constantinople* calleth the *Latin* tongue barbarous, though Pope *Nicolas* do storm at it: so the *Jews* long before *Christ* called all other nations *Lognazim*[1], which is little better than barbarous. Therefore as one complaineth that always in the Senate of *Rome* there was one or other that called for an interpreter; so, lest the Church be driven to the like exigent, it is necessary to have translations in a readiness. Translation it is that openeth the window, to let in the light; that breaketh the shell, that we may eat the kernel; that putteth aside the curtain, that we may look into the most holy place; that removeth the cover of the well, that we may come by the water; even as *Jacob* rolled away the stone from the mouth of the well, by which means

1 Cor. 14[11].

Clem. Alex. 1º *Strom.* [*cap.* XVI. p. 133].

S. Hieronym. Damaso.

Michael. Theophili fil. 2 *Tom. Concil. ex edit. Petri Crab.*

Cicero 5. *De Finibus* [*cap.* XXIX. (89)].

Gen. 29. 10.

---

[1] לוֹעֲזִים. from לֹעֵז Ps. cxiv. 1.

the flocks of *Laban* were watered. Indeed without translation into the vulgar tongue, the unlearned are but like children at *Jacob's* well (which was deep) without a bucket or something to draw with: or as that person mentioned by *Esay*, to whom when a sealed book was delivered with this motion, *Read this, I pray thee*, he was fain to make this answer, *I cannot, for it is sealed*. John 4. 11.
Isai. 29. 11.

While God would be known only in *Jacob*, and have his name great in *Israel*, and in none other place; while the dew lay on *Gideon's* fleece only, and all the earth besides was dry; then for one and the same people, which spake all of them the language of *Canaan*, that is, *Hebrew*, one and the same original in *Hebrew* was sufficient. But when the fulness of time drew near, that the Sun of righteousness, the Son of God, should come into the world, whom God ordained to be a reconciliation through faith in his blood, not of the *Jew* only, but also of the *Greek*, yea, of all them that were scattered abroad; then lo, it pleased the Lord to stir up the spirit of a *Greek* Prince, (*Greek* for descent and language) even of *Ptolemy Philadelph* king of *Egypt*, to procure the translating of the book of God out of *Hebrew* into *Greek*. This is the translation of the *Seventy* interpreters, commonly so called, which prepared the way for our Saviour among the *Gentiles* by written preaching, as Saint *John Baptist* did among the *Jews* by vocal. For the *Grecians*, being desirous of learning, were not wont to suffer books of worth to lie moulding in kings' libraries, but had many of their servants, ready scribes, to copy them out, and so they were dispersed and made common. Again, the *Greek* tongue was well known and made familiar to most inhabitants in *Asia* The translation of the Old Testament out of the Hebrew into Greek.

See *S. Aug. lib.* 12. *contra Faust. cap.* 32.

by reason of the conquest that there the *Grecians* had made, as also by the colonies which thither they had sent. For the same causes also it was well understood in many places of *Europe*, yea, and of *Africk* too. Therefore the word of God being set forth in *Greek*, becometh hereby like a candle set upon a candlestick, which giveth light to all that are in the house; or like a proclamation sounded forth in the market-place, which most men presently take knowledge of; and therefore that language was fittest to contain the Scriptures, both for the first preachers of the Gospel to appeal unto for witness, and for the learners also of those times to make search and trial by. It is certain, that that translation was not so sound and so perfect, but that it needed in many places correction; and who had been so sufficient for this work as the Apostles or apostolic men? Yet it seemed good to the Holy Ghost and to them to take that which they found, (the same being for the greatest part true and sufficient) rather than by making a new, in that new world and green age of the Church, to expose themselves to many exceptions and cavillations, as though they made a translation to serve their own turn, and therefore bearing witness to themselves, their witness not to be regarded. This may be supposed to be some cause, why the translation of the *Seventy* was allowed to pass for current. Notwithstanding, though it was commended generally, yet it did not fully content the learned, no not of the *Jews*. For not long after *Christ*, *Aquila* fell in hand with a new translation, and after him *Theodotion*, and after him *Symmachus:* yea, there was a fifth and a sixth edition, the authors whereof were not known. These with the *Seventy* made up the *Hexapla*, and were worthily and to great purpose compiled together by *Origen*. Howbeit the edition of the *Seventy* went away with the credit, and therefore not only was placed in the midst by *Origen*, (for the worth and excellency thereof above the rest, as *Epiphanius* gathereth) but also was used by the *Greek* Fathers for the ground and foundation of their commentaries. Yea, *Epiphanius* above-named doth attribute so much unto it, that he holdeth the authors thereof not only for interpreters, but also for prophets in some respect: and *Justinian* the Emperor, enjoining the *Jews* his subjects to use specially the Translation of the *Seventy*, rendereth this reason thereof, Because they were, as it were, enlightened with prophetical grace. Yet for all that, as the *Egyptians* are said of the Prophet to be men and not God, and their horses flesh and not spirit: so it is evident, (and Saint *Hierome* affirmeth as much) that the *Seventy* were interpreters, they were not prophets. They did many things well, as learned men; but yet as men they stumbled and fell, one while through oversight, another while through ignorance; yea, sometimes they may be noted to add to the original, and sometimes to take from it: which made the Apostles to leave them many times, when they left the *Hebrew*, and to deliver the sense thereof according to the truth of the word, as the Spirit gave them utterance. This may suffice touching the *Greek* translations of the Old Testament.

Epiphan. De mensuris et ponderibus [cap. 17].

See S. August. 2º De doctrin. Christian. c. 15.

Novel. diatax. 146.

Προφητικῆς ὥσπερ χάριτος περιλαμψάσης αὐτούς.

Isai. 31. 3.

S. Hieron. de optimo genere interpret. [ad Pammachium, passim. Aliud est enim vatem, aliud interpretem esse. Apol. adv. Ruff. lib. II. cap. 25].

There were also within a few hundred years after *Christ* translations many into the *Latin* tongue: for this tongue also was very fit to convey the law and the Gospel by, because in those times very many countries of the West, yea of the South, East, and North, spake or understood *Latin*, being made pro-

Translation out of Hebrew and Greek into Latin.

vinces to the *Romans*. But now the *Latin* translations were too many to be all good, for they were infinite; (*Latini interpretes nullo modo numerari possunt*, saith S. Augustine.) Again, they were not out of the *Hebrew* fountain, (we speak of the *Latin* translations of the Old Testament) but out of the *Greek* stream; therefore the *Greek* being not altogether clear, the *Latin* derived from it must needs be muddy. This moved S. *Hierome*, a most learned Father, and the best linguist without controversy of his age, or of any that went before him, to undertake the translating of the Old Testament out of the very fountains themselves; which he performed with that evidence of great learning, judgment, industry, and faithfulness, that he hath for ever bound the Church unto him in a debt of special remembrance and thankfulness.

Now though the Church were thus furnished with *Greek* and *Latin* translations, even before the faith of *Christ* was generally embraced in the Empire: (for the learned know that even in S. *Hierome*'s time the Consul of *Rome* and his wife were both Ethnicks, and about the same time the greatest part of the Senate also) yet for all that the godly learned were not content to have the Scriptures in the language which themselves understood, *Greek* and *Latin*, (as the good lepers were not content to fare well themselves, but acquainted their neighbours with the store that God had sent, that they also might provide for themselves) but also for the behoof and edifying of the unlearned which hungered and thirsted after righteousness, and had souls to be saved as well as they, they provided translations into the vulgar for their countrymen, insomuch that most nations under heaven did shortly after their conversion hear *Christ* speaking unto them in their mother tongue, not by the voice of their minister only, but also by the written word translated. If any doubt hereof, he may be satisfied by examples enough, if enough will serve the turn. First, S. *Hierome* saith, *Multarum gentium linguis Scriptura ante translata docet falsa esse quæ addita sunt*, &c. i. e. *The Scripture being translated before in the language of many nations doth shew that those things that were added* (by *Lucian* or *Hesychius*) *are false.* So S. *Hierome* in that place. The same *Hierome* elsewhere affirmeth that he, the time was, had set forth the translation of the *Seventy, suæ linguæ hominibus;* i. e. for his countrymen of *Dalmatia.* Which words not only *Erasmus* doth understand to purport, that S. *Hierome* translated the Scripture into the *Dalmatian* tongue; but also *Sixtus Senensis*, and *Alphonsus a Castro*, (that we speak of no more) men not to be excepted against by them of *Rome*, do ingenuously confess as much. So S. *Chrysostome*, that lived in S. *Hierome's* time, giveth evidence with him: *The doctrine of S.* John (saith he) *did not in such sort* (as the Philosophers did) *vanish away: but the Syrians, Egyptians, Indians, Persians, Ethiopians, and infinite other nations, being barbarous people, translated it into their (mother) tongue, and have learned to be (true) Philosophers*, he meaneth Christians. To this may be added *Theodoret*, as next unto him both for antiquity, and for learning. His words be these, *Every country that is under the sun is full of these words* (of the Apostles and Prophets) *and the Hebrew tongue* (he meaning the Scriptures in the Hebrew tongue) *is turned not only into the language of the Grecians, but also of the Romans, and Egyptians, and Persians, and Indians, and Armenians, and Scythians, and Sauromatians, and, briefly, into all the*

S. *Hieron. Præf. in 4. Evangel.*

S. *Hieron. Sophronio.*

Six. Sen. lib. 4. Alphon. a Castro, lib. 1. cap. 23.

S. *Chrysost. in Joann. cap. 1. hom. 1* [§ 2].

Theodor. [*Serm.*] 5. *Therapeut.* [pp. 839 –40].

languages which any nation useth. So he. In like
manner *Ulpilas* is reported by *Paulus Diaconus* and
Isidore, and before them by *Sozomen*, to have trans-
lated the Scriptures into the *Gothic* tongue: *John*
Bishop of *Sevil* by *Vasseus*, to have turned them into
Arabick about the year of our Lord 717: *Beda* by
Cistertiensis, to have turned a great part of them into
Saxon: *Efnard* by *Trithemius*, to have abridged the
French Psalter (as *Beda* had done the *Hebrew*) about
the year 800: King *Alured* by the said *Cistertiensis*, to
have turned the Psalter into *Saxon*: *Methodius* by
Aventinus (printed at *Ingolstad*) to have turned the
Scriptures into *Sclavonian*[||]: *Valdo* Bishop of *Frising*
by *Beatus Rhenanus*, to have caused about that time
the Gospels to be translated into *Dutch* rhythme, yet
extant in the library of *Corbinian*[1]: *Valdus* by divers,
to have turned them himself, or to have gotten them
turned into *French* about the year 1160: *Charles* the
fifth of that name, surnamed *The wise*, to have caused
them to be turned into *French*, about 200 years after
Valdus his time; of which translation there be many
copies yet extant, as witnesseth *Beroaldus*. Much
about that time, even in our King *Richard* the second's
days, *John Trevisa*[2] translated them into *English*, and
many *English* Bibles in written hand are yet to be
seen with divers; translated, as it is very probable, in
that age. So the *Syrian* translation of the New Testament is in most learned men's libraries, of *Widmin-
stadius* his setting forth; and the Psalter in *Arabick* is
with many, of *Augustinus Nebiensis*' setting forth. So

P. Diacon. lib. 12.
Isid. in Chron. Goth.
Sozom. lib. 6. cap. 37.
Vasseus in Chron. Hispan.

Polydor. Virg. 5. histor. Anglorum testatur idem de Aluredo nostro. Aventin. lib. 4.
|| Circa annum 900. B. Rhenan. rerum German. lib. 2.

Beroald.

[circa 1387.]

[1555.]

[1516.]

---

[1] S. Corbinian's Library at Freising on the Isar. See Ussher, *Historia Dogmatica*, A.D. 890.
[2] John Trevisa, the Cornishman's claim, as a Translator of the Bible, is roughly treated by Dr Eadie (*English Bible*, Vol. I. p. 60).

Postel[1] affirmeth, that in his travel he saw the Gospels in the *Ethiopian* tongue : And *Ambrose Thesius* allegeth the Psalter of the *Indians*, which he testifieth to have been set forth by *Potken* in *Syrian* characters[2]. So that to have the Scriptures in the mother tongue is not a quaint conceit lately taken up, either by the Lord *Cromwell* in *England*, or by the Lord *Radevil* in *Polonie*, or by the Lord *Ungnadius* in the Emperor's dominion, but hath been thought upon, and put in practice of old, even from the first times of the conversion of any nation; no doubt, because it was esteemed most profitable to cause faith to grow in men's hearts the sooner, and to make them to be able to say with the words of the Psalm, *As we have heard, so we have seen.* [Aethiopic.] [1513.] [1538.] *Thuan.* Ps. 48. 8.

Now the Church of *Rome* would seem at the length to bear a motherly affection towards her children, and to allow them the Scriptures in their mother tongue : but indeed it is a gift, not deserving to be called a gift*, an unprofitable gift: they must first get a license in writing before they may use them; and to get that, they must approve themselves to their Confessor, that is, to be such as are, if not frozen in the dregs, yet soured with the leaven of their superstition. Howbeit, it seemed too much to *Clement* the eighth that there should be any license granted to have them in the vulgar tongue, and therefore he overruleth and frustrateth the grant of *Pius* the fourth. So much are they afraid of the light The unwillingness of our chief adversaries that the Scriptures should be divulged in the mother tongue, &c. * Δῶρον ἄδωρον κοὐκ ὀνήσιμον. Sophocles [*Ajax*, ver. 665]. See the observation (set forth by *Clement* his authority) upon the 4th rule of *Pius* the 4th his making in the *Index lib. prohib. pag.* 15. *ver.* 5.

---

[1] If the reference is to the *Linguarum duodecim characteribus differentium Alphabetum* (1538) of the voluminous mystic W. Postel [1510—1581], the fact here named is rather implied than stated in sheet F, *de Indica lingua*.
[2] Walton, *Prolegomena*, XIV. 19, III.

of the Scripture, (*Lucifugæ Scripturarum*, as *Tertullian* speaketh) that they will not trust the people with it, no not as it is set forth by their own sworn men, no not with the license of their own Bishops and Inquisitors. Yea, so unwilling they are to communicate the Scriptures to the people's understanding in any sort, that they are not ashamed to confess that we forced them to translate it into *English* against their wills. This seemeth to argue a bad cause, or a bad conscience, or both. Sure we are, that it is not he that hath good gold, that is afraid to bring it to the touchstone, but he that hath the counterfeit; neither is it the true man that shunneth the light, but the malefactor, lest his deeds should be reproved; neither is it the plain-dealing merchant that is unwilling to have the weights, or the meteyard, brought in place, but he that useth deceit. But we will let them alone for this fault, and return to translation.

<small>*Tertul. de resur. carnis [cap. 47].*</small>

<small>John 3. 20.</small>

<small>The speeches and reasons, both of our brethren, and of our adversaries, against this work.</small> Many men's mouths have been open a good while (and yet are not stopped) with speeches about the translation so long in hand, or rather perusals of translations made before: and ask what may be the reason, what the necessity, of the employment. Hath the Church been deceived, say they, all this while? Hath her sweet bread been mingled with leaven, her silver with dross, her wine with water, her milk with lime? (*lacte gypsum malè miscetur*, saith S. *Ireney*.) We hoped that we had been in the right way, that we had had the oracles of God delivered unto us, and that though all the world had cause to be offended, and to complain, yet that we had none. Hath the nurse holden out the breast, and nothing but wind in it? Hath the bread been delivered by the Fathers of the Church, and the same proved to be *lapidosus*,

<small>*S. Iren. lib. 3. cap. 19 [cap. xvii. fin. Migne].*</small>

as *Seneca* speaketh? What is it to handle the word of God deceitfully, if this be not? Thus certain brethren. Also the adversaries of *Judah* and *Hierusalem*, like *Sanballat* in *Nehemiah*, mock, as we hear, both at the work and workmen, saying, *What do these weak Jews, &c. will they make the stones whole again out of the heaps of dust which are burnt? Although they build, yet if a fox go up, he shall even break down their stony wall.* Was their translation good before? Why do they now mend it? Was it not good? Why then was it obtruded to the people? Yea, why did the Catholicks (meaning Popish *Romanists*) always go in jeopardy for refusing to go to hear it? Nay, if it must be translated into *English*, Catholicks are fittest to do it. They have learning, and they know when a thing is well, they can *manum de tabulâ*. We will answer them both briefly: and the former, being brethren, thus with St. *Hierome, Damnamus veteres? Minimè, sed post priorum studia in domo Domini quod possumus laboramus.* That is, *Do we condemn the ancient? In no case: but after the endeavours of them that were before us, we take the best pains we can in the house of God.* As if he said, Being provoked by the example of the learned that lived before my time, I have thought it my duty to assay whether my talent in the knowledge of the tongues may be profitable in any measure to God's Church, lest I should seem to have laboured in them in vain, and lest I should be thought to glory in men (although ancient) above that which was in them. Thus S. *Hierome* may be thought to speak.

Neh. 4. 2, 3.

S. *Hieron. Apolog. adversus Ruffin* [*lib.* II. *cap.* 25: Migne, Tom. II. 520].

And to the same effect say we, that we are so far off from condemning any of their labours that travailed before us in this kind, either in this land,

A satisfaction to our brethren.

or beyond sea, either in King *Henry's* time, or King *Edward's*, (if there were any translation, or correction of a translation, in his time) or Queen *Elizabeth's* of ever renowned memory, that we acknowledge them to have been raised up of God for the building and furnishing of his Church, and that they deserve to be had of us and of posterity in everlasting remembrance. The judgment of *Aristotle* is worthy and well known :

Arist. 2
[βιβλίον α' τὸ ἔλαττον]
Metaphys.
cap. 1 [§ 3.]

If Timotheus had not been, we had not had much sweet musick: But if Phrynis (*Timotheus* his master) *had not been, we had not had Timotheus.* Therefore blessed be they, and most honoured be their name, that break the ice, and give the onset upon that which helpeth forward to the saving of souls. Now what can be more available thereto, than to deliver God's book unto God's people in a tongue which they understand?

S. Epiphan.
loco ante citato
[p. 279].

Since of an hidden treasure, and of a fountain that is sealed, there is no profit, as *Ptolemy Philadelph* wrote to the Rabbins or masters of the Jews, as witnesseth *Epiphanius:* and as S. *Augustine*

S. Augustin.
lib. 19. *de civit. Dei,*
cap. 7.

saith, *A man had rather be with his dog than with a stranger* (whose tongue is strange unto him). Yet for all that, as nothing is begun and perfected at the same time, and the latter thoughts are thought to be the wiser: so, if we building upon their foundation that went before us, and being holpen by their labours, do endeavour to make that better which they left so good; no man, we are sure, hath cause to mislike us; they, we persuade ourselves, if they were alive, would thank us. The vintage of *Abiezer*, that strake the stroke ; yet the gleaning of grapes of *Ephraim*

Judg. 8. 2.

was not to be despised. See *Judges* viii. *verse* 2.

2 Kin. 13. 18, 19.

Joash the king of *Israel* did not satisfy himself till he had smitten the ground three times ; and yet he offended the Prophet for giving over then. *Aquila*, of whom we spake before, translated the Bible as carefully and as skilfully as he could; and yet he thought good to go over it again, and then it got the credit with the *Jews* to be called κατὰ ἀκρίβειαν, that is, accurately done, as St. *Hierome* witnesseth. How many books of profane learning have been gone over again and again, by the same translators, by others? Of one and the same book of *Aristotle's* Ethics there are extant not so few as six or seven several translations. Now if this cost may be bestowed upon the gourd, which affordeth us a little shade, and which to-day flourisheth, but to-morrow is cut down; what may we bestow, nay, what ought we not to bestow, upon the vine, the fruit whereof maketh glad the conscience of man, and the stem whereof abideth for ever? And this is the word of God, which we translate. *What is the chaff to the wheat?* *saith the Lord.* *Tanti vitreum, quanti verum margaritum* (saith *Tertullian*,) if a toy of glass be of that reckoning with us, how ought we to value the true pearl? Therefore let no man's eye be evil, because his Majesty's is good; neither let any be grieved, that we have a Prince that seeketh the increase of the spiritual wealth of *Israel;* (let *Sanballats* and *Tobiahs* do so, which therefore do bear their just reproof) but let us rather bless God from the ground of our heart for working this religious care in him to have the translations of the Bible maturely considered of and examined. For by this means it cometh to pass, that whatsoever is sound already, (and all is sound for substance in one or other of our editions, and the worst of ours far better than their authentick Vulgar) the same will shine as gold more brightly, being

S. Hieron. in Ezech. cap. 3 [ver. 15].

Jer. 23. 28.

Tertul. ad Martyr. [cap. 4]. *Si tanti vitrum, quanti pretiosissimum Margaritum: Hieron. ad Salvin.* [cap. 7, p. 505].
[Neh. 4. 1—3.]

rubbed and polished; also, if any thing be halting, or superfluous, or not so agreeable to the original, the same may be corrected, and the truth set in place. And what can the King command to be done, that will bring him more true honour than this? And wherein could they that have been set a work approve their duty to the King, yea, their obedience to God, and love to his Saints, more, than by yielding their service, and all that is within them, for the furnishing of the work? But besides all this, they were the principal motives of it, and therefore ought least to quarrel it. For the very historical truth is, that upon the importunate petitions of the Puritans at his Majesty's coming to this crown, the conference at *Hampton Court* having been appointed for hearing their complaints, when by force of reason they were put from all other grounds, they had recourse at the last to this shift, that they could not with good conscience subscribe to the Communion book, since it maintained the Bible as it was there translated, which was, as they said, a most corrupted translation. And although this was judged to be but a very poor and empty shift, yet even hereupon did his Majesty begin to bethink himself of the good that might ensue by a new translation, and presently after gave order for this translation which is now presented unto thee. Thus much to satisfy our scrupulous brethren.

An answer to the imputations of our adversaries. Now to the latter we answer, that we do not deny, nay, we affirm and avow, that the very meanest translation of the Bible in *English* set forth by men of our profession (for we have seen none of theirs of the whole Bible as yet[1]) containeth the word of God, nay,

---

[1] *The Holy Bible faithfully translated into English out of the Authentical Latin:* Douay, 1609—1610, 2 vols. 4to. The

is the word of God: as the King's speech which he uttered in Parliament, being translated into *French, Dutch, Italian,* and *Latin,* is still the King's speech, though it be not interpreted by every translator with the like grace, nor peradventure so fitly for phrase, nor so expressly for sense, every where. For it is confessed, that things are to take their denomination of the greater part; and a natural man could say, *Verum ubi multa nitent in carmine, non ego paucis offendor maculis,* &c. A man may be counted a virtuous man, though he have made many slips in his life, (else there were none virtuous, for *in many things we offend all,*) also a comely man and lovely, though he have some warts upon his hand, yea, not only freckles upon his face, but also scars. No cause therefore why the word translated should be denied to be the word, or forbidden to be current, notwithstanding that some imperfections and blemishes may be noted in the setting forth of it. For whatever was perfect under the sun, where Apostles or apostolick men, that is, men endued with an extraordinary measure of God's Spirit, and privileged with the privilege of infallibility, had not their hand? The Romanists therefore in refusing to hear, and daring to burn the word translated, did no less than despite the Spirit of grace, from whom originally it proceeded, and whose sense and meaning, as well as man's weakness would enable, it did express. Judge by an example or two.

Plutarch writeth, that after that *Rome* had been burnt by the *Gauls,* they fell soon to build it again: but doing it in haste, they did not cast the streets,

Horace. [*Epist. ad Pisones,* ver. 351.]

James 3. 2.

Plutarch. in Camillo [Διὸ καὶ τεταραγμένην τοῖς στενωποῖς καὶ συμπεφυρμένην ταῖς οἰκήσεσιν ἀνήγαγον τὴν πόλιν ὑπὸ σπουδῆς καὶ τάχους. *cap.* 32].

writer must have seen the first volume of the Douay Bible, since neither *tunike* nor *rational* (see p. 302) occur in the Rhemish New Testament.

S.

nor proportion the houses, in such comely fashion, as had been most sightly and convenient. Was *Catiline* therefore an honest man, or a good patriot, that sought to bring it to a combustion? or *Nero* a good Prince, that did indeed set it on fire? So by the story of *Ezra* and the prophecy of *Haggai* it may be gathered, that the temple built by *Zerubbabel* after the return from *Babylon* was by no means to be compared to the former built by *Solomon :* (for they that remembered the former wept when they considered the latter) notwithstanding might this latter either have been abhorred and forsaken by the *Jews*, or profaned by the *Greeks?* The like we are to think of translations. The translation of the *Seventy* dissenteth from the Original in many places, neither doth it come near it for perspicuity, gravity, majesty; yet which of the Apostles did condemn it? Condemn it? Nay, they used it, (as it is apparent, and as Saint *Hierome* and most learned men do confess) which they would not have done, nor by their example of using of it so grace and commend it to the Church, if it had been unworthy the appellation and name of the word of God. And whereas they urge for their second defence of their vilifying and abusing of the *English* Bibles, or some pieces thereof, which they meet with, for that Hereticks forsooth were the authors of the translations: (Hereticks they call us by the same right that they call themselves Catholicks, both being wrong) we marvel what divinity taught them so. We are sure *Tertullian* was of another mind: *Ex personis probamus fidem, an ex fide personas?* Do we try men's faith by their persons? We should try their persons by their faith. Also S. *Augustine* was of another mind: for he, lighting upon

marginalia:
Ezra 3. 12.
[Hagg. 2. 3.]

Tertul. de præscript. contra hæreses [cap. 3].

certain rules made by *Tychonius* a *Donatist* for the better understanding of the Word, was not ashamed to make use of them, yea, to insert them into his own book, with giving commendation to them so far forth as they were worthy to be commended, as is to be seen in St. *Augustine's* third book *De Doctrinâ Christianâ.* To be short, *Origen*, and the whole Church of God for certain hundred years, were of another mind: for they were so far from treading under foot (much more from burning) the translation of *Aquila* a proselyte, that is, one that had turned *Jew*, of *Symmachus*, and *Theodotion*, both *Ebionites*, that is, most vile hereticks, that they joined them together with the *Hebrew* original, and the translation of the *Seventy*, (as hath been before signified out of *Epiphanius*) and set them forth openly to be considered of and perused by all. But we weary the unlearned, who need not know so much; and trouble the learned, who know it already.

S. August. 3. de doct. Christ. cap. 30.

Yet before we end, we must answer a third cavil and objection of theirs against us, for altering and amending our Translations so oft; wherein truly they deal hardly and strangely with us. For to whom ever was it imputed for a fault (by such as were wise) to go over that which he had done, and to amend it where he saw cause? Saint *Augustine* was not afraid to exhort S. *Hierome* to a *Palinodia* or recantation. The same S. *Augustine* was not ashamed to retractate, we might say, revoke, many things that had passed him, and doth even glory that he seeth his infirmities. If we will be sons of the truth, we must consider what it speaketh, and trample upon our own credit, yea, and upon other men's too, if either be any way a hinderance to it. This to the cause. Then to the

S. August. Epist. 9.

S. August. lib. Retractat. Video interdum vitia mea, S. August. Epist. 8.

persons we say, that of all men they ought to be most silent in this case. For what varieties have they, and what alterations have they made, not only of their service books, portesses[1], and breviaries, but also of their *Latin* translation? The service book supposed to be made by S. *Ambrose* (*Officium Ambrosianum*) was a great while in special use and request: but Pope *Adrian*, calling a council with the aid of *Charles* the Emperor, abolished it, yea, burnt it, and commanded the service book of Saint *Gregory* universally to be used. Well, *Officium Gregorianum* gets by this means to be in credit; but doth it continue without change or altering? No, the very *Roman* service was of two fashions; the new fashion, and the old, the one used in one Church, the other in another; as is to be seen in *Pamelius* a Romanist his preface before *Micrologus*. The same *Pamelius* reporteth out of *Radulphus de Rivo*, that about the year of our Lord 1277 Pope *Nicolas* the third removed out of the churches of *Rome* the more ancient books (of service) and brought into use the missals of the Friers Minorites, and commanded them to be observed there; insomuch that about an hundred years after, when the above named *Radulphus* happened to be at *Rome*, he found all the books to be new, of the new stamp. Neither was there this chopping and changing in the more ancient times only, but also of late. *Pius Quintus* himself confesseth, that every bishoprick almost had a peculiar kind of service, most unlike to that which others had; which

Durand. lib. 5. cap. 2.

---

[1] "*Portesses,*" i.e. manuals of devotion. Spelt also *portace, portus,* &c.

"And in his hand his portesse still he *bare.*"
Spenser, *F. Q.* I. 4.

moved him to abolish all other breviaries, though never so ancient, and privileged and published by Bishops in their Dioceses, and to establish and ratify that only which was of his own setting forth in the year 1568. Now when the Father of their Church, who gladly would heal the sore of the daughter of his people softly and slightly, and make the best of it, findeth so great fault with them for their odds and jarring; we hope the children have no great cause to vaunt of their uniformity. But the difference that appeareth between our translations, and our often correcting of them, is the thing that we are specially charged with; let us see therefore whether they themselves be without fault this way, (if it be to be counted a fault to correct) and whether they be fit men to throw stones at us: *O tandem major parcas insane minori:* they that are less sound themselves ought not to object infirmities to others. If we should tell them that *Valla, Stapulensis, Erasmus,* and *Vives,* found fault with their vulgar translation, and consequently wished the same to be mended, or a new one to be made; they would answer peradventure, that we produced their enemies for witnesses against them; albeit they were in no other sort enemies, than as S. *Paul* was to the *Galatians,* for telling them the truth: and it were to be wished, that they had dared to tell it them plainlier and oftener. But what will they say to this, That Pope *Leo* the tenth allowed *Erasmus's* translation of the New Testament, so much different from the Vulgar, by his apostolick letter and bull? That the same *Leo* exhorted *Pagnine* to translate the whole Bible, and bare whatsoever charges was necessary for the work? Surely, as the Apostle reasoneth to the *Hebrews,* that

Horat. [2 *Sat.* III. ver. 326].

Gal. 4. 16.

Sixtus Senens.

if the former Law and Testament had been sufficient, there had been no need of the latter: so we may say, that if the old Vulgar had been at all points allowable, to small purpose had labour and charges been undergone about framing of a new. If they say, it was one Pope's private opinion, and that he consulted only himself; then we are able to go further with them, and to aver, that more of their chief men of all sorts, even their own *Trent* champions, *Paiva* and *Vega*, and their own Inquisitors, *Hieronymus ab Oleastro*, and their own Bishop *Isidorus Clarius*, and their own Cardinal *Thomas a Vio Cajetan*, do either make new translations themselves, or follow new ones of other men's making, or note the Vulgar interpreter for halting, none of them fear to dissent from him, nor yet to except against him. And call they this an uniform tenor of text and judgment about the text, so many of their worthies disclaiming the now received conceit? Nay, we will yet come nearer the quick. Doth not their *Paris* edition differ from the *Lovaine*, and *Hentenius* his from them both, and yet all of them allowed by authority? Nay, doth not *Sixtus Quintus* confess, that certain Catholicks (he meaneth certain of his own side) were in such a humour of translating the Scriptures into *Latin*, that Satan taking occasion by them, though they thought no such matter, did strive what he could, out of so uncertain and manifold a variety of translations, so to mingle all things, that nothing might seem to be left certain and firm in them? &c. Nay further, did not the same *Sixtus* ordain by an inviolable decree, and that with the counsel and consent of his Cardinals, that the *Latin* edition of the Old and New Testament, which the Council of *Trent* would have to be authentick, is the same without controversy which he then set forth, being diligently corrected and printed in the printinghouse of *Vatican?* Thus *Sixtus* in his Preface before his Bible. And yet *Clement* the eighth, his immediate successor, published another edition of [1592] the Bible, containing in it infinite differences from that of *Sixtus*, and many of them weighty and material; and yet this must be authentick by all means. What is to have the faith of our glorious Lord *Jesus Christ* with yea and nay, if this be not? Again, what is sweet harmony and consent, if this be? Therefore, as *Demaratus* of *Corinth* advised [1] a great King, before he talked of the dissensions among the *Grecians*, to compose his domestick broils; (for at that time his queen and his son and heir were at deadly feud with him) so all the while that our adversaries do make so many and so various editions themselves, and do jar so much about the worth and authority of them, they can with no show of equity challenge us for changing and correcting. [1592] [Diodorus, XVI. 9.]

But it is high time to leave them, and to shew in brief what we proposed to ourselves, and what course we held, in this our perusal and survey of the Bible. Truly, good Christian Reader, we never thought from the beginning that we should need to make a new translation, nor yet to make of a bad one a good one; (for then the imputation of *Sixtus* had been true in some sort, that our people had been fed with gall of dragons instead of wine, with whey instead of milk;) but to make a good one better, or out of many good ones one principal good one, not justly to be excepted against; that hath been our endeavour, that our mark. To that purpose there

The purpose of the Translators, with their number, furniture, care, &c.

[1] Xerxes.

were many chosen, that were greater in other men's eyes than in their own, and that sought the truth rather than their own praise. Again, they came, or were thought to come, to the work, not *exercendi causâ*, (as one saith) but *exercitati*, that is, learned, not to learn: For the chief overseer and ἐργοδιώκτης under his Majesty, to whom not only we, but also our whole Church was much bound[1], knew by his wisdom, which *Nazianzen.* thing also *Nazianzen* taught so long ago, that it is a εἰς ρν'.ἐπισκ. παρουσ. preposterous order to teach first, and to learn after, [*Orat.* XLII, *cap.* 1]. yea that τὸ ἐν πίθῳ κεραμίαν μανθάνειν, to learn and *Idem in Apologet.* practise together, is neither commendable for the work- [*Orat.* II. *cap.* 47]. man, nor safe for the work. Therefore such were thought upon, as could say modestly with S. *Hierome*, *Et Hebræum sermonem ex parte didicimus, et in Latino penè ab ipsis incunabulis,* &c. *detriti sumus; Both we have learned the Hebrew tongue in part, and in the Latin we have been exercised almost from our very cradle.* S. *Hierome* maketh no mention of the *Greek* tongue, wherein yet he did excel; because he translated not the Old Testament out of *Greek*, but out of *Hebrew*. And in what sort did these assemble? In the trust of their own knowledge, or of their sharpness of wit, or deepness of judgment, as it were in an arm of flesh? At no hand. They trusted in him that [Rev. 3. 7.] hath the key of *David*, opening, and no man shutting; they prayed to the Lord, the Father of our Lord, to *S. Aug. lib.* the effect that St. *Augustine* did; *O let thy Scriptures* 11. *Confess. cap.* 2. *be my pure delight; let me not be deceived in them, neither let me deceive by them.* In this confidence, and with this devotion, did they assemble together; not too many, lest one should trouble another; and yet

---

[1] Richard Bancroft, Archbishop of Canterbury, died Nov. 2, 1610.

many, lest many things haply might escape them. If
you ask what they had before them, truly it was the
Hebrew text of the Old Testament, the *Greek* of the
New. These are the two golden pipes, or rather
conduits, wherethrough the olive branches empty them- [Zech. iv. 12.]
selves into the gold. Saint *Augustine* calleth them *S. August.* 3.
precedent, or original, tongues; Saint *Hierome*, foun- *de doctr. c.* 3, &c.
tains. The same Saint *Hierome* affirmeth, and *Gratian* *S. Hieron. ad Suniam*
hath not spared to put it into his decree, That *as the et Fretel.*
credit of the old books (he meaneth of the Old Testa- *S. Hieron. ad Lucini-*
ment) *is to be tried by the Hebrew volumes; so of the* *um, Dist.* 9. Ut veterum.
New by the Greek tongue, he meaneth by the original
Greek. If truth be to be tried by these tongues, then
whence should a translation be made, but out of them?
These tongues therefore (the Scriptures, we say, in
those tongues) we set before us to translate, being
the tongues wherein God was pleased to speak to
his Church by his Prophets and Apostles. Neither
did we run over the work with that posting haste that
the *Septuagint* did, if that be true which is reported of *Joseph. Antiq.*
them, that they finished it in seventy two days; neither *lib.* 12.
were we barred or hindered from going over it again, [cap. 2. 13].
having once done it, like St *Hierome*, if that be true *S. Hieron.*
which himself reporteth, that he could no sooner *ad Pammac. pro lib.*
write any thing, but presently it was caught from him, *advers. Jovinian.*
and published, and he could not have leave to mend
it: neither, to be short, were we the first that fell in πρωτόπειροι.
hand with translating the Scripture into *English*, and [Steph. *Thesaur.*
consequently destitute of former helps, as it is written Tom. III. p. 153.]
of *Origen*, that he was the first in a manner, that put
his hand to write commentaries upon the Scriptures,
and therefore no marvel if he overshot himself many
times. None of these things: the work hath not
been huddled up in seventy two days, but hath cost

the workmen, as light as it seemeth, the pains of twice seven times seventy two days, and more. Matters of such weight and consequence are to be speeded with maturity : for in a business of moment a man feareth not the blame of convenient slackness. Neither did we think much to consult the translators or commentators, *Chaldee*, *Hebrew*, *Syrian*, *Greek*, or *Latin;* no, nor the *Spanish*, *French*, *Italian*, or *Dutch*[1]; neither did we disdain to revise that which we had done, and to bring back to the anvil that which we had hammered : but having and using as great helps as were needful, and fearing no reproach for slowness, nor coveting praise for expedition, we have at the length, through the good hand of the Lord upon us, brought the work to that pass that you see.

Some peradventure would have no variety of senses to be set in the margin, lest the authority of the Scriptures for deciding of controversies by that show of uncertainty should somewhat be shaken. But we hold their judgment not to be so sound in this point. For though *whatsoever things are necessary are manifest*, as S. *Chrysostome* saith ; and, as S. *Augustine*, *in those things that are plainly set down in the Scriptures all such matters are found that concern faith, hope, and charity:* yet for all that it cannot be dissembled, that partly to exercise and whet our wits, partly to wean the curious from loathing of them for their every where plainness, partly also to stir up our devotion to crave the assistance of God's Spirit by prayer, and lastly, that we might be forward to seek aid of our brethren by conference, and never scorn those that be not in all respects so complete as they should be, being to seek in many things ourselves,

---

[1] See above, p. 140 note.

The Translators to the Reader.

it hath pleased God in his Divine Providence here and there to scatter words and sentences of that difficulty and doubtfulness, not in doctrinal points that concern salvation, (for in such it hath been vouched that the Scriptures are plain) but in matters of less moment, that fearfulness would better beseem us than confidence, and if we will resolve, to resolve upon modesty with S. *Augustine*, (though not in this same case altogether, yet upon the same ground) *Melius est dubitare de occultis, quam litigare de incertis: It is better to make doubt of those things which are secret, than to strive about those things that are uncertain.* There be many words in the Scriptures which be never found there but once, (having neither brother nor neighbour, as the *Hebrews* speak) so that we cannot be holpen by conference of places. Again, there be many rare names of certain birds, beasts, and precious stones, &c. concerning which the *Hebrews* themselves are so divided among themselves for judgment, that they may seem to have defined this or that, rather because they would say something, than because they were sure of that which they said, as S. *Hierome* somewhere saith of the *Septuagint*. Now in such a case doth not a margin do well to admonish the Reader to seek further, and not to conclude or dogmatize upon this or that peremptorily? For as it is a fault of incredulity, to doubt of those things that are evident; so to determine of such things as the Spirit of God hath left (even in the judgment of the judicious) questionable, can be no less than presumption. Therefore as S. *Augustine* saith, that variety of translations is profitable for the finding out of the sense of the Scriptures: so diversity of signification and sense in the margin, where

S. August. li. 8. de Genes. ad liter. cap. 5.

ἅπαξ λεγό- μενα.

S. Aug. 2⁰. de doctr. Christian. c. 14.

the text is not so clear, must needs do good; yea, is necessary, as we are persuaded. We know that *Sixtus Quintus* expressly forbiddeth that any variety of readings of their Vulgar edition should be put in the margin[1]; (which though it be not altogether the same thing to that we have in hand, yet it looketh that way;) but we think he hath not all of his own side his favourers for this conceit. They that are wise had rather have their judgments at liberty in differences of readings, than to be captivated to one, when it may be the other. If they were sure that their high priest had all laws shut up in his breast, as *Paul* the second bragged, and that he were as free from error by special privilege, as the dictators of *Rome* were made by law inviolable, it were another matter; then his word were an oracle, his opinion a decision. But the eyes of the world are now open, God be thanked, and have been a great while; they find that he is subject to the same affections and infirmities that others be, that his skin is penetrable, and therefore so much as he proveth, not as much as he claimeth, they grant and embrace.

Sixtus V. Præf. Bibl.

Plat. in Paulo secundo.

ὁμοιοπαθής.

Τρωτός γ' οἱ χρώς ἐστι. [Compare *Homer, Iliad* XXI. 568.]

Reasons inducing us not to stand curiously upon an identity of phrasing.

Another thing we think good to admonish thee of, gentle Reader, that we have not tied ourselves to an uniformity of phrasing, or to an identity of words, as some peradventure would wish that we had done, because they observe, that some learned men somewhere have been as exact as they could that way. Truly, that we might not vary from the sense of that

---

[1] So that even Vercellone, as late as 1860, when publishing his collection of *Variæ Lectiones Vulg. Lat. Bibl.*, probably was prevented by this rule from printing the text with them, "and so deprived them of a great deal of their value" (Canon Wordsworth, *Gospel from the St German MS.* (g), Introduction, p. XVI. note 3).

which we had translated before, if the word signified the same thing in both places, (for there be some words that be not of the same sense every where) we were especially careful, and made a conscience, according to our duty. But that we should express the same notion in the same particular word; as for example, if we translate the *Hebrew* or *Greek* word once by *purpose*, never to call it *intent*; if one where *journeying*, never *travelling*; if one where *think*, never *suppose*; if one where *pain*, never *ache*; if one where *joy*, never *gladness*, &c. thus to mince the matter, we thought to savour more of curiosity than wisdom, and that rather it would breed scorn in the atheist, than bring profit to the godly reader. For is the kingdom of God become words or syllables? Why should we be in bondage to them, if we may be free? use one precisely, when we may use another no less fit as commodiously? A godly Father in the primitive time shewed himself greatly moved, that one of newfangleness called κράββατον, σκίμπους, though the difference be little or none; and another reporteth, that he was much abused for turning *cucurbita* (to which reading the people had been used) into *hedera*. Now if this happen in better times, and upon so small occasions, we might justly fear hard censure, if generally we should make verbal and unnecessary changings. We might also be charged (by scoffers) with some unequal dealing towards a great number of good *English* words. For as it is written of a certain great Philosopher, that he should say, that those logs were happy that were made images to be worshipped; for their fellows, as good as they, lay for blocks behind the fire: so if we should say, as it were, unto certain words, Stand up higher, have a

[margin: πολύσημα. A bed. *Niceph. Calist. lib.* 8. *cap.* 42. *S. Hieron. in* 4. *Jona.* See *S. Aug. epist.* 10.]

place in the Bible always; and to others of like quality, Get ye hence, be banished for ever; we might [James 2. 4.] be taxed peradventure with S. *James* his words, namely, *To be partial in ourselves, and judges of evil* λεπτολογία. *thoughts.* Add hereunto, that niceness in words was ἀδολεσχία. always counted the next step to trifling; and so was τὸ σπουδάζειν ἐπὶ ὀνόμασι. to be curious about names too: also that we cannot See *Euseb.* προπαρασκευ. follow a better pattern for elocution than God himself; therefore he using divers words in his holy writ, *lib.* 12. *ex Platon.* and indifferently for one thing in nature; we, if we will not be superstitious, may use the same liberty in our *English* versions out of *Hebrew* and *Greek*, for that copy or store that he hath given us. Lastly, we have on the one side avoided the scrupulosity of the Puritans, who leave the old Ecclesiastical words, and betake them to other, as when they put *washing* for *Baptism*, and *Congregation* instead of *Church:* as also on the other side we have shunned the obscurity of the Papists, in their *Azimes, Tunike, Rational, Holocausts, Præpuce, Pasche*, and a number of such like, [Isai. 19. 18.] whereof their late translation[1] is full, and that of purpose to darken the sense, that since they must needs translate the Bible, yet by the language thereof it may be kept from being understood. But we desire that the Scripture may speak like itself, as in the language of *Canaan*, that it may be understood even of the very vulgar.

Many other things we might give thee warning of, gentle Reader, if we had not exceeded the measure of a preface already. It remaineth that we commend thee to God, and to the Spirit of his grace, which is

---

[1] *The New Testament...translated faithfully into English out of the authentical Latin.* Rheims, 1580, 4to. See also p. 288, note.

able to build further than we can ask or think. He removeth the scales from our eyes, the vail from our hearts, opening our wits that we may understand his word, enlarging our hearts, yea, correcting our affections, that we may love it above gold and silver, yea, that we may love it to the end. Ye are brought unto fountains of living water which ye digged not; do not cast earth into them, with the Philistines, neither prefer broken pits before them, with the wicked Jews. Others have laboured, and you may enter into their labours. O receive not so great things in vain: O despise not so great salvation. Be not like swine to tread under foot so precious things, neither yet like dogs to tear and abuse holy things. Say not to our Saviour with the *Gergesites*, Depart out of our coasts; neither yet with *Esau* sell your birthright for a mess of pottage. If light be come into the world, love not darkness more than light: if food, if clothing, be offered, go not naked, starve not yourselves. Remember the advice of *Nazianzene*, *It is a grievous thing* (or dangerous) *to neglect a great fair, and to seek to make markets afterwards:* also the encouragement of S. *Chrysostome*, *It is altogether impossible, that he that is sober* (and watchful) *should at any time be neglected:* lastly, the admonition and menacing of S. *Augustine, They that despise God's will inviting them shall feel God's will taking vengeance of them.* It is a fearful thing to fall into the hands of the living God; but a blessed thing it is, and will bring us to everlasting blessedness in the end, when God speaketh unto us, to hearken; when he setteth his word before us, to read it; when he stretcheth out his hand and calleth, to answer, Here am I, here we are to do thy will, O God. The Lord work a care and conscience in us to know him and serve him, that we may be acknowledged of him at the appearing of our Lord JESUS CHRIST, to whom with the Holy Ghost be all praise and thanksgiving. Amen.

INDEX

OF PERSONS AND SUBJECTS.

N.B.—A.V. denotes the Authorized Bible (1611).

Abbot, Ezra, Prof. 243
Abbot, G., Archp. .... 19 n.
Accuracy only comparative 33
Addison, Jos. .... 25 n. 1
Adjectives used for adverbs 112
Adonai Jehovah, how represented in A.V. .... 147 n. 1
Aldus, Greek Bible (1518) .... 47, 48 and n. 2, 52 n., 140, 176 n., 199 n. 2, 200 n., 229 n. 2
Alford, H., Dean .... 91, 105 n.
Alternative renderings ("∥Or") alleged superior to those in the Text 43
American failure of attempt at revision of A.V. (1851)...36 and n. 2, 37-8, 46, 113, 114, 208 n.
Anderson, Chr. .... 12 n. 4
Andrewes, Lancelot, Bp 137
Angus, Joseph, Dr .... 108 n. 2
Antedating books, fraud of ...16 n. 2
Apocrypha, omitted in Bibles ...19 and n.
———— signatures and order as bound in 1769 .... 29 n. 2
———— mode of representing italic type in A.V. 34, 72
———— Tremellius' Latin version of 44
———— marginal notes in...46—55
———— Text used in translation of 47-8

Apocrypha, first printed in English by Coverdale .... 52 n.
———— resembles Bishops' version more closely than Canonical Books 73
———— parallel refs. to, expunged .... 119, 195 n. 2
———— Translators of 140
Apodosis suppressed in orig. texts, how treated in A.V. 65-6
Apostrophe, before s in poss. cases plur. of pers. pronouns 100
———— before or after s to indicate poss. case sing. or plural ...... 110, 152 n., 196 n., 235 n. 1
Appendices (A—E) of this work...3, 6, 7, 14, 15, 17, 19, 21, 22, 23, 24, 29, 30, 31, 32, 33, 36 and n. 1, 38, 49, 51, 58 n. 2, 59, 63, 68, 69, 71, 80, 88, 91, 98, 110 and n. 1, 111 and n., 113, 132, 133, 145, 153 n. 2, 161 n. 1, 173 n., 187, 202, 205, 217 n. 4, 233 n. 3, 234 n.
Archaic style of A.V. corrected...30, 94, 101
Arnald, Richard 52
Article in original Texts, how represented in A.V. 74-7
Assembly of Divines ...... 25 and n. 3
Athanasius, quoted in margin of Apocrypha 46

S.

20

Index of persons and subjects.

Bagster's Hexapla .... 15 n.
―――― Polyglott (1828) 121
Bain, Eng. Grammar, 75, 110 n. 2
Baker papers .... 12 n. 1
Bancroft, Rich., Archp .... 13 n. 2, 296 n.
Basketts, the, their Bibles (1744—56) ... 28, 201 n.
Bayward, Thomas ...... 239 and n. 3
Bensly, R. L. .... 49 n. 1
Bentley, Wm., his correct Bibles (1646—51) 26
Beza, Theodore, influence of, on Revisers of N.T. ... 57, 60; 58 nn. 3 and 4
―――― his Greek Testaments ...... 60, 243, 248 and n. 1, 257
―――― his Latin N.T. (1556) ... 61, 248 n. 1
Bibles: English
 A.V. (1611) ...... 1 *passim*, 5—15
 Bishops' (1568—72) ... 9, 12 n. 1, 40, 43, 47, 48 and n. 2, 55, 57, 58 n. 1, 61, 73, 89, 113, 131 n. 2, 132, 136, 140, 144, 176 n., 203 n. 2, 267 n.
 Coverdale's (1535) ...... 40, 52 n., 73, 92, 93 n., 105, 131 n. 2
 Douay (1609—10) .... 288 n.
 Geneva (1557 N.T., 1560) ... 40, 45 n., 57, 61, 62, 92, 127, 132, 267 n.
 Great (1539) ... 5 n., 61, 92, 132, 139
 Recent (or modern) 2, 3
 Revised (1871) 1
 Rhemish (1582) ... 262, 288 n., 302 n.
 Tyndale's (1525—34) ... 40, 92, 262
 Wicklif's (about 1380?) ... 207 n. 1, 250, 252, 255, 262
French, R. P. Olivetan's (Geneva, 1535) .... 140 n.
―――― The Pastors' (1588) ... 140 n.
German, Luther's (1522) ...... 140 n.
Greek, Aldus (1518) ... 47, 48 and n. 2, 52 n., 140, 176 n., 199 n. 2, 200 n., 229 n. 2
―――― Elzevir (1624) 132
Italian, Bruccioli's (1532) ... 140 n.
―――― Diodati's (1607) ...... 140 n.

Spanish (Valencia, 1478) ...... 140 n.
―――― Pinel (Ferrara, 1553) ... 140 n.
―――― C. de Reyna's (1569) ... 140 n.
―――― De Valera's revision of Valencia, 1478 (Amsterdam, 1602) ... 140 n.
Bilson, Thomas, Bp .... 12 n. 4, 136 n., 264
Blayney, B. ... 4 n., 23, 28—35, 38, 45, 71, 80, 101, 117 n., 121, 133, 145, 242 n.
―――― his *Report* to the Delegates of the Oxford Press ... 28, 71, 121, 133, 238—42
Blunt, J. H. .... 13 n. 2, 25 n. 1
Bodleian MSS. .... 13 n. 2
Boel, Corn. .... 10, 17 n.
Bois, Anne .... 13 n. 1
Bois (or *Boyse* or *Boys*), *J.* ... 12, 13 and nn., 22 and n. 1, 140
Brady, Nicholas 133
British and Foreign Bible Society ... 36 nn. 1 and 2
British Museum, copies of A.V. there 5, 203, 214
―――――――――― of later editions ... 25 n. 1, 201 n.
―――――――――― Grenville Library in 40
Brown, J. (of Haddington), his Bible 121
Buchanan, Gilb. .... 8 n. 1
Burgon, J. W., Dean ...... 22 n. 1
Burnet, Gilb., Bp .... 139 n.

"*Caesural comma*" .... 92 n.
Calendar and Tables of Lessons no part of A.V. 39
Cambridge University Press 6
―――― editions of A.V., their merits 20-2
Canne, John ... 121 and n., 240 n. 2
Capital letters, employment of ... 2, 114—6
―――― intimating change of speaker .... 115 and n.
―――― representing JEHOVAH ... 116 n. 5, 147 n. 1, 161 n., 163, 168, 174, 210, 223 n. 3

Index of persons and subjects. 307

Carafa, *John Peter*, Cardinal (Pope Paul IV.) ......47 n.
Cardinal numbers used for ordinal... 111, 147 n. 2, 185 n., 233 n. 1
Cardwell, *Edw.* ......3 n., 35, 93 n., 168 n. 1, 193 n. 1, 219 n. 4
Carleton, *G.*, Bp 264
Changes (later) for the better from A.V. should be retained...3, 4, 94
Chaucer, *Geoffrey* ......93 n., 105
Chetiv or Hebrew text ......41-2, 68 and nn. 1 and 2, 219 n. 3
Child, *John*, his evidence before a Parliamentary Committee 33 n. 1
Christian *II.* of Denmark ...139 n.
Chronology of Jewish Kings, attempt to set right 45-6, 134
Clarke, *Adam* 121
Classics, *English* 1
Codex Alexandrinus......47, 90 n. 2, 131, 176 n.
—— Bezae 59, 250, 257
—— Sangermanensis ......49 n.
—— Vaticanus...47 n., 48 and n. 1, 52
Common *Prayer Book* sometimes bound up with A.V. ...17, 21, 39
Complutensian *Polyglott* (1517)...43, 47, 48 and n. 2, 52, 60, 140, 176 n., 200 n., 255 n.
Convocation of Province of Canterbury......1, 26, 27 and n. 1
Copies of A.V., where deposited...5, 6, 7 and n. 1, 203, 214
—— of later editions ......15, 16 and n. 1, 17 n., 18 n., 19 n., 20 n., 22, 23 n., 25 n. 1, 201 n., 207 n. 2
copulative, absence of Hebr., how noted by Translators 77
Corbinian, S......282 n. 1
Corrie, *G. E.* 18
Coverdale's *Bible* (1535)...40, 52 n., 93 n., 131 n. 2, 139 and n.
Cox, *Richard*, Bp 139
Critical edition of Authorized Bible ...1
—— resources of Translators of N.T. very scanty......59
Crutwell's edition......121, 242 n.
Cumberland, *R.*, Bp, his Tables...27

Curtis, *Th.* ......35 and n.
Dandolini, Lexicon...... ......13 n. 2
Daniel, *Wm.*, Archp. ......13 n. 2
Dates in margin of Bibles ...27, 30, 45-6, 133-5, 240
Davenant, *John*, Bp 264
Deane, *W. J.* 131
Delegates of Oxford University Press ..6, 29, 35
Delitzsch, *F.* ......68 n. 1, 88, 129
Departures of modern Bibles from A.V. 3
Diphthongs œ and æ in A.V. ...114
Division of this work into sections 2
—— of the Bible into chapters and verses ......127, 132 n.
—— marks of paragraph (¶) in A.V. 128
Dod, *B.*, publisher ......29 and n. 1
Dort, Synod of ......12 n. 4, 264
Doubtful *authority*, words or clauses of, how indicated in A.V. 68, 73, 254
Downes, *And.*...12 and n. 3, 140 n.
Dresden, Latin MS. at ......49 n. 1
Drusius......73 n. 2
Dryden, *John* 96
Durell, *David*......239 and n. 1
Eadie, *John*......12 n. 4, 139 n., 240 n. 2, 282 n. 2
Editions (later) of A. V. (1611)... 5 n.
—— dated 1612 8vo. 15
—— —— 1613 fol. 16, 63
—— —— 1616 8vo. 17
—— —— 1617 fol. 18
—— —— 1619 8vo. 18
—— —— 1629 4to. 19
—— —— 1630 4to. 19
—— Cambridge 1629 fol. ...3, 21, 45, 63, 65, 68, 69, 70, 73 n. 3, 75, 118, 149 n. 1, 164 n., 264 n.
—— Cambridge 1637 4to. ... 23 n.
—— Cambridge 1638 fol. ...3, 21, 22 n. 2, 26, 45, 54, 55, 63, 64, 68, 69, 70, 71 and n., 72, 77, 92, 114, 118, 164 n.

Editions, dated 1634 fol. 24
—— —— 1640 fol. 24
—— Cambridge 1683 ....56, 82, 92
—— Large folio of 1701 26
—— Basketts' (1744—56)...28, 201 n.
—— Paris, Cambridge 1762 ... 29, 45, 54, 55, 56, 59, 63, 71, 94, 103, 104, 110, 119, 132 n. 2, 134, 135, 172 n., 238
—— Blayney, Oxford 1769... 29, 45, 55, 56, 59, 63, 68, 69, 71, 78, 79, 81, 92, 94, 103, 104, 110, 117 n., 119, 132 n. 2, 133, 134
—— D'Oyly and Mant's 4to. 1817...23, 32, 87, 91, 132 n. 2, 156 n. 2
—— Oxford reprint, 1833 ... 6, 7, 16, 18, 35, 86, 94, 203
—— —— 1835 ....32, 33
—— Coldstream 1845 33
—— Bagster 1846 ....32, 34, 36 n. 1, 90, 121, 134
—— American 1867 ....23, 31, 32, 35, 37 and n. 2, 87, 91, 92, 105, 134
—— Cambridge nonpareil 1857 ...38
—— Cambridge 1858, our model ...32, 38, 69, 79 n. 2, 80, 86, 88, 94, 99, 117, 119, 122, 128, 129, 134, 135, 143, 147 and n. 2, 164 n., 172 n., 194, 215
—— Cambridge 1863 4to., our model for Apocrypha ......33 n. 3
—— "Scotch Edition,"...120, 121 n., 240 and n. 2, 241
—— Canne (Edin. 1747) ...... 121 n.
—— Amsterdam, 8vo. ...121 n.
—— Nourse's Paragraph Bible (Boston 1836).................90, 91, 92, 128 n., 130
—— Relig. Tract Society's "Annotated Parag. Bible" 1861 ...88, 91, 92, 122
—— Blackadder 1864...91, 92
—— — Newberry 1870 91
Erasmus, editions of Greek Test. ...60, 255 n.

Ellipsis, in original texts, how treated in A. V. 64, 79
Errors, notable in typography of A. V. (1611) 8
—— and of later editions ....4 and n. 1, 17, 22 n. 1, 23, 25 n. 1, 30-1, 32, 33-4, 38-9
—— in the seventh commandment (1632) ....25 and n. 1
—— many due to Tremellius' Version 44
-*eus*, terminations in ....188 n.
Eyre (or *Eyers* or *Ayers*), *W.* ...13 n. 2, 136 n.

Falmouth, Visc. 17
Favour, Dr ....275 n.
"*Fenowed*"......................275 n.
Field's Bibles shamefully inaccurate ......25 n. 2, 26, 28. See *Hills*.
—— ...56, 91, 191 n. 2, 193 n. 2
—— *F.*, Dr 103, 127
Fine inflicted for misprint in Bible ... 25 n. 1
"*Five Clergymen*", Revision of the ... 85, 91, 135 n.
Fletcher, John ....135 n.
Fritzsche, O. T. ....49 n., 73 n. 2, 131, 199 n. 2
Fry, Francis ....5—11 and nn., 13, 15 n., 18 and n., 20, 24, 39

Gell, Robt., Dr ....43 n., 141 n.
Genealogical charts, maps, &c. attached to A.V. 39
Genitive, double ....110, 216 n. 1, 217
—— sign of, suppressed ...... 110 and n. 2, 207 n. 1, 217 n. 2
George I., his four rules to secure an accurate Bible 27
George II., degrees conferred by ... 12 n. 1
Gerundial Infinitive of Hebrew, different methods of rendering in A.V........................142
Gifford, William..................93 n.
Ginsburg, C. D., Dr ....44 n.
Goad, J., Dr 22
Gorle, J. ....79 and n. 2, 115

Goulburn, E. M., Dean ......142 n.
Gower, John ....93 n.
Grabe, J. E. ....200 n.
Graduation of punctuation 92
Grammatical peculiarities ......2, 30, 109—12
―― inflections, old ...101
Gravamina of Convocation ...27 n.
Greenfield, Wm. ....36 n. 1
Griffith, Mr, Pemb. Coll. Oxon. 239
Grote, J., his MS. cited ......23 n., 32, 57 n. 1, 74, 81, 82, 91, 92 and n., 121 n., 133, 191 n. 2

h initial, use of *a* or *an* before, in A. V. ....105—8
Hall, Joseph, Bp 264
Hampton Court Conference (1603-4) ...138
Harding, John, Dr 138
Harleian MSS. ....12 nn. 1 and 3, 13 n. 1
Hayes, John, his Cambridge Bibles, 1677—83 26
Headings of columns and chapters... 132, 239
Hebrew Text used in A. V. 42
―― compactness of, how treated in A. V. 65
―― old accus. termination in, how treated in A. V. 76
Herodotus, quoted in margin of Apocrypha 46
Hervey, Lord *A. C.*, Bp ...131 n. 2
Hewlett's Commentary ....117 n.
High Commission Court ......25 n. 1
Hills and *Field* bought their privilege by a bribe 26
―――――― their Bibles of 1653-7 very inaccurate ...25 n. 2, 26, 28
History of text of A. V. ...2, 3—39
Hobson, Th. ....18 n.
Holland, producer of misprinted Bibles ....25 and nn. 2 and 3
Hooker, Richard 137
Hopkins, John 133
Horne, T. H. ....4 n., 117 n.
Hort, F. J. A., Prof. 132

Importation of Bibles forbidden by statute ....25 and n. 3

Intensive forms 113
Isaiah, single authorship of prophecies of 126
Issues of A. V. (1611) two extant... 5—12, 15
―― relative value and priority of each ....7 and n. 2—12
Italic type of Authorized Bible ...2, 23, 29, 31, 38
―― very defectively represented... 34
―― use of, by Translators...61—81

James I. curtails marginal notes in A. V........ 40
―― orders the Bishops' Bible to be closely followed 43-4
―― his *Instructions*...40, 136
JEHOVAH, Hebr., how represented in A. V. ....116 n. 5, 147 n. 1, 161 n. 1, 223 n. 3
Jehovah Adonai, how represented in A. V. ....147 n. 1
Jerome's Latin Version 48, 131
Jerusalem, the form "Hierusalem" ...186 n.
Job, book of, influence of its diction upon its successors 126
―― unsatisfactory rendering of, in A. V. 139
Johnson, Samuel 96
Jonson, Ben ....93 n., 217 n. 2
Josephus quoted in margin of A. V. ...46 and n., 227 n. 2; 74, 90
Junius, Francis.....................44, 46; 47, 50 n., 51 n., 55, 57, 73 and n. 2, 153 n. 1, 176 n., 198 n. 1, 199 n. 1

Keri, or Hebrew margin ....16, 41-2, 68 and nn. 1 and 2, 219 n. 3
Kilburne, Wm. ....22 n. 2, 24, 25 and n. 1, 26
Kilbye, Richard, Dr ....138 and n. 2
Killingworth, John ....13 n. 1
King James's Bible 1
King's Printers ...5, 20, 25, 27, 28, 35, 127

Latin MSS. ....49 n. 1

Latin translation of O. T. by Immanuel Tremellius............44, 57, 90 n. 1, 153 n. 1, 170 n., 172 n.
—— —— by Sebastian Munster (1534) 61
—— —— of Apocrypha by Francis Junius..................44
—— —— of N. T. by Theodore Beza (1556) ......57, 248 n. 1
—— Version, Old ...47, 48, 90, 144
Laud, Wm., Archp. ....25 n. 1
Lectionary, New Church 129
Lenox, Mr ....25 n. 1
Lewis, John ....12 n. 1, 27 nn. 1 and 2
Lightfoot, J. B., Bp ......23 n.
Litany, English 105
Lively, Edward 139
Lloyd, Wm., Bp.............26-7, 30, 57, 133, 134, 168 n. 1, 238, 240
Longfellow, H. W. ....25 n. 2
Lowth, Robert, Bp ......129, 131 n. 1
Luard, H. R. ....13 n. 2

Macalpine, J. M. ....139 n.
Manley, W. L. 19
Marginal dates 27, 30, 45-6, 133-5, 240
—— marks of A. V., errors in... 180 n. 2
—— notes of A. V. ......2, 27, 31, 40—60
—— notes, additional 26, 27, 45
—— —— their number and character in O. T. 41-6
—— —— in Apocrypha ...46—55
—— —— in N. T. ...55—60
—— textual references of A. V. ...2, 8, 26, 27, 30, 116—27
—— —— in Epistle of "Translators to the Reader" ......267 n.
Marsh, G. P..........93 n., 207 n. 1
Mary, Queen ....139 n.
Masoretic revisers of Hebrew text ...41
—— points 78, 130
—— notes 42
McLane, J. W. 36

Mead (or *Mede*), *Jos.*............22 and n. 1, 134
Milton, John 96
Misprints, see *Errors*.
Missing fragment of 4th book of Esdras ....49 n.
Models of Cambridge Paragraph Bible 32, 38, 80, 86, 99
Modernizers of diction of A. V. 30, 94, 101, 133
Morinus, Peter ....47 n.
Moses cornutus 9
Moule, H. C. G. 91
Moulton, W. F. 90, 92
Munster, Sebastian 61

Negative, archaic double 111
Newth, S., Dr ....19, 138 n. 1
New York Bible Society, ...46
North, James ....207 n. 2
Number of final Committee on A. V. ...12 and n. 4, 13 n. 2, 39, 264

O and *Oh*, distinction between ... 113
Objective case used for nominative ...112
Omissions through same beginning of clauses 17
Origen's Hexapla, Dr Field's edition of 127
Original texts from which A. V. was rendered 2, 42, 47, 57, 60
"|| *Or*" the word prefixed to alternative renderings 41, 55
Orthography ....2, 93—109
Overall, John, Bp 137
"*own*," use of in A. V. representing simple poss. pron. of original text 78
Oxford University Press 6, 28, 29, 35, 127, 133, 238
—— Bibles, see *Editions*.

Palmer, J., Prof. ....49 n.
Paragraphs, custom of printing the Bible in 127
—— marks (¶) of division into, in A. V. 128
Parentheses, replaced by commas in modern Bibles 81

Index of persons and subjects. 311

Paris, Dr, 28—35, 45, 46, 57, 72, 101, 238
Participles past, archaic forms of... 103, 217 and n. 3
Particles, various forms of... 103 & n.
Paston letters (1470) ....93 n.
Patrick, Simon, Bp 122
Paul, C. K. ....132 n. 2
Peck, Francis, "*desiderata curiosa*" ...12 nn. 1—3
Perowne, J. J. S., Dean 83, 88
Philoxenian Syriac version 59
Pleonastic pronouns ......111 and n.
Pliny, quoted in margin of Apocrypha 46
Plural, archaic ....87 and n., 228 and n. 1
———— regarded as sing....229 and n. 1
Poetical portions of Bible, arrangement of, in Camb. Par. Bible...129
Polyglott, Bagster's (1828) 121
———— Complutensian (1517) ... 43, 47, 48 and n. 2, 52, 60, 140, 176 n., 200 n., 255 n.
———— Walton's (1657)...47, 283 ...n. 2
"*Portesses*" ....292 n.
Pope, Alex. ....13 n. 2
Postel, William ....283 n. 1
Preterite, archaic 101-3
Pronoun pers., omission of with Hebr. infin., how indicated by Translators 78
Proper Names explained in the additional marginal notes ...45, 239
———— alternative forms of ...55, 94
———— introduced into A.V. on authority of Josephus.........73
———— absolute uniformity in spelling of, not to be aimed at ...97 n.
———— parallel references relating to, in Camb. Par. Bible ... 124
Psalms, Pr.-Book version of ...139
Punctuation of A.V....2, 27, 81—92
Pursuivant fetcht to a reviser of A.V. ....12 n. 3
Pusey, E. B., Canon ...... 82 n. 2

Rainolds, John, Dr......138 and n. 1
Rashe tevoth ....13 n. 2
Reeves, John 127
References, parallel ....116—27
Reprinted leaves (244) in A. V. Bibles ....5, 6 and n., 10, 12
Revised version of the Bible.........1
Rheims, Vulgate N.T. of (1582) ... 262, 288 n., 302 n.
Richardson, Charles............275 n.
Rivalry, generous between English versions 1
Rivington, C. R. ....19 n.
Robinson, Ed. 36
Rules laid down by Translators but not carried out..................74
———— the four, of George I. 27

s after Hebrew termination -*im*....113
Saravia, Adrian de 137
Savile, Sir *Henry* 140
Scattergood, Ant., Dr......26, 57 n. 1
Schaff, Phil. ...37 n. 1, 203 n. 1, 243
Scholefield, James, Prof. ......35, 79 n. 1, 90, 91, 233 n. 2
Schultens, Albert 139
Scott, Thomas 121
Secker, Th., Archp. ......30, 240 n.
Sections, this work divided into seven 2
Selden, John ......19 n., 140 n. 1
Septuagint Greek version of Old Test. 41, 68
———— Roman (1586) ...47 and n., 48 and n. 2, 90 n. 2, 140, 176 n., 229 n. 2
Shakespeare, different ways of spelling his name...................94
———— quoted......108 n. 2, 110 n. 3; 229 n. 1
Singular, archaic use of, for plural ...111
Smith, Miles, Bp ....12 n. 4, 39, 136 n., 264
Spalding, R. 139
Speed, Jo., his patent for genealogical charts, &c. 39
Spenser, Edmund ....292 n.
Standard copies of A.V. (1611) ...6
———— of Cambridge Paragraph Bible 38

Index of persons and subjects.

Status Emphaticus of Chaldee ...... 222 n. 1
Stephen, Robert, his Greek Test....60, 243, 248 and n. 1, 255 n., 257
———————— division into verses invented by ....127, 132 n. 1
Sterne, Rich. 22
Sternhold, Thomas 133
Stevens, H. ....25 n. 1
Superlative, double..................112
Syndics of the Cambridge University Press ....6, 35, 79 n. 2

Tables of Scripture Measures, &c.... 27
———— of Kindred, Time, Offices, &c.......................................27
Targum, or Chaldee paraphrase...41
Tate, Nahum.........................133
Tenison, Th., Archp.................26
Texts, original, used for A.V....2, 42, 47, 57, 60
—— of Scripture, parallel in A.V. ...2, 116—27
Time spent in translating A.V....... 12 and n. 2
Tischendorf, Aen. F. C., his Septuagint...47 n.; 90, 92
Tomson, Lawr. 132, 251
Transition from *oratio obliqua* to *o. directa* in Hebr., how indicated in A.V. 67, 73
Translators to the Reader ...12 n. 2, 39, 262, 267—304
Tregelles, S. P., Dr 90
Tremellius, Immanuel.........44, 57, 90 n. 1, 153 n. 1, 170 n., 172 n.
Trench, R. C., Archp........85, 114, 233 n. 2
Trevisa, John ....282 n. 2
Turin, Latin MS. at ....49 n. 1
Turton, T., Bp ....21, 33 n. 2, 35-6, 41 n., 57, 61 n. 1, 65, 168 n. 1, 223 n. 3
Type, variation of in Bible, method of and reasons for employment ... 61, 62
Tyrrell, James ....13 n. 2

un- prefix in place of *im-* or *in-*...112
Unequal execution of A.V. 136
Uniformity of practice in marking grammatical divergences not followed in A.V. 70
Ussher (or Usher), James, Archp.... 13 n. 2, 24, 46 n., 133, 282 n. 1

Verbs, transitive and intransitive confounded........................112
Vercellone, C.....................300 n.
Vulgate ...52 n., 61, 69 n., 73 n. 2, 117, 118, 176 n., 262, 300 n.

Wake, W., Archp., his care for an accurate Bible 27
Walker, Ant., Dr ......12 and nn. 2 and 3, 13
Waller, G. C.......................92 n.
Walpole, Sir R. 27
Walton, Brian, Bp, his Polyglott (1657) ....47, 283 n. 2
Walton, Isaac ....138 and n. 2
Ward, S. Dr ....22, 264 and n.
Westcott, B. F., Canon ......12 n. 2, 136 n., 243, 248 nn. 2 and 3, 253 n.
Wetstein, J. J. 126
Wheeler, Prof............239 and n. 2
Whitelocke, Buls...............25 n. 3
Wicklif, John ...207 n. 1, 250, 252, 255, 262
Wigram's "Hebr. Vade Mecum" ...127
Wilson, Lea 21, 22, 214
—— Thomas, Bp ...121, 242 n.
—— William, Canon 126
Winer, G. B. 90, 92
Wolfenbuttel Bible ....25 n. 1
Wordsworth, Chr., Bp ...86, 89, 92
———— John, Canon...300 n.
———— Charles, Bp ...132 n. 2
Wright, W. Aldis...........110 n. 2, 217 n. 2

Ximenes, Francisco de Cisneros, Cardinal ....48 n. 1

Zeugma, Hebraic use of, how treated in A.V. 66, 73

CAMBRIDGE: PRINTED BY C. J. CLAY, M.A. AND SON, AT THE UNIVERSITY PRESS.

UNIVERSITY PRESS, CAMBRIDGE.
April, 1892.

PUBLICATIONS OF

The Cambridge University Press.

THE HOLY SCRIPTURES, &c.

HEBREW.

A short Commentary on the Hebrew and Aramaic Text of the Book of Daniel, by A. A. BEVAN, M.A., Fellow of Trinity College. Demy 8vo. 8s.

GREEK.

The Old Testament in Greek according to the Septuagint. Edited by the Rev. Professor H. B. SWETE, D.D. Crown 8vo. Vol. I. Genesis—IV Kings. 7s. 6d. Vol. II. I Chronicles—Tobit. 7s. 6d.
[Vol. III. *In the Press.*

The Book of Psalms in Greek according to the Septuagint. Being a portion of Vol. II. of the above work. Crown 8vo. 2s. 6d.

The Parallel New Testament Greek and English. The New Testament, being the Authorised Version set forth in 1611 Arranged in Parallel Columns with the Revised Version of 1881, and with the original Greek, as edited by the late F. H. A. SCRIVENER, M.A., D.C.L., LL.D. Crown 8vo. 12s. 6d. (*The Revised Version is the joint Property of the Universities of Cambridge and Oxford.*)

Greek and English Testament, in parallel columns on the same page. Edited by J. SCHOLEFIELD, M.A. *New Edition, with the marginal references as arranged and revised by* DR SCRIVENER. 7s. 6d.

Greek and English Testament. THE STUDENT'S EDITION of the above on *large writing paper*. 4to. 12s.

See also p. 22, *Cambridge Greek Testament.*

The New Testament in the Original Greek, according to the Text followed in the Authorised Version, together with the Variations adopted in the Revised Version. Edited by the late F. H. A. SCRIVENER, M.A., D.C.L., LL.D. Small Crown 8vo. 6s.

Biblical Fragments from Mount Sinai, edited by J. RENDEL HARRIS, M.A. Demy 4to. 10s. 6d.

Notitia Codicis Quattuor Evangeliorum Græci membranacei viris doctis hucusque incogniti quem in museo suo asservat Eduardus Reuss Argentoratensis. 2s.

London: Cambridge Warehouse, Ave Maria Lane.

1500
19/4/92

SYRIAC.

The Harklean Version of the Epistle to the Hebrews, Chap. XI. 28—XIII. 25. Now edited for the first time with Introduction and Notes on this version of the Epistle. By ROBERT L. BENSLY. Demy 8vo. 5s.

LATIN.

The Latin Heptateuch. Published piecemeal by the French printer WILLIAM MOREL (1560) and the French Benedictines E. MARTÈNE (1733) and J. B. PITRA (1852—88). Critically reviewed by JOHN E. B. MAYOR, M.A. Demy 8vo. 10s. 6d.

The Missing Fragment of the Latin Translation of the Fourth Book of Ezra, discovered and edited with Introduction, Notes, and facsimile of the MS., by Prof. BENSLY, M.A. Demy 4to. 10s.

Codex S. Ceaddae Latinus. Evangelia SSS. Matthaei, Marci, Lucae ad cap. III. 9 complectens, circa septimum vel octavum saeculum scriptvs, in Ecclesia Cathedrali Lichfieldiensi servatus. Cum codice versionis Vulgatae Amiatino contulit, prolegomena conscripsit, F. H. A. SCRIVENER, A.M., LL.D. Imp. 4to. £1. 1s.

The Codex Sangallensis (Δ). A Study in the Text of the Old Latin Gospels, by J. RENDEL HARRIS, M.A. Royal 8vo. 3s.

The Origin of the Leicester Codex of the New Testament. By J. R. HARRIS, M.A. With 3 plates. Demy 4to. 10s. 6d.

ANGLO-SAXON.

The Four Gospels in Anglo-Saxon and Northumbrian Versions. By Rev. Prof. SKEAT, Litt.D. One Volume. Demy Quarto. 30s. Each Gospel separately. 10s.

ENGLISH.

The Authorised Edition of the English Bible (1611), its Subsequent Reprints and Modern Representatives. By the late F. H. A. SCRIVENER, M.A., D.C.L., LL.D. Crown 8vo. 7s. 6d.

The Cambridge Paragraph Bible of the Authorized English Version, with the Text revised by a Collation of its Early and other Principal Editions, the Use of the Italic Type made uniform, the Marginal References remodelled, and a Critical Introduction, by the late F. H. A. SCRIVENER, M.A., LL.D. Crown 4to., cloth gilt, 21s.

THE STUDENT'S EDITION of the above, on *good writing paper*, with one column of print and wide margin to each page for MS. notes. Two Vols. Crown 4to., cloth, gilt, 31s. 6d.

The Lectionary Bible, with Apocrypha, divided into Sections adapted to the Calendar and Tables of Lessons of 1871. Cr. 8vo. 3s. 6d.

(*See also pp.* 21, 22, *Cambridge Bible for Schools.*)

London : Cambridge Warehouse, Ave Maria Lane.

HOLY SCRIPTURES.

The Book of Ecclesiastes. Large Paper Edition. By the Very Rev. E. H. PLUMPTRE, late Dean of Wells. Demy 8vo. 7s. 6d.

The Gospel History of our Lord Jesus Christ in the Language of the Revised Version, arranged in a Connected Narrative, especially for the use of Teachers and Preachers. By Rev. C. C. JAMES, M.A. Crown 8vo. 3s. 6d.

A Harmony of the Gospels in the words of the Revised Version with copious references, tables &c. Arranged by Rev. C. C. JAMES, M.A. Crown 8vo. 5s.

Wilson's Illustration of the Method of explaining the New Testament, by the early opinions of Jews and Christians concerning Christ. Edited by T. TURTON, D.D. Demy 8vo. 5s.

SERVICE-BOOKS.

A Comparative Index to the Leonine, Gelasian, and Gregorian Sacramentaries of Muratori. By H. A. WILSON, M.A., Fellow of Magdalen College, Oxford. Demy 8vo. [*Nearly ready*.

Breviarium ad Usum Sarum. A Reprint of the folio edition by Chevallon and Regnault, Paris, 1531. Edited by F. PROCTER, M.A. and CHR. WORDSWORTH, M.A. Demy 8vo.

Vol. 1. Kalendar and Temporale. 18s.
Vol. 2. Psalter &c. 12s.
Vol. 3. Sanctorale. With an Introduction, lists of editions from the papers of H. Bradshaw, and complete Indexes. 15s.
The three volumes together £2. 2s.

Breviarium Romanum a FRANCISCO CARDINALI QUIGNONIO editum et recognitum iuxta editionem Venetiis A.D. 1535 impressam curante JOHANNE WICKHAM LEGG. Demy 8vo. 12s.

The Greek Liturgies. Chiefly from original Authorities. By C. A. SWAINSON, D.D., late Master of Christ's College. Cr. 4to. 15s.

The Pointed Prayer Book, being the Book of Common Prayer with the Psalter or Psalms of David, pointed as they are to be sung or said in Churches. Royal 24mo, cloth, 1s. 6d.

The same in square 32mo. cloth, 6d.

Wheatly on the Common Prayer, edited by G. E. CORRIE, D.D., late Master of Jesus College. Demy Octavo. 7s. 6d.

The Cambridge Psalter, for the use of Choirs and Organists. Specially adapted for Congregations in which the "Cambridge Pointed Prayer Book" is used. Demy 8vo. cloth, 3s. 6d. Cloth limp cut flush, 2s. 6d.

The Paragraph Psalter, arranged for the use of Choirs by the Right Rev. B. F. WESTCOTT, D.D., Lord Bp. of Durham. Fcp. 4to. 5s.

The same in royal 32mo. Cloth, 1s. Leather, 1s. 6d.

London: Cambridge Warehouse, Ave Maria Lane.

The Homilies, with Various Readings, and the Quotations from the Fathers given at length in the Original Languages. Edited by G. E. CORRIE, D.D., late Master of Jesus College. Demy 8vo. 7s. 6d.

Two Forms of Prayer of the time of Queen Elizabeth. Now First Reprinted. Demy Octavo. 6d.

THEOLOGY.

Sayings of the Jewish Fathers, comprising Pirqe Aboth and Pereq R. Meir in Hebrew and English, with Critical Notes. By C. TAYLOR, D.D., Master of St John's College. [*New Edition. Preparing.*

The Palestinian Mishna. By W. H. LOWE, M.A. Royal 8vo. 21s.

Chagigah from the Babylonian Talmud. A Translation of the Treatise with Notes, etc. by A. W. STREANE, B.D. Demy 8vo. 10s.

Psalms of the Pharisees, commonly known as the Psalms of Solomon, by H. E. RYLE, B.D. and M. R. JAMES, M.A. Demy 8vo. 15s.

Fragments of Philo and Josephus. Newly edited by J. RENDEL HARRIS, M.A. With two Facsimiles. Demy 4to. 12s. 6d.

The Rest of the Words of Baruch: A Christian Apocalypse of the year 136 A.D. The Text revised with an Introduction by J. RENDEL HARRIS, M.A. Royal 8vo. 5s.

The Teaching of the Apostles. Newly edited, with Facsimile Text and Commentary, by J. R. HARRIS, M.A. Demy 4to. 21s.

A Collation of the Athos Codex of the Shepherd of Hermas. Together with an Introduction by SPYR. P. LAMBROS, PH.D., translated and edited with a Preface and Appendices by J. ARMITAGE ROBINSON, B.D. Demy 8vo. 3s. 6d.

The Philocalia of Origen. The Greek Text edited from the Manuscripts, with Critical Apparatus and Indexes, and an Introduction on the Sources of the Text. By J. ARMITAGE ROBINSON, B.D.
[*In the Press.*

Theodore of Mopsuestia's Commentary on the Minor Epistles of S. Paul. The Latin Version with the Greek Fragments, edited from the MSS. with Notes and an Introduction, by Professor H. B. SWETE, D.D. Vol. I., containing the Introduction, and the Commentary upon Galatians—Colossians. Demy Octavo. 12s.

Volume II., containing the Commentary on 1 Thessalonians—Philemon, Appendices and Indices. 12s.

The Acts of the Martyrdom of Perpetua and Felicitas; the original Greek Text now first edited from a MS. in the Library of the Convent of the Holy Sepulchre at Jerusalem, by J. RENDEL HARRIS and SETH K. GIFFORD. Royal 8vo. 5s.

The Diatessaron of Tatian. By J. RENDEL HARRIS, M.A. Royal 8vo. 5s.

London: Cambridge Warehouse, Ave Maria Lane.

TEXTS AND STUDIES: CONTRIBUTIONS TO BIBLICAL AND PATRISTIC LITERATURE.

Edited by J. ARMITAGE ROBINSON, B.D., Fellow and Assistant Tutor of Christ's College.

Vol. I. No. 1. **The Apology of Aristides on behalf of the Christians.** Edited from a Syriac MS., with an Introduction and Translation by J. RENDEL HARRIS, M.A., and an Appendix containing the chief part of the Original Greek, by J. ARMITAGE ROBINSON, B.D. Demy 8vo. 5s. Net.

No. 2. **The Passion of S. Perpetua:** the Latin Text freshly edited from the Manuscripts with an Introduction and Appendix containing the Original Latin Form of the Scillitan Martyrdom; by J. ARMITAGE ROBINSON, B.D. 4s. Net.

No. 3. **The Lord's Prayer in the Early Church:** with Special Notes on the Controverted Clauses; by F. H. CHASE, B.D., Christ's College. 5s. Net.

No. 4. **The Fragments of Heracleon:** the Greek Text with an Introduction by A. E. BROOKE, M.A., Fellow of King's College. 4s. Net.

Vol. II. No. 1. **A Study of Codex Bezae:** by J. RENDEL HARRIS, M.A. 7s. 6d. Net.

No. 2. **The Testament of Abraham.** By M. R. JAMES, M.A., with an Appendix containing Translations from the Arabic of the Testaments of Abraham, Isaac and Jacob, by W. E. BARNES, B.D. Demy 8vo. [Nearly ready.

Tertullianus de Corona Militis, de Spectaculis, de Idololatria with Analysis and English Notes, by G. CURREY, D.D. Crown 8vo. 5s.

Sancti Irenæi Episcopi Lugdunensis libros quinque adversus Hæreses, edidit W. WIGAN HARVEY, S.T.B. Collegii Regalis olim Socius. 2 Vols. Demy Octavo. 18s.

Theophili Episcopi Antiochensis Libri Tres ad Autolycum. Edidit Prolegomenis Versione Notulis Indicibus instruxit GULIELMUS GILSON HUMPHRY, S.T.B. Post Octavo. 5s.

Theophylacti in Evangelium S. Matthæi Commentarius. Edited by W. G. HUMPHRY, B.D. Demy Octavo. 7s. 6d.

M. Minucii Felicis Octavius. The text newly revised from the original MS. with an English Commentary, Analysis, Introduction, and Copious Indices. By H. A. HOLDEN, LL.D. Cr. 8vo. 7s. 6d.

S. Austin and his place in the History of Christian Thought. Being the Hulsean Lectures for 1885. By W. CUNNINGHAM, D.D. Demy 8vo. Buckram, 12s. 6d.

London: Cambridge Warehouse, Ave Maria Lane.

Works of Isaac Barrow, compared with the original MSS. A new Edition, by A. NAPIER, M.A. 9 Vols. Demy 8vo. £3. 3s.

Treatise of the Pope's Supremacy, and a Discourse concerning the Unity of the Church, by I. BARROW. Demy 8vo. 7s. 6d.

Select Discourses, by JOHN SMITH, late Fellow of Queens' College, Cambridge. Edited by H. G. WILLIAMS, B.D., late Professor of Arabic. Royal Octavo. 7s. 6d.

Pearson's Exposition of the Creed, edited by TEMPLE CHEVALLIER, B.D. 3rd Edition revised by R. SINKER, D.D. Demy 8vo. 12s.

An Analysis of the Exposition of the Creed, written by the Right Rev. Father in God, JOHN PEARSON, D.D. Compiled by W. H. MILL, D.D. Demy Octavo. 5s.

De Obligatione Conscientiæ Prælectiones decem Oxonii in Schola Theologica habitæ a ROBERTO SANDERSON, SS. Theologiæ ibidem Professore Regio. With English Notes, including an abridged Translation, by W. WHEWELL, D.D. Demy 8vo. 7s. 6d.

Lectures on Divinity delivered in the University of Cambridge. By JOHN HEY, D.D. Third Edition, by T. TURTON, D.D., late Lord Bishop of Ely. 2 vols. Demy Octavo. 15s.

Cæsar Morgan's Investigation of the Trinity of Plato, and of Philo Judæus. 2nd Ed., revised by H. A. HOLDEN, LL.D. Cr. 8vo. 4s.

Christ the Life of Men. Being the Hulsean Lectures for 1888. By Rev. H. M. STEPHENSON, M.A. Crown 8vo. 2s. 6d.

SYRIAC AND ARABIC.

Lectures on the Comparative Grammar of the Semitic Languages from the Papers of the late WILLIAM WRIGHT, LL.D. Demy 8vo. 14s.

The History of Alexander the Great, being the Syriac version of the Pseudo-Callisthenes. Edited from Five Manuscripts, with an English Translation and Notes, by E. A. W. BUDGE, Litt.D. Demy 8vo. 25s.

The Chronicle of Joshua the Stylite edited in Syriac, with an English translation and notes, by W. WRIGHT, LL.D. Demy 8vo. 10s. 6d.

Kalīlah and Dimnah, or, the Fables of Bidpai; with an English Translation of the later Syriac version, with Notes, by the late I. G. N. KEITH-FALCONER, M.A. Demy 8vo. 7s. 6d.

The Poems of Beha ed dín Zoheir of Egypt. With a Metrical Translation, Notes and Introduction, by the late E. H. PALMER, M.A. 2 vols. Crown Quarto.
Vol. I. The ARABIC TEXT. Paper covers. 10s. 6d.
Vol. II. ENGLISH TRANSLATION. Paper covers. 10s. 6d.

London: Cambridge Warehouse, Ave Maria Lane.

SANSKRIT AND PERSIAN.

Maḳála-i-Shakhsí Sayyáḥ ki dar Kaziyya-i-Báb Navishta-Ast (a Traveller's Narrative written to illustrate the Episode of the Báb). Persian text, edited, translated and annotated, in two volumes, by E. G. BROWNE, M.A., M.B. Crown 8vo. 15s. net. Vol. II. (containing the Translation and Notes) separately, 10s. 6d. net.

Nalopàkhyànam, or, The Tale of Nala; containing the Sanskrit Text in Roman Characters, with Vocabulary. By the late Rev. T. JARRETT, M.A. Demy 8vo. 10s.

Notes on the Tale of Nala, for the use of Classical Students, by J. PEILE, Litt. D., Master of Christ's College. Demy 8vo. 12s.

The Divyâvadâna, a Collection of Early Buddhist Legends, now first edited from the Nepalese Sanskrit MSS. in Cambridge and Paris. By E. B. COWELL, M.A. and R. A. NEIL, M.A. Demy 8vo. 18s.

GREEK.

(*See also* pp. 23, 24.)

The Agamemnon of Aeschylus. With a translation in English Rhythm, and Notes Critical and Explanatory. **New Edition, Revised.** By the late B. H. KENNEDY, D.D. Crown 8vo. 6s.

Aeschyli Fabulae.—ΙΚΕΤΙΔΕΣ ΧΟΗΦΟΡΟΙ in libro Mediceo mendose scriptae ex vv. dd. coniecturis emendatius editae cum Scholiis Graecis et brevi adnotatione critica, curante F. A. PALEY, M.A., LL.D. Demy 8vo. 7s. 6d.

Aristotle.—ΠΕΡΙ ΨΥΧΗΣ. Aristotle's Psychology, in Greek and English, with Introduction and Notes, by E. WALLACE, M.A. Demy 8vo. 18s.

Aristotle. The Rhetoric. With a Commentary by the late E. M. COPE, Fellow of Trinity College, Cambridge, revised and edited by J. E. SANDYS, Litt.D. 3 Vols. Demy 8vo. 21s.

Demosthenes against Androtion and against Timocrates, with Introductions and English Commentary by WILLIAM WAYTE, M.A. Crown 8vo. 7s. 6d.

Select Private Orations of Demosthenes with Introductions and English Notes, by F. A. PALEY, M.A., & J. E. SANDYS, Litt.D.

Part I. Contra Phormionem, Lacritum, Pantaenetum, Boeotum de Nomine, de Dote, Dionysodorum. Cr. 8vo. *New Edition.* 6s.

Part II. Pro Phormione, Contra Stephanum I. II.; Nicostratum, Cononem, Calliclem. Crown 8vo. *New Edition.* 7s. 6d.

Demosthenes, Speech of, against the Law of Leptines. With Introduction and Critical and Explanatory Notes, by J. E. SANDYS, Litt.D. Demy 8vo. 9s.

London: Cambridge Warehouse, Ave Maria Lane.

Euripides. Bacchae, with Introduction, Critical Notes, and Archæological Illustrations, by J. E. SANDYS, Litt. D. Third Edition. Crown 8vo. 12s. 6d.

Euripides. Ion. The Greek Text with a Translation into English Verse, Introduction and Notes by A. W. VERRALL, Litt.D. Demy 8vo. 7s. 6d.

Homer's Odyssey. The text edited in accordance with modern criticism by ARTHUR PLATT, M.A., late Fellow of Trinity College, Cambridge. Crown 8vo. 4s. 6d.

Pindar. Olympian and Pythian Odes. With Notes Explanatory and Critical, Introductions and Introductory Essays. Edited by C. A. M. FENNELL, Litt. D. Crown 8vo. 9s.

— **The Isthmian and Nemean Odes** by the same Editor. 9s.

Plato's Phædo, literally translated, by the late E. M. COPE, Fellow of Trinity College, Cambridge. Demy Octavo. 5s.

The Theætetus of Plato, with a Translation and Notes by the late B. H. KENNEDY, D.D. Crown 8vo. 7s. 6d.

The Nuptial Number of Plato: its solution and significance, by J. ADAM, M.A., Fellow and Tutor of Emmanuel College, Cambridge. Demy 8vo. 2s. 6d. Net.

Sophocles: the Plays and Fragments. With Critical Notes, Commentary, and Translation in English Prose, by R. C. JEBB, Litt. D., LL.D., Regius Professor of Greek in the University of Cambridge.

Part I. Oedipus Tyrannus. Demy 8vo. *Second Edit.* 12s. 6d.

Part II. Oedipus Coloneus. Demy 8vo. *Second Edit.* 12s. 6d.

Part III. Antigone. Demy 8vo. *Second Edit.* 12s. 6d.

Part IV. Philoctetes. Demy 8vo. 12s. 6d.

Part V. Trachiniae. Demy 8vo. 12s. 6d.

Fragments of Zeno and Cleanthes, an Essay which obtained the Hare Prize in the year 1889. By A. C. PEARSON, B.A., Christ's College, Cambridge. Crown 8vo. 10s.

Pronunciation of Ancient Greek translated from the Third German edition of Dr BLASS by W. J. PURTON, B.A. Demy 8vo. 6s.

An Introduction to Greek Epigraphy. Part I. The Archaic Inscriptions and the Greek Alphabet. By E. S. ROBERTS, M.A., Fellow and Tutor of Gonville and Caius College. Demy 8vo. 18s.

London : Cambridge Warehouse, Ave Maria Lane.

LATIN.

(*See also* pp. 24, 25.)

M. Tulli Ciceronis ad M. Brutum Orator. A Revised Text Edited with Introductory Essays and Critical and Explanatory Notes by J. E. SANDYS, Litt.D. Demy 8vo. 16s.

M. T. Ciceronis de Finibus Bonorum Libri Quinque. The Text revised and explained by J. S. REID, Litt.D. [*In the Press.*
Vol. III., containing the Translation. Demy 8vo. 8s.

M. T. Ciceronis de Natura Deorum Libri Tres, with Introduction and Commentary by JOSEPH B. MAYOR, M.A. Demy 8vo. Vol. I. 10s. 6d. Vol. II. 12s. 6d. Vol. III. 10s.

M. T. Ciceronis de Officiis Libri Tres with Marginal Analysis, an English Commentary, and Indices. New Edition, revised, by H. A. HOLDEN, LL.D., Crown 8vo. 9s.

M. T. Ciceronis de Officiis Libri Tertius, with Introduction, Analysis and Commentary by H. A. HOLDEN, LL.D. Cr. 8vo. 2s.

M. Tulli Ciceronis pro C. Rabirio [Perduellionis Reo] Oratio ad Quirites. With Notes, Introduction and Appendices. By W. E. HEITLAND, M.A. Demy 8vo. 7s. 6d.

P. Vergili Maronis Opera, cum Prolegomenis et Commentario Critico pro Syndicis Preli Academici edidit BENJAMIN HALL KENNEDY, S.T.P. Extra fcp. 8vo. 3s. 6d.

A Latin-English Dictionary. Printed from the (Incomplete) MS. of the late T. H. KEY, M.A., F.R.S. Demy 4to. £1. 11s. 6d.

Graduated Passages from Greek and Latin Authors for First-Sight Translation. Selected and supplied with short Notes for beginners by H. BENDALL, M.A., Head Master, and C. E. LAURENCE, B.A., Assistant Master, of Blackheath Proprietary School. Crown 8vo. Part I. EASY. 1s. 6d. Part II. MODERATELY EASY. 2s. Part III. MODERATELY DIFFICULT. [*In the Press.*

CAMBRIDGE PHILOLOGICAL SOCIETY'S PUBLICATIONS.

Transactions. Vol. I. 1872—1880. 15s. Vol. II. 1881—1882. With Index to Vols. I., II. and Proceedings for 1882. 12s. Vol. III. Pt. I. 1886. 3s. 6d. Pt. II. 1889. 2s. Pt. III. 1890. 2s. 6d.

Proceedings. I—III. 2s. 6d. IV—VI. 2s. 6d. VII—IX. 2s. 6d. X—XII. 2s. 6d. XIII—XV. 2s. 6d. XVI—XVIII. 2s. 6d. XIX—XXI. 2s. 6d. XXII—XXIV. 1889. 1s. XXV—XXVII. With Laws and List of Members for 1891. 1s. net.

Spelling Reform and English Literature by H. SWEET. 2d. PRONUNCIATION OF LATIN in the Augustan Period. 3d.

An Eighth Century Latin-Anglo-Saxon Glossary preserved in the Library of Corpus Christi College, Cambridge, edited by J. H. HESSELS. Demy 8vo. 10s.

London: Cambridge Warehouse, Ave Maria Lane.

FRENCH.

Random Exercises in French Grammar, Homonyms and Synonyms for Advanced Students, by L. BOQUEL, Lecturer at Emmanuel and Newnham Colleges. Crown 8vo. 3s. 6d.

Key to the above by the same. Crown 8vo. 10s. 6d. (net).

Exercises in French Composition for Advanced Students. By the same. Demy 8vo. 5s. 6d. (net).

CELTIC.

A Grammar of the Irish Language. By Prof. WINDISCH. Translated by Dr NORMAN MOORE. Crown 8vo. 7s. 6d.

ENGLISH LITERATURE AND LITERARY HISTORY.

Chapters on English Metre. By Rev. JOSEPH B. MAYOR, M.A. Demy 8vo. 7s. 6d.

Studies in the Literary Relations of England with Germany in the Sixteenth Century. By C. H. HERFORD, M.A. Crown 8vo. 9s.

From Shakespeare to Pope. An Inquiry into the causes and phenomena of the Rise of Classical Poetry in England. By E. GOSSE, M.A. Crown 8vo. 6s.

Gray and his Friends. Letters and Relics in great part hitherto unpublished. Edited by the Rev. D. C. TOVEY, M.A. Crown 8vo. 6s.

OTHER MODERN EUROPEAN LITERATURE.

Contributions to the Textual Criticism of the Divina Commedia. Including the complete collation throughout the *Inferno* of all the MSS. at Oxford and Cambridge. By the Rev. E. MOORE, D.D. Demy 8vo. 21s.

The Literature of the French Renaissance. An Introductory Essay. By A. A. TILLEY, M.A. Crown 8vo. 6s.

MATHEMATICS, PHYSICS AND CHEMISTRY.

The Collected Mathematical Papers of ARTHUR CAYLEY, Sc.D., F.R.S. Demy 4to. 10 vols.
Vols. I., II., III. and IV. 25s. each. [Vol. V. *In the Press*.

Mathematical and Physical Papers. By Sir G. G. STOKES, Sc.D., LL.D. Reprinted from the Original Journals and Transactions, with additional Notes by the Author. Vol. I. Demy 8vo. 15s. Vol. II. 15s.
[Vol. III. *In the Press*.

Mathematical and Physical Papers. By Lord KELVIN (Sir W. THOMSON), LL.D., F.R.S. Collected from different Scientific Periodicals from May, 1841, to the present time. Vol. I. Demy 8vo. 18s. Vol. II. 15s. Vol. III. 18s.

London: Cambridge Warehouse, Ave Maria Lane.

MATHEMATICS, PHYSICS AND CHEMISTRY. 11

The Scientific Papers of the late Prof. J. Clerk Maxwell. Edited by W. D. NIVEN, M.A. 2 vols. Royal 4to. £3. 3s. (net.)

Scientific Papers compiled by the Royal Society of London, Catalogue of. Vols. I.—VI., for the years 1800—1863, Royal 4to. cloth (Vol. I. in half-morocco), £4 (net); half-morocco, £5. 5s. (net). Vols. VII.—VIII. for the years 1864—1873, cloth, £1. 11s. 6d. (net); half-morocco, £2. 5s. (net). Single volumes cloth, 20s., or half-morocco, 28s. (net). Vol. IX. New series for the years 1874–1883, cloth, 25s., half-morocco, 32s. (net). [Vol. X. *In the Press.*

A History of the Study of Mathematics at Cambridge. By W. W. ROUSE BALL, M.A. Crown 8vo. 6s.

Diophantos of Alexandria; a Study in the History of Greek Algebra. By T. L. HEATH, M.A. Demy 8vo. 7s. 6d.

A History of the Theory of Elasticity and of the Strength of Materials, from Galilei to the present time. Vol. I. GALILEI TO SAINT-VENANT, 1639–1850. By the late I. TODHUNTER, Sc.D., edited and completed by Prof. KARL PEARSON, M.A. Demy 8vo. 25s. Vol. II. By the same Editor. [*In the Press.*

The Elastical Researches of Barre de Saint-Venant (extract from Vol. II. of TODHUNTER's History of the Theory of Elasticity), edited by Professor KARL PEARSON, M.A. Demy 8vo. 9s.

A Short History of Greek Mathematics. By J. GOW, Litt. D., Fellow of Trinity College. Demy 8vo. 10s. 6d.

A Treatise on Plane Trigonometry. By E. W. HOBSON, Sc.D. Demy 8vo. 12s.

A Treatise on the Theory of Determinants and their Applications in Analysis and Geometry. By R. F. SCOTT, M.A. Demy 8vo. 12s.

Theory of Differential Equations. Part I. Exact Equations and Pfaff's Problem. By A. R. FORSYTH, Sc.D., F.R.S. Demy 8vo. 12s.

An Elementary Treatise on Quaternions. By P. G. TAIT, M.A. *Second Edition.* Demy 8vo. 14s.

A Treatise on Natural Philosophy. By Lord KELVIN (Sir W. THOMSON), LL.D., and P. G. TAIT, M.A. Part I. Demy 8vo. 16s. Part II. 18s.

Elements of Natural Philosophy. By Lord KELVIN (Sir W. THOMSON), and P. G. TAIT. *Second Edition.* Demy 8vo. 9s.

A Treatise on Analytical Statics. By E. J. ROUTH, Sc.D., F.R.S. Vol. I. Demy 8vo. 14s.

A Treatise on Dynamics. By S. L. LONEY, M.A. New and Enlarged Edition. Crown 8vo. 7s. 6d.

Solutions of the Examples in a Treatise on Elementary Dynamics. By the same Author. Crown 8vo. 7s. 6d.

A Treatise on Geometrical Optics. By R. S. HEATH, M.A. Demy 8vo. 12s. 6d.

London: Cambridge Warehouse, Ave Maria Lane.

An Elementary Treatise on Geometrical Optics. By R. S. HEATH, M.A. Crown 8vo. 5s.

Hydrodynamics, a Treatise on the Mathematical Theory of Fluid Motion, by HORACE LAMB, M.A. Demy 8vo. 12s.

A Treatise on the Mathematical Theory of Elasticity. By A. E. H. LOVE, M.A., Fellow of St John's College. In Two Volumes.
[Vol. I. *Nearly ready.*

An attempt to test the Theories of Capillary Action, by F. BASHFORTH, B.D., and the late J. C. ADAMS, M.A. Demy 4to. £1. 1s.

A Revised Account of the Experiments made with the Bashforth Chronograph, to find the resistance of the air to the motion of projectiles. By FRANCIS BASHFORTH, B.D. Demy 8vo. 12s.

Astronomical Observations made at the Observatory of Cambridge from 1846 to 1860, by the late Rev. J. CHALLIS, M.A.

Astronomical Observations from 1861 to 1865. Vol. XXI Royal 4to., 15s. From 1866 to 1869. Vol. XXII. 15s.
[Vol. XXIII. *In the Press.*

The Mathematical Works of Isaac Barrow, D.D. Edited by W. WHEWELL, D.D. Demy Octavo. 7s. 6d.

The Analytical Theory of Heat. By JOSEPH FOURIER. Translated with Notes, by A. FREEMAN, M.A. Demy 8vo. 12s.

Elementary Thermodynamics, by J. PARKER, M.A., Fellow of St John's College, Cambridge. Crown 8vo. 9s.

The Electrical Researches of the Honourable Henry Cavendish, F.R.S. Written between 1771 and 1781. Edited by J. CLERK MAXWELL, F.R.S. Demy 8vo. 18s.

Practical Work at the Cavendish Laboratory. Heat. Edited by W. N. SHAW, M.A. Demy 8vo. 3s.

A Treatise on the General Principles of Chemistry, by M. M. PATTISON MUIR, M.A. Second Edition. Demy 8vo. 15s.

Elementary Chemistry. By M. M. PATTISON MUIR, M.A., and CHARLES SLATER. M.A., M.B. Crown 8vo. 4s. 6d.

Practical Chemistry. A Course of Laboratory Work. By M. M. PATTISON MUIR, M.A., and D. J. CARNEGIE, M.A. Cr. 8vo. 3s.

Notes on Qualitative Analysis. Concise and Explanatory. By H. J. H. FENTON, M.A., F.C.S. New Edit. Crown 4to. 6s.

(*See also p.* 28, *Pitt Press Mathematical Series.*)

BIOLOGY AND GEOLOGY.

Lectures on the Physiology of Plants, by S. H. VINES, Sc.D., Professor of Botany in the University of Oxford. Demy 8vo. 21s.

Studies from the Morphological Laboratory. Edited by ADAM SEDGWICK, M.A., Fellow and Lecturer of Trinity College, Cambridge. Vol. II. Part I. Royal 8vo. 10s. Vol. II. Part II. 7s. 6d: Vol. III. Parts I. and II. 7s. 6d. each. Vol. IV. Part I. 12s. 6d. Vol. IV. Part II. 10s. Vol. IV. Part III. 5s. Vol. V. Part I. 7s. 6d.

London: Cambridge Warehouse, Ave Maria Lane.

BIOLOGY AND GEOLOGY.

A Catalogue of Books and Papers on Protozoa, Coelenterates, Worms, etc. published during the years 1861–1883, by D'ARCY W. THOMPSON, M.A. Demy 8vo. 12s. 6d.

A Catalogue of the Collection of Birds formed by the late Hugh EDWIN STRICKLAND, now in the possession of the University of Cambridge. By O. SALVIN, M.A., F.R.S. £1. 1s.

Illustrations of Comparative Anatomy, Vertebrate and Invertebrate. Second Edition. Demy 8vo. 2s. 6d.

Catalogue of Osteological Specimens contained in the Anatomical Museum of the University of Cambridge. Demy 8vo. 2s. 6d.

Catalogue of Type Fossils in the Woodwardian Museum, Cambridge. By H. WOODS, B.A., F.G.S., with Preface by Professor T. M^cKENNY HUGHES. Demy 8vo. 7s. 6d.

A Catalogue of the Collection of Cambrian and Silurian Fossils contained in the Geological Museum of the University of Cambridge, by J. W. SALTER, F.G.S. Royal Quarto. 7s. 6d.

A Catalogue of Australian Fossils. By R. ETHERIDGE, Jun., F.G.S. Demy 8vo. 10s. 6d.

The Fossils and Palæontological Affinities of the Neocomian Deposits of Upware and Brickhill, being the Sedgwick Prize Essay for 1879. By W. KEEPING, M.A. Demy 8vo. 10s. 6d.

The Jurassic Rocks of Cambridge, being the Sedgwick Prize Essay for the year 1886, by the late T. ROBERTS, M.A. Demy 8vo.

[*In the Press.*

The Bala Volcanic Series of Caernarvonshire and Associated Rocks, being the Sedgwick Prize Essay for 1888, by A. HARKER, M.A., F.R.S. Demy 8vo. 7s. 6d.

LAW.

Digest XIX. 2. Locati Conducti, with a Translation and Notes by C. H. MONRO, M.A., Fellow of Gonville and Caius College. Crown 8vo. 5s.

An Introduction to the Study of Justinian's Digest. By HENRY JOHN ROBY. Demy 8vo. 9s.

Justinian's Digest. Lib. VII., Tit. I. De Usufructu, with a Legal and Philological Commentary by H. J. ROBY. Demy 8vo. 9s.
The Two Parts complete in One Volume. Demy 8vo. 18s.

Selected Titles from the Digest, by BRYAN WALKER, M.A., LL.D.
Part I. Mandati vel Contra. Digest XVII. 1. Cr. 8vo. 5s.

Part II. De Adquirendo rerum dominio, and De Adquirenda vel amittenda Possessione, Digest XLI. 1 and 2. Crown 8vo. 6s.

Part III. De Condictionibus, Digest XII. 1 and 4—7 and Digest XIII. 1—3. Crown 8vo. 6s.

The Commentaries of Gaius and Rules of Ulpian. Translated and Annotated, by J. T. ABDY, LL.D., and BRYAN WALKER, M.A., LL.D. New Edition by BRYAN WALKER. Crown 8vo. 16s.

London: Cambridge Warehouse, Ave Maria Lane.

The Institutes of Justinian, translated with Notes by J. T. ABDY, LL.D., and BRYAN WALKER, M.A., LL.D. Cr. 8vo. 16s.

The Fragments of the Perpetual Edict of Salvius Julianus, Arranged, and Annotated by the late BRYAN WALKER, LL.D. Cr. 8vo. 6s.

Grotius de Jure Belli et Pacis, with the Notes of Barbeyrac and others; an abridged Translation of the Text, by W. WHEWELL, D.D. Demy 8vo. 12s. The translation separate, 6s.

The Science of International Law. By T. A. WALKER, M.A., LL.M. of the Middle Temple. Demy 8vo. [*Nearly ready*.

An Analysis of Criminal Liability. By E. C. CLARK, LL.D., Regius Professor of Civil Law. Crown 8vo. 7s. 6d.

Practical Jurisprudence. A comment on AUSTIN. By the same. Crown 8vo. 9s.

The Constitution of Canada. By J. E. C. MUNRO, LL.M. Demy 8vo. 10s.

Elements of the Law of Torts. A Text-book for Students. By MELVILLE M. BIGELOW, Ph.D. Crown 8vo. 10s. 6d.

A Selection of Cases on the English Law of Contract. By GERARD BROWN FINCH, M.A. Royal 8vo. 28s.

Bracton's Note Book. A Collection of Cases decided in the King's Courts during the Reign of Henry the Third, annotated by a Lawyer of that time, seemingly by Henry of Bratton. Edited by F. W. MAITLAND. 3 vols. Demy 8vo. £3. 3s. (net.)

A Selection of the State Trials. By J. W. WILLIS-BUND, M.A., LL.B. Crown 8vo. Vols. I. and II. In 3 parts. 30s.

Commons and Common Fields, or the History and Policy of the Laws of Commons and Enclosures in England. Being the Yorke Prize Essay for 1886. By T. E. SCRUTTON, M.A. Demy 8vo. 10s. 6d.

History of Equity as administered in the Court of Chancery. Being the Yorke Prize Essay for 1889. By D. M°KENZIE KERLY, M.A., St John's College. Demy 8vo. 12s. 6d.

History of Land Tenure in Ireland. Being the Yorke Prize Essay for 1888. By W. E. MONTGOMERY, M.A., LL.M. Demy 8vo. 10s. 6d.

History of the Law of Tithes in England. Being the Yorke Prize Essay for 1887. By W. EASTERBY, B.A., LL.B. Demy 8vo. 7s. 6d.

The History of the Law of Prescription in England. Being the Yorke Prize Essay for 1890. By T. A. HERBERT, B.A., LL.B. Demy 8vo. 10s.

Land in Fetters. Being the Yorke Prize Essay for 1885. By T. E. SCRUTTON, M.A. Demy 8vo. 7s. 6d.

Tables shewing the Differences between English and Indian Law. By Sir ROLAND KNYVET WILSON, Bart., M.A., LL.M. Demy 4to. 1s.

London: Cambridge Warehouse, Ave Maria Lane.

HISTORY.

Cambridge Historical Essays.

Political Parties in Athens during the Peloponnesian War, by L. WHIBLEY, M.A. (Prince Consort Dissertation, 1888.) Second Edition. Crown 8vo. 2s. 6d.

Pope Gregory the Great and his relations with Gaul, by F. W. KELLETT, M.A. (Prince Consort Dissertation, 1888.) Crown 8vo. 2s. 6d.

The Constitutional Experiments of the Commonwealth, being the Thirlwall Prize Essay for 1889, by E. JENKS, M.A., LL.B. Crown 8vo. 2s. 6d.

On Election by Lot at Athens, by J. W. HEADLAM, M.A. (Prince Consort Dissertation, 1890.) Crown 8vo. 2s. 6d.

The Influence and Development of English Gilds. (Thirlwall Prize Essay, 1891.) By F. AIDAN HIBBERT, B.A. Crown 8vo. 3s.

The Somerset Religious Houses. By W. A. J. ARCHBOLD, B.A., LL.B. (Prince Consort Dissertation, 1890.) Crown 8vo. 10s. 6d.

The Early History of Frisia, with special relation to its Conversion. By W. E. COLLINS, B.A. (Prince Consort Dissertation, 1890.) Cr. 8vo. [*Preparing*.

The Origin of Metallic Currency and Weight Standards. By W. RIDGEWAY, M.A., Professor of Greek, Queen's College, Cork, and late Fellow of Gonville and Caius College. Demy 8vo. 15s. Net.

The Growth of English Industry and Commerce during the Early and Middle Ages. By W. CUNNINGHAM, D.D. Demy 8vo. 16s.

The Growth of English Industry and Commerce in Modern Times. By the same Author. [*Nearly ready*.

A History of Epidemics in Britain. From A.D. 664 to the extinction of the Plague in 1666. By CHARLES CREIGHTON, M.D., M.A., formerly Demonstrator of Anatomy in the University of Cambridge. Demy 8vo. 18s.

Two Unfinished Papers by the late HENRY BRADSHAW. 1. The Collectio Canonum Hibernensis. 2. On the Chartres and Tours MSS. of the Hibernensis. (64 pp.) Demy 8vo. 2s. 6d.

Statutes of Lincoln Cathedral. Arranged by the late HENRY BRADSHAW, with illustrative Documents. Edited by Chr. WORDSWORTH, M.A. Part I. containing the complete text of 'Liber Niger' with Mr Bradshaw's Memorandums. Demy 8vo. 12s. 6d.

London: Cambridge Warehouse, Ave Maria Lane.

Ecclesiae Londino-Batavae archivum. TOMVS PRIMVS. ABRAHAMI ORTELII et virorum eruditorum ad eundem et ad JACOBVM COLIVM ORTELIANVM Epistulae, (1524—1628). TOMVS SECVNDVS. EPISTVLAE ET TRACTATVS cum Reformationis tum Ecclesiae Londino-Batavae Historiam Illustrantes 1544—1622. Ex autographis mandante Ecclesia Londino-Batava edidit JOANNES HENRICVS HESSELS. Demy 4to. Each vol., separately, £3. 10s. Taken together £5. 5s. *Net.*

The Growth of British Policy, by J. R. SEELEY, M.A.
[*In the Press.*

The Despatches of Earl Gower, English Ambassador at the court of Versailles, June 1790 to August 1792, and the Despatches of Mr Lindsay and Mr Monro. By O. BROWNING, M.A. Demy 8vo. 15s.

Life and Times of Stein, or Germany and Prussia in the Napoleonic Age, by J. R. SEELEY, M.A. Portraits and Maps. 3 vols. Demy 8vo. 30s.

Rhodes in Ancient Times. By CECIL TORR, M.A. With six plates. 10s. 6d.

Rhodes in Modern Times. By the same Author. With three plates. Demy 8vo. 8s.

Chronological Tables of Greek History. By CARL PETER. Translated from the German by G. CHAWNER, M.A. Demy 4to. 10s.

History of Nepāl, edited with an introductory sketch of the Country and People by Dr D. WRIGHT. Super-royal 8vo. 10s. 6d.

Kinship and Marriage in early Arabia, by W. ROBERTSON SMITH, M.A., LL.D. Crown 8vo. 7s. 6d.

Natural Religion in India. The Rede Lecture, delivered in the Senate-House, Cambridge, on June 17, 1891, by Sir ALFRED LYALL, K.C.B., K.C.I.E. Cloth, 2s. Paper Covers, 1s.

BIOGRAPHY.

Erasmus. The Rede Lecture, delivered in the Senate-House, Cambridge, June 11, 1890, by R. C. JEBB, Litt.D. Cloth, 2s. Paper Covers, 1s.

The Life and Letters of the Reverend Adam Sedgwick, LL.D., F.R.S. (Dedicated, by special permission, to Her Majesty the Queen.) By JOHN WILLIS CLARK, M.A., F.S.A., and THOMAS M^cKENNY HUGHES, M.A. 2 vols. Demy 8vo. 36s.

Memorials of the Life of George Elwes Corrie, D.D., formerly Master of Jesus College. By M. HOLROYD. Demy 8vo. 12s.

TRAVELS.

Travels in Arabia Deserta in 1876 and 1877. By CHARLES M. DOUGHTY. With Illustrations. Demy 8vo. 2 vols. £3. 3s.

A Journey of Literary and Archæological Research in Nepal and Northern India, 1884—5. By C. BENDALL, M.A. Demy 8vo. 10s.

London: Cambridge Warehouse, Ave Maria Lane.

ART, &c.

Illuminated Manuscripts in Classical and Mediaeval Times, their Art and their Technique, by J. HENRY MIDDLETON, Slade Professor of Fine Art. Royal 8vo. [*Nearly ready.*

The Engraved Gems of Classical Times with a Catalogue of the Gems in the Fitzwilliam Museum by J. H. MIDDLETON, M.A. Royal 8vo. 12s. 6d.

The Lewis Collection of Gems and Rings, in the possession of Corpus Christi College, Cambridge, with an Introductory Essay on Ancient Gems by J. H. MIDDLETON, M.A. Royal 8vo. 6s.

A Catalogue of Ancient Marbles in Great Britain, by Prof. ADOLF MICHAELIS. Translated by C. A. M. FENNELL, Litt.D. Royal 8vo. Roxburgh (Morocco back). £2. 2s.

Some Interesting Syrian and Palestinian Inscriptions, by J. RENDEL HARRIS, M.A. Royal 8vo. 4s.

The Types of Greek Coins. By PERCY GARDNER, Litt.D., F.S.A. With 16 plates. Impl. 4to. Cloth £1. 11s. 6d. Roxburgh (Morocco back) £2. 2s.

Essays on the Art of Pheidias. By C. WALDSTEIN, Litt.D., Phil.D. Royal 8vo. With Illustrations. Buckram, 30s.

The Woodcutters of the Netherlands during the last quarter of the Fifteenth Century. By W. M. CONWAY. Demy 8vo. 10s. 6d.

The Literary remains of Albrecht Dürer, by W. M. CONWAY. With Transcripts from the British Museum Manuscripts, and Notes upon them by LINA ECKENSTEIN. Royal 8vo. 21s.

The Collected Papers of Henry Bradshaw, including his Memoranda and Communications read before the Cambridge Antiquarian Society. *With 13 facsimiles.* Edited by F. J. H. JENKINSON, M.A. Demy 8vo. 16s.

MUSIC.

Counterpoint. A practical course of study. By the late Prof. Sir G. A. MACFARREN, Mus. D. 5th Edition, revised. Cr. 4to. 7s. 6d.

EDUCATIONAL SCIENCE, &c.

Eighteen Years of University Extension. By R. D. ROBERTS, M.A., D.Sc., Organizing Secretary for Lectures to the Local Examinations and Lectures Syndicate. With Map and Diagrams. Crown 8vo. 1s.

Occasional Addresses on Educational Subjects. By S. S. LAURIE, M.A., F.R.S.E. Crown 8vo. 5s.

Lectures on Language and Linguistic Method in the School. By S. S. LAURIE, M.A., LL.D. Crown 8vo. 4s.

London: Cambridge Warehouse, Ave Maria Lane.

Lectures on Teaching, delivered in the University of Cambridge. By J. G. FITCH, M.A., LL.D. Cr. 8vo. 5s.

Lectures on the Growth and Training of the Mental Faculty, delivered in the University of Cambridge. By FRANCIS WARNER, M.D., F.R.C.P. Crown 8vo. 4s. 6d.

SHORTHAND.

A Primer of Cursive Shorthand. By H. L. CALLENDAR, M.A. 6d.

Essays from the Spectator in Cursive Shorthand, by H. L. CALLENDAR, M.A. 6d.

Reading Practice in Cursive Shorthand. Easy extracts for Beginners. St Mark, Pt. I. Vicar of Wakefield, Chaps. I.—IV. Alice in Wonderland, Chap. VII. Price 3d. each.

A System of Phonetic Spelling, adapted to English by H. L. CALLENDAR, M.A. Extra Fcap. 8vo. 6d.

A Manual of Orthographic Cursive Shorthand. By H. L. CALLENDAR, M.A. 1s.

A Manual of Cursive Shorthand, by H. L. CALLENDAR, M.A. Extra Fcap. 8vo. 2s.

MISCELLANEOUS.

Town and Gown. Some five years of work in St George's, Camberwell. By J. TETLEY ROWE, M.A., Trinity College Missioner, with a few words of Preface by Rev. A. MONTAGU BUTLER, D.D., Master of Trinity College, Cambridge. Crown 4to. 1s.

CAMBRIDGE.

The Architectural History of the University of Cambridge and of the Colleges of Cambridge and Eton, by the late Professor WILLIS, M.A., F.R.S. Edited with large Additions and a Continuation to the present time by J. W. CLARK, M.A. 4 Vols. Super Royal 8vo. £6. 6s.

Also a limited Edition of the same, consisting of 120 numbered Copies only, large paper Quarto; the woodcuts and steel engravings mounted on India paper; of which 100 copies are now offered for sale, at Twenty-five Guineas net each set.

The University of Cambridge from the Earliest Times to the Royal Injunctions of 1535. By J. B. MULLINGER, M.A. Demy 8vo. 12s.
—— Part II. From the Royal Injunctions of 1535 to the Accession of Charles the First. Demy 8vo. 18s.

Scholae Academicae: some Account of the Studies at the English Universities in the Eighteenth Century. By CHRISTOPHER WORDSWORTH, M.A. Demy 8vo. 10s. 6d.

History of the College of St John the Evangelist, by THOMAS BAKER, B.D., Ejected Fellow. Edited by JOHN E. B. MAYOR, M.A., Fellow of St John's. Two Vols. Demy 8vo. 24s.

London: Cambridge Warehouse, Ave Maria Lane.

CAMBRIDGE.

Admissions to Gonville and Caius College in the University of Cambridge March 1558—9 to Jan. 1678—9. Edited by J. VENN, Sc.D., and S. C. VENN. Demy 8vo. 10s.

A Chronological List of the Graces, etc. in the University Registry which concern the University Library. 2s. 6d.

Trusts, Statutes and Directions affecting (1) The Professorships of the University. (2) The Scholarships and Prizes. (3) Other Gifts and Endowments. Demy 8vo. 5s.

Graduati Cantabrigienses: sive catalogus exhibens nomina eorum quos gradu quocunque ornavit Academia Cantabrigiensis (1800—1884). Cura H. R. LUARD, S.T.P. Demy 8vo. 12s. 6d.

Letters patent of Elizabeth and James the First, addressed to the University of Cambridge, with other Documents. Edited (with a translation of the letters of Elizabeth) by J. W. CLARK, M.A. Demy 8vo. 2s. 6d.

Statutes for the University of Cambridge and for the Colleges therein, made, published and approved (1878—1882) under the Universities of Oxford and Cambridge Act, 1877. Demy 8vo. 16s.

Statutes of the University of Cambridge. 3s. 6d.

Ordinances of the University of Cambridge. 7s. 6d. Supplement to ditto. 1s. Bound in one volume. 8s. 6d.

A Compendium of University Regulations. Demy 8vo. 6d.

Cambridge University Reporter (*Published by authority*). Containing all the Official Notices of the University Reports of Discussions in the Schools, and Proceedings of the Cambridge Philosophical, Antiquarian and Philological Societies. 3d. weekly.

CATALOGUES.

University Library.

A Catalogue of the Manuscripts. Demy 8vo. 5 vols. 10s. each. Index to Catalogue. 10s.

A Catalogue of Adversaria and printed books containing MS. notes. Demy 8vo. 3s. 6d.

Catalogus Bibliothecæ Burckhardtianæ. Demy Quarto. 5s.

A Catalogue of the Hebrew Manuscripts. By the late Dr S. M. SCHILLER-SZINESSY. 9s.

Catalogue of the Buddhist Sanskrit Manuscripts. Edited by C. BENDALL, M.A. 12s.

Bulletin (weekly), containing titles of new books added to the Library. Crown 8vo. 6s. a year, paid in advance.

Catalogue of the collection of books on Logic presented by J. VENN, Sc.D. 2s. 6d.

A Catalogue of the Portsmouth Collection of Books and Papers written by or belonging to SIR ISAAC NEWTON. Demy 8vo. 5s.

The Illuminated Manuscripts in the Library of the Fitzwilliam Museum, Cambridge, by W. G. SEARLE, M.A. 7s. 6d.

London: Cambridge Warehouse, Ave Maria Lane.

CAMBRIDGE UNIVERSITY EXAMINATION PAPERS.

These Papers are published in occasional numbers every Term, and in volumes for the Academical year.

Vol. XVII. Papers for the year 1887—88. Vol. XVIII. Papers for the year 1888—89. Vol. XIX. Papers for the year 1889—90. Vol. XX. Papers for the year 1890—91. 15*s*. each.

COLLEGE EXAMINATION PAPERS.

Examination Papers for Entrance and Minor Scholarships and Exhibitions in the Colleges of the University of Cambridge. Part I. Mathematics and Science. Part II. Classics, Mediaeval and Modern Languages and History (Michaelmas Term, 1890). Part III. Mathematics and Science. Part IV. Classics, Law and History (Lent Term, 1891). 2*s*. each. Parts V. and VI. [*Nearly ready*.

CAMBRIDGE LOCAL EXAMINATIONS.

Examination Papers, for various years, with the Regulations for the Examination. Demy 8vo. 2*s*. each, or by post 2*s*. 2*d*.

Class Lists, for various years. Boys 1*s*. Girls 6*d*.

Annual Reports of the Syndicate, with Supplementary Tables showing the success and failure of the Candidates. 2*s*. each, by post 2*s*. 3*d*.

CAMBRIDGE HIGHER LOCAL EXAMINATIONS.

Examination Papers, for various years, with the Regulations for the Examination. Demy 8vo. 2*s*. each, by post 2*s*. 2*d*.

Class Lists, for various years. 1*s*. each. By post 1*s*. 2*d*.

Reports of the Syndicate. Demy 8vo. 1*s*., by post 1*s*. 2*d*.

TEACHERS' TRAINING SYNDICATE.

Examination Papers for various years with the Regulations for the Examination. Demy 8vo. 6*d*., by post 7*d*.

OXFORD AND CAMBRIDGE SCHOOLS EXAMINATIONS.

Papers set in the Examination for Certificates, July, 1891. 2*s*.

Papers set in the Examination for Commercial Certificates, July, 1891. 6*d*.

List of Candidates who obtained Certificates at the Examination held in 1891; and Supplementary Tables. 9*d*.

Regulations of the Board for 1892. 9*d*.

Regulations for the Commercial Certificate, 1892. 3*d*.

Report of the Board for the year ending Oct. 31, 1891. 1*s*.

London: Cambridge Warehouse, Ave Maria Lane.

The Cambridge Bible for Schools and Colleges.

GENERAL EDITOR: J. J. S. PEROWNE, D.D., BISHOP OF WORCESTER.

"It is difficult to commend too highly this excellent series."—*Guardian.*

Now Ready. Cloth, Extra Fcap. 8vo. With Maps.
Book of Joshua. By Rev. G. F. MACLEAR, D.D. 2s. 6d.
Book of Judges. By Rev. J. J. LIAS, M.A. 3s. 6d.
First Book of Samuel. By Rev. Prof. KIRKPATRICK, B.D. 3s. 6d.
Second Book of Samuel. By Rev. Prof. KIRKPATRICK, B.D. 3s. 6d.
First Book of Kings. By Rev. Prof. LUMBY, D.D. 3s. 6d.
Second Book of Kings. By Rev. Prof. LUMBY, D.D. 3s. 6d.
Book of Job. By Rev. A. B. DAVIDSON, D.D. 5s.
Book of Psalms. Book I. By Rev. Prof. KIRKPATRICK, B.D. 3s. 6d.
Book of Ecclesiastes. By Very Rev. E. H. PLUMPTRE, D.D. 5s.
Book of Jeremiah. By Rev. A. W. STREANE, B.D. 4s. 6d.
Book of Ezekiel. By Rev. A. B. DAVIDSON, D.D. 5s.
Book of Hosea. By Rev. T. K. CHEYNE, M.A., D.D. 3s.
Books of Obadiah and Jonah. By Arch. PEROWNE. 2s. 6d.
Book of Micah. By Rev. T. K. CHEYNE, M.A., D.D. 1s. 6d.
Books of Haggai, Zechariah & Malachi. By Arch. PEROWNE. 3s. 6d.
Book of Malachi. By Archdeacon PEROWNE. 1s.
Gospel according to St Matthew. By Rev. A. CARR, M.A. 2s. 6d.
Gospel according to St Mark. By Rev. G. F. MACLEAR, D.D. 2s. 6d.
Gospel according to St Luke. By Archdeacon FARRAR. 4s. 6d.
Gospel according to St John. By Rev. A. PLUMMER, D.D. 4s. 6d.
Acts of the Apostles. By Prof. LUMBY, D.D. 4s. 6d.
Epistle to the Romans. Rev. H. C. G. MOULE, M.A. 3s. 6d.
First Corinthians. By Rev. J. J. LIAS, M.A. 2s.
Second Corinthians. By Rev. J. J. LIAS, M.A. 2s.
Epistle to the Galatians. By Rev. E. H. PEROWNE, D.D. 1s. 6d.
Epistle to the Ephesians. Rev. H. C. G. MOULE, M.A. 2s. 6d.
Epistle to the Hebrews. By Archdeacon FARRAR, D.D. 3s. 6d.
Epistle to the Philippians. By Rev. H. C. G. MOULE, M.A. 2s. 6d.
Epistles to the Thessalonians. By Rev. G. G. FINDLAY, B.A. 2s.
General Epistle of St James. By Very Rev. E. H. PLUMPTRE. 1s. 6d.
Epistles of St Peter and St Jude. By the same Editor. 2s. 6d.
Epistles of St John. By Rev. A. PLUMMER, M.A., D.D. 3s. 6d.
Book of Revelation. By Rev. W. H. SIMCOX, M.A. 3s.

London: Cambridge Warehouse, Ave Maria Lane.

Preparing.
Book of Genesis. By the BISHOP OF WORCESTER.
Books of Exodus, Numbers and Deuteronomy. By Rev. C. D. GINSBURG, LL.D.
First and Second Books of Chronicles. By Very Rev. Dean SPENCE, D.D.
Books of Ezra and Nehemiah. By Rev. Prof. RYLE, B.D.
Book of Isaiah. By Prof. W. ROBERTSON SMITH, M.A.
Epistles to Colossians & Philemon. By Rev. H. C. G. MOULE, M.A.
Epistles to Timothy and Titus. By Rev. A. E. HUMPHREYS, M.A.

The Smaller Cambridge Bible for Schools.

"The notes elucidate every possible difficulty with scholarly brevity and clearness."—*Saturday Review.*

"We can cordially recommend this series of text-books, not only to those for whom it is primarily intended, but also to the clergy and other workers for use in Bible-classes."—*Church Review.*

"Accurate scholarship is obviously a characteristic of their productions, and the work of simplification and condensation appears to have been judiciously and skilfully performed."—*Guardian.*

Now ready. Price 1s. *each.*

Book of Joshua. By J. S. BLACK, M.A.
Book of Judges. By J. S. BLACK, M.A. [*Preparing.*
First and Second Books of Samuel. By Prof. KIRKPATRICK, B.D.
First and Second Books of Kings. By Rev. Prof. LUMBY, D.D.
Gospel according to St Matthew. By Rev. A. CARR, M.A.
Gospel according to St Mark. By Rev. G. F. MACLEAR, D.D.
Gospel according to St Luke. By Archdeacon FARRAR, D.D.
Gospel according to St John. By Rev. A. PLUMMER, D.D.
Acts of the Apostles. By Professor LUMBY, D.D.

THE CAMBRIDGE GREEK TESTAMENT
FOR SCHOOLS AND COLLEGES

with a Revised Text, based on the most recent critical authorities, and English Notes, prepared under the direction of the General Editor,

J. J. S. PEROWNE, D.D., BISHOP OF WORCESTER.

Gospel according to St Matthew. By Rev. A. CARR, M.A. 4s. 6d.
Gospel according to St Mark. By Rev. G. F. MACLEAR, D.D. 4s. 6d.
Gospel according to St Luke. By Archdeacon FARRAR. 6s.
Gospel according to St John. By Rev. A. PLUMMER, D.D. 6s.
Acts of the Apostles. By Prof. LUMBY, D.D. 4 Maps. 6s.
First Corinthians. By Rev. J. J. LIAS, M.A. 3s.
Second Corinthians. By Rev. J. J. LIAS, M.A. 3s.
Epistle to the Hebrews. By Archdeacon FARRAR, D.D. 3s. 6d.
Epistles of St John. By Rev. A. PLUMMER, M.A., D.D. 4s.

London: Cambridge Warehouse, Ave Maria Lane.

THE PITT PRESS SERIES.

⁎ *Copies of the Pitt Press Series may generally be obtained in two volumes, Text and Notes separately.*

I. GREEK.

Aristophanes. Aves—Plutus—Ranae. By W. C. GREEN, M.A., late Assistant Master at Rugby School. 3s. 6d. each.
Euripides. Heracleidæ. By E. A. BECK, M.A. 3s. 6d.
Euripides. Hercules Furens. By A. GRAY, M.A., and J. T. HUTCHINSON, M.A. 2s.
Euripides. Hippolytus. By W. S. HADLEY, M.A. 2s.
Euripides. Iphigeneia in Aulis. By C. E. S. HEADLAM, M.A. 2s. 6d.
Herodotus. Book V. By E. S. SHUCKBURGH, M.A. 3s.
Herodotus. Book VI. By the same Editor. 4s.
Herodotus. Books VIII., IX. By the same Editor. 4s. each.
 [*Nearly ready.*
Herodotus. Book VIII., Ch. 1—90. Book IX., Ch. 1—89. By the same Editor. 3s. 6d. each.
Homer. Odyssey, Book IX. Book X. By G. M. EDWARDS, M.A. 2s. 6d. each.
Homer. Odyssey, Book XXI. By the same Editor. 2s.
Homer. Iliad. Book VI. By the same Editor. 2s.
Homer. Iliad. Books XXII., XXIII. By the same Editor. 2s. each.
Luciani Somnium Charon Piscator et De Luctu. By W. E. HEITLAND, M.A., Fellow of St John's College, Cambridge. 3s. 6d.
Lucian. Menippus and Timon. By E. C. MACKIE, B.A. 3s. 6d.
Platonis Apologia Socratis. By J. ADAM, M.A. 3s. 6d.
—— **Crito.** By the same Editor. 2s. 6d.
—— **Euthyphro.** By the same Editor. 2s. 6d.
Plutarch's Lives of the Gracchi.—Sulla—Timoleon. By H. A. HOLDEN, M.A., LL.D. 6s. each.
Plutarch's Life of Nicias. By the same Editor. 5s.
Sophocles.—Oedipus Tyrannus. School Edition. By R. C. JEBB, Litt.D., LL.D. 4s. 6d.
Thucydides. Book VII. By Rev. H. A. HOLDEN, M.A., LL.D. 5s.
Xenophon—Agesilaus. By H. HAILSTONE, M.A. 2s. 6d.

London: Cambridge Warehouse, Ave Maria Lane.

Xenophon—Anabasis. By A. PRETOR, M.A. Two vols. 7s. 6d.
—— —— **Books I. III. IV. and V.** By the same Editor.
Price 2s. each. **Books II. VI. and VII.** 2s. 6d. each.
Xenophon—Cyropaedeia. Books I. II. By Rev. H. A. HOLDEN, M.A., LL.D. 2 vols. 6s.
—— —— **Books III. IV. and V.** By the same Editor. 5s.
—— —— **Books VI. VII. and VIII.** By the same Editor. 5s.

II. LATIN.

Beda's Ecclesiastical History, Books III., IV. Edited by J. E. B. MAYOR, M.A., and J. R. LUMBY, D.D. Revised Edit. 7s. 6d.
—— —— **Books I. II.** [*In the Press.*
Caesar. De Bello Gallico Comment. I. By A. G. PESKETT, M.A. 1s. 6d. **Com. II. III.** 2s.
—— **Comment. I. II. III.** 3s. **Com. IV. V.** 1s. 6d. **Com. VI. and Com. VIII.** 1s. 6d. each. **Com. VII.** 2s.
—— **De Bello Civili. Comment. I.** By the same Editor. 3s.
M. T. Ciceronis de Amicitia.—de Senectute.—pro Sulla Oratio. By J. S. REID, Litt.D., Fellow of Gonville and Caius College. 3s. 6d. each.
M. T. Ciceronis Oratio pro Archia Poeta. By the same. 2s.
M. T. Ciceronis pro Balbo Oratio. By the same. 1s. 6d.
M. T. Ciceronis in Gaium Verrem Actio Prima. By H. COWIE, M.A., Fellow of St John's College. 1s. 6d.
M. T. Ciceronis in Q. Caecilium Divinatio et in C. Verrem Actio. By W. E. HEITLAND, M.A., and H. COWIE, M.A. 3s.
M. T. Ciceronis Oratio pro Tito Annio Milone. By JOHN SMYTH PURTON, B.D. 2s. 6d.
M. T. Ciceronis Oratio pro L. Murena. By W. E. HEITLAND, M.A. 3s.
M. T. Ciceronis pro Cn. Plancio Oratio, by H. A. HOLDEN, LL.D. Second Edition. 4s. 6d.
M. Tulli Ciceronis Oratio Philippica Secunda. By A. G. PESKETT, M.A. 3s. 6d.
M. T. Ciceronis Somnium Scipionis. By W. D. PEARMAN, M.A. 2s.
Horace. Epistles, Book I. By E. S. SHUCKBURGH, M.A. 2s. 6d.
Livy. Books IV., IX. By H. M. STEPHENSON, M.A. 2s. 6d. each.
—— **Book V.** By L. WHIBLEY, M.A. 2s. 6d.
—— **Book VI.** By H. M. STEPHENSON, M.A. [*In the Press.*
—— **Books XXI., XXII.** By M. S. DIMSDALE, M.A. 2s. 6d. each.
—— **Book XXVII.** By H. M. STEPHENSON, M.A. 2s. 6d.
M. Annaei Lucani Pharsaliae Liber Primus. By W. E. HEITLAND, M.A., and C. E. HASKINS, M.A. 1s. 6d.

London: Cambridge Warehouse, Ave Maria Lane.

Lucretius, Book V. By J. D. DUFF, M.A., Fellow of Trinity College. *Price* 2s.

P. Ovidii Nasonis Fastorum Liber VI. By A. SIDGWICK, M.A. 1s. 6d.

Ovidii Nasonis Metamorphoseon Liber I. By L. D. DOWDALL, LL.B., B.D. [*Nearly ready.*

Quintus Curtius. A Portion of the History (Alexander in India). By W. E. HEITLAND, M.A. and T. E. RAVEN, B.A. 3s. 6d.

Vergil. The Complete Works. By A. SIDGWICK, M.A. Two Vols. Vol. I. Introduction and Text. 3s. 6d. Vol. II. Notes. 4s. 6d.

P. Vergili Maronis Aeneidos Libri I.—XII. By the same Editor. 1s. 6d. each.

P. Vergili Maronis Bucolica. By the same Editor. 1s. 6d.

P. Vergili Maronis Georgicon Libri I. II. By the same Editor. 2s. Libri III. IV. By the same Editor. 2s.

III. FRENCH.

Bataille de Dames. By SCRIBE and LEGOUVÉ. By Rev. H. A. BULL, M.A. 2s.

Dix Années d'Exil. Livre II. Chapitres 1—8. Par MADAME LA BARONNE DE STAËL-HOLSTEIN. By the late G. MASSON, B.A. and G. W. PROTHERO, M.A. New Edition, enlarged. 2s.

Histoire du Siècle de Louis XIV. par Voltaire. Chaps. I.—XIII. By GUSTAVE MASSON, B.A. and G. W. PROTHERO, M.A. 2s. 6d. Chaps. XIV.—XXIV. 2s. 6d. Chap. XXV. to end. 2s. 6d.

Frédégonde et Brunehaut. A Tragedy in Five Acts, by N. LEMERCIER. By GUSTAVE MASSON, B.A. 2s.

Jeanne D'Arc. By A. DE LAMARTINE. By Rev. A. C. CLAPIN, M.A. Revised Edition by A. R. ROPES, M.A. 1s. 6d.

La Canne de Jonc. By A. DE VIGNY. By H. W. EVE, M.A. 1s. 6d.

La Jeune Sibérienne. Le Lépreux de la Cité D'Aoste. Tales by COUNT XAVIER DE MAISTRE. By GUSTAVE MASSON, B.A. 1s. 6d.

La Picciola. By X. B. SAINTINE. By Rev. A. C. CLAPIN, M.A. 2s.

La Guerre. By MM. ERCKMANN-CHATRIAN. By the same Editor. 3s.

La Métromanie. A Comedy, by PIRON. By G. MASSON, B.A. 2s.

Lascaris ou Les Grecs du XVE Siècle, Nouvelle Historique, par A. F. VILLEMAIN. By the same. 2s.

La Suite du Menteur. A Comedy by P. CORNEILLE. By the same. 2s.

Lazare Hoche—Par EMILE DE BONNECHOSE. With Four Maps. By C. COLBECK, M.A. 2s.

Le Bourgeois Gentilhomme, Comédie-Ballet en Cinq Actes. Par J.-B. Poquelin de Molière (1670). By Rev. A. C. CLAPIN, M.A. 1s. 6d.

London: Cambridge Warehouse, Ave Maria Lane.

Le Directoire. (Considérations sur la Révolution Française. Troisième et quatrième parties.) Revised and enlarged. By G. MASSON, B.A. and G. W. PROTHERO, M.A. 2s.
Les Plaideurs. RACINE. By E. G. W. BRAUNHOLTZ, M.A., Ph.D. 2s.
—— —— (Abridged Edition.) 1s.
Les Précieuses Ridicules. MOLIÈRE. By E. G. W. BRAUNHOLTZ, M.A., Ph.D. 2s.
—— —— (Abridged Edition.) 1s.
L'École des Femmes. MOLIÈRE. By GEORGE SAINTSBURY, M.A. 2s. 6d.
Le Philosophe sans le savoir. Sedaine. By Rev. H. A. BULL, late Master at Wellington College. 2s.
Lettres sur l'histoire de France (XIII—XXIV). Par AUGUSTIN THIERRY. By G. MASSON, B.A. and G. W. PROTHERO. 2s. 6d.
Le Verre D'Eau. A Comedy, by SCRIBE. Edited by C. COLBECK, M.A. 2s.
Le Vieux Célibataire. A Comedy, by COLLIN D'HARLEVILLE. With Notes, by G. MASSON, B.A. 2s.
M. Daru, par M. C. A. SAINTE-BEUVE (Causeries du Lundi, Vol. IX.). By G. MASSON, B.A. Univ. Gallic. 2s.
Polyeucte. By CORNEILLE. By E. G. W. BRAUNHOLTZ, M.A.
[Nearly ready.
Recits des Temps Merovingiens I—III. THIERRY. By the late G. MASSON, B.A. and A. R. ROPES, M.A. Map. 3s.

IV. GERMAN.

A Book of Ballads on German History. By W. WAGNER, Ph.D. 2s.
A Book of German Dactylic Poetry. By W. WAGNER, Ph.D. 3s.
Benedix. Doctor Wespe. Lustspiel in fünf Aufzügen. By KARL HERMANN BREUL, M.A., Ph.D. 3s.
Culturgeschichtliche Novellen, von W. H. RIEHL. By H. J. WOLSTENHOLME, B.A. (Lond.). 3s. 6d.
Das Jahr 1813 (THE YEAR 1813), by F. KOHLRAUSCH. By WILHELM WAGNER, Ph.D. 2s.
Der erste Kreuzzug (1095—1099) nach FRIEDRICH VON RAUMER. THE FIRST CRUSADE. By W. WAGNER, Ph. D. 2s.
Der Oberhof. A Tale of Westphalian Life, by KARL IMMERMANN. By WILHELM WAGNER, Ph.D. 3s.
Der Staat Friedrichs des Grossen. By G. FREYTAG. By WILHELM WAGNER, PH.D. 2s.
Die Karavane, von WILHELM HAUFF. By A. SCHLOTTMANN, Ph.D. 3s.
Goethe's Hermann and Dorothea. By W. WAGNER, Ph. D. Revised edition by J. W. CARTMELL. 3s. 6d.

London: Cambridge Warehouse, Ave Maria Lane.

Goethe's Knabenjahre. (1749—1761.) **Goethe's Boyhood.** By W. WAGNER, Ph.D. Revised edition by J. W. CARTMELL, M.A. 2s.

Hauff, Das Bild des Kaisers. By KARL HERMANN BREUL, M.A., Ph.D. 3s.

Hauff, Das Wirthshaus im Spessart. By A. SCHLOTTMANN, Ph.D., late Assistant Master at Uppingham School. 3s. 6d.

Mendelssohn's Letters. Selections from. By JAMES SIME, M.A. 3s.

Schiller. Wilhelm Tell. By KARL HERMANN BREUL, M.A., Ph.D. 2s. 6d.

—— —— (Abridged Edition.) 1s. 6d.

—— Geschichte des Dreissigjährigen Kriegs. By the same Editor. [*Nearly ready.*

Selected Fables. Lessing and Gellert. By KARL HERMANN BREUL, M.A., Ph.D. 3s.

Uhland. Ernst, Herzog von Schwaben. By H. J. WOLSTENHOLME, B.A. (Lond.). 3s. 6d.

Zopf und Schwert. Lustspiel in fünf Aufzügen von KARL GUTZKOW. By H. J. WOLSTENHOLME, B.A. (Lond.). 3s. 6d.

V. ENGLISH.

An Apologie for Poetrie by Sir PHILIP SIDNEY. By E. S. SHUCKBURGH, M.A. The text is a revision of that of the first edition of 1595. 3s.

A Discourse of the Commonwealf of thys Realme of Englande. First printed in 1581, and commonly attributed to W. S. Edited from the MSS. by the late ELIZABETH LAMOND. [*In the Press.*

An Elementary Commercial Geography. A Sketch of the Commodities and Countries of the World. By H. R. MILL, Sc.D., F.R.S.E. 1s.

An Atlas of Commercial Geography. (Companion to the above.) By J. G. BARTHOLOMEW, F.R.G.S. With an Introduction by Dr H. R. MILL. 3s.

Ancient Philosophy from Thales to Cicero, A Sketch of, by JOSEPH B. MAYOR, M.A. 3s. 6d.

Bacon's History of the Reign of King Henry VII. By the Rev. Professor LUMBY, D.D. 3s.

British India, a Short History of. By Rev. E. S. CARLOS, M.A. 1s.

Cowley's Essays. By Prof. LUMBY, D.D. 4s.

General Aims of the Teacher, and Form Management. Two Lectures by F. W. FARRAR, D.D. and R. B. POOLE, B.D. 1s. 6d.

John Amos Comenius, Bishop of the Moravians. His Life and Educational Works, by S. S. LAURIE, A.M., F.R.S.E. 3s. 6d.

Locke on Education. By the Rev. R. H. QUICK, M.A. 3s. 6d.

Milton's Arcades and Comus. By A. W. VERITY, M.A. 3s.

Milton's Ode on the Morning of Christ's Nativity, L'Allegro, Il Penseroso, and Lycidas. By the same Editor. 2s. 6d.

London: Cambridge Warehouse, Ave Maria Lane.

Milton's Samson Agonistes. By the same Editor. 2s. 6d.
Milton's Paradise Lost. Books XI., XII. By the same Editor.
[Immediately.
Milton's Paradise Lost. Books V., VI. By the same Editor.
[In the Press.
Milton's Tractate on Education. A facsimile reprint from the Edition of 1673. Edited by O. BROWNING, M.A. 2s.
More's History of King Richard III. By J. RAWSON LUMBY, D.D. 3s. 6d.
On Stimulus. A Lecture delivered for the Teachers' Training Syndicate at Cambridge, May 1882, by A. SIDGWICK, M.A. New Ed. 1s.
Outlines of the Philosophy of Aristotle. Compiled by EDWIN WALLACE, M.A., LL.D. Third Edition, Enlarged. 4s. 6d.
Sir Thomas More's Utopia. By Prof. LUMBY, D.D. 3s. 6d.
Theory and Practice of Teaching. By E. THRING, M.A. 4s. 6d.
The Teaching of Modern Languages in Theory and Practice. By C. COLBECK, M.A. 2s.
The Two Noble Kinsmen. By Professor SKEAT, Litt.D. 3s. 6d.
Three Lectures on the Practice of Education. I. On Marking, by H. W. EVE, M.A. II. On Stimulus, by A. SIDGWICK, M.A. III. On the Teaching of Latin Verse Composition, by E. A. ABBOTT, D.D. 2s.

VI. MATHEMATICS.

Arithmetic for Schools. By C. SMITH, M.A., Master of Sidney Sussex College, Cambridge. 3s. 6d.
Elementary Algebra (with Answers to the Examples). By W. W. ROUSE BALL, M.A. 4s. 6d.
Euclid's Elements of Geometry. Books I. and II. By H. M. TAYLOR, M.A. 1s. 6d. Books III. and IV. By the same Editor. 1s. 6d.
——— ——— Books I.—IV. in one volume. 3s.
Solutions to the Exercises in Euclid, Books I.—IV. By W. W. TAYLOR, M.A. *[In the Press.*
Elements of Statics and Dynamics. By S. L. LONEY, M.A. 7s. 6d. Or in Two Parts. Part I. Elements of Statics. 4s. 6d. Part II. Elements of Dynamics. 3s. 6d.
Elementary Treatise on Plane Trigonometry for the use of Schools. By E. W. HOBSON, Sc.D., and C. M. JESSOP, M.A. *[In the Press.*

London: C. J. CLAY AND SONS,
CAMBRIDGE WAREHOUSE, AVE MARIA LANE.
Glasgow: 263, ARGYLE STREET.
Cambridge: DEIGHTON, BELL AND CO. **Leipzig:** F. A. BROCKHAUS.
New York: MACMILLAN AND CO.

www.ingramcontent.com/pod-product-compliance
Lightning Source LLC
Chambersburg PA
CBHW030309240426
43673CB00040B/1109